Community Health and Social Services

Fifth Edition

Brian Meredith Davies
MD (London), FFPHM, DPH

Formerly Director of Social Services, Director of Personal Health and Social Services, city of Liverpool. Lecturer in Public Health and (Preventive) Paediatrics, University of Liverpool.

Edward Arnold
A division of Hodder & Stoughton
LONDON MELBOURNE AUCKLAND

362
.10425
DAV

© 1991 Brian Meredith Davies

First published as *Preventive Medicine for Nurses and Social Workers*, 1965
Second edition 1972, reprinted with extensive revisions, 1975
Third edition 1977, reprinted with extensive revisions, 1980
Fourth edition 1984, fourth impression 1988
Fifth edition 1991

British Library Cataloguing in Publication Data

Davies, Brian Meredith *1920–*
    Community health and social services.
    1. Great Britain. Community health services
    I. Title
    362.10425

    ISBN 0-340-52761-7

Typeset by Rowland Phototypesetting Limited, Bury St Edmunds, Suffolk. Printed and bound in Great Britain for Edward Arnold, a division of Hodder and Stoughton Limited, Mill Road, Dunton Green, Sevenoaks, Kent TN13 2YA by Biddles Ltd, Guildford and King's Lynn

Contents

Preface

This fifth edition is being published at a time of great change in the National Health Service (NHS). After a long and heated period of debate and consultation, the National Health Service and Community Care Act received the Royal Assent at the end of June 1990. The date of implementation has been fixed for 1 April 1991 although a number of changes, including the establishment of NHS Hospital Trusts, will be phased in gradually. An important part of these changes, the new general practitioner contract, is already in being (April 1990) and the next year should see many opportunities develop in the family doctor services (primary health care), especially in the preventive field. Nurses and health visitors will undoubtedly play a major role in these new ventures especially when, from 1991, all family doctors will have to make certain that every one of their patients aged 16 to 74 years who has not seen the doctor during the last three years will have to be given an appointment when certain health checks and a medical examination must be carried out. Nurses working in primary health care (and an increasing number now are attached to or visit general practices) will carry out many of these essential health checks.

For patients aged 75 years and over a wider and more extensive system will be introduced, whereby the family doctor must see and examine everyone each year and, if need be, offer to make a home visit. Another radical change to be introduced is the setting up of Child Health Surveillance and Minor Surgery services in general practice and, in both, health visitors and nurses will again play an important part.

Another advance will be the complete modernisation of patients' records and data collection in the family doctor services. With financial help from the Department of Health, computers are being installed into general practices. These will not only assist with the regular health checks to be made by family doctors in future but will enable quicker and more efficient methods to be used to recall patients for immunisations and screening tests. At the same time, it will be easily possible for the complete medical history to be sent with patients when they visit or are admitted to hospital.

As well as the new legislative changes, the demographic ones forecast during the past 15 years have already become a reality. The numbers of very elderly people in the community (over 85 years of age) has increased rapidly. From a figure of 1 in 104 in 1978, it has already reached 1 in 71 (1990) and is well on course to reach 1 in 65 by the turn of the century. With these changes have come many problems for it is this group of very old people who necessarily make most demands on health care and social services of all kinds.

In addition, longer survival times and new cures for many diseases which used to be fatal have meant that there are now a greater number of handicapped and dependent people living in the community.

All these factors have emphasised how important it will be in the future for the NHS and social services to become more efficient. The changes introduced by the National Health Service and Community Care Act 1990 and the new general practitioner contract (which also for the first time makes it possible for part-time doctors to be principals in the NHS) and the various community care initiatives made by local authorities and voluntary bodies, are designed to help achieve a better service for patients and clients. Efficiency will only come with more flexibility, more choice and more delegation but these will only follow provided that all *professional staff and especially nurses fully understand the reasons and objectives behind these initiatives*. It is hoped that this book will help in this respect.

The format of the book remains largely the same. As before it is divided into two parts – the Health Services and the Social Services. This division must not be taken to indicate that both services can operate efficiently in isolation. In particular many parts of the Social Services and especially in the field of child care, child abuse, care of the physically handicapped, the mentally disordered and the elderly involve both the social and health services and especially many nurses working in them. Under the community care changes, local authorities, who are in charge of the local personal social services, will be encouraged to appoint nurses to help, especially with elderly persons.

In Chapter 13, there is a report on the impending changes in community care announced in 1989 and expected to be implemented in April 1991. As explained in that chapter the Secretary of State for Social Services announced, in July 1990, that the implementation is going to be in three stages. Phase 1 (April 1991) will see the introduction of a specific grant for mentally ill persons and a specific grant for voluntary bodies providing a service for drug and alcohol abusers. New inspection units will also be set up and a complaints procedure introduced. Phase 2 (April 1992) will implement the planning and development services while the major part of the changes, the proposed new benefit arrangements for the elderly and physically handicapped, will now be fully implemented in April 1993. These delays increase problems and there has been much comment and doubt expressed about whether adequate financial resources will be available by then.

All nurses, not only those in training, should completely understand the scope of these changes and how they can be used to make preventive health care more readily available to all groups of patients, including those who are chronically ill, for even in such serious cases much can be done (tertiary prevention) to avoid further deterioration and many complications.

The new edition has 20 chapters (two extra) but is roughly the same length as before. The chapter on Social Security has been omitted as it is no longer possible to give an adequate description of all the benefits in such a short book. References are still made to maternity benefits (in Chapter 4), to attendance allowances and mobility allowances (in Chapter 16) and to retirement pensions (in Chapter 18). A completely new chapter (8) covers the important topic of AIDS and the opportunity has been taken to include in this chapter sexually transmitted diseases and viral hepatitis as all show many epidemiological similarities. A second new chapter (15) deals solely with all forms of child abuse, including sexual abuse. This very important subject became headline news in the Cleveland crisis of 1986. This problem is fully discussed as well as the findings of the Lord Butler-Schloss Inquiry which followed. The Children Act 1989 is, at present, being implemented. It represents a real advance and is intended to simplify all child care law and to give better protection to children especially in all forms of child abuse. It is also hoped that it will strike a fairer balance between protecting children and the interference with parents and families which follow full investigations of any child care problem. There is also another very important basic objective behind the Act – to make certain that, in future, there is a better consultation and partnership between parents and those responsible for caring for children in need. Chapter 14 has been completely rewritten and it is hoped that it gives a short readable account of these changes. The subject of child abuse has never been more important – there are now over 40 000 children's names on the child protection registers of England and Wales. Prevention of child abuse will always be difficult but it is essential for everyone to realise that it is a subject which can only be tackled effectively if all professionals in the NHS and social services understand that they must work together – it represents an ideal example of how the NHS and personal social services are so often dependent upon each other. A necessary starting point to a better understanding and joint working together must depend on staff in both services having available a short, readable account of the legal changes in child care.

The legislative changes which followed the Children Act 1989 are fully discussed in Chapters 14 and 15. In the last new chapter (20) drug and alcohol abuse are covered in detail for the first time. Drug abuse is discussed fully and two types are studied briefly – illegal 'hard' drugs, which are becoming an increasing problem in many countries; and where a drug, which has been used medicinally, is followed by increasing dependence in that patient. Both are subjects which the nurse now needs to understand fully.

Two chapters have been changed in emphasis and content, Chapters 10 and 12. The first of these (10) now concentrates upon the role of nurses in the field of health education especially in primary health care. Many very effective preventive health measures depend on the awareness of the general public being heightened so that they use the increasing numbers of excellent screening tests now available – regular medical examinations, cervical cytology, mammography, eye tests. Most nurses have an important role here as the most valuable health education is that undertaken in everyday professional life – when patients are being treated and seen in general practice and in hospitals. Chapter 12 now deals with both nutrition and environmental health and special mention is made of the usefulness of fibre in all diets as it assists in fat metabolism (especially of dairy fats) and also helps to protect the colon and to reduce the incidence of diverticulitis and other forms of colitis.

Times of radical change are never easy – all professionals mistrust alterations to their services and it is essential that all nurses know exactly what the changes involve. It is all too easy to rely on the biased views of the press or media, many of which are often quite wrong in their facts. If nurses really understand the details of the changes they will be able to form their own opinions of them. It is hoped that this short book will give a clear indication of what the impending changes in the health and social services involve. Most of these changes, if used and developed properly, should lead to an improved health care and better social support in this country.

Once again I would like to thank my wife for all her patient help with the typing of the script, the correction of the proofs and for the compilation of the index as well as for her constant encouragement.

Brian Meredith Davies
1990

1 The structure of the health services

Before discussing the various parts of the community health services and the ways in which disease is prevented, it is important that the structure of the health services is fully understood.

The National Health Service (NHS) in the United Kingdom was introduced in 1948 and was completely reorganised in 1974 and 1982. It is an essential part of a much wider system of social security in which the whole state makes compulsory provision for various inevitable happenings in life, including the prevention of disease and the treatment of illness. During the last five years various administrative changes have been introduced, including the appointment of Regional, District and Unit General Managers. These changes followed the recommendations of the Griffiths report of 1983. The National Health Service is a comprehensive health service covering the whole country and its benefits and services are available to everyone. There is no contracting out of the service and it is financed centrally from both Exchequer general taxation and specific levies paid within National Insurance contributions.

Since 1988, all control of the various Social Security Benefits are under the Department of Social Security with the Secretary for Social Security in charge.

The following descriptions are mainly based on the NHS in England. The principles are the same for Scotland, Wales and Northern Ireland but there are minor administrative differences which are described on pages 15–17.

Function of the Secretary of State for Health

The Secretary of State for Health has full overall responsibility for the health services and, being a member of the Cabinet, is responsible directly to Parliament. The responsibilities of the Secretary of State for Social Services for local social services undertaken by local authorities are discussed in Chapter 13.

The Secretary of State for Health must arrange to provide, to an extent which he or she considers necessary, the following services.

- Accommodation for any services under the National Health Service Acts (clinics, health centres etc.).

- Hospital accommodation.
- Medical, dental, nursing and ambulance services.
- Facilities for the care of expectant and nursing mothers and very young children.
- Facilities for the prevention of illness and the after-care of persons either recovering from various illnesses or continuing to suffer from some chronic condition. These include vaccination and immunisation and a full range of rehabilitation services (including physiotherapy and occupational therapy).
- Such other services which are required for the diagnosis and treatment of illness (these include full pathological, bacteriological and blood transfusion services.
- School Health Services (in conjunction with Local Education Authorities).
- Family Planning Services.

There are a number of Standing Advisory Committees (such as the Standing Advisory Committee on Prevention of Disease by Immunisation) to which the Secretary of State may refer various specific problems. From time to time, particularly pressing problems occur which need very careful study and the Secretary of State may then arrange for them to be examined in detail by a special *ad hoc* Expert Committee. An example of an Expert Committee was the Court Committee which, in 1974–7, studied the future of the child health services (under the chairmanship of Professor Court) or an Inquiry such as the Inquiry into Child Sexual Abuse in Cleveland in 1987–8 under Lord Justice Butler-Schloss. Such a Committee or Inquiry collects evidence from various sources, studies that evidence, and recommends a course of action. It then becomes the responsibility of the Secretary of State for Social Services to assess the report and decide whether to recommend Parliament to implement the changes suggested.

In some instances, the subject to be studied is so important that a Royal Commission may be appointed by Parliament to consider the subject and draw up a report on it. Examples include the Royal Commission on the National Health Service, set up in 1976, which reported in 1979.

In addition to these expert committees, the Secretary of State has a large staff of experts to advise him or her, based at the Department of Health in London and locally in various regional offices. These include administrators, doctors, nurses and architects who deal with the detailed administration.

Method of control exercised by the Department of Health

The method used to control health services locally varies. Although all day-to-day administration of the health services is dealt with locally at the District Health Authority level, the Department of Health has three methods of controlling overall development.

1 **Financial** This is the most important method. All the finance needed for the health services is supplied from the Department of Health and covers running costs (*revenue expenditure*) and new buildings (*capital expenditure*).

   The Department of Health passes regional budgets for each Regional Health Authority which then allocates finances to each individual District Health Authority. In allocating finance to Regional Health Authorities, the Department of Health will take regard to special developments which it wishes to encourage. In this way, the Department of Health will be able to encourage (by providing the finances necessary) services which it considers urgently need developing.

   As regards capital, the Department of Health provides finance for hospital building on a 'once and for all' basis and not on any loan basis. All new health centres are financed centrally which ensures a more uniform development of health centres.

2 **Advisory** Advice on the development of all aspects of the health services is constantly being issued by the Department of Health in the form of memoranda and circulars. In many instances, the advice covers both health and social services.

   In the publication *Working Together*, issued by the Department of Health in 1988 after the Lord Butler-Schloss report on child sexual abuse in Cleveland, there is a comprehensive review of all forms of child abuse and outlines of the recommended action for the health and social services. Such a publication therefore forms the basis of an ideal service and is a model indicating how local services should be organised. It also defined exactly the duties and responsibilities of Area Child Protection Committees (see also pp. 257–8). This assists in ensuring a uniformly high standard of care all over the country but retains the ability of local health and social services to adjust their services to meet local problems.

3 **Planning and policy** The development of an integrated national health service calls for careful planning to ensure that the most urgent needs are met and that services are balanced between the different parts (i.e. between hospital, general practice and the community). It is, for instance, no use advocating a reduction in the number of hospital places for a certain group of patients (for example, the mentally ill) if there are not enough community

services to help these patients when discharged from hospitals.

In the reorganised health service future planning is more carefully carried out and involves local staff of all types through the *Health-Care Planning Teams* (see page 9). A future long range plan for all the health and social services is developed each year so that carefully integrated and balanced development will take place. In particular the planning aspect should always consider the *effectiveness of health services* as judged by their benefit to the ordinary people – i.e. are the health services managing to produce better health and less disease and is the health of the majority of the population better?

The Department of Health acts as a master planner for the health services. By these various methods, the Secretary of State is able to exert an indirect control over the services – strengthening them where they are weakest and constantly encouraging an improvement in standards of care.

Parliamentary control

Because the Secretary of State is answerable to Parliament for the conduct of the health services, it is always open to any member of Parliament to raise any question, however detailed, and this must be answered by the Secretary of State verbally at question time or in writing.

In very serious instances the Secretary of State can set up an Inquiry which then considers all aspects of the question and reports to the Secretary of State who then presents that report to Parliament. Recent examples have included fires in certain hospitals and allegations about the maltreatment of patients in mental hospitals.

A further method of control was introduced in 1973 by the setting up of a Health Service Commissioner for England and a separate one for Wales (see page 30).

Administration of the National Health Service

The simplest way to understand the functioning of the National Health Service is to look at the plan of its administration (see Fig. 1.1). It will be seen that there are two tiers of health authorities – 14 Regional Health Authorities (RHAs) and 192 District Health Authorities (DHAs) and a similar number of Family Health Services Authorities (FHSAs), the population of each rarely exceeding 500 000.

Regional Health Authorities (RHAs)

Generally the Regional Health Authority (RHA) is responsible for the main planning of health services, for capital building programmes, for postgraduate medical, dental and nurse training and for the allocation of financial resources between the constituent District Health Authorities (DHAs) and Family Health Services Authorities (FHSAs).

There are 14 RHAs in England and their distribution is shown in Fig. 1.2. Each has at least one University providing medical education within its boundaries. The RHA forms part of the chain of responsibility from the Secretary of State to the DHAs. The main functions of the RHAs include:

- The development of strategic plans based on the needs identified by the DHAs;
- The allocation of financial resources between its constituent DHAs;
- The allocation of financial resources to each FHSA;
- Monitoring the performance and policies of each DHA to ensure that they are consistent with the needs of the whole region;

Secretary of State for Health
(advised by officers of the
Department of Health situated
centrally and at various regions)

14 Regional Health Authorities (RHAs)
(each advised by a Regional General
Manager, Regional Medical Officer,
Finance Officer, Regional Nursing
Officer, Regional Works Manager)
Functions include:
Planning and priorities
Appointments of consultants (except
in DHAs with teaching responsibilities)
Allocation of resources between DHAs and FHSAs
Capital building
Postgraduate medical, dental and nurse training
Ambulance duties (may be delegated to DHA)
Blood transfusion service

192 District Health
Authorities (DHAs)
Functions include:
Day to day running of all hospital
services (except when given to
NHS Hospital Trusts)
Maternity and child welfare
Community and hospital midwifery
Health visiting
District nursing
Vaccination and immunisation
Prevention of disease, care after-care
Appointment of consultants (in DHAs
containing teaching hospitals)
Ambulance services (when delegated)

Family Health Service
Authorities (FHSAs)
Functions include:
General practitioner services
General dental services
Pharmaceutical services
Ophthalmic services

Community Health Councils
(represent the patients' interests)

Fig. 1.1 The administration of the National Health Service, England.

Fig. 1.2 The Regional Health Authorities in England and Wales. **1** Northern **2** Yorkshire **3** Trent **4** East Anglia **5** North East Thames **6** North West Thames **7** South East Thames **8** South West Thames **9** Wessex **10** Oxford **11** South Western **12** West Midlands **13** Mersey **14** North Western **15** Wales.

- The development of a regional plan for specialist services, i.e. deciding the location and provision of the rarer specialities such as chest surgery, radiotherapy, neurosurgery etc.
- Ensuring with the DHAs that there are adequate medical and dental teaching and research facilities available (this includes postgraduate teaching);
- Provision of an ambulance service – day-to-day control may be delegated to larger DHAs with the exception of the large conurbations, i.e. London, Birmingham, Liverpool etc.
- The design and construction of all large capital building developments (i.e. new hospitals). Small capital projects (i.e. health centres) are usually carried out by DHAs subject to the approval and guidance of the RHA.
- The blood transfusion service.

For details of membership of each RHA see page 20.

Regional General Manager (RGM)

The Regional General Manager (RGM) is responsible for the development of strategic plans and priorities for the Region and the allocation of financial resources to the District Health Authorities. These are based on an analysis from each DHA as well as the advice from the Regional Team of Officers. This includes the Regional Treasurer, Regional Medical Officer, Regional Nursing Officer and the Regional Works Officer. The RGM is also responsible for ensuring that the capital building programme is kept up to date and modified where necessary. Another task of the RGM is to set clear objectives for each of the District General Managers (DGMs) and to monitor their performance.

District Health Authorities (DHAs)

There are 192 District Health Authorities (DHAs) in England. Generally, DHAs are responsible for the main day-to-day management of the local health services except the general practitioners.

The DHA is responsible for all the hospital and community health services and is in charge of:

- District General Hospitals and other hospitals;
- maternity and child health services;
- community midwifery;
- health visiting;
- district nursing/community nursing;
- vaccination and immunisation;
- prevention of disease, care and after care (health education,

chiropody, tuberculosis after care, occupational therapy and some types of convalescence);
— school health services (in conjunction with the corresponding local education authority).

Nineteen of the DHAs also act as centres for medical teaching (in conjunction with the medical schools of the corresponding university). In addition all DHAs which act as centres for medical teaching are responsible for all consultants and senior registrar appointments. (In the rest of the health service, such appointments are undertaken by the RHA.)

The administration of each DHA is delegated to a District General Manager (DGM) who has the assistance of a number of Unit General Managers (UGMs) each of whom are responsible for the administration of a group of hospitals and/or community health services. In addition each DHA has the following chief officers:

• District Treasurer;
• District Medical Officer;
• District Nursing Officer;
• Two clinicians (one consultant and one general practitioner).

Working within each district will be all types of clinicians in consultant practice, as well as a unified hospital and community nursing service covering all aspects – general nursing, midwifery in hospitals and the community, psychiatric nursing, health visiting and district nursing services. There are also various specialists in community medicine working in the district although each DHA has the responsibility of deciding how these functions will be distributed between the local specialists in community medicine.

From 1991 a new self-governing status called NHS Hospital Trusts will be introduced (see page 18 for details).

Specialists in community medicine and community nursing

Although each DHA has to decide the allocation of duties between its specialists in community medicine, the following tasks have to be undertaken:

• The giving of medical and nursing advice to the relevant local education authority on child health and school health matters. It is expected that most DHAs will appoint staff equivalent to the former Specialists in Community (Child Health) and Area Nurse (Child Health) to assist in the organisation and management of the school health service.
• The giving of medical advice to the relevant local authority on

environmental health matters. Such a doctor will also have to act as *'proper officer'* to each local authority in the District who has environmental health responsibilities. Such a Specialist in Community Medicine also helps to control outbreaks of communicable diseases or food poisoning and works closely with the environmental health officers of the local authorities. Notification of communicable and infectious diseases is reported by the patient's doctor to the 'proper officer'. In the cases of outbreaks of infectious diseases the 'proper officer' has, for the purpose of carrying out an epidemiological investigation, executive control over environmental health officers, port health inspectors or health visitors as regards that investigation.

Health-Care Planning Teams

Health-Care Planning Teams are multidisciplinary working parties of officers set up in each District to analyse and assess the needs of the health services. There are two types of Health-Care Planning Teams.

- Permanent teams continuously dealing with the following:
  — children;
  — maternity services;
  — mentally ill people;
  — mentally handicapped people;
  — elderly people.
- *Ad hoc* teams set up to consider a special subject. Such teams may be disbanded after they have studied and reported on a specific subject. They cover many aspects and examples include:
  — review of primary health care services;
  — introduction of day surgery in hospitals;
  — diagnosis, treatment and prevention of non-accidental injury in babies.

Each Health-Care Planning Team contains a wide range of professionals in the health service – general practitioners, consultants, hospital and community nursing staff (midwives, district nurses, health visitors), radiographers, physiotherapists, occupational therapists, chiropodists, hospital social workers – from the corresponding local authority. The Health-Care Planning Teams provide an opportunity for views on special subjects within each district to be studied in detail and to be presented to the DGM and from there to the District Health Authority and Regional Health Authority and to the Department of Health. The District Health Authority through the Joint Consultative Committee (see below) will discuss with the local authority the views of the Health-Care Planning Teams.

Joint Care Planning – Health and Local Authorities

Because services provided by local authorities (particularly those of the social services departments) have a considerable impact on health services and vice versa, it has been decided by the Department of Health that effective arrangements should be made for joint planning.

Joint Care Planning Teams have therefore been set up by all District Health Authorities and the relevant local authorities (including social services and education departments). Joint planning will cover all aspects of health and social services but is particularly important to ensure the correct balance of services for the elderly, the disabled, the mentally handicapped, the mentally ill, children and families and for socially handicapped groups such as alcoholics and drug addicts.

In 1986, at the request of the Secretary of State for Health, Sir Roy Griffiths began a review of all forms of community care and his report was published in 1988. The full description of this report and the Government's response to it (which was reported to the House of Commons in July 1989 by the Secretary of State) is given in Chapter 13, pages 228–30.

Joint Consultative Committees

Every District Health Authority and the matching local authority/ authorities must set up a Joint Consultative Committee (JCC) which has the responsibility of advising on the planning and operation of the health services and the social, environmental and education services run by the local authority. The aim of such a committee is to improve cooperation.

Community Health Councils

Community Health Councils were introduced into the health service by the National Health Service (Reorganisation) Act, 1973. There is approximately one for each District. Their main function is to represent the local consumers' interests and to ensure that the development of the local health service does take regard of local opinion. Each contains 18–30 members, one third of whom are drawn from voluntary bodies active within the district. About half the members are appointed by the corresponding local authority and one sixth by the Regional Health Authority (who provide any permanent staff). No member of a Regional Health Authority, District Health Authority, Family Health Service Authority, nor any doctor or other National Health Service employee may serve on a Community Health Council.

Each Community Health Council has the following list of matters which it can investigate:

— the effectiveness of the health services in that district;
— planning of health services;
— variations in local health services – closure of hospitals or hospital departments;
— collaboration between the health services and the local authority environmental health, education and social services;
— standards of service – number of hospital beds in the district and the average number of patients on family doctors' lists;
— patient facilities including hospital out-patients, open visiting of children, waiting times, amenities for hospital patients and arrangements for rehabilitation of patients;
— waiting periods for in-patients' and out-patients' treatments and for domiciliary services;
— quality of catering in hospitals and in other health service institutions;
— complaints (*not* individual complaints from patients, see below, but the general type of complaint);
— advice to individual members of the public on how and where they should lodge a complaint and the facts that should be provided.

Each Community Health Council must issue an annual report which must then be sent to the Regional Health Authority and District Health Authority. It is hoped that Community Health Councils will provide an opportunity for local people to maintain a careful watch over the development of local health services.

General practitioner services

Family Health Services Authority (FHSA)

A special committee called the Family Health Services Authority (FHSA) (formerly the Family Practitioner Committee) is responsible to the Department of Health on all matters concerning the local family doctor services, the dental services and the optical and pharmaceutical services (Fig. 1.3). All these professionals are independent contractors and hold their contracts with the Family Health Services Authority.

The National Health Service and Community Care Act 1990 reduced the number of members of each FHSA from 30 to 11 (see page 21).

There is a special machinery set up nationally by the Secretary of State – the *Medical Practices Committee* – which is constantly assessing the number of general practitioners in any area compared with its population. It then classifies each area into one of four types.

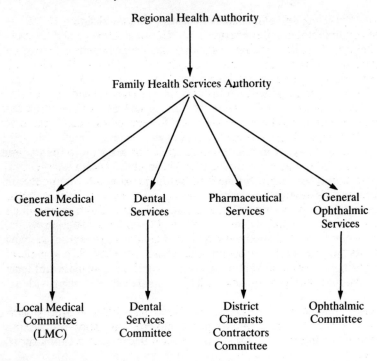

Regional Health Authority

Family Health Services Authority

| General Medical Services | Dental Services | Pharmaceutical Services | General Ophthalmic Services |

| Local Medical Committee (LMC) | Dental Services Committee | District Chemists Contractors Committee | Ophthalmic Committee |

Fig. 1.3   Organisation of the Regional Health Authority and Family Health Services Authority.

Designated area   An area in which there is an inadequate number of doctors. Doctors are encouraged to practise in such an area and will receive a special inducement payment.

Open area   An area with a fair number of doctors where the doctor/patient ratio is between 1/2100 and 1/2400. Permission will always be granted to practise in such an area.

Intermediate area   An area with the doctor/patient ratio between 1/1700 and 1/2100. Applications to practise in such areas will never automatically be granted. Each area is considered on its merits with special reference to the trends in the area.

Restricted area   An area which is over-doctored and where the number of patients per doctor is below 1/1700. Permission is never granted to start a new practice in a restricted area and entry can only be obtained by applying for a vacancy or partnership or assistantship.

Any doctor wishing to start a new practice or to apply for a vacant single handed practice must first apply to the FHSA.

Size of practice and choice of patient and doctor   A limit of 3500 is fixed on the total number of patients any single doctor may have on his or her list. If the doctor employs an assistant (the doctor must have the permission of the Family Health Services Authority to do this), the limit is raised by a further 2000 patients.

The new general practitioner contract (1990) introduced an age limit for family doctors of 70 years and arrangements for facilities for part-time doctors to become principals in general practice for the first time (see page 29 for further details).

The public have a completely free choice of doctor and the doctor also has a free choice in deciding whether or not to accept a patient on to his or her list. Once the patient has been accepted, the doctor is required to render all proper and necessary treatment. If the doctor has agreed to give maternity medical services, then this treatment will include such services for which there will be an additional payment. The doctor must arrange further treatment for patients, such as admission to hospital or attendance at out-patients. Every general practitioner is responsible for ensuring adequate medical cover during absence on holiday or for sickness.

General practitioner vocational training   Since 1976, all new principals to general practice must have completed an approved training scheme (lasting three years) or be exempt because of earlier experience.

Medical List   Each Family Health Services Authority is required to keep a list of all doctors practising in the area. This list, called the Medical List, must indicate separately the general medical practitioners who undertake maternity services. This list is available at the local Family Health Services Authority headquarters and main post offices, where it may be examined by any member of the public to help in the choice of a doctor.

If a patient has difficulty in finding a doctor to accept him or her an application can be made to the Allocation Committee (a sub-committee of the Family Health Services Authority) which will then allocate the patient to a convenient doctor. There are facilities for patients to change their doctor if they wish to do so, or for a doctor to indicate that he or she no longer wishes to look after a particular patient.

Methods of controlling local general medical practice

Local Medical Committee   The Local Medical Committee of doctors acts as the local medical advisory committee to the Family Health Services Authority. Any difficulties connected with particular practices or with local policies are referred to the Local Medical Committee who then advises the Family Health Services Authority. In the case of a doctor who is considered by the Secretary of State to be prescribing excessive drugs and appliances for his or her patients, the Local Medical Committee has the task of carrying out an investigation. If, as a result of their inquiry, the Local Medical Committee come to the conclusion that there has been excessive prescribing, then they must report the case to the Family Health Services Authority who may then recommend the Secretary of State for Health to withhold a certain sum from the remuneration of the doctor as a penalty. Such action is rarely taken, a warning first being given to the doctor.

Other similar expert committees help with the administration of other services, for example:

— Dental Services Committee;
— Area Chemists Contractors Committee (pharmaceutical services);
— Ophthalmic Services Committee.

Methods of controlling general practice

A *Medical Services Committee* appointed by the Family Health Services Authority investigates any serious complaints raised by a patient about the services provided by his or her doctor. This consists of the Chairman of the Family Health Services Authority plus six other members, three of whom must be from the Local Medical Committee. There is a set procedure laid down for the investigation of such complaints. Minor complaints can be investigated by the Administrator to the Family Health Services Authority and major complaints by the Medical Services Committee. The hearing is always in private and the doctor's name is never made public. The Medical Services Committee reports its findings to the Family Health Services Authority which then sends its decision to the Secretary of State. The doctor may also appeal to the Secretary of State. In the case of a proved complaint, a doctor may be warned, have a special limit as to the number of patients on his or her list imposed, or have a sum withheld from his or her remuneration. There is no appeal beyond the Secretary of State whose decision is final.

In very serious cases, the Family Health Services Authority can refer the case to a central *Tribunal* set up by the Secretary of State for Health with a chairman who must be a barrister or solicitor of at least ten years' standing. The Tribunal holds an inquiry and, if satisfied that the case is serious enough, can order the removal of the doctor from general practice in the Health Service. In such a case, there is a right of appeal to the Secretary of State. This is quite different from action by the General Medical Council which can determine the fitness for a doctor to practise in any medical field.

Value of general medical services There is little doubt that, although the hospital and specialist services cost so much more, the standard of medical service provided for each individual patient depends as much on the standard of the general medical services as on any other factor. Although there is no compulsion on any person to register with a doctor, the vast majority of people (about 97–98% of the population have so registered).

Charges to patients There is no additional cost to the individual in obtaining all the medical services provided by hospitals or by general practitioners. Some charges are levied for prescription. Prescriptions for the following people can be obtained without charge by completing the declaration on the back of the prescription form: children aged 16 years and under, women aged 60 and over and men aged 65 and over, and people holding exemption certificates. These are issued to expectant and nursing mothers, people suffering from certain medical conditions, persons and their dependents receiving supplementary benefit and family income supplement. A part charge is made for all dental treatment and other charges are levied for dentures, but these are free for young persons (anyone under 16 or in full-time attendance at school) and expectant and nursing mothers. Charges are also made for spectacles and eye tests.

Scotland

The Scottish Home and Health Department is responsible to the Secretary of State for Scotland for the administration of the National Health Service in Scotland. Its head office is at New St Andrews House, Edinburgh.

There are 15 local health boards in Scotland which administer on behalf of the Secretary of State for health services in Scotland (other than those carried out by the Common Services Agency – see below). These boards take the major policy decisions such as the allocation of resources and the long term planning of services.

Board General Managers (BGMs) have been appointed. Their responsibility is similar to the District General Managers in England but the BGM has more specific authority for public accounting. Unit General Managers have also been appointed in Scotland but many of these posts are part-time. Each Board also has a Chief Administrative Medical Officer whose main task is the identification, measurement and coordination of medical health care.

The Secretary of State for Scotland is responsible to Parliament and there is a Scottish Health Service Planning Council set up to advise the Secretary of State on:

— the identification of health priorities in relation to the resources available and the necessary measures to meet them;
— the implementation, review and evaluation of health planning in Scotland's national health services;
— the integration of health care with other kinds of care to ensure a coordinated policy for the treatment of people in need.

To assist it, the Council has set up a number of advisory groups.

An interesting difference in Scotland is that a central body – the Common Services Agency – has been set up to provide on behalf of the Secretary of State and the health boards a range of specialised services which are more effectively organised on a national basis including ambulance and blood transfusion services, the buying of equipment and other supplies, the planning and design of health service buildings, legal services and health education. Responsibility for the administration of these services rests with a management committee appointed by the Secretary of State. The Common Services Agency whose headquarters are at Trinity Park House, Edinburgh, has a number of separate units including the Scottish Health Services Council, the Scottish Health Education Unit, the Communicable Diseases (Scotland) Unit, the central Legal Office of the health services in Scotland and the Information Services Division.

In addition there are the following.

- A series of *local area consultative committees* to advise health boards on the provision of services in their area. These represent doctors, dentists, pharmacists and ophthalmic and dispensing opticians and advise on all professional matters.
- *University liaison committees* which advise on undergraduate and postgraduate teaching and on research.
- A series of 48 *local health councils* which represent the 'consumer' interests of patients.

In the Scottish Health Services much emphasis has been laid on integration of services for patients and not only at senior management level. Services are planned mainly to meet the needs of patients and to make the best possible use of the staff, money and physical resources. Team work in all aspects of the health services is stressed as well as the involvement of doctors and clinical workers in management matters.

Wales

There are important differences between the health services in England and Wales for no regional tier of health authorities has been set up in Wales.

The Secretary of State for Wales has overall authority to Parliament for the health services in Wales and has four main duties:

— to determine the health policies in Wales;
— to allocate resources between the nine District Health Authorities in Wales;
— to ensure that the objectives of the services are achieved;
— to ensure that the standards of the health services in Wales are satisfactory.

There are nine District Health Authorities in Wales: Dyfed, Clwyd, Gwent, Gwynedd, Mid Glamorgan, Powys, South Glamorgan, West Glamorgan and West Dyfed. These DHAs are responsible to the Secretary of State for Wales for all the day to day health services (with the exception of those carried out by the Welsh Health Technical Services Organisation – see below).

District and Unit General Managers have been appointed in Wales with similar responsibilities to their counterparts in England.

The *Welsh Health Technical Services Organisation* is directly accountable to the Secretary of State for Wales and has three main functions:

— the designing and building of all major hospital and other capital works for the health services in Wales;
— the control and running of a central computer service for the health services in Wales;
— the negotiation of all central supply contracts for health services in Wales.

Northern Ireland

A unified structure exists in Northern Ireland which is outside local political control and deals with all the health services and social services. At provincial level, the Department of Health acts as a government agency and is responsible for policies and the allocation of resources. There are four Boards and each has a General Manager who is personally accountable to the Board for the effective and efficient use of services for patients and clients. There is also an *Area Executive Team* of chief officers and clinicians (including a consultant and a general practitioner).

The National Health Service and Community Care Act 1990

At the end of June 1990, the Bill introducing the National Health Service and Community Care Act 1990 received the Royal Assent.

The majority of the new Act will come into operation on 1 April 1991 although the community care sections, which will place upon local authorities (through their Social Service Departments) the responsibility for carrying out assessments of the needs of certain clients (or patients), will not be introduced until April 1993.

The National Health Service and Community Care 'Act 1990 provides a new framework for the operation of the NHS. The exact details will be determined by various regulations which will be laid before Parliament by the Secretary of State for Health, as well as by various advisory memoranda. To ensure that the general public fully understands the main objectives of the Act a free booklet entitled 'The NHS Reforms and You' was delivered to every household in the UK during July 1990. All health care professionals are strongly advised to study this booklet carefully, as well as the White Paper entitled 'Working for Patients' which was issued in 1988.

The objectives behind the new Act include seven key measures.

1   To ensure more delegation of responsibility to local level so that all the health and community services become more responsive to the individual needs of patients. This principle of delegation also aims at making the community care services for patients (and especially for the mentally ill, mentally handicapped persons, the physically handicapped and the increasing numbers of elderly persons in the country) more flexible. New measures for community care should ensure that the larger local authorities (those responsible for the personal social services) support the increasing numbers of vulnerable people within the United Kingdom. It is also hoped that these community services will become more relevant and responsive to local needs.

2   To make the hospital services more flexible and to give a number of hospitals more freedom to make decisions which, in the end, will benefit patients. A new self-governing status called *NHS Hospital Trusts* is being introduced and the aim of this change is to give certain hospitals more control over their budgets. Health authority property will be transferred to such Trusts and health authority staff working in such hospitals will be employed directly by these Trusts, who will also have the power to determine rates of pay etc. These changes are being introduced to encourage certain hospitals to serve a wider population than just the local one. NHS Trust hospitals will remain within the NHS and will have to continue to provide essential local services. Hospitals will only be allowed to become NHS Trusts when they are judged to be ready to make the best use of *the freedom of NHS Trust status to benefit NHS patients*.

3   New funding arrangements will be introduced to ensure that the finances needed to care for patients in the community will be more

readily available. From a statement made in Parliament by the Secretary of State it now appears that these arrangements will be postponed until April 1993. Many of the details are yet to be determined and there will be a constant process of widespread consultation within the health service professions during the period of the introduction of the new Act.

4   These new financial arrangements will include the family doctor services (primary health care) and large general practices will be able to apply for their own NHS budgets. However, even if any practice were to overspend its budget, there is no question of patients not getting the treatment they need.

A new general practitioner contract (see page 23), aimed at improving the preventive health initiatives undertaken by individual family doctors, has already been introduced (on 1 April 1990). Many features of the new general practitioner contract depend on a much improved data collection service as well as an ongoing analysis of the individual needs of patients in the practice, such as a constant check on when each patient was last seen by the doctor. Under the contract patients aged 16–74 years must be given an invitation to see the doctor every three years and those aged 75 years and over every year. To enable general practitioners to carry this out, a wide re-organisation of record keeping is taking place in all general practices. With the financial help of the Department of Health, the majority of general practices will have their own computers operating for their patients' records by April 1991. In addition these computers keep a check on all prescriptions issued and, when any patient is referred to hospital, provide a full history of the health of the patient. Such systems are bound to improve the quality of clinical care within the NHS.

5   A further important objective is the *reduction of hospital waiting lists for patients needing consultant advice and for operations* or expert treatments only available within hospitals. At least 100 new permanent consultant medical posts are being created over a three year period.

The final two main reforming measures concentrate upon various management changes, including the following.

6   Reform of the various Health Authorities. The Regional Health Authorities (RHAs) and District Health Authorities (DHAs) will have the number of their members reduced and the selection process will be changed.

The Family Practitioner Committees was renamed *Family Health Services Authorities* and their membership reduced and changed radically. A further reform is that, in future, they will be answerable to the RHA (and not the Department of Health as at present). They will be in a similar administrative position as the DHA to the RHA.

7   A *new medical audit service* will be introduced throughout the NHS. These changes will involve the creation of a new *Clinical Standards Advisory Group* who will undertake studies and advise the Secretary of State and other various health bodies on standards of clinical care. In future, the Audit Commission will carry out the audit of the financial accounts of health authorities and other NHS bodies. These changes are aimed at ensuring that wide ranging studies will constantly be carried out. The aim is to ensure that output measurements occur as well as input calculations – the results will be judged on what has actually been achieved for patients. This entails attempting to assess results rather than just give a list of various treatments carried out.

Detailed changes introduced by the National Health Service and Community Care Act 1990

The composition of the new Health Authorities will be as follows.

Regional Health Authority (RHA)

These will cover existing geographical boundaries. The two main changes include the numbers and types of members and the responsibilities of the RHA.

With effect from July 1990 each RHA will consist of the following:

—   chairman;
—   five non-executive members, to include the chairman of a Family Health Service Authority as well as someone from a University with a medical or dental school;
—   up to five executive members, to include the General Manager and Director of Finance.

The main changes can be summarised by noting that the RHA in future will be smaller and will no longer contain members representing local authorities and, for the first time, will include executive members (officers). Note that, including the chairman, there will always be a majority of members from outside the health professions – this is assuming the executive members will always be drawn from doctors, nurses and other health care professionals or administrative staff.

District Health Authority (DHA)

These will cover the same geographical area as at present. The number of members making up each DHA is reduced to a maximum of 11 (similar to RHA) and these will consist of:

— chairman;
— five non-executive members (if the DHA is a 'teaching district' there will be one member from either a University or medical school);
— up to five executive members, to include both the General Manager and the Director of Finance.

In general the responsibilities of each DHA are unchanged. Where, however, NHS Trusts are formed within the District, this will have the effect, in practical terms, of reducing the responsibility of the DHA because they will no longer be responsible for the finance or the administration of that hospital as both functions would then be undertaken by the respective NHS Hospital Trust.

Family Health Services Authority (FHSA)

This body will undertake the same responsibilities as the former Family Practitioner Committee (see pages 11–15) but will contain a smaller number of members. Each FHSA will have 11 members made up as follows:

— chairman;
— General Manager;
— nine non-executive members, to include a general practitioner, a dentist, a pharmacist, a community nurse plus five lay members.

Note that, in future, all appointments to the Health Authorities will be appointed by the Secretary of State for Health. Apart from a university or medical or dental school in respect of an RHA or a university or medical school in the case of a teaching DHA, no specific organisation can claim it must be represented. This means that local authorities will no longer have a right of representation although individual members of local authorities can be directly appointed by the Secretary of State.

Another significant change is that the General Manager must be appointed to the RHA, DHA or FHSA and the Director of Finance to the RHA. In the past these officers have advised their Health Authorities but have not been voting members. Such officers will now have both an advisory and a voting role on their respective health authorities.

Community care changes in the National Health Service and Community Care Act 1990

The Act places on large local authorities (in practice on their Social Service Departments) the responsibility for carrying out assessments of the needs of individual clients. These would include those who are chronically ill or physically handicapped, mentally ill persons, those who are mentally handicapped and elderly persons who are infirm and who need help to enable them to continue to live in the community. In some instances such vulnerable people may, at present, be looked after in hospital (this is particularly the case with mentally ill persons). To make certain that each local authority will have the financial means to do this, new specific financial grants will, in future, be paid for community care for mentally ill persons. The principle likely to be followed will involve grants specifically calculated for each mentally ill patient transferred from hospital to the community. These grants will be determined after consultation with health, housing, voluntary and other interests. They will cover the funding of nursing home care and the provision of other services either directly by the local authority or by making arrangements with other bodies. The exact methods of doing this are yet to be determined and will probably vary from area to area although the principle will remain the same.

The method of funding community care services for other groups of clients (physically handicapped persons, chronically ill people and vulnerable elderly persons) will not be by specific financial grants but by the Government increasing its general grant to large local authorities. This decision to give specific grants only for mentally ill persons and to exclude other vulnerable groups has been widely criticised as many fear that community care services will be very unequally developed or even postponed.

Section 50 of the Act establishes a new complaints procedure to assist users of community care services and also widens the Secretary of State's power to set up inquiries where there is evidence of a possible misuse of power by the relevant local authority responsible for arranging the extended system of community care.

Other parts of the National Health Service Act 1990 include the following.

- Giving wider powers of inspection to the Social Service Inspectorate of the Department of Health.
- In future there will be easier staff transfer arrangements for staff to move from the NHS to local authority as community care services develop. These should assist the smooth transfer of certain home nursing care services (now not due until 1993).
- The remaining Crown immunities in the NHS are abolished by the Act.

- The present power of the Secretary of State for Health to control the development of private hospitals will be removed by the Act.

Details of individual sections of the National Health Service and Community Care Act 1990

The main detailed provisions of the Act are given in Table 1.1.

New general practitioner contract

A new general practitioner contract was introduced in April 1990 as part of the reforms of the NHS. The following short account describes those changes which are of particular importance to patients and the general public. All health care professionals should be familiar with these details so that they can help patients to make the best use of the family doctor service.

Many of the changes introduced are intended to improve the preventive medical care which general practitioners undertake.

Information to patients

In future the Family Health Services Authority must draw up a list called the '*Local Directory of Family Doctors*'. This is in addition to the 'Medical List' (see page 13). The following information will be included.

- The date of the first registration of the doctor.
- The sex of the doctor.
- Details of any medical qualification of the doctor.
- The nature of any clinic provided by the doctor for the patients.
- The number of assistants and trainee general practitioners employed by the doctor.
- Details of:
  - the number of persons employed or available at the practice premises to assist the doctor;
  - the nature of the services provided by each such person;
  - the average number of hours normally worked by such person during the week;
  - if the doctor so desires, details of any languages, other than English, spoken by the doctor or other person employed in the practice.

This local Directory is readily available for consultation by the general public.

Table 1.1   The main detailed provisions of the National Health Service and Community Care Act 1990.

1. Replacing existing Regional Health Authorities (RHAs) and District Health Authorities (DHAs) and Family Practitioner Committees, renamed Family Health Services Authorities (FHSAs), with smaller bodies consisting of a mix of executive and non-executive and, in the case of RHAs and teaching DHAs, a member drawn from a university. (Sections 1–2, Schedule 1)

2. Enabling health service bodies to make NHS contracts for better matching of money to the provision of services, providing for urgent need for treatment where time does not allow NHS contracts to be arranged in advance, and setting up procedures for resolving disputes between NHS contracts. (Sections 3–4)

3. Establishing NHS trusts after statutory consultation, setting out their powers and duties, their financial arrangements, the mechanism for transferring health authority staff and property to them, and the Secretary of State's reserve powers over them. (Sections 5–11 and 21, Schedule 2 and 3)

4. Putting FHSAs in a management relationship with RHAs which parallels the present position of DHAs. (Sections 12, 13 and 19)

5. Setting out the arrangements for GP practices to apply for fund-holding status, the method of funding and the use of practice funds. (Sections 14–17)

6. Requiring GP practices to be given annual indicative prescribing amounts. (Section 18)

7. Transferring responsibility for the statutory audit of NHS accounts from the Department of Health and the Welsh Office to the Audit Commission. (Section 20, Schedule 4)

8. Changes in general practice, including allowing entry of part-time doctors to the medical list and reserve powers over the number of doctors and dentists entering general practice. (Sections 22–4)

Practice Leaflet

All family doctors *must in future publish a 'Practice Leaflet'* (and keep it up to date each year). The leaflet will provide the following information for patients.

- Names and addresses of doctors in the practice with their medical qualifications and dates when obtained.
- The times when the doctor is available for consultation and how appointments can be made.
- How requests for home visits should be made.
- How emergency calls should be made.
- The method of obtaining repeat prescriptions.
- Details of the reception staff available at the surgery premises.

9. Removing the need for the Secretary of State's authorisation of private patient facilities in NHS hospitals, but retaining his or her power to intervene if this freedom is abused. (Section 25)

10. Placing on local authorities the responsibility for carrying out assessments of the needs of individual clients, planning community care services for their locality (in consultation with health, housing, voluntary and user interests), funding nursing home care and providing other services, either directly or by making arrangements with other bodies. (Sections 42–7)

11. Giving wider powers of inspection to the Social Services Inspectorate and other appointees of the Secretary of State. (Section 48)

12. Providing for easier staff transfer from the NHS to Local Authorities as community care services develop. (Section 49)

13. Establishing new complaints procedures to help users of community care services and widening the Secretary of State's power to set up inquiries. (Section 50)

14. Establishing for new specific grants for mental illness services and services for drug and alcohol misusers provided by voluntary bodies. (Section 50)

15. Abolishing the remaining Crown immunities in the NHS, with a small number of essential exceptions. (Sections 60 and 61, Schedule 8)

16. Establishing the Clinical Standards Advisory Group to undertake studies and advise the Secretary of State and health service bodies on standards of clinical care. (Section 62)

17. Removing the Secretary of State's power to control the development of private hospitals. (Section 63)

Parts II and IV of the Act make analogous changes to the National Health Service and the community care services in Scotland.

- Whether practice nurse/nurses are employed.
- How to contact the district nurse, midwife and health visitor who work with the practice.
- Details of other medical services available – immunisation sessions held, antenatal clinics (if maternity services are provided), contraceptive advice (if provided), cervical smears as well as details of child health surveillance and minor surgery (if these are undertaken).
- Details of regular medical examinations held. Three groups of patients must be seen by all family doctors in the future (for full details see page 27):
    (*i*)   patients registering with the practice for the first time;
    (*ii*) patients aged 16–74 years of age who have not been seen by

the doctor during the last three years. These must be invited to a consultation at the surgery premises;

(*iii*)   patients aged 75 years and over – these must be offered a consultation and home visit annually.

- An indication of the practice area normally covered. Usually the doctor will only agree to provide medical services for those living within the practice area but may accept patients from outside the area in certain circumstances.
- Details of the surgery premises including whether they can accommodate handicapped persons and wheelchairs.

New family doctor services

Child health surveillance

In future, all family doctors will be encouraged to provide child health surveillance for children under the age of five years. This involves the doctor undertaking a monitoring procedure and an examination of the child on a number of occasions at spaced intervals to check that the progress of the child is normal.

In all instances, records must be maintained by the doctor which will later be used for school health and other checks then carried out. Notes will be recorded of both the medical condition of the child and the responses (if any) to offers made to the child's parents for the child to undergo any examination.

Each Family Health Services Authority must maintain a '*Child health surveillance list*' of the names of family doctors who have satisfied the Authority that they have such medical experience and training to enable them properly to provide child health surveillance.

An extra fee will be paid to doctors providing this service.

Minor surgery procedures

In future all doctors who are trained and have experience in minor surgical procedures will be encouraged to undertake them in their practices. These include the following.

Injections	Intra articular
	Peri articular
	Varicose veins
	Haemorrhoids
Aspirations	Joints
	Cysts
	Bursae
	Hydrocoele

Incisions   Abscesses
            Cysts
            Thrombosed piles

Each Family Health Services Authority must keep a *Minor Surgery List* of the names of the family doctors who have the medical experience, training and facilities to enable them properly to provide minor surgical procedures. Extra fees are paid for such services.

Maternity and contraceptive services

The arrangements for doctors to be approved to carry out maternity and contraceptive services are unchanged and will continue as at present.

Regular medical examinations

The regular medical examination which all family doctors have, in future, to undertake will cover three groups of patients: (*i*) newly registered; (*ii*) those aged 16–74 years; and (*iii*) those aged 75 years and over.

Newly registered patients   In all consultations for newly registered patients the doctor must, in the course of the examination, undertake the following.

- Seek details from the patient as to his or her medical history and, so far as may be relevant to the patient's medical history, as to that of his or her consanguineous family, in respect of:
  — illnesses, immunisations, allergies, hereditary conditions, medication and tests carried out for breast or cervical cancer;
  — social factors (including employment, housing and family circumstances) which may affect the patient's health;
  — factors of the patient's lifestyle (including diet, exercise, use of tobacco, consumption of alcohol, and misuse of drugs or solvents) which may affect health;
  — the current state of the patient's health.
- Offer to undertake a physical examination of the patient, comprising:
  — the measurement of height, weight and blood pressure;
  — the taking of a urine sample and its analysis to identify the presence of albumin and glucose.
- Record in the patient's medical records the doctor's findings arising out of the details supplied by, and any examination of, the patient.

- Assess whether and, if so, in what manner and to what extent the doctor should render personal medical services to the patient.
- In so far as it would not, in the opinion of the doctor, be likely to cause serious damage to the physical or mental health of the patient to do so, offer to discuss with the patient (or, where the patient is a child, the parent) the conclusions the doctor has drawn as to the state of the patient's health. The invitation to a patient (or parent) must be in writing or, if given verbally, be confirmed in writing and recorded in the patient's records.

Patients aged 16–74 years   A similar procedure and medical examination, as outlined above, must take place for patients aged between 16 and 74 years who have not been seen within three years.

Patients aged 75 years and over   In the case of patients aged 75 years and over the doctor must, in addition to the procedures outlined above, undertake the following.

- Invite each patient to participate in a consultation.
- Offer to make a domiciliary visit to each patient, for the purpose of assessing whether the doctor needs to render personal medical services to that patient.
- When making an assessment the doctor shall record in the patient's records the observations made on any matter which appears likely to affect the patient's general health, including, where appropriate, the patient's:
  — sensory functions;
  — mobility;
  — mental condition;
  — physical condition including continence;
  — social environment;
  — use of medicines.

A record of any observations made in the course of a domiciliary visit must be filed with the patient's medical records.

General nature of medical services offered

A general practitioner working in the NHS must render to his or her patients all necessary and appropriate medical services of the type usually provided by general medical practitioners. These services shall include the following.

- Giving advice, where appropriate, to a patient in connection with the patient's general health, and in particular about the signifi-

cance of diet, exercise, the use of tobacco, the consumption of alcohol, and the misuse of drugs and solvents.
- Offering consultations to patients and, where appropriate, physical examinations for the purpose of identifying, or reducing the risk of, disease or injury.
- Offering to patients, where appropriate, vaccination or immunisation against Measles, Mumps, Rubella, Pertussis, Poliomyelitis, Diphtheria and Tetanus.
- Arranging for the referral of patients, as appropriate, for the provision of any other services under the National Health Service Act 1977.
- Giving advice, as appropriate, to enable patients to avail themselves of services provided by a local social services authority.

A doctor is not required to provide to any person contraceptive services, child health surveillance services, minor surgery services nor, except in an emergency, maternity medical services, unless he or she has previously undertaken to the Family Health Services Authority to provide such services to that person.

A part-time principal (see below) is only required to provide those medical services which he or she has agreed to undertake.

Alterations to the conditions of service for family doctors

The following are the main changes to general practitioners' contracts which are of interest to other health professionals and the general public.

Age limit   In future all family doctor principals will have to retire from the NHS when reaching 70 years of age.

Part-time doctors   For the first time, doctors may act as principals in the NHS even if they only practise part-time. Three groups of doctors are envisaged:
  (*i*)   those working 26 hours a week or more but less than full-time;
  (*ii*)   those working 19–25 hours a week; and
  (*iii*)   those working 13–18 hours a week.
It is expected that this change will help women with families to return part-time to the family doctor service thus strengthening the service as more doctors will be encouraged to work in general practice.

Changing the family doctor   The method of a patient changing his or her family doctor has been simplified in the new contract. Any patient who is on a doctor's list may now apply to any other doctor to register, providing the second doctor agrees. The arrangements whereby any patient who has been refused acceptance can apply to the Family

Health Services Authority for assignment to a doctor on the Authority's list remains unchanged (see page 13).

Health Service Commissioners

Health Service Commissioners for England and Wales were introduced in 1973 to investigate complaints against the relevant health bodies.

Both these commissioners are only removable on an address from both Houses of Parliament and their salaries are paid directly by the Treasury (out of the Consolidated Fund). They are therefore in the same independent position as High Court Judges.

The main function of these Health Service Commissioners is to investigate the following.

— An alleged failure in a service provided by a relevant health body – Regional Health Authority, District Health Authority, Family Practitioner Committee, Public Health Laboratory Service Board or any special body appointed before and after 1 April 1974.
— An alleged failure of a relevant body to provide a service which it was a function of that body to provide.
— Any other act taken by or on behalf of a relevant body in a case where it is alleged any person has sustained injustice or hardship in consequence of the failure or of maladministration.

It is important to note that the Health Service Commissioner is specifically excluded from dealing with the following.

— Professional complaints against decisions of individual doctors or nurses in regard to individual patients.
— Any action which is dealt with by the tribunal set up to deal with serious complaints (see page 14).
— Any complaint which is subject to action in a court of law.

2   The measurement of health

The measurement or assessment of the health of a community is an important feature of any preventive health programme. Rarely is it possible to attempt to carry out all desirable preventive health work in any area at once. It is, therefore, essential to be able to assess the fluctuations in the health of the community from time to time, and to decide which are the worst problems so that they may be tackled first. It is also valuable to be able to compare the health of, say, one city or country with another. Often, in this way, marked variations will be shown in the health of different places and then a search can be started to discover the reasons behind such differences.

The assessment of the health of any group of individuals may occasionally be made by a series of medical examinations held on all the people in, say, a factory or a school. But this is only possible where there is complete control over the persons involved and is never practicable for a whole community such as a city, town or country. The measurement of the health of such populations is only possible by indirect methods, by studying various factors such as mortality of the population from different diseases and studies of the incidence of disease. The collection and interpretation of such information is called the study of *Vital Statistics*.

Most of these studies concern either the incidence of disease (*morbidity*) or the proportion of persons within the community dying from disease (*mortality*). Although accurate records of incidence of disease are the more valuable, it is rarely possible to get such figures as there is no method of ensuring that all or even a fixed proportion of cases are reported. It is, however, necessary to know the cause of all deaths (for legal purposes), and mortality statistics are usually very complete and certainly more reliable when dealing with very large communities. But even with mortality statistics, difficulties may arise from different standards of diagnosis and from the introduction of new forms of treatment which may change the mortality completely. For example, the mortality rate of typhoid fever has fallen over 10% to less than 1% following the introduction of ampicillin treatment. Thus, the present mortality rate cannot be used as a reliable indicator of the incidence of this disease.

It is obviously desirable to refer to all statistics in terms of the same unit of population and this is normally per 1000 or per 100 000 persons. Thus the *Birth Rate* is the number of persons who are born per year per 1000 persons. The *Infant Mortality Rate* is the number of infants under the age of one year who die per 1000 births per year. The *Maternal Mortality Rate* is the number of women who die from causes associated with childbirth per 100 000 total births.

It is essential to know the population accurately to calculate various death rates. A Census – when the population is counted – is undertaken every ten years and was last carried out in April 1981. The Registrar General calculates the estimated population of all areas in the intermediate years between each Census. Studies have already commenced in preparation of the next Census in 1991.

Age distribution of the population

The distribution of the various age groups within the population is of interest and is shown in Table 2.1. Note that although there are larger numbers of males in the population at the younger age groups, the reverse occurs in old age – there are many more old women alive than old men. In 1988 in the UK there were 196 000 men aged 85 years and over compared with more than three times as many women, 600 000.

Birth rate

The birth rate is the number of children born per year per 1000 of the population. This is affected by many factors such as the numbers of persons of reproductive age within a population – the higher their proportion, the higher is likely to be the birth rate. The social habits of a country will cause great changes in birth rate – in 1988 the rate in Eire (a predominantly Roman Catholic country) was 15.3 compared with a rate of 11.6 in the UK. A rapidly developing country will usually show a high birth rate – e.g. Israel whose rate in 1985 was 23.5.

Table 2.1   Age and sex structure of the population of the United Kingdom, 1988 (thousands). (From Population Trends, 1990.)

Age group	Persons	Males	Females
0–4	3747 (6.56%)	1920	1827
5–14	7013 (12.29%)	3600	3413
15–24	8977 (15.73%)	4588	4389
25–34	8387 (14.69%)	4227	4160
35–44	7853 (13.77%)	3933	3920
45–59	9264 (16.23%)	4602	4662
60–64	2940 (5.15%)	1411	1529
65–74	5031 (8.81%)	2228	2803
75–84	3068 (5.39%)	1108	1960
85+	796 (1.39%)	196	600

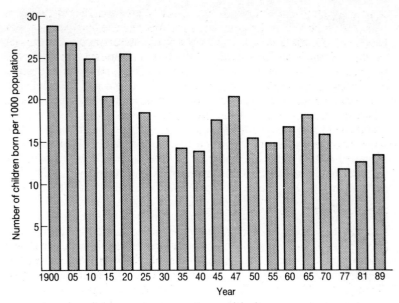

Fig. 2.1 Birth rate, United Kingdom, 1900–89.

The accompanying graph of the birth rate in England and Wales from 1900 to present day (Fig. 2.1) shows many fascinating changes. It will be seen that the rate fell steadily to a very low figure in 1933; it fell during the Second World War, rose to a peak in 1947, and fell again, only to rise once more to the figure of 17.9 in 1966. Since that year, it fell steadily to 11.6 in 1977, but since then has risen and in 1989 was 13.6.

These changes tell much about the pattern of human life in this century. The high rate in 1900 was associated with a very high death rate among children (15% died before their first birthday) so that although the birth rate was high a much smaller proportion of children reached adult life than today. The low birth rate of the 1930s was connected with the very unstable living conditions between the two world wars. The 1947 peak was the result of many families being re-united after the war. The 1965 high figure is dependent upon many factors, including earlier marriage and greater prosperity. During the last 20 years, increasing use of effective contraceptives (for example, the pill) and abortion have all played an important part in reducing the birth rate.

The most recent rise is due mainly to technical reasons, there being a higher proportion of persons of child bearing age in the community caused by the high birth rates in the 1947–55 period.

Various death rates

The *Crude Death Rate* (the number of persons dying per 100 population) is of little value, as the relative population in towns is never known accurately. When there is a large number of aged inhabitants, the number of deaths in such a community is bound to be higher, irrespective of the living conditions in that area. More important is the Standardised Mortality Ratio (SMR).

Standardised Mortality Ratios make allowances for changes in the age structure of the population. By convention the levels in one year are called 100 (in Table 2.2 that year is 1980). Table 2.2 gives the SMRs for selected causes in 1987 for England as published by the Department of Health. Note that, for all causes, the mortality had fallen to 88 for males and to 90 for females compared with the base year 1980. It will be noticed that there have been many unequal changes in mortality between the sexes. Whereas pneumonia, bronchitis, hypertensive disease and motor vehicle and other accidents have fallen fairly equally, there has been a sharp increase in the mortality for diabetes in both sexes. Marked differences have been observed in suicide (103 in

Table 2.2 Standardised Mortality Ratios (SMRs) in selected causes,England, 1987 (SMR 1980 = 100). (From Health and Personal Social Service Statistics (1989). Department of Health.)

Males		Females	
All causes	88	All causes	90
Pneumonia	34	Pneumonia	42
Bronchitis	38	Pregnancy/Labour	45
Hypertensive disease	60	Bronchitis	51
Tuberculosis (respiratory)	60	Hypertensive disease	64
Hyperplasia of prostate	64	Meningococcal infection	64
Chronic rheumatic heart disease	64	Suicide	67
Ulcer of stomach	75	Motor vehicle accidents	71
Motor vehicle accidents	78	Chronic rheumatic heart disease	74
Ulcer of duodenum	79	Tuberculosis (respiratory)	75
Meningococcal infection	81	Cancer of stomach	78
Cancer of stomach	84	Ulcer of stomach	79
Cerebrovascular disease	85	Cerebrovascular disease	87
Cancer of lung	88	Cancer of cervix uteri	89
Ischaemic heart disease	90	Congenital malformations	91
Nephritis/nephrosis	91	Nephritis/nephrosis	94
Congenital malformations	94	Ischaemic heart disease	96
Leukaemia	98	Ulcer of duodenum	99
Suicide	103	Cancer of lung	104
Cancer of breast	104	Leukaemia	108
Diabetes	152	Cancer of breast	110
		Diabetes	147

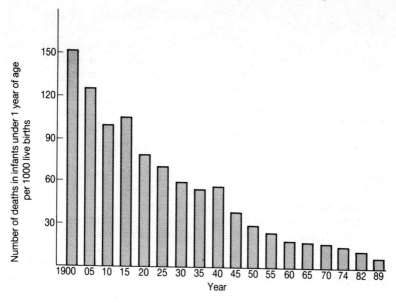

Fig. 2.2   Infant mortality rate, United Kingdom, 1900–89.

men and 67 in women) while cancer of the lung mortality has fallen to 88 in men but risen to 104 in women. Ischaemic heart disease has fallen in men to 90 and in women to 96.

The *Infant Mortality Rate* is one of the most useful death rates to give an indication of the living conditions of any area. The infant mortality rate is the number of infants who die under one year of age per 1000 live related births. It is a measure of the number of children who die before reaching their first birthday per 1000 born alive. In 1989 in the United Kingdom the rate was 8.4 which means that 0.84% of infants born alive, died in their first year of life.

The improvement in the infant mortality rate, and consequently in the living conditions in the United Kingdom is shown in Fig. 2.2. It will be seen that there has been a general improvement throughout the last 80 years. There have, however, been periods such as the 1930s when the change was very slow due to the slowing down of the improvement in the living conditions. The infant mortality rate is a sensitive indicator of changes in the living conditions. It can, for instance, be used to compare the living conditions of large cities in the same country. The rates for different District Health Authorities in England are shown in Table 2.3.

Many people find it difficult to believe that the excellent paediatric services available in some cities do not improve matters. They do play their part in keeping the deaths lower than they might otherwise be, but the *main factors affecting an infant's health are the conditions in the*

Table 2.3   Infant mortality rates of District Health Authorities in England, 1986–88. (From OPCS, Monitor DH3, 89/1.)

Huntingdon	5.1	Nottingham	8.2	Huddersfield	11.6
Bexley	5.9	Newcastle	8.3	Central Birmingham	11.8
Warrington	6.1	Liverpool	8.8	Camberwell	12.2
Oxfordshire	6.4	East Surrey	9.1	Exeter	12.5
Hillingdon	6.8	Scunthorpe	9.9	Kettering	12.6
Enfield	7.1	Bristol & Frenchay	10.7	Central Manchester	12.9
Solihull	7.6	Rugby	10.8	Isle of Wight	13.5
Plymouth	8.1	Salisbury	11.5	Bradford	14.3

home. An increase of unemployment leading to deterioration of living conditions would increase infant deaths. Indeed a political decision which reduced unemployment might do more to prevent infant deaths than many medical improvements. There are considerable variations in the infant mortality rates of different District Health Authorities (see Table 2.3).

The infant mortality rate is lowest in Social Class I and II and highest in Social Class V (see Table 2.4 and page 45 for a description of social classes). The infant mortality rate for legitimate births in the United Kingdom for 1989 was 8.2 and 11.6 for illegitimate births. This difference, which is usual, reflects the greater hazards to illegitimate babies. There are wide variations between the infant mortality rates of different countries of the world (Table 2.5).

An important part of the infant mortality rate is the number of infant deaths which occur in the first four weeks of life – the *Neonatal Mortality Rate*. In 1989 in the United Kingdom this was 4.7 per 1000 live related births showing that 57% of the first year deaths occur within the first four weeks of life. The majority of neonatal deaths occur in the first week of life and this is now called the *Early Neonatal Mortality Rate*. Thus in 1989 in the UK the neonatal mortality rate was made up as follows:

Early neonatal mortality rate	3.8
Late neonatal mortality rate	0.9
	4.7

Table 2.4   Infant mortality rate by social class, United Kingdom, 1987 (all classes infant mortality rate = 9.0). (From OPCS, Monitor DH3 Series.)

Social class	Infant mortality rate
I	6.9
II	6.7
IIIN	7.1
IIIM	7.7
IV	9.6
V	11.8

Table 2.5 Infant mortality in different countries, 1986. (From World Health Organisation Statistics, 1987.)

Japan	5.2	United States of America	10.4
Canada	7.9	New Zealand	10.9
Netherlands	8.0	Israel	11.4
France	8.3	Greece	14.1
Germany	9.0	Portugal	17.8
United Kingdom	9.5	USSR	25.3
Australia	9.8	Yugoslavia	27.3
Italy	10.3	Guatemala	56.0

The *Perinatal Mortality Rate* is a combination of the number of stillbirths and deaths that occur within the first week of life per 1000 total births – early neonatal death rate. In 1989 in the United Kingdom, the perinatal mortality rate was 8.8 (5.0 stillbirth rate plus 3.8 deaths in the first week of life). The value of the perinatal mortality rate is that it gives a very good indication of the hazards to a baby immediately before and after birth.

There are four factors which influence perinatal mortality – maternal age, parity, social class and legitimacy (see Table 2.6). Note that the perinatal mortality rate is high in both very young mothers (under the age of 20) and in mothers over the age of 35. The rate is lowest for mothers with one child and highest for those with three or more children. Perinatal mortality is lowest in Social Class I (6.8) and then rises steadily until it reaches 10.8 in Social Class V. Note that the perinatal mortality rate in illegitimate births is higher than in legitimate births.

The *Maternal Mortality Rate*, which is the number of women who die from causes associated with childbirth per 100 000 total births, is another very interesting death rate. It is a measure of the risk attached to childbirth, as deaths are only counted if they are directly related to the pregnancy.

Since 1900 the maternal mortality rate has improved dramatically (Fig. 2.3). In 1985 it was 6.9 compared with 481 in 1900. But examin-

Table 2.6 Perinatal mortality by maternal age, parity and social class, England and Wales, 1987. All births show a perinatal mortality rate in legitimate births of 8.9 and in illegitimate births of 11.1. (From OPCS Monitor Services, DH1.)

Maternal age	Rate	Parity	Rate	Social class	Rate
Less than 20	10.3	0	9.0	I	6.8
20–24	9.0	1	6.6	II	7.0
25–29	7.9	2	8.5	IIIN	7.8
30–34	8.6	3 and		IIIM	8.1
35 and over	11.6	over	10.6	IV	9.9
				V	10.8

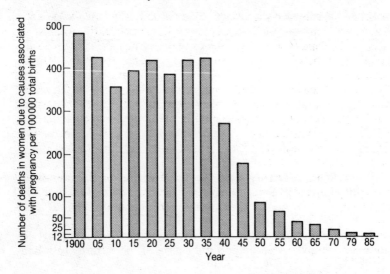

Fig. 2.3 Maternal mortality rate (including abortion), England and Wales, 1900–85.

ation of the way in which this rate has improved shows that it did so quite differently compared with the infant mortality rate. Comparison of the two graphs shows that the infant mortality rate gradually and steadily improved throughout the last 80 years, whereas the maternal mortality rate hardly altered from 1900 to 1930 and at the beginning of the 1930s had actually risen to 410. It then fell very quickly after 1937. The reason for this difference is that the maternal mortality rate is affected by entirely different factors – whereas the infant mortality rate is mainly connected with living conditions, *the maternal mortality rate is related to the standard of obstetric practice*. An advance in obstetrics, particularly the introduction of chemotherapy and antibiotics, cut down the dangers of deaths from puerperal infection dramatically after 1937. It was later followed by further advances reducing the danger of toxaemias and haemorrhage.

Morbidity measurement

One of the most interesting studies of morbidity (incidence of disease) was made in the second national study of morbidity statistics in general practice. This was carried out in the United Kingdom in 1981–2, covered 48 different practices of all types and involved 332 270 patients. Just over 71% of persons at risk consulted their general practitioner during the study year. The consultation rate varied with the age of the patient – the highest consultation rate was the under fives (98%). More females saw their doctor than did males (77% compared with 65%) and, on average, each person consulted their general practitioner one and a half times per episode of illness.

Seven main diagnostic groups were used although under 'Remainder' a number of different conditions were included as well as 'symptoms, signs and ill-defined conditions' and these involved abdominal pain, cough, rashes and skin eruptions, headache, malaise and tiredness and dizziness and giddiness. The results are given in Table 2.7.

Table 2.7 Results of a national study of morbidity statistics in general practice in England and Wales, 1981–82. (From Morbidity Statistics in General Practice, 1981–82, OPCS.)

	Diagnostic group	% of patient/doctor consultations
1	Remainder	41.5
2	Diseases of respiratory system	16.0
3	Prophylatic procedures, medical examinations, oral contraceptive advice etc.	13.9
4	Diseases of circulatory system	8.9
5	Disease of central nervous system and sense organs	7.6
6	Mental disorders	6.8
7	Infectious and parasitic diseases	5.3

Hospital statistics

Another interesting way of studying the incidence of disease is to study hospital statistics. These are taken from the Hospital Inpatient Enquiry (England) which is published by the Office of Population Censuses and Surveys (OPCS). If the proportion of hospital beds occupied (Fig. 2.4) is compared with the discharge and deaths of patients (Fig. 2.5) some interesting differences are noted. Elderly patients occupy 33% of all hospital beds and surgical patients 30%; but of all discharges and deaths surgical cases make up no less than 45.9% whereas elderly patients only total 7.1%. This is mainly because the length of stay of elderly patients is so much longer than that of most surgical cases. This example emphasises the increasing problem an ageing population presents to hospitals.

Communicable diseases

Before any effective preventive measures can be planned, it is essential to know the levels of incidence of the disease in question.

Most serious communicable diseases must be notified to the 'proper

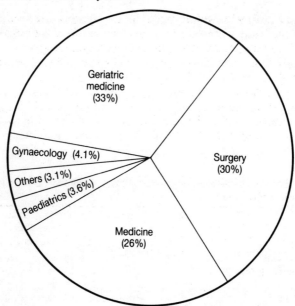

Fig. 2.4   Percentage of hospital beds in daily use (excluding maternity cases and mental disorders), England, 1985. (Based on figures from *Hospital Inpatient Enquiry*, OPCS, 1985.)

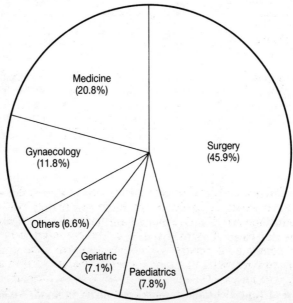

Fig. 2.5   Percentage of discharges and deaths (excluding mental disorders), England, 1985. (Based on figures from *Hospital Inpatient Enquiry*, OPCS, 1985.)

officer' (see p. 9) who will normally be the appropriate Community Physician or District Medical Officer. This allows the disease to be completely investigated and its source of infection discovered, as well as allowing a complete record of the incidence of the disease to be maintained.

Figures of notifiable communicable diseases reported in England and Wales are given in Table 2.8. Most are fairly typical although there has been a marked fall in the number of cases of whooping cough and the food poisoning figures are very high. Tuberculosis again shows a fall.

Table 2.8 Communicable diseases notified in England and Wales, 1988. (From OPCS, Monitor MB 2, 90/1.)

Measles	86001
Food poisoning	39713
Scarlet fever	5949
Whooping cough	5117
Tuberculosis (respiratory)	4022
Dysentery	3692
Viral hepatitis	5063
Acute meningitis	2987
Malaria	1271
Other forms of tuberculosis	1083
Ophthalmia neonatorum	374
Paratyphoid fever	180
Typhoid fever	174
Acute encephalitis	65
Leptospirosis	36
Tetanus	12
Acute poliomyelitis	2
Typhus	1
Diphtheria	1
Rabies	1

AIDS

Some communicable diseases have never been made notifiable because to do so would be likely to lead to concealment of the illness. Examples include AIDS and sexually transmitted diseases (see Chapter 8). In the case of AIDS, statistics are prepared from direct voluntary confidential reports by clinicians to the Public Health Laboratory Service (PHLS) Communicable Disease Centre and the Communicable Disease (Scotland) Unit (see Table 8.1 for full details). By the end of June 1990, the cumulative total of cases of AIDS in the UK had reached 3433 (3280 men and 153 women) with 1869 deaths. Details of sexually transmitted diseases are collected from special

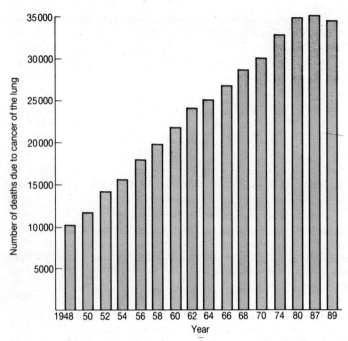

Fig. 2.6   Deaths from cancer of the lung, England and Wales, 1948–89.

hospital clinics and published annually in the Health and Personal Social Service Statistics (Department of Health).

Non-communicable disease

The value of a study into the incidence of non-communicable diseases is that it emphasises the relative problems of different diseases and stimulates research into factors which are connected with their incidence. Very often special research studies are started in this way and lead to important preventive factors being demonstrated. A good example of this is given by cancer of the lung, which has increased so alarmingly from 6439 deaths in 1940 to 34 581 in 1989 (see Fig. 2.6) that much research has been undertaken to find out the reasons for this increase. Many studies, carried out in different countries, have shown a direct connection between smoking cigarettes and cancer of the lung. At present deaths from cancer of the lung in men have slightly fallen (see Table 2.2), but, in women, deaths have risen sharply.

Another disease which has increased dramatically this century is ischaemic heart disease, although the greatest increases took place during the 1950s. Since 1961 there has been a much slower increase

Table 2.9 Deaths from ischaemic heart disease England and Wales (rates per 100000 population.) 1961–1989. (From Population Trends, 1989.)

Year	Males	Females
1961	297.3	210.1
1966	323.1	222.3
1971	347.5	237.9
1976	371.1	266.6
1981	368.8	259.4
1986	365.0	271.1
1989	338.5	262.9

(see Table 2.9) although the death rate in women has increased by 25.13% compared with 13.8% in men.

Within the UK there are marked regional differences in the mortality from ischaemic heart disease – the lowest levels are found in East Anglia (SMR 86 for men and 89 for women) and the highest in Scotland (SMR 126 for men and 118 for women). Another interesting finding is that there are wide variations in the level of ischaemic heart disease in different countries (see Table 2.10).

Table 2.10 Deaths from ischaemic heart disease per 100000 population 1986 (unless otherwise stated). (From World Health Annual Statistics, 1987.)

Japan	49.5	Canada	213.8
Hong Kong	52.9	USA**	237.1
Spain	111.1	Austria	257.8
Argentina**	116.5	Germany (Federal)	265.4
Portugal	121.7	New Zealand	270.2
Yugoslavia**	134.2	Malta	271.5
Mauritius*	144.8	Netherlands	284.5
Italy*	150.0	Australia*	290.0
France*	155.4	Ireland**	382.1
Bulgaria	160.1	England and Wales	427.8
Israel	187.2	Scotland	547.7

*1985
**1984

Social class differences have always shown a much greater increase in Social Classes IV and V than in Classes I and II (see Fig. 2.7).

All these statistical findings suggest possible factors connected with the incidence of ischaemic heart disease. At least seven important factors have been identified with the cause of ischaemic heart disease:

— hypertension;
— cigarette smoking;
— genetic factors – often linked to high cholesterol levels in the blood;

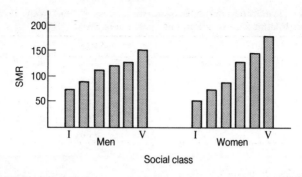

Fig. 2.7 Mortality from ischaemic heart disease for men and women aged 20–64 years, England and Wales, 1979–80, 1982–83. (From *Occupational Mortality*, OPCS, 1987.)

— physical activity;
— obesity;
— diabetes.

When so many different causative factors are identified, complicated combinations of factors can produce curious results. For instance, the occupational group which has the lowest level of ischaemic heart disease in men is farmers and farm workers yet their intake of dairy products (cream, butter, fats, etc.) is among the highest in the United Kingdom. In this case the multifactorial effect of the various factors involved is very clear – the consumption of large amounts of dairy products is more than compensated by (*i*) the high intake of fibre in the diet and (*ii*) the high level of physical activity in these workers.

Prevention of ischaemic heart disease can best be achieved by reducing as many 'risk factors' as possible: by lowering the total consumption of fat, by substituting polyunsaturated fats for saturated ones (by taking vegetable rather than animal fats); by increasing the fibre content of foodstuffs; by early diagnosis and effective treatment of hypertensive disease; by stopping cigarette smoking (there is much evidence that this association is not strongly cumulative and that anyone who stops smoking returns to the low risk group of non-smokers within a few months); by increased physical activity; and by avoiding obesity.

One of the most dramatic falls in the death rate of any non-communicable disease over the last 25 years has been seen in hypertensive disease (see Table 2.11). Note that the rate of fall in mortality from hypertensive disease has been very marked over this period – a reduction of just over five times in men and women.

Table 2.11 Deaths from hypertensive disease England and Wales 1961–1989 (rates per 100000). (From various OPCS Monitors Series DH2.)

Year	Males	Females
1961	31.7	40.5
1966	21.6	27.7
1971	17.6	20.4
1976	14.2	16.8
1980	10.6	12.0
1989	6.28	8.0

Social factors in disease

A further method that can be employed to study disease is to compare the mortality of illness by grouping the family by occupation. The Registrar General divides the population in England and Wales into six different social classes based on the occupation of the chief wage earner of the family.

Non-Manual

Class I	Professional occupations (lawyers, doctors etc.)
Class II	Managerial and lower professional occupations (i.e. teachers, nurses, sales managers)
Class III N	Non-manual skilled occupations (clerks, shop assistants)

Manual

Class III M	Skilled manual occupations (bricklayers, underground coal miners etc.)
Class IV	Partly skilled occupations (bus conductors, postmen)
Class V	Unskilled occupations (porters, labourers etc.).

The social class classification can be used to compare the relative mortality of various groups in society. These results are published by OPCS every ten years in a report entitled *Occupational Mortality*; the latest report was published in 1987. The results are given as the Standardised Mortality Ratio (SMR) (see pages 46–7). This is given as a ratio 100. A group experiencing exactly the national expected mortality would have an SMR of 100. If the SMR was 75, then the group has 75/100 or three-quarters of the expected mortality (it is enjoying less mortality than expected). If the SMR is 200, it means that the mortality is 200/100 or twice as great as normal.

Table 2.12 demonstrates the wide variations found between the social classes. In men for 'all causes of death' the SMR is two and one half times greater in Social Class V compared with Social Class I. In women the difference is slightly less but the trend is similar. Most

Table 2.12   Standardised Mortality Ratios (SMR) by cause and social class, England and Wales, 1979–80, 1982–83 (national expected SMR would be 100). (From Occupational Mortality, OPCS, 1987.)

Cause of death	Social class					
	I	II	IIIN	IIIM	IV	V
All causes (men)	66	76	94	89	116	165
All causes (women)	75	83	93	111	125	160
Cancer of lung (men)	43	63	80	120	126	178
Cancer of lung (women)	50	73	81	122	138	170
Cancer of breast (women)	109	104	106	101	99	94
Cancer of cervix uteri (women)	29	60	73	112	124	186
Diabetes (men)	67	76	113	100	123	155
Diabetes (women)	47	59	92	114	145	247
Ischaemic heart disease (men)	70	82	104	109	117	144
Ischaemic heart disease (women)	46	75	80	122	144	194
Bronchitis (men)	34	48	85	110	115	211

diseases show this tendency, especially cancer of the cervix uteri where deaths in women in Social Class V are over six times greater than in Social Class I. This emphasises the importance of educating women, particularly those from Social Class V, as to the value of screening tests (smears) for this condition. Bronchitis is another disease where there is a marked social class gradient (SMR 34 in Social Class I but 211 in Social Class V in men). There are probably many factors causing this difference, including the larger proportion of men in Social Class V who smoke heavily. An unusual and unexplained result is shown in cancer of the breast in women where there is an inverse social class gradient – deaths are highest in Social Class I and lowest in Social Class V.

Table 2.13 shows the SMRs for different occupations and, again, wide variations are seen. Even in the health services this is the case – physiotherapists (80), ambulancemen (84), hospital ward orderlies (87), dentists (89), medical practitioners (97), pharmacists (121) and nurses (151). Although professional groups generally have low rates, there are exceptions – judges, barristers and solicitors have an SMR of 113, almost double that of the lowest group which is local government administrators. These differing mortality rates not only indicate particular hazards of different occupations but are also influenced by the type of individual who is attracted to a particular job.

Value of vital statistics

Nurses are constantly concerned with the taking of various measurements in assessing the health of the individual patient – taking temperatures, collection of specimens, assisting with biochemical or radio-

Table 2.13 Standardised Mortality Ratios (SMRs) for all causes for men aged 20–64, England and Wales 1979–80, 1982–3. (From Occupational Mortality, OPCS, 1987.)

Local government administrators	64	Masons	100
Roadmen	67	Clergymen	102
Dustmen	69	Librarians	108
Postmen	72	Bus and coach drivers	111
University academic staff	72	Judges, barristers and solicitors	113
Teachers (higher education)	73	Crane drivers	116
Board and paper workers	75	Waiters and bar staff	117
Physiotherapists	80	Pharmacists	121
Bookbinders	80	Police officers	126
Forestry workers	80	Environmental health officers	127
Teachers (main group)	81	Miners (not coal), quarrymen	133
Ambulancemen	84	Butchers	134
Company secretaries	86	Actors	138
Hospital ward orderlies	87	Shoe repairers	146
Railway engine drivers	88	Prison officers	147
Dentists	89	Nurses	151
Rubber and plastic workers	90	Scaffolders	159
Textile workers	91	Musicians	181
Farmers	93	Steel erectors and benders	184
Carpenters and joiners	94	Fishermen	194
Coal miners (underground)	96	Printers	202
Medical practitioners	97	Brewery, vinery process workers	266

logical investigations. Vital statistics, in their various forms, can be looked upon in the same way, for they represent the most reliable means available to measure the health of the community. It is not necessary for the health professional to become an expert in vital statistics, but a simple knowledge and understanding of their uses is likely to make the work more interesting. Community health problems change continuously and if the rudiments of the subject are understood, then the effects of these changes are likely to mean so much more.

3   Maternal health services

In the United Kingdom about 760 000–790 000 births occur each year and the task of caring for the health of each mother is an important part of the health services.

Unlike almost any other speciality in medicine, the care of women in pregnancy is mainly a physiological one – there is nothing abnormal in the process itself. This has helped to create a very strong preventive service and the emphasis of all the maternity services is to avoid and prevent abnormalities occurring, and to recognise and diagnose them early so that, if they do occur, their effects are minimised.

The maternity services are more closely coordinated than almost any other type of medical care. This is essential as the maternity service is shared between hospitals and the primary health services.

Hospital confinements

The proportion of mothers having their babies in hospitals varies with the area but in 1988 in the United Kingdom nearly 99% had their confinements in hospital or in a nursing home with the remainder at home. However, there were many variations and many towns showed a hospital delivery rate over 99%. The following are the groups of mothers who should *always be delivered in hospital*.

- Those in whom there is an abnormality (such as toxaemia of pregnancy or malpresentation, i.e. breech, or illness in the mother, for example diabetes).
- Previous caesarean section.
- Mothers with four or more children.
- Mothers over the age of 35 years.
- Low birth weight baby in a previous pregnancy.
- Primary infertility.

It is also sound practice to ensure that all primigravidae (mothers in their first pregnancy) are, at least, delivered in a general practitioner maternity unit.

There is an increasing tendency for mothers to be discharged during the first week following confinement. By 1988, 80% of mothers whose babies were delivered in hospital were discharged home on or before the seventh day of confinement.

The average stay in consultant maternity beds in hospital in the UK is 4.7 days and 3.6 days in general practitioner beds. The indications are that the tendency towards early discharge will be increased and some mothers are discharged home as early as 6 hours following delivery – the Domino scheme (Domiciliary midwife in and out). There are many social and community care problems created by such early discharge, for no mother is fit to look after her home at such an early stage of the puerperium and must have special help.

Administration of the maternity services

In the UK there is very strict control maintained over all maternity services by a central authority created for the purpose – the United Kingdom Central Council for Nursing, Midwifery and Health Visiting (UKCC). This body lays down rules for the conduct of all midwives. In addition, under the Midwives Acts, all unqualified persons, who are not either midwives or doctors (or students in training to become midwives or doctors), are prohibited from attending any woman in childbirth except to assist under the personal direction of a midwife or doctor, except in a sudden or urgent necessity. This rule prevents unskilled and untrained persons attending women in childbirth and so ensures indirectly that every woman is looked after by a fully-trained qualified person. The rules of the UKCC are supervised locally by the Regional Health Authority who usually delegates this responsibility to the District Health Authority. These rules include the following.

- Supervision over all certified midwives practising in the area. This covers midwives in maternity hospitals as well as those in nursing homes or employed as community midwives; in practice, the detailed supervision of midwives in maternity hospitals is left to the senior staff of those hospitals. The district health authority supervises midwives in nursing homes and community practice. No midwife may practise until she has given her notice to do so to the local supervising authority.
- Power to suspend a midwife from practice if it appears necessary to do so to prevent spread of infection, for example it would be dangerous for a midwife who was a nasal carrier of pathogenic streptococci, to continue midwifery.

The UKCC itself lays down a code of practice and rules for all midwives. These specify the records which must be kept, the standards which must be followed in midwifery practice, the drugs which may be used, the anaesthetics which may be used, as well as making it quite clear in what medical emergencies the midwife has a duty to call in medical aid. In addition, the UKCC insists that every practising midwife shall attend a refresher course once every five years.

The rôle of the general practitioner and midwife

If the mother is to be delivered at home there are three possibilities open to her.

(*i*)   In a minority of cases, her own general practitioner carries out the ante-natal care, delivers the baby and the midwife acts as a maternity nurse. Post-natal care is undertaken by the general practitioner.

(*ii*)   In most cases, the general practitioner does the ante-natal care but the midwife delivers the baby calling the doctor only in case of need. The midwife reports the delivery to the general practitioner who then completes the post-natal care.

(*iii*) The mother may choose to have the baby delivered solely by a midwife who, in this instance, accepts full responsibility for looking after the patient in the ante-natal period and in her confinement.

In practice, it is usual for the mother to choose alternatives (*i*) or (*ii*) as her own doctor is in an excellent position to help and advise in the event of complications. General practitioners who have had special experience in midwifery and who undertake regular midwifery, are placed on the 'obstetric list'. They are then remunerated at a higher rate for each confinement than doctors who are not on the list.

Organisation of a community midwifery service

Each District Health Authority employs the midwives who carry out the community work. The midwife can best be described as an expert practitioner of normal child bearing in all its varied aspects, working very closely with the health visitor who should, wherever possible, be introduced to the mother during her ante-natal care (see page 71).

The District Health Authority arranges an adequate midwifery coverage for the whole area. Often each midwife is provided with a house or flat from which to practise, and it is usual for the midwife to have a car. This is particularly important in order to reach patients quickly at any hour of the day or night, and to carry heavy equipment (including mobile gas and oxygen analgesia equipment).

Maternity outfits, which include all the necessary sterile dressings for the confinement and puerperium, are supplied free to each mother. It therefore is not necessary for the general practitioner to have to supply extra dressings for the confinement.

All midwives are trained in giving gas/oxygen analgesia. A medical certificate of fitness for analgesia must be obtained from the patient's own doctor during the pregnancy. Analgesia is available today to all mothers confined at home who wish to use it. Modern apparatus is very reliable and is designed to allow the patient to give herself (after tuition), her own gas/oxygen anaesthetic during the first stage of labour. The patient lies on her side, presses the mask with a pressure valve on it over her nose and breathes a mixture of gas and oxygen. As she loses consciousness, her grip relaxes, the mask falls away shutting off the valve and the supply of gas is cut off. She regains consciousness and may repeat the cycle if necessary.

Ante-natal care

The prevention of many complications of pregnancy rests more with careful ante-natal care than with any other factor. It is the responsibility of the midwife to ensure that adequate ante-natal care is carried out on his or her patients.

Mothers due to be delivered in hospital usually receive *shared ante-natal care*. The hospital obstetrician will see the patient when booking and later organise an ultrascan and, if all is well, will only see the patient two or three times before delivery. The remainder of the ante-natal care will be undertaken by the general practitioner and/or midwife who will refer back to the hospital obstetrician if any complications occur.

The pressure on most hospital ante-natal clinics is often so great that it is not always possible to carry out health education or parentcraft clinics in hospitals. Mothers are encouraged to attend special health education parentcraft clinics, often arranged by the local health visitors and/or community midwives. Fathers are also encouraged to attend at least some sessions at these clinics. The National Childbirth Trust (NCT) also holds parentcraft classes in many areas.

The first ante-natal examination usually takes place at the time of confirmation of the pregnancy, at about the third month of pregnancy. A complete general medical examination must then be undertaken to ensure the woman has no undetected illness. At this time, a complete record should be obtained of past medical history paying particular attention to any past history of tuberculosis, diabetes and any virus infections from which the patient may have suffered. Chest X-rays are now only carried out if history or symptoms indicate that this would be wise.

The next stage is for a complete obstetric history of any previous pregnancies to be taken, paying particular attention to any difficulties and abnormalities which may have occurred, either in her own or the baby's health. In all cases, blood tests should be taken and sent to the laboratory and include:

- A *Wassermann* or *Kahn* test to make certain that the mother *has no hidden infection of syphilis*. If it is found that she has a latent syphilitic infection at the third month of pregnancy and immediate treatment is started, then a possible congenital infection in the infant can be avoided.
- *Haemoglobin* estimation to check the level in each mother. If this is lower than normal, immediate treatment must be started. This is important as haemorrhage may occur later, and the results of such haemorrhage are bound to be more serious in cases where the haemoglobin level is lower than normal.
- *Blood group* should be estimated and recorded. In an emergency, such information will be invaluable to enable a blood transfusion to be given quickly.
- *Rubella serology* to detect antibodies and thus immunity to Rubella (German measles).
- *Rhesus factor* estimation should be carried out. If the mother is Rhesus positive then no problems will arise. If, however, the mother is Rhesus negative, difficulties may occur later affecting the health of her second and subsequent children. If the father is Rhesus positive, which is more likely, then a further blood examination must be undertaken at the 34th week of pregnancy to check whether antibodies have developed in the mother's blood. If they have, then it is likely that the baby will develop serious haemolytic jaundice after birth and may need an exchange transfusion. For this reason, the patient must be delivered in hospital and the neighbouring paediatric unit should be alerted before the birth.

  Even when antibodies are absent from a Rhesus negative mother's blood, blood from the baby's umbilical cord should be collected at birth and sent to a laboratory to be tested for antibodies.

In addition to the blood tests, a midstream specimen of *urine* is taken to exclude a urinary infection.

German measles and pregnancy

An attack of german measles (rubella) during the first three months of pregnancy can result in harmful effects to the fetus. These include a higher proportion of abortion and stillbirths and an increased incidence of congenital abnormalities, especially congenital cataract in the child, congenital heart disease or deafness. Research has also shown a much higher infant mortality in children of mothers who develop rubella during the first three months of pregnancy. Active immunisation is advocated for all girls aged 11–13 years (see page 108). From October 1988, a combined measles, mumps and rubella immunisation (MMR) has been offered to all children at the age of 15 months. Vaccination of women of childbearing age is not recommended routinely. If an adult woman wishes to have a vaccination, a serological test, which can be carried out by the Public Health Laboratory Service, should always be undertaken. Vaccination should only be offered to those who are seronegative (approximately 10% of adult women without a history of rubella). *It is most important that a woman is not pregnant at the time of the vaccination, and does not become pregnant for at least two months after vaccination.*

Any mother who has never had german measles or has not been immunised and who comes into contact with the disease during the first three months of pregnancy should be promptly immunised with immunoglobulin. This normally prevents an attack of german measles developing and protection lasts for six weeks and so avoids subsequent congenital deformities in the child.

It is, however, essential to realise that any danger from german measles only occurs within the first three/four months of pregnancy and that a later attack does no harm. Therefore, reassurance is often needed when this occurs.

Prevention of Rhesus incompatibility by immunisation

It is now possible to prevent many of the problems of Rhesus incompatibility by immunisation with Anti-D immunoglobulin of Rhesus negative women immediately after their first confinement or miscarriage. The problem in Rhesus incompatibility is due to red blood cells from a Rhesus positive child crossing the placental barrier and entering the mother's blood stream. Shortly after the birth of the first child, the Rhesus negative mother manufactures antibodies against these Rhesus positive red blood cells of her child which, in this way, are then destroyed. In second and subsequent pregnancies, these antibodies increase and, when they recross the placental barrier and enter the baby's blood stream, they lead to massive destruction of the baby's blood cells usually after birth, but in serious cases, before birth which may lead to a stillbirth.

Immunisation with Anti-D immunoglobulin should be given *immediately following the first delivery* of a child or after *a first miscarriage or abortion*. An Anti-D immunoglobulin then destroys the Rhesus positive red blood cells of the baby within the mother's blood stream and there is not time enough for the mother to develop antibodies. Therefore a consequent pregnancy will be like a first pregnancy and no problems will arise. It is, however, necessary in such cases to *reimmunise the mother after all subsequent pregnancies or miscarriages to prevent antibody formation.*

Recommendations in regard to treatment are as follows:

- In all cases the Anti-D immunoglobulin should be given within 60 hours of delivery or termination of pregnancy (miscarriage or abortion).
- All Rhesus negative women giving birth to a Rhesus positive baby after the 20th week should be screened for fetal cells so that women who have large transplacental haemorrhages can be given large doses of Anti-D immunoglobulin.
- The usual dose of Anti-D immunoglobulin for all Rhesus negative women having had Rhesus positive babies regardless of parity or ABO group, should initially be 100 microgrammes. Further doses may be necessary for cases in which large transplacental haemorrhages have occurred.
- A standard dose of 50 microgrammes should be provided for all women known to be Rhesus negative, having therapeutic abortions up to and including the 20th week of pregnancy, except for those who are sterilised at the same operation. Rhesus negative women whose pregnancy with a Rhesus positive fetus is terminated after the 20th week should receive a dose of 100 microgrammes.
- The decision to use Anti-D immunoglobulin for Rhesus negative women having spontaneous abortions should be left to the individual clinician.

Dental care in pregnancy

Dental care in pregnancy is very important as the mother's teeth can deteriorate rapidly at this time. Every mother should, therefore, have a dental examination carried out immediately after the first ante-natal visit and arrangements made for any dental treatment needed to be done at once. Because care of the teeth is so important in pregnancy, special arrangements are made to treat, at no cost, all pregnant and nursing mothers (up to one year after confinement) – this free treatment includes the provision of dentures if needed. District Health Authorities arrange for this dental treatment to be carried out by their own dental staff at clinics.

Health education in pregnancy

The first ante-natal visit should be concluded by arranging for the mother to attend various health educational clinics to learn parentcraft. This is especially important for the mother having her first child (primipara) and gives her the opportunity to meet the health visitors who will help her after her baby's birth. Fathers are now also encouraged to attend some parentcraft clinics and an increasing number of fathers are responding and coming to such clinics.

A visit should next be paid by the midwife or health visitor to the home. At this meeting, there should be frank discussion about many aspects of the pregnancy. Advice should especially be given concerning the diet for the mother.

Recent research has emphasised that there is a greater risk to the baby of a mother who smokes during pregnancy, and it has been found that smoking by the mother can lead to the baby being underweight at birth.

Prescription charges are waived to expectant mothers and until their baby is one year old. A Family Health Service Authority Exemption certificate is needed; this is obtained by filling in Form FW8 obtainable from the doctor, midwife or health visitor.

Diet for pregnancy

A well-balanced diet with a good proportion of high-class protein is required. Many mothers have odd ideas about diet in pregnancy and the midwife must be patient and make certain that the diet required is fully understood. At least a pint of milk should be drunk per day and foodstuffs rich in iron, calcium, phosphorus and vitamins should be eaten. One or two eggs (properly cooked) and a good helping of meat, fish or poultry should be eaten per day. Cheese is also a most valuable food in pregnancy particularly for vegetarians.

Vitamin preparations either in the form of tablets or orange juice and codliver oil may be obtained from the local clinic, or alternatively these may be taken in the diet by fresh fruit and various fats. Good well-balanced meals will reduce the likelihood of unexplained prematurity and the incidence of toxaemia of pregnancy.

It is becoming increasingly important for all expectant mothers to understand that certain foodstuffs should not be eaten by expectant mothers. This is because of the special dangers of listeriosis to both the expectant mother and her baby. Any food which has been associated with listeriosis should be avoided throughout pregnancy. These include many pre-cooked foods which are stored and sold as 'chilled foods'. All such foods (such as pre-cooked chicken) should always be stored below 3° (37°F); recent studies have shown that many commercial refrigerators in shops do not achieve such low temperatures, adding to the danger of multiplication of any listeriosis if the food is infected. Expectant mothers should avoid eating such foods, as well as soft cheeses and pâtés. The special dangers to expectant mothers and their new-born babies are described in Chapter 7 (see pages 132–3).

Screening in pregnancy

Ultrascan

It is of great value to carry out a routine ultrascan test on all expectant mothers at 16 weeks. This is undertaken by the hospital maternity department and can confirm that everything is normal or detect abnormalities. It is also essential to do such a test before amniocentesis. Ultrascan will also reveal whether a multiple pregnancy exists which can itself be very useful.

Screening by amniocentesis

Amniocentesis is the removal, usually during the 16th week of pregnancy, of a small amount of amniotic fluid by means of a needle inserted through the uterine wall usually via the abdominal wall. This fluid can then be examined in two ways.

— *Microscopically*   The baby is surrounded by amniotic fluid in the uterus and a few cells will be cast off from the baby's skin and mucous membranes. These can be examined to give the chromosome pattern of the child (see Down's syndrome, page 57).
— *Chemically*   To estimate the level of alphafeta protein (AFP) which will, at 16 weeks of pregnancy, be raised in 99% of cases of open neural tube defects.

In both instances, the object of carrying out the amniocentesis is to give an opportunity to the mother to have her pregnancy terminated by the 20th week if the results show that her baby is congenitally deformed. It is therefore most important that *counselling takes place before the 16th week*, and that *both parents fully understand the reasons for the investigation* and agree that, if the child is found to be abnormal, a termination of pregnancy should be carried out. If for any reason (religious or ethical) the parents would not agree to termination then this should be known before any tests are carried out for it is then better that they should not be done at all.

Amniocentesis produces slight risks to the fetus. It is not easy to estimate these accurately but the most recent studies have indicated that there is approximately 1% extra risk of fetal death. This is a maximum figure and is likely to be lower. There is also an increased possibility of respiratory difficulties in the fetus at birth and of orthopaedic postural deformities which may require immediate treatment. Hence, after amniocentesis, the birth should always take place in a maternity hospital with full paediatric support. At present, in the UK, about 3% of mothers have amniocentesis carried out.

Amniocentesis is useful in families with a history of either Duchenne muscular dystrophy or haemophilia for the sex of the unborn child can be determined. Both diseases are sex-linked conditions where the sufferer is invariably a boy although both diseases can be passed on by mothers. Clearly, if the baby is known to be a girl, there is no risk of either disease in the expected child (although a girl may pass the disease on to any male children which she may later bear).

Screening to diagnose Down's syndrome

It is possible to diagnose, by amniocentesis, whether the fetus is suffering from Down's syndrome. It is advisable only to carry out amniocentesis where the risks of Down's syndrome exceed those to the fetus during the procedure of amniocentesis (approximately 1%). In practice, this means that amniocentesis to discover Down's syndrome should only be carried out on pregnant women aged 35 years and over, or if there has been a previous Down's syndrome baby born, or if there is a family history of such births. If all such mothers were screened in this way it has been estimated that the birth of about 18–20% of babies with Down's syndrome could be prevented. The chances of any mother having a child with Down's syndrome increase as the age of the mother rises (see Table 17.1, page 304).

Screening tests to identify open neural tube defects

The following are the stages in the screening tests to identify open neural tube defects.

— Dating of the pregnancy accurately and counselling of the parents before the 16th week.
— 16th week – sample of mother's blood collected and alphafetaprotein (AFP) level estimated.
— If AFP level is high repeat the test during 17th week.
— If second test is also positive, carry out ultrascan (if this has not already been done), to check the duration of pregnancy and to exclude multiple pregnancy (twins).
— Undertake amniocentesis during 16th week and calculate the level of AFP in the amniotic fluid.
— If raised, then the chance of the fetus having an open neural tube defect is very high (99%) and an immediate termination of pregnancy should be carried out.

Counselling

Skilled counselling is essential after any termination of pregnancy which has taken place because of some known defect in the baby, for example open neutral tube defect or Down's syndrome. Counselling enables the parents to have explained to them

— the nature of the malformation found in the fetus; and
— the risks of a likely recurrence in another pregnancy.

After one abnormal pregnancy resulting in an open neural tube defect, the chance will be higher in a second (approximately 1 in 20); after two abnormal pregnancies the risk rises to approximately 1 in 8. However, it is still possible to carry out the screening tests in further pregnancies and, if this is done, the risks of any abnormal child being born are minimal.

It is also important to offer counselling to the parents after any other termination of pregnancy (including abortion and natural miscarriage) to enable parents to be given the correct advice about future pregnancies and/or birth control.

Continued ante-natal care

Further ante-natal examinations are regularly carried out during pregnancy – at least once a month until the 28th week, then every two weeks until the 36th week, then once a week until delivery. The following examinations should be carried out at each visit:

— *Abdominal examination*   The position of the child is carefully observed and recorded during the last weeks of pregnancy and, particularly in the primipara, the early engagement of the head in the pelvis is checked.
— *Blood pressure*   This should never rise above 130/90 during pregnancy.
— *Urine test*   Urine is tested for albumin.
— The legs should be palpated for oedema.
— *Weight*   A careful record is kept of weight gain during pregnancy, especially between the 20th and 30th weeks. If the weight gain exceeds 3.3 kg (7 lbs) in this period, especially in young primipara, this should be regarded as a sign of hypertensive disease of pregnancy. Such patients should be treated accordingly with a high-protein low-carbohydrate diet and observed very carefully at frequent intervals.

If other signs of impending hypertensive disease of pregnancy develop, especially raised blood pressure and/or development of albuminuria, the patient should be given strict bed rest. The patient must be admitted to hospital for further treatment if, in spite of bed rest, signs of toxaemia persist.

Value of ante-natal care in preventing serious abnormalities of pregnancy

It cannot be emphasised too strongly that good ante-natal care can reduce the dangers of serious abnormalities of pregnancy. Early in the ante-natal care programme of any mother, the possible danger of an ectopic pregnancy must be borne in mind. In the 1982–4 study of maternal deaths (see Table 3.1) ectopic pregnancy was the sixth commonest cause of maternal death and accounted for ten deaths in England and Wales. Immediate operation is most important as soon as the diagnosis has been made. Resuscitation should not precede operation but be co-incidental with it.

The main dangers of hypertensive disease of pregnancy and haemorrhage can both be greatly reduced by careful ante-natal care. Any abnormality discovered in ante-natal work must be completely investigated. The following are some of the more important ones.

- A raised blood pressure.
- Albuminuria.
- Oedema.
- A loss of blood per vaginam. Even if this is only slight – a 'show' – it may be a sign of placenta praevia.
- The head of the child not fully engaging into the mother's pelvis. This is a very important factor in the primipara in whom the head should be fully engaged by the 36th week and often earlier. If the baby's head in the primipara is not engaged by this time, there is usually something wrong. Either the presentation is faulty, or there may be an abnormally small pelvis, which is rare today except in immigrant populations, or the pelvis may already contain the placenta – placenta praevia.

As the pregnancy nears its end regular ante-natal examinations become even more important. If a patient defaults from attending an ante-natal visit it is essential that the doctor or midwife call on the patient to find out the reason. In many instances, the reason may only be slackness on the part of the patient but it may be that she has developed some symptom which she does not recognise as serious but which gives her the excuse to postpone her visit. If such symptoms are the signs of an impending hypertensive disease of pregnancy, the midwife's visit may well be instrumental in ensuring that proper treatment is carried out promptly. This could make the difference between, in extreme cases, a live child plus healthy mother, or the tragedy of a maternal death with probably a stillbirth.

Pulmonary embolism is one of the commonest causes of maternal mortality. Its risk rises with age and parity of the mother and is increased by caesarean section. It is important that the early signs of pulmonary embolism are not missed – not infrequently pleuritic pain is present but its significance is often not recognised and the patient is treated with antibiotics. In pregnancy such pain should always be treated seriously as it may indicate a pulmonary embolism.

Preventive aspects of maternal mortality

At present one mother per 14 666 pregnancies loses her life as a result of childbearing. Each maternal death is very carefully investigated to find the cause and whether there was any element of substandard care in that death. This enquiry is carried out by a consultant obstetrician and the community physician. The most recent series of such investigations carried out by the Department of Health showed that about half of all present day maternal deaths have some 'substandard care' factor. In other words, half the deaths could have been avoided if some mistake or omission had not occurred. The type of 'substandard care' varies from mistakes and omissions on the part of the doctors and midwives to lack of cooperation on the part of the patient herself.

When the great improvement over the last 55 years in the safety of child bearing is examined (1 mother per 230 pregnancies died in 1936) it is easy to be complacent, but the fact remains that if all the preventable factors were reduced, and theoretically this is quite possible, only 1 in (approximately) 29 000 women would die, not 1 in 14 666 as at present. Detailed examination of the types of mistake which lead to most of these deaths shows that lack of adequate ante-natal care was the most important reason.

The nine most common causes of maternal mortality in the 1979–81 survey of maternal deaths in England and Wales are given in Table 3.1.

Management of labour in community practice

Although only approximately 1% of births now occur at home, the following account is still given in detail as all home deliveries may present special hazards to the mother and child. Whether or not a doctor has been booked, usually the midwife is first notified when labour starts. The midwife visits the mother, examines her and, upon confirming that labour has started, arranges for the care of the mother. The midwife will bring to each patient the anaesthetic apparatus plus all the equipment for the labour.

As explained earlier, the mother may give herself a whiff of anaesthetic using gas and oxygen. The midwife then reports to the doctor when labour has started. As most doctors have to carry on their busy practices, the midwife continues to look after the mother, only calling the doctor if some difficulty occurs.

A high degree of surgical cleanliness is maintained by using sterile

Table 3.1 Maternal Deaths by cause-numbers and rates per million pregnancies 1982–84 England and Wales. (From Report on Confidential Enquiries into Maternal Deaths in England and Wales, 1982–84, HMSO, 1989. ISBN 0 11 321204 6.)

Cause of maternal death	Numbers	Percentage	Rate per million pregnancies
Hypertensive disease of pregnancy	25	18.2	10.0
Pulmonary embolism	25	18.2	10.0
Anaesthesia	18	13.0	7.2
Amniotic fluid embolism	14	10.1	5.6
Abortion	11	8.0	4.4
Ectopic pregnancy	10	7.2	4.0
Haemorrhage	9	6.5	3.6
Ruptured uterus	3	2.2	1.2
Sepsis-excluding abortion	2	1.4	0.8
Other direct causes	21	15.2	8.4
All deaths	138	100.0	55.2

gowns, masks, cap and sheets. Increasing use is being made of disposable sterile materials and these now include towels, masks, caps and syringes. Any sterile gowns which are used remain at the patient's house to reduce any risk of carrying infection from patient to patient.

Midwives may leave the patient for a short time in the first stage of labour. They can give either pethidine or more commonly pethidine which has less depressant effect upon the child. Because labour often progresses rapidly after giving such drugs, no midwife should leave the patient after administering pethilorfin.

After delivery, the midwife may have to resuscitate the child. The midwife should have a special mucus sucker to clear the air passages of the child and also a sparklet oxygen resuscitator, a most valuable and neat apparatus which supplies oxygen at a measured rate for the baby to breathe and has made the problem of resuscitation much safer and surer.

If, during the labour, the midwife meets with any abnormality, medical aid must be summoned immediately while the midwife stays to continue the delivery. Some district health authorities provide their midwives with portable radio transmitters so that they can summon medical aid without having to leave their patient. In most cases, medical aid will be provided by the doctor who is booked, but, if no doctor has been booked, the midwife sends for the nearest doctor who is on the obstetric list.

In more urgent and serious problems, the midwife may send for a special mobile hospital team, the 'flying squad'.

Use of hospital emergency team (flying squad)

Each maternity hospital has a mobile team (flying squad) consisting of an experienced obstetrician (consultant or registrar) plus an anaesthetist and an experienced hospital midwife, who will go to the home of a patient to deal with any emergency in labour. Usually such a team is taken to the patient's home by an ambulance. The most usual reasons for the flying squad to be sent for are:

- *Sudden haemorrhage* (particularly post-partum haemorrhage)   In this instance the flying squad helps to resuscitate the patient and for this purpose they carry blood and plasma for transfusion. They may also have to control bleeding and deal with its cause (say retained placenta). It is much safer to resuscitate the patient first and then move her to hospital.
- *A complication of labour*   An example would be difficulty in the second stage of labour such as unexpected breech presentation.

Flying squads have proved themselves to be most valuable especially in large cities and one of their great assets is that they are readily available at all times. The general practitioner may be out on his or her rounds when help is urgently needed and it is reassuring to the midwife to know that skilled help can always be obtained by calling out the flying squad.

The flying squad is called out to one in approximately 70 community births – the causes being for haemorrhage in a third of the cases, for retained placenta in half the cases and for varying difficulties in the remainder.

The cooperation card

Although community midwifery usually does not involve the hospital service, cooperation, as shown by the value of the flying squad, is of great importance. Cooperation between services is helped by every woman whether booked to have her baby in hospital or at home always carrying a special cooperation card with her. This is a simple record of her ante-natal care, containing all the information which is invaluable in an emergency. If a patient booked for home confinement suddenly requires urgent hospital admission, this cooperation card is of great value in arranging for prompt and proper treatment. It records the results of all tests carried out including blood group, and can therefore save valuable time.

Post-natal care

Six weeks after delivery a full post-natal examination should be carried out either at the hospital where the baby was born or at the doctor's surgery or at the clinic. By this time the health visitor should be acting as one of the most important advisors to the mother (see Chapter 4).

Social aspects

Maternity benefits

Considerable changes have occurred in these benefits during the last few years. There are now three types of maternity benefit available.

Statutory maternity pay (SMP) This is operated by the employer and there does not need to be an intention to return to work to claim. SMP is payable if the woman has been in employment without a break for at least six months by her 26th week of pregnancy, and her average weekly earnings are above the amount where National Insurance contributions are paid. There are two rates of SMP. The greater amount is paid to a woman if she has been working for at least 16 hours a week full time for at least two years, or at least eight hours a week part time for at least five years. The first six weeks of SMP are paid at 90% of her average earnings. After that, the lower rate is paid for the remaining 12 weeks.

For a woman who has been in the same employment for between 26 weeks and two years, the lower rate is paid for the whole period. To receive SMP three weeks' notice must be given and the employer given the maternity certificate (form MAT B1).

Maternity allowance This is payable by the local Social Security Office for up to 18 weeks to someone who has changed jobs, or has become self employed provided that the standard rate National Insurance contributions have been paid for at least 26 weeks in the 52 weeks leading up till the 26th week of pregnancy. This maternity allowance is slightly less than the lower rate of SMP.

Maternity payment This is paid from the social fund (in 1988/89 it was £85 for every baby expected, born or adopted) and is payable if the mother or partner are getting Income Support or Family Credit. The full amount is only paid if there are savings of less than £500. Applications should be made 11 weeks before the baby is due until the baby is three months old. For an adopted baby, the claim may be made up to the time he or she is one year old.

Free milk

Free milk is available to expectant mothers and all children under school age where the family income is below a certain level i.e. where the family is on Income Support or Family Income Supplement. Free milk is also available to all handicapped children aged 5–16 who are not registered at school and to children attending a registered day nursery.

Care of unmarried mothers

The care of the unmarried mother in pregnancy can be a special problem, especially in those women who are on their own and who have no stable relationship with the father. In the UK, between 18 and 20% of all births are illegitimate (to parents who are not married at the time of the birth) although a proportion occur to women who have a stable relationship. In those who have not, many difficulties can occur and, from the preventive health point of view, the most serious immediate problem is that the social circumstances surrounding an unmarried mother produce greater hazards to both mother and child. These are mainly connected with the fact that no ante-natal care may be carried out because of concealment of the pregnancy, or the mother may be forced to leave her home due to unsympathetic parental reaction. The extra hazard to the baby in an illegitimate birth is shown quite dramatically in an increased infant mortality rate of 11.6 for illegitimate births compared with a rate of 8.2 for legitimate births (1989).

Wherever possible, arrangements should be made to help the very young unmarried mother-to-be (e.g. a teenager) to stay at home, and to help in healing any rifts which may have been created between the mother-to-be and her parents. If this can be done, problems tend to be reduced and hospital delivery and possible early adoption may provide the best outcome.

In about half of the cases, however, the unmarried mother cannot and does not wish to stay at home. In such instances the best solution is for her to be helped by a social services department who can usually arrange a suitable hostel or similar unit, many of which are run by church or voluntary organisations. After the birth of the child in hospital many unmarried mothers need time to decide whether they wish to care for the child or arrange adoption. An increasing number now care for their children and are accommodated in flats or sheltered housing.

Sheltered housing for unmarried mothers

Independent accommodation for the unmarried mother where she can live with her baby for 1½–2 years after confinement has been intro-duced in a few areas and has proved very successful. By using day nursery services the mother is able to go out to work and lead a more normal independent life than is possible in hostels. Late permanent housing is often arranged and with the help of a day nursery run by the social services department the mother can undertake a full-time job.

Family planning

Family planning advice should always be available to all women as part of their post-natal care. As the majority of post-natal care in the UK is carried out by the general practitioner, the majority of family planning consultations after pregnancy are now also undertaken by the general practitioner. General practitioners can prescribe oral contraceptive pills and other forms of contraception (e.g. the diaphragm) on the usual prescription forms.

The following are the forms of contraception available to women.

- *Combined oral contraceptive pill* (oestrogens and progesterone) which stops ovulation. It is taken for three weeks out of four. It may suppress breast milk and therefore should not be taken by any mother who is breast feeding.
- *Progesterone only pill* This is taken every day. It does not suppress breast milk and is therefore used on mothers who are breast feeding. It does not stop ovulation and is a less effective contraceptive pill than the combined one. Irregular menstruation or amenorrhoea (no periods) may follow.
- *Injectable progesterones* These are only used after rubella vaccination in the adult woman to ensure absolutely certain contraception. It is only used for three months. The menstrual cycle may be affected.
- *Intrauterine devices* (the coil) This is usually copper-coated and can be left in for five years. It works by setting up a low grade inflammation. It is best fitted six weeks after delivery. The coil can lead to infections, heavier bleeding and, very rarely, perforation of the uterus.
- *Diaphragm* This needs special fitting and must be used with a spermicide. It is intended to cause a physical barrier which prevents sperms entering the cervix.
- *Female sterilisation* This is only advocated where the couple have already had their family or where, in an earlier pregnancy, the mother was very ill and it now is essential for her not to risk another pregnancy. The fallopian tubes are either cut or tied or clamped. In many instances this can be carried out through a laparoscope.
- The man can practise contraception by using a condom (not available on prescription) or be sterilised by vasectomy. Coitus interruptus (withdrawal) and the rhythm method are still used but both methods are very uncertain.

Skilled counselling is essential before female sterilisation or vasectomy to ensure that both parents realise the finality of both procedures.

Although breast feeding often delays the resumption of menstruation, it is important that mothers realise that further pregnancies can occur – in no way does breast feeding act as a contraceptive.

Abortion

Since the introduction of the Abortion Act, 1967, abortion is legal in the United Kingdom where it can be shown by two doctors that the physical or mental health of the mother or children would be seriously affected by the birth.

The abortion (except in an emergency) must be performed either in a National Health Service hospital, or in one of the approved services hospitals, or in a place for the time being approved by the Secretary of State for the purposes of the Act.

The details of the present law are capable of considerable variations of interpretation; pregnancy may be terminated by a doctor if two registered medical practitioners are of the opinion, formed in good faith:

- that the continuance of the pregnancy would involve risk of the life of the pregnant woman or of injury to the physical or mental health of the pregnant woman or any existing children of her family, greater than if the pregnancy were terminated; or
- that there is a substantial risk that if the child were born it would suffer from such physical or mental abnormalities as to be seriously handicapped.

In assessing the former, account may be taken of the pregnant woman's actual or reasonably foreseeable environment.

Abortions should, as far as possible, be completed by the 18th week of pregnancy at the latest.

Nursing homes undertaking abortion and pregnancy advice bureaux have to be approved by the Secretary of State.

4 Preventive child health services

Care in the neo-natal period (birth to 28 days)

The first month of any child's life, the neo-natal period, is one of the most critical, for it is then that the majority of infant deaths occur. In 1989 in the UK the rate of infant deaths under one year per 1000 live births was 8.4 but the rate for deaths in the first month (neo-natal mortality) was 4.7. It is, therefore, very essential that great care is taken with the newborn child. Reference is made below to the dangers of extreme cold to babies shortly after birth. It is equally important that any baby should not be kept too hot as this has also been shown to be hazardous.

Haemolytic disease of the newborn (see also pages 53–54)

Cases which are not immunised with Anti-D immunoglobulin At birth every baby of a Rhesus negative mother should have some blood removed from the umbilical cord to test for antibodies which, if present, will gradually destroy the baby's red blood corpuscles by haemolysis. If the blood test shows antibodies to be present, *the baby must be immediately admitted to hospital for treatment.* This may include an exchange blood transfusion, which sets out to dilute continuously the antibodies and thus reduces the danger of blood destruction.

A simple perspex device for estimating the depth of jaundice in a newborn child (an icterometer) should be carried by every midwife and is useful to help judge the depth of any jaundice. It is especially useful to record the intensity of jaundice in low birth weight babies.

Neo-natal cold injury

Although the very small low birth weight baby is liable to suffer from chilling, it is now recognised that this is also a hazard in babies of normal birth weight. If any baby in its first month of life becomes seriously chilled, its body temperature may fall dangerously low to 32.2°C (90°F) or lower. The baby then becomes quiet and difficult to rouse and feed, and is cold to touch, and later oedematous. It may have a deceptively florid red complexion.

The prevention of this condition involves making certain that the temperature of the room in which the baby is sleeping does not fall below 18°C (65°F). Each midwife has a wall thermometer which should be left near the baby's cot to record the present temperature and the minimum temperature. This check and control is most important in winter but is still needed in summer, when unexpectedly low air temperatures may occur at night.

The low birth weight baby

Problems of the low birth weight baby

The majority of illnesses and death occur in babies of low birth weight (premature babies). As it is never possible to predict with complete accuracy the length of any pregnancy, a baby whose birth weight is less than 2500 g (5½ lbs) is classified as needing special care. Approximately 6.8% of all babies come into this category. The chance of survival falls rapidly as the birth weight of the baby falls. With babies between 2000 g (5 lbs) and 2499 g (5½ lbs) birthweight 2.1% die within 28 days but, for babies whose birth weight is between 1500 g and 1999 g the death rate is 5.7% and for those under 1500 g 30.2% die within 28 days. The special hazards for a low birth weight baby child are shown by the neo-natal death rate (deaths within first 28 days of life) for such children, which is 7–8 times greater than for all children.

The reduction of mortality from prematurity can be achieved in two ways:

(*i*)   by avoiding prematurity; and
(*ii*) by improving care facilities for low birth weight babies when born.

Avoidance of low birth weight babies

In many instances the exact cause of low birth weight is unknown. However, in some cases it will be associated with severe hypertensive disease of pregnancy, and first-class ante-natal care which reduces the incidence of this condition will also lessen the risk of it occurring.

Another important cause is chronic malnutrition in the mother and this is why the diet of each mother in pregnancy should be carefully watched. Generally, poor living conditions, overwork and increased frequency of infection, are also associated with a larger incidence of low birth weight babies. Cigarette smoking has also been identified with a greater risk of a low birth weight baby. There is a greater frequency of low birth weight babies being born to women in Social Class IV and V than in Social Class I and II. Improvements in living conditions will help reduce its incidence.

Care of low birth weight babies

It is convenient to subdivide all low birth weight babies into two groups – those under 2000 g (4½ lbs) and who should be admitted to a special intensive care unit, while the second group, from 2000 g (4½ lbs) to 2500 g (5½ lbs), can be looked after at home, provided the home is satisfactory and there is a special domiciliary nursing service (see page 70).

Intensive care units for low birth weight babies

Special intensive care units for low birth weight babies should be provided in all large maternity departments. Such units are usually designed to look after a small number of such infants. The care of the very small baby calls for skilled nursing using many modern techniques.

Incubator care will be needed for the very tiny babies. The value of the incubator is that it makes it easier to control the atmosphere in which the baby lives. There are three main factors:

- The *temperature* of the incubator should be maintained so that the baby's temperature is kept constant at just below 36.6°C (98°F).
- There should also be a constancy in the *relative humidity* within the incubator. It is best to keep the relative humidity (level of water vapour in the air) constantly at 60%.
- The *supply of oxygen* should be controlled. As many such babies have difficulties in pulmonary ventilation (they often develop hyaline membrane disease after birth) oxygen can be most helpful, but *great care must be taken not to increase the level of oxygen too high*, for if this is done, there is danger of damaging the retina of the new-born child and producing blindness (retrolental fibroplasia). Thus, the level of oxygen is always kept at the lowest which will give adequate relief to the child.

Feeding

There are many different methods of feeding used. Because of the effort of sucking, breast feeding is rarely possible for very tiny babies. But some mothers wish to express breast milk which can then be fed to their own baby through a nasogastric tube. Various forms of artificial feeding are also used – often carefully graduated weaker feeds of dried milks. These are always given more frequently than usual, two or three hourly, and often given by nasal catheter, allowing the measured feed to flow by gravity.

Prevention of infection

To all very small babies, infections represent their greatest hazard. The development of a respiratory infection in a small baby may be so sudden and dramatic that death can result after a few hours. The prevention of infection is, therefore, one of the most important tasks of the nurses in charge of a premature baby unit. Strict rules must always be observed. No one (other than the parents) should enter an intensive care unit unless his or her presence is essential. No one should enter if suffering from an infection (cold or upper respiratory tract infection). Everyone must wear sterile cap, mask and gown. Hand washing must be scrupulously carried out.

Great care must be taken not to carry infection from one cot to another and very high nursing standards are essential. New admissions, especially if admitted from home, should be separated from those already being nursed within the unit. In some units, air sterilisation is practised using ultra-violet light filters.

Prevention of hypoxia and cerebral palsy

There is increasing evidence that low levels of oxygen in a baby's bloodstream (hypoxia) can damage the brain. This is most likely to occur with the low birth weight baby and can produce cerebral palsy. This damage can occur either late in pregnancy, due to death of part of the placenta, or in the first few days after the birth. Continuous monitoring of the level of oxygen in the baby's bloodstream, which is now possible in the best intensive care units, has been shown to reduce the incidence of cerebral palsy by 35–40%. Although such preventive treatment is only possible in certain centres, it is hoped to extend its use in the future.

Domiciliary care of low birth weight babies

The larger low birth weight babies, between 2000 g (4½ lbs) and 2500 g (5½ lbs) weight, can be looked after adequately at home provided the home is reasonable and that there is a special domiciliary nursing baby service. This is run by the District Health Authority and consists of specially trained nurses, who may also be midwives, whose task it is to look after the small baby at home. The nurse has special equipment such as cots, feeding equipment and thermometers, which can be loaned to the mother. The nurse teaches the mother all the necessary information especially about feeding problems, and follows this up by daily or twice-daily visits to each baby, to ensure that care is continuing properly. In this way, continuous advisory help is available to the mothers and it also ensures that, if any difficulty or illness occurs, it can be promptly treated. In many cases ignorance plays a large part in producing problems in the low birth weight baby looked after at home. The great value of a domiciliary nursing baby service is that it reduces the effects of such ignorance.

The nurses who staff the service must do nothing else and must be careful to avoid introducing infection to the home. Visitors to the baby must be as carefully controlled as in hospital. In practice, infection is not as large a problem at home as in the hospital intensive care unit; there is much less danger of cross infection from other patients and staff as the human contacts with the baby at home are so limited.

Care of the normal baby

Rôle of the health visitor in home care

The standard of care and help given to the mother within a month after her confinement in helping with the care of her child is most important. It is during this period that the basis of sound health in the child can be formed.

The care of the child immediately after birth will be by the staff of the maternity ward, if a hospital birth, or by the midwife who delivered the baby if the birth took place at home. When the mother leaves hospital after delivery, the midwife will take over the care of the baby for a few days. After the 14th day, the main adviser to the mother (apart from the family doctor who is usually only consulted if some illness or extreme difficulty occurs) is the health visitor.

The health visitor is a highly trained nurse who, after gaining an RGN qualification and attending an obstetrics course, must then attend a year's full-time course in social and preventive medicine and qualify by examination for a Health Visitor's Certificate. The main task of the health visitor is to ensure that all the family and especially the children are as healthy as possible. This is achieved by a continuous process of health education and the health visitor strives to become the welcomed adviser to the mother and family in all health matters.

If possible, the health visitor meets and gets to know the mother during her pregnancy, at mothercraft and/or ante-natal classes. The health visitor takes over from the midwife the responsibility of the mother and child at the 14th day after delivery. It is best if this can be done by the midwife and health visitor meeting at the mother's home on the 14th day. Increasingly it is becoming usual for the link up between the general practitioner and health visitor to be closer and closer and so the health visitor today will usually be working in the primary health care team with the general practitioner who is also in charge of the patient.

Infant feeding

The first important factor upon which the health visitor concentrates is the feeding of the child. Wherever possible, breast feeding is recommended. To establish breast feeding much patience and encouragement is needed. The temptation to give up the effort because of difficulties is often great and much anxiety is felt by mothers who fear the baby is not getting enough milk on the breast.

In 1988 a national committee looked into present day practice in infant feeding DHSS Report on Health and Social Subjects No. 32 and unanimously agreed that the best food for babies is human breast milk, and that, when successfully managed, breast feeding of four to six months duration offers many advantages to both mother and infant. Since the risks of ill health are greater when the baby is very young, breast feeding for even as short a period as two weeks is an advantage. The increased tendency for some mothers to return to work after two months, and the ease and convenience of artificial feeding have tended to reduce breast feeding. It is, however, important to realise that the infant who is breast fed for five to six months has the best possible start in life. There is a lot of evidence that the incidence of all types of infection is lowest in breast fed children. In outbreaks of infantile gastroenteritis, which can be a dangerous disease in young infants, the breast fed child almost invariably escapes. There is also evidence that the personal bond between mother and child is never closer than between the mother and her child whom she has breast fed.

Health visitors therefore do all they can to encourage breast feeding. If, however, this is not possible, then the health visitor constantly helps the mother by giving her advice regarding artificial feeding. Today the majority of artificial feeding is by use of dried milks which are reconstituted just before the baby's feed. There are many different kinds. Suitable dried milks are available at health authority maternity and child health clinics at low cost. It is also usual to sell other proprietary baby foods at such clinics.

The health visitor also advises and helps the mother with all the small day-to-day problems of bringing up a baby. Frequency of feeding, clothing to be used, room temperature, general hygiene and the sleep patterns of babies, are all dealt with. An important aspect of a health visitor's work is that, in visiting the home of the mother, practical advice and health education can be given in the mother's own environment, that which the mother herself will have to use. The health visitor can make certain the mother fully understands all the intricacies attached to caring for a small baby. Each health visitor hopes that the mother will look forward to her or his visits as those of a friend and adviser.

Child health clinics

By the end of the first month, it is expected that the feeding of the baby will be progressing satisfactorily and the mother is invited to bring her baby along to the nearest child health clinic.

The child health clinic is designed as a place to which the mother can bring her baby at any time for help and advice. No ill child should ever be taken to such a clinic but should be seen by the general practitioner at the normal surgery. In cases of doubt, the health visitor will call to see the baby at home. It is important to avoid bringing ill babies to child health clinics because of the risk of spreading infection.

Each child health clinic is staffed by the same health visitors who do the home visiting in the area. The functions of the clinic include the following.

- *Education in parentcraft*   This is carried out by individual tuition or group tuition with the help of leaflets, posters, lectures and films. All health education topics are discussed, including the avoidance of accidents in the home.
- *Sale of infant foods* including:
  — suitable dried milks;
  — vitamin drops for infants;
  — vitamin tablets for expectant and nursing mothers (these also contain calcium, phosphate and iodine);
  — certain other baby foods.

Mixed feeding in infants usually starts any time between 12 and 15 weeks. There is a wide variety of special baby foods now available, usually sold in tins or jars and made up from many types of meats and vegetables. There are also many different cereals available so that any baby can get used to a wide variety of new tastes.

- *Routine medical inspection*   A doctor, often the family general practitioner, attends the clinic and sees the mother and examines her child on the first visit and usually at three months, six months and one year, and subsequently annually. The doctor is also available if the health visitor or mother wants a consultation between routine examinations, the purpose of which is to check that the baby is perfectly fit and to discover any abnormalities as soon as possible.
- *To give advice on minor problems* as they arise. Much of this will be done by the health visitor during home visits but mothers are also encouraged to visit the clinic if they have problems in between home visits. Feeding problems and difficulties connected with the development of the child are usual reasons for such visits.
- *To give protective immunisations to infants*   These immunisations,

which can also be given by the general practitioner in the surgery, are fully discussed in Chapter 6 and include immunisation against whooping cough, diphtheria, tetanus, poliomyelitis and measles, mumps and rubella (MMR).

Screening tests to discover unsuspected illness

During the first few months of a baby's life, it is important to carry out various checks on the health of the child to make certain that all abnormalities are spotted (such tests are called 'screening' tests).

Phenylketonuria

This is a rare metabolic disease (incidence approximately 1 in 10 000) in which the metabolism of the infant is faulty and poisonous phenylalanine metabolites are produced which eventually lead to a marked retarded mental development, and the child develops severe mental handicap. If treatment is started when the first symptoms of mental handicap show themselves, it is too late. However, if the disease can be diagnosed within a few weeks of birth, and the child given a special diet, this mental deterioration can be avoided.

Every child has a simple blood test – the Guthrie test – carried out on a specimen of blood taken from the baby between the sixth and fourteenth day of life. Several spots of blood from the young infant are collected from a heel prick on to specially absorbent filter paper. In the laboratory a small disc is punched out of each of the blood-impregnated filter papers and up to 100 individual discs are placed on a special agar plate containing a spore suspension of *Bacillus subtilis* and an inhibitory substance, Phenylalanase, acts as an antagonist to the inhibitor; after incubation in positive tests growth of the organism will be observed around the blood disc.

At present about 95% of babies born in the United Kingdom are tested for phenylketonuria.

Neo-natal hypothyroidism

It is now possible to screen new born babies for hypothyroidism which, if undetected, can lead to permanent brain damage within a few months and mild to severe mental handicap. The incidence of neo-natal hypothyroidism is about 1 in 5000. Provided the condition is recognised and treated before the third month of life, 74% achieve an IQ of 90 or greater whereas if the diagnosis is delayed until the fourth to sixth month, only 33% come into this category. The test involves measuring by radio immuno assay, the thyroid hormone (T4) or the Thyroid Stimulating Hormone (TSH) of the pituitary in the baby's blood. The TSH test is more specific and is always used to make the final diagnosis, but the advantage of the T4 test is that the blood collected for the phenylketonuria test can be used for both. It is therefore cheap and relatively easy to introduce. Such screening is now widely carried out throughout the United Kingdom. With widespread screening for neo-natal hypothyroidism, it has been estimated that 150 infants a year will be prevented from developing brain damage and mental handicap.

Congenital dislocation of the hip

Another good example of a condition which, if diagnosed very early, can be simply and completely treated but which, if diagnosed later, is difficult to treat and may lead to permanent disability, is congenital dislocation of the hip. It is now known that the main cause of this condition is inadequate development of the acetabulum of the pelvis.

There is a simple test (eliciting Ortolani's or von Rosen's sign) which the midwife or health visitor should carry out on all babies at birth and at monthly intervals until the child is four months old. In this test, the hip of the child is manipulated from the adducted to the abducted position while the thigh is flexed. A positive result is indicated by a 'click' or 'snap' being produced during the test and corresponds with the dislocated femoral head moving into the proper position in the acetabulum.

If the test is abnormal, the child should be referred without delay to an orthopaedic surgeon. Treatment is simple and consists of maintaining the hips continuously in abduction until the subluxation has been corrected. The constant pressure of the head of the femur in the centre of the acetabulum causes it to deepen and develop normally. After treatment for six to nine months, the danger of congenital dislocation of the hip disappears.

Screening for deafness

The recognition of congenital deafness is difficult and depends on careful observation of the infant during the first eight months of life, and on recognising the different vocalisation patterns in the normal and deaf child from three to eight months of age. Both develop in the same way until three months old, making reflex sounds and responding to a loud noise. But from three months onwards, the deaf child's vocalisation diminishes steadily so that by eight months, little effort is made to produce sounds, although the child will still remain alert, attentive and interested in its surroundings. By comparison, the normal child increases his or her sounds which become more tuneful, and is clearly copying what is heard. This changing pattern in the deaf child is often more easily recognised by the health visitor who plays an important part in diagnosing congenital deafness.

Sudden infant death syndrome (cot death)

The sudden infant death syndrome – often called 'cot death' – is a very distressing event, for such a death occurs very suddenly and unexpectedly. The aetiology of the condition is not fully known but it is now recognised that there is not one simple cause.

In 1984 in England and Wales there were 1242 such deaths traced (716 in boys and 526 in girls – boys have always shown a greater tendency to be affected); 58% of cot deaths occur between two and five months of age and such deaths are rare after the first year of life.

Many different causes have been postulated including mechanical obstruction, smothering, a disorder of the respiratory centre in the brain which may cause prolonged apnoea (cessation of breathing), hypothermia, overheating, and metabolic disorders especially those connected with calcium, sodium and magnesium metabolism.

There is a higher risk of a cot death in a low weight baby and where a previous baby in the family has died from such a cause. Babies of mothers who are heroin addicts have up to an 80 times greater chance of dying from a cot death.

Any child who has already nearly died from a cot death continues to be at high risk. Use of electronic alarms connected to the skin of the baby which alert the parents when the child has stopped breathing have proved to be useful and can give the parents much peace of mind. If the baby suddenly stops breathing, the child should be picked up and gently stimulated by being tapped on the bottom. This causes the baby to cry, and to take a deep breath. This action can be very effective provided it is taken immediately breathing has stopped (hence the value of alarms). Cot deaths occur more frequently in families in Social Classes IV and V.

Prevention, in the present stage of knowledge, is inexact but studies in Sheffield suggest that it may be possible to identify families whose children may be at potential risk. Such families need more concentrated ante-natal and post-natal care and health education and support from health visitors and services in such areas should be structured to enable this to occur.

Importance of follow-up of certain infants

Although screening for congenital abnormalities is now undertaken on all infants by doctors and health visitors, a high proportion are found in children in whom:

- *Family history* is suggestive of
  — any deafness, blindness or cerebral palsy
  — any known congenital abnormalities
  — mental disorder.

- **Obstetric history** is abnormal. This includes any illness or abnormality of the mother in pregnancy – rubella, excessive vomiting, threatened abortion, toxaemia, multiple pregnancy, premature birth, asphyxia, prolonged labour.
- **Post-natal problems** occur, including difficulties in sucking, convulsions or any serious illness in the first few months of life.

For all children coming within this group, special attention should be paid during the first five years of life and their follow-up is the responsibility not only of the health visitor but also the general practitioner and paediatric departments.

Care of normal children, six months to five years of age

The preventive care of children from six months to five years of age continues along similar lines. Periodic visits are made to the child's home and progress is checked from time to time at the child health clinic or by visits to the family doctor. The two approaches which are followed are:

(*i*) checking that normal progress is being maintained; and
(*ii*) complete investigation of any illness or abnormality discovered.

Normal stages of development in children

Normal progress in any child is checked by watching the various stages of growth reached, and checking that these are not late in appearing.

Mobility The normal baby should be able to sit with support by the 3rd or 4th month and by the 7th to sit alone. By the 8th or 9th month standing should be possible with support and without support between the 10th and 14th months. Walking will follow shortly after the infant can stand without support. Crawling or creeping usually occurs about the 9th or 10th month but may not always be shown.

Weight In the past, probably too much attention was paid to a baby's weight as indicating progress. It is still useful in indicating change in progress – a sudden loss of weight or halting in the gain in weight always calls for further investigation. However, due to the wide variations commonly seen in normal children, no reliance should be placed on tables giving 'normal' weights for children of different ages.

Usually a baby will double his birth weight by 5 months and treble it by 12 months. Sudden changes in weight, e.g. suddenly ceasing to gain weight, are indicators for further investigation. There is much individual variation. In particular, care must be taken not to stress too much to the parent the baby's weight, for it should never be the main guide to progress. It is interesting to note that some of the fittest babies who have been breast fed are often lighter than average but are very active and alert.

Behaviour   The general behaviour of the child is also an important guide to normal development. The child should be happy and active, and constantly exploring the home in an inquisitive way. It is important that the child always feels secure.

Bladder control   Sphincter control of the bladder is slow to develop. It usually does so at the end of the first year and may not be completely reliable until the child is 2½ to 3 years old. It is important that parents realise this for futile attempts to train the baby too young may only cause undue irritation and tensions, and may later produce the opposite effect in enuresis. These and other problems should be freely discussed between the parent and health visitor and, in this way, most of the difficulties will be avoided.

Weaning   Weaning from either breast milk or from bottled feeds commences between three and six months of age. Today, with the many specially prepared foods for weaning (including tinned foods), this is simple. In many clinics, such foods are sold and the health visitor is always there to advise on their use.

Speech development   The development of speech in a child is a very important stage. The first primitive efforts to produce speech start at 7 or 8 months of age. The child begins to imitate what is heard and to associate people and objects with the sounds. By 1½ years of age, a child should be using simple words and simple sentences.

A very slow development of speech should always lead to a careful re-testing of hearing. The completely deaf child hears nothing to imitate and, unless taught by special methods, will never speak. The other important reason for severe retardation of speech is lack of normal mental development. Further examination in such a case will show retardation in other stages of physical development.

Clothing and shoes

As the child begins to walk, it is important that his or her clothing and shoes always fit. Many crippling deformities of the feet have been produced by ill-fitting shoes at all ages. As far as possible, shoes with wide fitting toes should be selected. It is also important to make certain that the child's socks are the correct size. If they have shrunk and are too short, they will exert constant pressure on the toes and may lead to overlapping of toes and other deformities. Because no two children have similar shaped feet, it is always wise not to pass on shoes to younger children in the same family. This can, however, be safely done for loose fitting footwear such as wellington boots.

A constant watch should be kept on the way in which the feet of the toddler are developing. Minor deformities such as flat feet, pes cavus and rigid feet can be spotted easily. All response much more readily to treatment at this age than later. Early diagnosis can thus do much to prevent subsequent problems.

Intestinal infestations

Minor infestations with threadworms are quite commonly seen at this age. The worms often migrate from the rectum to the buttocks at night time leading to much itching and irritation. This is often the cause of toddlers sleeping fitfully. Diagnosis is easy – examination of the anus shows the tiny migrating worms. Once diagnosed, treatment with modern drugs is easy using piperazine phosphates, and prevents further problems.

Care of acute illness in the child aged one to five years

In families it is not unusual for the younger children to become infected with the common childhood infectious diseases, such as measles, whooping cough and scarlet fever, although an increasing number are prevented by immunisation. Treatment is similar to that for older children but it is always important to remember that such illnesses may be the starting point for various chronic minor inflammatory and catarrhal conditions such as tonsillitis, sinusitis, or otitis media. With modern chemotherapy and antibiotic treatment many of the serious chronic conditions such as otitis media can be avoided *provided that early diagnosis is made and treatment started promptly.*

The treatment of a child with enlarged tonsils depends on

(*i*)   whether the child has successive attacks of tonsillitis;
(*ii*) whether there is associated respiratory obstruction from enlarged and inflamed adenoids; and
(*iii*) whether infection spreads to involve the ear.

If any of the above three occur tonsillectomy should be carried out as soon as the child is well again. Prompt removal of the adenoids in such children is likely to prevent serious otitis media. Tonsils today are rarely removed just because they are enlarged.

Various squints may become obvious in this age group and the doctor or health visitor should always check if there is any sign of such defects. Early diagnosis and effective treatment will do much to reduce the likelihood of chronic and serious problems later.

Congenital malformations

Congenital malformations are notifiable to the Office of Population Censuses and Surveys (OPCS). Pre-natal infections such as rubella or the use of certain drugs in early pregnancy such as thalidomide can cause congenital abnormalities and it is hoped that by careful continuous analysis any increase would be noticed more quickly. Approximately 13 000 babies in England and Wales are born with congenital abnormalities each year (see Table 4.1). The age and parity of the mother are factors in determining the levels of incidence: the lowest rates are in the younger mothers having their second child, while the highest rates are in mothers over 40 having their fourth child.

Table 4.1   Principal causes of congenital malformations by site, England, 1988. Total number of malformations = 14764. (From OPCS Report, MB3, 1989.)

Site	Numbers
Deformities of feet	2080
Other congenital abnormalities of the limbs	1968
Congenital abnormalities of the skin	1869
Hypo- and epispadias	1102
Congenital dislocation of the hip	992
Ear, face and neck malformations	739
Malformations of the heart and circulatory system	726
Polydactyly	646
Other congenital malformations	641
Cleft lip	529
Syndactyly	519
CNS malformations	509
Down's syndrome	428
Malformations of urinary system	392
Reduction deformaties of the limbs	301
Cleft palate (excluding lip)	274
Other abnormalities of the digestive system	253
Spina bifida	157
Exomphalos, gastroschisis	147
Atresia and stenosis of large intestine, rectum and anal canal	138
Hydrocephalus	137
Eye malformations	106
Tracheo-oesophageal fistula and oesophageal atresia and stenosis	70
Anencephalus	41

Of the babies born with congenital abnormalities, 11% have more than one malformation (see Table 4.2). It will be seen that 89% of babies who are born with a congenital abnormality have only one malformation, 8.2% have two and 1.7% have three. Although these represent a very small proportion of all babies born in 1988, 14 babies had eight or more congenital abnormalities.

Table 4.2 Multiple congenital malformations, England and Wales, 1988. (From OPCS Report, DH3, 1989.)

Total number of babies born with congenital malformations	13020
Babies born with 1 congenital malformation	11592 (89.0%)
Babies born with 2 congenital malformations	1070 (8.2%)
Babies born with 3 congenital malformations	222 (1.7%)
Babies born with 4 congenital malformations	66
Babies born with 5 congenital malformations	33
Babies born with 6 congenital malformations	16
Babies born with 7 congenital abnormalities	7
Babies born with 8 or more congenital abnormalities	14

Safety of children

As children grow up they become more and more inquisitive and thus may become liable to accidents and illnesses. As seen in Table 4.3, in 1988 in England and Wales 1131 children died as a result of an accident. Traffic accidents were responsible for 31.7% of the deaths

Table 4.3 Accidental deaths in children aged 0–14 years by type and sex, England and Wales, 1988. (From OPCS Report DH3, 1989.)

Type	Under 1 year		1–4 years		5–14 years		Total	
	Male	Female	Male	Female	Male	Female	Male	Female
All accidents in the home	26	16	63	47	464	157	553	220
Main causes of accidents in the home								
Accidental poisoning (drugs and medicines)	1	0	2	0	147	56	150	56
Falls	6	0	2	6	78	21	86	27
Accidents caused by fire and flame	3	5	29	27	17	11	49	43
Accidental mechanical suffocation	4	1	6	3	11	1	21	5
Accidental drowning	1	3	10	4	0	0	11	18
Inhalation, ingestion of food causing obstruction of respiratory tract and suffocation	5	3	2	1	3	0	10	4
Electrocution	1	1	0	1	0	1	1	3
Other causes	5	3	12	5	208	67	225	75
Accidents outside the home								
Motor traffic accidents	5	7	34	34	203	75	242	116
Motor non-traffic accidents	0	0	1	1	4	1	5	2

(358 children). Seat belts should always be used for children of all ages, including in the rear seats where the use of belts has now been made compulsory in the UK. Baby car seats should be tethered by safety straps. Kerb drill should be taught at an early age and parents, as well as schools, should train their children continuously. Note that the largest numbers of deaths from traffic accidents occurred in the age group 5–14 years and that boys made up almost double the number of deaths than for girls.

In 1988 home accidents resulted in the deaths of 773 children in England and Wales. The four commonest causes of accidental death are accidental poisoning with drugs and medicines (150 in boys and 56 in girls), falls (86 in boys, and 27 in girls), accidents caused by fire or flame (49 in boys and 43 in girls) and accidental mechanical suffocation (21 in boys and 5 in girls). Many of these accidents lead also to much hospitalisation and handicap. All are preventable and continuous efforts must be made by health visitors to reduce these casualties. Parents should be taught the dangers of letting young children play with unsuitable objects such as plastic bags, the importance of fireguards and flameproof clothing, the dangers of unprotected stairs and of brightly coloured medical tablets, many of which are poisonous to young children and which look so like sweets to them.

Climate

Excessive heat or cold can be dangerous (see also page 67 for neo-natal cold injury). Older babies can also be affected by a lesser degree; no infant should go out of doors in very cold or foggy weather. Babies should also avoid intense heat and it must be remembered that a pram can become a heat trap. In sunny weather the hood should be kept down and a sun canopy used. Under no circumstances should a baby be left in an unventilated car in warm weather.

Prams and pushchairs

Brakes should be tested regularly. For very young infants lying down, cat nets must be used to avoid the possibility of suffocating the baby if the cat snuggles against his or her face. A harness should be used for all infants when sitting up.

Cots and bedding

Pillows are unnecessary and dangerous to young babies for their use may lead to suffocation. Under no circumstances should a cot be painted with a lead based paint as the child may suck the sides of the cot and be poisoned.

Feeding

It is possible for a baby to choke on a bottle propped up in a cot or pram. No baby should ever be left alone with a bottle and all feeding must be carefully supervised.

Coordination of child health services and education and social services

At all times, it is essential to ensure coordination between the child health services and the education and social services. Health visitors and social workers should work closely together (see page 277) and both should undertake domiciliary care for children who are either handicapped or have special problems.

In many handicapped children, the special education (see page 93) which they need should start before two years of age. Such children, when they reach the age of 17 years, will become the responsibility of the social services, although all education authorities continue to have some responsibility as regards continuing education until they reach the age of 25. By arranging a well coordinated service involving health visitors, teachers and social workers, continuity of care will make certain that the best possible success in each individual is achieved. The Griffiths Report on Community Care (see page 228) included reference to both physically and mentally handicapped of all ages. Hence local authorities, through their education and social services committees, should ensure that a very close liaison is maintained with the health and employment authorities, especially in the case of handicapped school leavers.

The Warnock Committee (see Chapter 5, page 92) emphasised that health visitors have an important role with very young handicapped children under the age of five years, and that, generally, the health visitor should act as the 'named person' in such cases.

Child abuse (non-accidental injury)

Another area in which cooperation between child health, education and social services departments is essential is in the control of child abuse. This is dealt with in detail in Chapter 13 (see pages 252–66).

5 Health services for schoolchildren

The prevention of disease in schoolchildren is the concern of all branches of the health services, but special arrangements are made under the various Education Acts to safeguard the health of children at school. Each Health Authority must organise a comprehensive range of integrated health services for children including a *school health service* run in conjunction with the relevant local education authority. Each Health Authority appoints a Specialist in Community Medicine (Child Health) who is responsible to the local education authority for providing and organising the health staff for the school health services. Many doctors are employed within the school health service by the District Health Authority – some being specially trained to deal with handicapped children – and are either employed full-time or part-time on a sessional basis. In this respect increasing use is made of general practitioners.

Aims of the school health service

The move of a child to school when aged five years is one of the more important changes in life. The child has to leave the comparative peace and security of home and mix with dozens of other children in the competitive atmosphere of the classroom and playground. Even for the child with brothers and sisters the move to school is important, but, for the first or only child, the impact of school represents a very great change.

School life in all children covers the next 11 years and many remain at school until 18 years of age when they move on to a university.

Preventive medicine for any child of school age is largely connected with school life. In order to help children to get the most benefit from their education the School Health Service, a highly developed preventive medical service, has been built up to ensure that every child's health is safeguarded throughout his or her school career. There are two main functions of the school health service.

• To make certain that every child is *as fit as possible*. This includes many services designed to diagnose disabilities as early as possible, to allow for correction before they have a lasting effect upon the health of the child. This function also includes the promotion of *positive health* – it is not just sufficient to see that no disease occurs, but there must be a positive programme designed to make every school child as fit as possible.

- To assist with the care of various groups of *handicapped children*.

Nursery school

The normal child can gain much from attending a nursery school when aged three to five years. The value of such schools, which the children usually attend for half a day, is in the social contact made. The child gets used to working with others and this is especially useful and makes the entry into primary school easier. The medical care of children in nursery schools is important and is undertaken by the school health service. Special care must be taken with outbreaks of communicable disease as conditions such as dysentery can spread rapidly in nursery schools if not recognised early (see page 134).

Steps taken to ensure every school child is as fit as possible

The present method of medical examination in schools is a combination of *full routine medical examinations* on all children either just before or immediately after entry into school (five years) combined with *selective medical examinations during school life.* Just before leaving school (15 years) there is another full examination including a fitness test for employment.

Occasionally the initial examination is replaced by a *pre-school initial medical inspection* at four years of age. This has the advantage that a dental examination is possible earlier (when conservative dentistry is more effective) and enables any medical defect discovered to be investigated fully and treated before entry to school.

Routine medical inspections

Each school is visited at least once a year by the team carrying out the routine medical inspection – the school doctor, the health visitor and/or school nurse, and a clerk to assist with clerical work. The medical examination takes place at school, if possible in a medical inspection room. Parents are invited to be present and their presence is most important especially at the first medical inspection. It is best to summon parents on a single appointment system so that they are kept waiting as little as possible. About 12 children are examined each morning and afternoon.

A careful *medical history* is taken from the parent and this is supplemented by records from the child health service and from the general practitioner. These should provide a complete story of the child's progress from infancy with full details of any illness, medical problems, immunisations, as well as a brief record of the health of the parents and family. It is best if the health visitor who dealt with the child when a baby also looks after the school which the child attends. This is not always possible but is usually the case, for the infant's school is normally in the same district as the child's home. To have the same health visitor working with pre-school children and with the infant and junior schools, means that she knows a great deal about the background of each child. Any unusual point in the medical history is noted and problems should be carefully watched.

A full *medical examination* then takes place by the school doctor. All systems are carefully examined, including the special senses. Apart from testing for abnormalities particular attention is paid to posture, nutrition and minor orthopaedic problems such as foot deformities, for example pes cavus and flat foot. The intelligence of each child is not tested routinely but if the teacher raises any doubt about a child's mental ability a special intelligence test is arranged at once.

Sight testing is carried out routinely on five-year-olds and the Keystone machine which tests visual acuity, colour vision and muscle balance is often used. If any defect is found, a full ophthalmic examination is arranged. *Any child with a squint must be treated immediately.* Treatment can be carried out at the nearest eye hospital or special orthoptic treatment can be arranged by the school health service.

The *hearing* of every child should be examined *individually* in the first medical examination when aged five. This can conveniently be carried out by a doctor or health visitor using a sweep test with a portable pure tone audiometer. This is a light, portable machine which produces sound of varying volume at frequency ranges from 128 to 8000 cycles per second. Each ear is tested independently – the child being given a small wooden mallet and asked to strike the table each time a sound is heard. Each frequency is tested starting with a loud volume of sound and gradually the volume is reduced until the child can no longer hear anything. This indicates the threshold of hearing – the lowest volume of sound at that particular frequency which the child can hear. This test is repeated for each frequency so that a pattern of hearing is established for both ears and at a number of different frequencies. It is important to test at different frequencies as occasionally there is a loss of hearing at one particular part of the sound scale (high-frequency deafness).

Testing the hearing of a five-year-old with this machine in expert hands takes between two and three minutes. About 5% of those tested initially fail the tests. All who fail should be retested immediately and this usually results in about a third of those who originally failed the test, passing it on the second occasion (they failed the first time not because of hearing loss but because they failed to understand the test). Usually about 3% of the original group finally fail. These children must all be investigated further by an Ear, Nose and Throat Department to establish the cause of their hearing loss. In many cases, the hearing loss is quite small and, without a special test, might never be discovered. It is, however, most important that any hearing loss, even if small, is discovered early, otherwise it is likely to interfere with the educational progress of the child – the child will probably not be working to his or her full potential although, if intelligent, may still be progressing quite well compared to other children.

All children with a hearing loss are carefully followed up and, where necessary, a hearing aid is prescribed by the hospital department. Those with minimal hearing loss are always put at the front of the class to make certain they have the best opportunity to hear each lesson.

If any illness or disability is discovered in the routine medical examination, the parent is told about it and a note sent to the child's own general practitioner who then arranges for treatment. The school health service is really a diagnostic service and not a treatment service, although it is careful to check that the treatment ordered by the doctor is properly carried out by the child. In some cases, the treatment may affect the child's ability to play a full part in the activities of the school, for example games. Wherever possible, interference in this way is always kept to a minimum for it is important that no child should ever think some activity cannot be undertaken unless this is essential. Close liaison must be maintained between the family doctor and school doctor in this respect.

After the school medical examination, the school doctor indicates those children who need to be seen again. Whenever any disability is discovered, arrangements are always made to see the child and parent again in a few weeks after treatment. This succeeding examination will take place at one of the follow-up school clinics held weekly. All children who have been found to have disabilities should also be seen on the next routine medical examination which the doctor carries out at that school. This will normally be the following year. A perfectly normal child would not be seen by the doctor following the initial medical inspection at four or five years until the child is about to leave school (15 years).

The exceptions to this would be if a sudden illness developed in the meantime or if the parents or teachers were worried about the health of the child. In this case, the child would be seen either at the next visit of the doctor to school or be referred to the follow-up clinic.

A few examples of how routine medical inspection works are given by the following.

Normal child   The child is medically examined at school when aged five years and 15 years. In addition the health visitor/school nurse visits the school each term to check on minor illnesses and absentees. A questionnaire is completed by parent and teacher when the child is aged eight years and 12 years. Selective medical examination is carried out where the answers cause concern.

Child with constant disability   A child with defective vision, or some chronic disability such as a scoliosis, would be seen when five years old at school, and then on each annual routine medical examination carried out by the doctor on the next visit to the school. Also the child may be seen at any time at follow-up clinics.

Normal child on entry to school who later develops severe illness   An example would be a child found to be quite normal on entering school at five years but who developed rheumatic fever when aged seven. This child would have been medically examined at five, found normal, and marked to be seen again at 15. However, when rheumatic fever developed at seven, the child would be referred immediately on return to the school doctor and would then be seen as regularly as needed and on each subsequent routine medical examination at the school (often called surveillance).

This careful 'watching over' process of the health of all schoolchildren should always be carried out in such a way as to help and assist parents, general practitioners and teachers. All children are seen after any recent serious illness, or if the teacher, parent or health visitor/school nurse is concerned because of unsatisfactory progress or difficulty of any kind.

Other functions of the school medical officer

The good school doctor will visit schools in between the more lengthy visits to carry out routine medical inspections and check up other points which are important to the health of the child. These include the following.

- *Helpful advice about the hygiene in the school*   This will include examination of buildings, heating, washing facilities and kitchen premises.
- *Investigation of all communicable diseases*   There are always likely to be outbreaks of communicable disease in schools, especially in infant and junior schools. Much further illness can be prevented by prompt and proper investigation. Bacteriological investigations should be carried out on the close family contacts of certain communicable diseases (such as diphtheria, dysentery, salmonella or enteric infections) and may prevent much unnecessary disease by defining carriers who may spread the disease.

    Whenever a case of tuberculosis occurs within a school, complete and careful examination of all contacts (staff and children) must be carried out to make certain that an unsuspected case has not been the cause.

It is best always for all such investigations to be undertaken by the regular school doctor and health visitor for they know so much about the school and its staff and children, and will thus be able to ensure that fullest investigations are undertaken with the minimum interference to school work.

The difficult question of any possible danger of any HIV positive children in schools (see Chapter 8 for a full discussion of risks) should always be dealt with by the school medical officer. In such instances, the only risk could be in the event of an accident or nose bleed when there could be a danger from infection from blood. Sensible precautions (the provision and use of *clean rubber gloves to be used in all such instances for all children*) should be introduced in every school and carefully discussed with all teachers, some of whom may not understand the remoteness of the danger.

Health education should always be one of the most important functions of the school health team. The aim is to *promote positive health* – to assist the teaching staff to improve the health of children as far as possible. This means encouraging certain non-athletic and underdeveloped children to improve their physique in various ways. Every school doctor should take an interest in the games schedules of the school. But it is also important not to neglect that group of children who, for one reason or another (e.g. bad eyesight) never seem able to excel at traditional ball games. Other forms of active recreation should always be encouraged and special activities such as walking, camping, cycling, rock climbing, skiing, fishing, sailing, skating and riding should, wherever possible, be part of the sporting activities of the school. To benefit from such sports is within the compass of any school today, for the Central Council of Physical Recreation runs a multitude of excellent courses in all areas of the country especially designed to introduce the older school child to such activities. Such an introduction may readily play an important part in maintaining the health of the adult later in life.

Special subjects in health education must be tackled such as sex education, care of teeth and education to prevent children starting to smoke. None of these topics are easy to put over successfully and often more can be gained by example. In this respect, the behaviour of all the teaching staff is most important – a campaign to stop children from smoking is unlikely to succeed unless staff are also prepared to help. Attempts must always be made to see that health education becomes a part of ordinary education wherever possible so that it is a continuously active process rather than a sudden strenuous campaign.

- *Immunisations* should be encouraged in schoolchildren. Booster doses of diphtheria and poliomyelitis immunisation should be given to those who have had prior courses. For children who have never been immunised, primary courses of immunisation should be arranged at school. The aim should be to make it as easy as possible for the child to be immunised.

  BCG vaccination against tuberculosis should be offered to all schoolchildren aged 12 to 13 years who are then Mantoux negative (see page 122).

  Arrangements should be made to immunise all girls between the ages of 11 and 13, and who have not previously had measles, mumps and rubella (MMR) immunisation, against rubella.
- The discovery or ascertainment of all groups of *handicapped children* is another function of the school doctor.

Routine inspections by health visitors

In addition to the health inspection visit, the health visitor visits each school frequently in order to

- note which children are absent from school so that the health visitor can pay a home visit to help and advise;
- carry out certain screening tests – repeat any hearing tests and test the vision of 7 year old children;
- carry out regular cleanliness inspections on schoolchildren.

A small percentage of all schoolchildren are found to have evidence of infestation with head lice. These infestations are mainly in the form of nits – the eggs of the head louse. Arrangements are then made for the cleansing of the child at a convenient clinic and for subsequent examination to make certain that there has not been a recurrence. It is essential for the health visitor to also visit the home, for often other members of the family are involved and, in such cases, to treat the schoolchildren only will achieve little. On such visits particular attention must be paid to examining the hair of the older members of the family.

Another disease in which it is important to treat all the family and which occasionally is found in schoolchildren is *scabies*. Modern treatment with benzyl benzoate solution is most efficient and soon controls such infestations, provided all infected members of the family are treated simultaneously.

School clinics

School clinics are provided so that schoolchildren can attend follow-up clinics and have minor ailments treated without having to spend too much time away from school. Treatment is not really the function of the school health service but there are so many problems connected with getting children's eyes tested for glasses that it has often been found most convenient for an eye specialist periodically to hold an *ophthalmic clinic* in a school clinic. The District Health Authority cooperates with the Education Committee in arranging this service. Special *orthopaedic clinics* are held in school clinics by orthopaedic consultants to treat and follow up the large number of minor orthopaedic problems always found in a school population. Such clinics are of special importance in country areas where attendance at a hospital outpatient department may be difficult.

Preventive dental treatment in schoolchildren

A comprehensive preventive dental service is an important part of the school health service. Unlike the rest of the school health service, the school dental service is both a diagnostic and a treatment service.

A visit is paid by the dental surgeon to each school every six months and every child is examined dentally and notes made of all defects. Each child is then called for individual treatment by the dentist in the following weeks. Treatment is free and usually carried out at the dental clinic which is normally attached to the school clinic. In remote country areas dental clinics may be mounted in a mobile caravan so that the treatment centre can be taken and parked at the school. This arrangement allows treatment of every child to be carried out without taking the children away from school for long periods.

Most school dental services have facilities to carry out orthodontic treatment on children with crowded and misplaced teeth. Effective orthodontic treatment in the school child can prevent many dental problems later. It is, however, important that orthodontic treatment is started early enough to enable the permanent teeth to develop correctly.

In the school dental service *dental hygienists* work under the personal direction of dentists, tackling certain tasks such as the scaling of teeth and doing some fillings.

A recent study of the dental health of children aged 5–15 years in maintained schools showed that very few children avoid dental decay – seven out of ten of the five year old children had evidence of past or present decay. Among teenagers the proportion was more than 95 out of 100. Some evidence of gingivitis was found in half of the children by the age of 17. There was also marked regional variation and this is often connected with either the natural or artificial fluoridation of water supplies.

Care of the handicapped school child

An important subsidiary function of the school health service is to assist in the diagnosis, discovery and special care for all handicapped school children whether the handicap or disability is physical or mental.

The education of children and young people who are handicapped or, to use a more modern phrase, have disabilities or significant difficulties was studied in detail by an expert Committee set up by the Department of Education and Science under the chairmanship of Mary Warnock. This Committee reported in 1978 and, since then, governments have generally accepted many of its recommendations and the Education Act, 1981, has changed the law where necessary.

Definition of special educational needs under the Education Act, 1981

The Education Act, 1981 accepts the recommendation of the Warnock Committee that the narrow definition of handicapped children (which only includes blind, partially sighted, deaf, partially deaf, delicate, educationally backward, emotionally and behaviourally disturbed, physically handicapped, epileptic, speech defect children) should be extended to include any child who requires some form of special educational provision (including 'remedial' education). This will mean that approximately 16–17% of the school population (one in six) will be involved at any one time (or 20% or one in five at some time during their school life). Special educational provision may take the form of special teaching techniques or equipment, a specially modified curriculum or help with social or emotional problems.

Duties of local education authorities (LEAs)

Under the Education Act, 1981, all LEAs must assess any child whom the LEA considers has a special educational need. Medical, psychological and educational advice *must* be sought in each assessment and assistance may also be obtained from social services where this is appropriate.

Once any child has been assessed to have a special educational need, the LEA will be under a legal duty to arrange special educational provision in accordance with the statement outlining that need. Parents also *must* receive a copy of the statement – indeed much emphasis in the Act is placed on parental involvement and cooperation. Parents *must* also be given the name and address of a person to whom they may apply for information and advice about their child's special educational needs.

The Education Act, 1981 requires all LEAs to provide for the needs of children requiring special education and to keep them under review.

This should include making arrangements to educate children with special needs with ordinary children (i.e. integration) and parental wishes should be met wherever possible. Where it would be inappropriate for special educational provision to be made at school, LEAs will be able to arrange for it to be made elsewhere.

At present, a local education authority (LEA) can legally insist on a medical and other examination of any child whom they have reason to believe requires special education once that child has reached the age of two years.

Under the Education Act, 1981 the LEA is required to determine the special educational provision which needs to be made and to assess the child's needs. However, *parents must be involved in the making of the assessments and may appeal against the decisions*. LEAs are also empowered, with the consent of parents, to assess these special educational needs of children under two years of age and to maintain records and statements about them.

In addition, parents are able to request that the LEA assesses the special needs of their child whether or not statements or records are being maintained for them.

Recording of handicapped children

A detailed statement must be maintained for each child. This record should contain the results of multi-professional assessment and should carefully define the individual handicaps or disabilities and the child's special needs and difficulties. It should also indicate the special form of education required for the child. The LEA then has to meet such needs.

Parents must be consulted in the drawing up of the record and it is a legal requirement for the LEA to review, modify and maintain the record. In the event of a disagreement between the parents and the LEA, there is an appeal to a special appeal committee and a final right of appeal to the Secretary of State.

Principles applying to meeting special educational needs

Certain basic principles apply to the education of children with special needs.

- Every effort should be made to discover the extent of the disability and special needs of the child as early as possible. In some instances, such as congenital deafness, this will be within the first year of life.
- Special education and care should be started early and continued well after the normal school leaving age.
- The aim should be to make each child as independent as possible.

- Each child should be dealt with individually and improvisation is always helpful.
- The best solution is usually that which is as near normal as possible. All forms of integration into the ordinary school system are therefore very useful.
- The after-care of children with disabilities or significant difficulties when they leave school is most important. Wherever possible, special vocational training and/or work preparation should be arranged.

To encourage early discovery and identification of special educational needs, all DHAs, under the Education Act 1981, have a legal duty to inform parents and the LEA where they form the opinion that a child under the age of five has, or is likely to have, special educational needs. The DHA must also afford the parents an opportunity to discuss their opinion before bringing the child to the attention of the LEA.

There are many ways in which a handicapped child can be educated: in an ordinary school; in a special class in an ordinary school; in a day special school; in a residential special school; at home with a peripatetic teacher; or in a combination of these.

Discovery of disabilities and disclosure to parents

The importance of early discovery of any disability in a child has already been stressed. Depending on the nature of the handicap or problem, it may be discovered shortly after birth by the parents, doctors, health visitor, or during the first few years or not even until the child attends a day nursery, nursery school or primary school. In all instances, it is essential that a full explanation of the disability is given in a sensitive way to the parents. Many may find it difficult to grasp the full meaning and significance, especially in the case of a serious disability or mental handicap and such parents *will need constant support* and will require *information, advice and practical help*. It is best if parents have nominated to them one individual professional to act as a 'Named Person' who can introduce the parents to the right services, explain any problems and generally act as a guide and counsellor. For any child of pre-school age, the health visitor will normally act in this capacity, although in exceptional cases (e.g. a deaf child) another professional (e.g. peripatetic teacher) may act as Named Person. For children with special needs at school, the head teacher should undertake this role. Parents should be encouraged to discuss their doubts and fears openly for concealment only adds to their problems.

Assessment of special educational needs

The assessment of a child with a disability or significant difficulty should always include the following.

- *Parents should always be involved* No estimation of a child's needs can be complete without the fullest help from parents. The aim should be to treat parents as partners and parents must be kept fully informed of all expert investigation.
- *Multi-professional assessment should always be undertaken* This will include expert medical examination by hospital paediatricians as well as assessment by health visitors, educational psychologists, teachers, social work staff and day nursery matrons, where appropriate. Assessment should aim at discovering how the child learns and responds over a period of time.
- There must be full *investigations of any aspect of the child's performance which is causing concern.*
- The *family and home circumstances* should always be taken into account.

Range of special education provided

The special educational needs of children are extremely complex and varied. It may be possible for even the seriously disabled to be educated in ordinary schools provided special ramps are available to accommodate wheelchairs, special teaching equipment is on hand and transport is provided to enable the child to get to school.

For most children with severe disabilities and for those who have already attended a primary school but made little progress, attendance at a special school may be needed at least for an initial period. Special schools are provided by LEAs and voluntary bodies and, under the Education Act 1981, the Secretary of State can make regulations in respect of the approval of special schools and independent schools.

In general, special schools are needed for three groups of children.

- Children with *very severe or complex disabilities*. This group includes a wide range of conditions including complete blindness or deafness, severe congenital disabilities such as spina bifida and the worst cerebral palsies, and progressive diseases such as Duchenne muscular dystrophy.
- Children with *severe emotional or behavioural disorders* whose behaviour is extreme and unpredictable. Such children were formerly called 'maladjusted' but this is a term no longer in general use.
- Children who for various reasons have *done badly in ordinary school* and who need the more intimate atmosphere of smaller teaching groups.

Integration

Wherever possible, children with special educational needs should be educated in ordinary schools (integration). There are three forms of integration.

- *Locational*   This is where a special school unit is sited within the same grounds as an ordinary school, but is run as a separate school. This is a first step in integration and is helpful in reducing isolation and stigma felt by parents and children who attend a 'special school'. It also enables seriously disabled children to attend the 'same school' as their brothers and sisters, and helps the children in ordinary schools to understand better the needs and problems of handicapped children.
- *Social integration* is a further step and here the children play, eat and mix with the children from the adjacent ordinary school and may even share some of their out-of-classroom activities. Classroom teaching, however, remains separate.
- *Functional integration* achieves all the above mixing but, in addition, the disabled children share most of their classes with ordinary children. Such an arrangement still allows some specialised teaching but enables the handicapped children to gain access to a wider range of teaching than is usually possible in a special school. It also enables the potential of most disabled children to be better reached.

For severely disabled children who have to spend most of their school life in a special school, it is important for them to experience some degree of social and functional integration during the last two to three years at school. This is the best way to avoid overprotection of such children which, to some degree, is inevitable for any child attending a small special school.

Special problems of the disabled child in the transitional period from school into adult life

All children with disabilities or significant difficulties meet special problems on leaving school. They are likely to find more difficulty in getting a job or in being accepted for higher education. Careful preparation is therefore important and re-assessment should always take place during the last two or three years at school. As well as the usual professionals, careers guidance officers, Disablement Resettlement Officers and special social workers from the social services department should be involved.

Special linked courses whereby children may spend part of their time in a nearby college of further education and 'work preparation' schemes can be of considerable value. For disabled young persons over school leaving age, there are also Employment Rehabilitation Centres run by the Department of Employment. There are also a number of specialised residential assessment courses at special units such as the Queen Elizabeth's Foundation at Banstead Place. *Special Careers Officers* are employed by most LEAs to give special help to disabled school leavers.

Young persons who are mentally handicapped and have been attending special schools will usually transfer to local Adult Training Centres run by social services departments (see page 306) and hopefully later to sheltered workshops.

Importance of further education

Many disabled young persons experience difficulties in finding work unless they can become qualified in some way. Therefore, they should, wherever possible, be encouraged to attend a college of further education or some form of higher education (polytechnic or university).

At Coventry, the LEA runs a very modern residential further education college (Hereward College). There are also a number of voluntary bodies who run excellent residential training colleges.

Special groups of children with disabilities or significant difficulties

Although handicapped children are no longer categorised, those with certain types of disabilities still require specialised help. Brief notes describing the needs of children with particular disabilities are given below.

Children who are blind or partially sighted

Blind children have no useful sight and must be educated by non-visual methods. Education in nearly all cases takes place in a residential school except in the largest cities. Blind children often start their training at the age of two years in the Sunshine Homes run by the Royal National Institute for the Blind.

Partially sighted children have very poor eyesight but, with special assistance, they can be taught using visual methods. Classes must be very small, not more than ten in a class, and special equipment is needed. In most instances, partially sighted children can be taught in special day schools or special classes within day schools.

Children who are deaf or partially deaf

Deaf children have no useful hearing and cannot be taught by auditory methods. *It is essential that their training and education should start very young (as soon as diagnosed)* and that it is very specialised. By remarkable methods which have translated the teaching of sounds into visual tuition, it has been possible to teach speech to totally deaf children who have never heard human speech. In the absence of such teaching, the totally deaf child will also be dumb, as speaking is learnt by the child copying what is heard. Most deaf children are educated in special residential schools.

Partially deaf children can be educated in small classes using auditory methods provided special hearing aids are used. Such tuition usually takes place in special day schools but may be carried out in residential schools.

Delicate children

This group is a large mixed group containing many medical and surgical conditions which interfere with a child's education. Chest diseases (such as asthma), heart conditions (rheumatic heart or congenital heart disease), blood diseases, diabetes and alimentary diseases make up this group, which includes any rare disease of childhood which makes a child's education difficult.

Many of these children need at first to be admitted to a residential school to allow their medical condition to be fully determined and their educational potential assessed. In many instances, education will have been very badly interrupted by repeated illnesses and the children may become very backward in their education. Many parents of such children worry so much about the child's health that they overprotect the child and this adds to the problems.

Having assessed the child in a residential school and having introduced some degree of stability into his or her education, it is often possible later to return the child to a special day school.

In the case of children undergoing a series of operations, the regime at a residential school will often build up the children and help their treatment as well as maintaining, as far as possible, continuity with their education.

Children with intellectual impairment

The degree of intellectual impairment in children can vary from those who have difficulties in learning and keeping up with their peers at school to those who need long term specialist education in order to accomplish even the most basic of everyday personal skills. Children in this last group are usually said to be 'mentally handicapped'.

Many children who are handicapped in this way exhibit more behaviour difficulties than normal children. Their rate of juvenile delinquency is always higher and a continuing problem for the school health and social services. Girls may reach sexual maturity quite early and may be in moral danger, being more easily led astray. It is important therefore that this is anticipated and fully discussed with the parents or guardian to reduce such a risk. Surveys of adolescent unmarried mothers have tended to show that a greater proportion of these young people have some form of intellectual impairment.

Until recently children with intellectual handicap were classified rather rigidly as 'educationally subnormal (moderate) – ESN(M)', and 'educationally subnormal (severe) – ESN(S)' (e.g. mental handicap). These terms are no longer used. It is now recognised that many children can achieve far more if, from the outset, all their qualities, such as their social adjustment, emotional and behavioural patterns are taken into consideration when deciding what type of educational opportunities or help may be available to them. More severe intellectual handicap or 'mental handicap' is also covered in Chapter 17. It should be noted that whilst 'intellectual handicap' or 'impairment' are frequently used in preference to 'mental handicap', they should not be confused with 'mental impairment' as defined in the Mental Health Act 1983, see page 301.

Intelligence tests

Although it should not be isolated from other aspects of a person's character and behavioural pattern, the intelligence test is a means of estimating the mental age of a child or adult. It consists of a series of tests, questions and exercises designed to demonstrate knowledge gained and reasoning power.

The *Intelligence Quotient (IQ)* $= \dfrac{\text{Mental Age}}{\text{Real Age}} \times 100$

Examples   A child aged 10 years who has a mental age of 12 years would have an intelligence quotient (IQ) of 120.

$$IQ = \frac{\text{Mental Age}}{\text{Real Age}} \times 100 = \frac{12}{10} \times 100 = 120$$

A child aged 10 years who has a mental age of 10 years would have an intelligence quotient of 100.

$$IQ = \frac{\text{Mental Age}}{\text{Real Age}} \times 100 = \frac{10}{10} \times 100 = 100$$

A child aged 10 years who has a mental age of 8 years would have an intelligence quotient of 80.

$$IQ = \frac{\text{Mental Age}}{\text{Real Age}} \times 100 = 80$$

It will thus be seen that a perfectly normal average child would have an intelligence quotient of 100. Above average intelligence gives an intelligence quotient over 100 and below average intelligence an intelligence quotient below 100.

Value of the intelligence quotient   Intelligence quotients vary roughly as follows:

	120–125+	University entrant
	115+	Bright school child
	90–115+	Average school child
	80–90	Retarded school child
	55–79	Intellectual impairment/mental handicap of
Under	50–55	varying degree

It is important to realise that *these levels are guides only* and that exceptions occur in this grouping.

In grading a backward child, it is necessary to carry out probably two or more intelligence tests and also to try the child out with a highly experienced teacher before the final decision is made. A very careful search must always be made for any signs of an accompanying physical deformity, such as deafness, which could be responsible for the low result.

Intellectually handicapped children may need to be educated in either a residential or special day school where the curriculum contains a greater proportion of practical teaching, and where the pace of the teaching is slower than at a normal school. A child who does well in special school may later be able to move back to an ordinary school.

Children with severe emotional or behavioural disorders

A child in this group is a 'problem child' showing many behaviour difficulties. Because of this, the child may become retarded educationally, although his or her intelligence may be normal.

There are many causes of this condition. Some of these children show emotional instability and even a psychological disorder, but many just reflect unstable home conditions including marital difficulties, divorce or separation of parents.

Complete careful diagnosis of the problem is essential. This is rarely a simple procedure. Often repeated visits of the child and the parents to the *Child Guidance Clinic*, where a psychiatrist and psychiatric social worker are in attendance, will be necessary before the complete causative factors are unravelled. It is usual for the social worker attached to the child guidance clinic to be a member of the Social Services Department so that there is maximum coordination between the social work undertaken in the child guidance clinics and the community social services.

These children are best educated in ordinary schools for they gain from contact with normal children although if their home is very unsatisfactory they may have to be in residential (boarding) school. Any psychological disorders in the children must be treated appropriately. It will, however, be necessary to attempt to improve the home conditions. Because it can be hard or impossible to improve conditions in a divided home, treatment is often difficult and calls for much patience. Relapses in behaviour occur and delinquency may complicate the picture. Continued encouragement and understanding by teaching and medical staff will sometimes eventually succeed.

Failure in such children may have serious consequences later for they may drift into criminal behaviour and may even become chronic criminals. There is no doubt that much crime could be prevented by more concentrated medico-social work upon schoolchildren who exhibit extreme forms of behaviour.

Children who are physically handicapped

This group contains the very severely handicapped children. Many have serious handicaps, often with paralysis, and include children handicapped by such diseases as muscular dystrophies and other serious orthopaedic conditions. Some children may never have attended normal schools since their illness commenced. It is usual to educate such children in special residential or day schools in which the classes are very small so that each child can receive much personal attention.

In those diseases which are not progressive it is important, towards the end of the child's education, to do everything possible to make him or her as independent as possible. In this respect, it is always wise to try and arrange for the child to spend the last year of school life at an ordinary school even if this can only be achieved by much improvisation – such as organising special transport. If the child can learn such independence there is more likelihood that, on leaving school, a job will be found.

Children with epilepsy

The majority of children with epilepsy can be educated in an ordinary school provided that:

(*i*)   the fits do not occur very often;

(*ii*)   there is no marked behaviour difficulty, i.e. the emotional stability of the child is reasonably normal; and

(*iii*)   there is a good liaison between the school doctor and teacher who realises that no other child in the class will come to any harm from witnessing the occasional epileptic fit.

In the case of very frequent major fits or of marked emotional instability, it is wise to arrange for the child to be admitted at once to a special residential school for epileptic children for assessment and treatment. Such a school may be run in conjunction with an epileptic colony and its medical and teaching staff will have great experience of such problems. After assessment and correct treatment, in a proportion of cases, it may be possible for the child to return to an ordinary school.

It is, however, stressed that only a small proportion of children with epilepsy ever need to go to such a school, for most can be educated at an ordinary school quite satisfactorily.

Children with speech defects

Any defect of speech in a school child can be serious unless corrected. Such children may quickly develop emotional difficulties from the frustration of being unable to make themselves readily understood. This in turn will tend to aggravate their speech defect.

A most careful physical examination is needed to exclude a physical cause (defective hearing or deformities of palate) and then regular speech therapy must be started. Speech therapists are employed by each school health service to carry out this treatment by relaxation and speech training. It is most important that the child with a speech defect stays in a normal school with normal children. Special schools are, therefore, not needed.

Children with dyslexia

Dyslexia is an interesting condition in which there is a specific language difficulty which shows itself in a series of ways affecting spelling, reading and other language skills. There is always a marked discrepancy between the mental potential of the child (which is often normal) and the educational level attained. The incidence of dyslexia is as high as 3% although many minor cases are missed. In many instances the condition is not recognised until very late with consequent serious loss of learning potential. Many such children may later become language-disabled adults.

The cause of dyslexia is not fully understood but most agree that it is caused by a lesion in the central nervous system which has been present either from birth or shortly afterwards. Many children suffering from dyslexia do well if the condition is recognised early, they attend nursery schools and later receive individual teaching or teaching in very small groups in which it is possible to mould a teaching programme to an individual child.

6 Prevention of disease by immunisation

In many communicable diseases, an attack of the disease is followed by a varying period of immunity from further attacks. Not all communicable diseases are followed by such an immunity (for example, the common cold is followed by only a very transient immunity) but in many, the length of immunity is substantial, lasting years or even a lifetime. Whenever a person develops an immunity in this way, the body manufactures special disease resistant bodies called antibodies.

It is possible to copy this mechanism artificially by introducing into the human body modified bacteria, viruses or their products so that the individual does not suffer from the disease but does develop antibodies and, therefore, does develop an immunity to a natural attack. Artificial immunisation and vaccination relies on this principle. Immunity can be either active or passive.

In *active immunity* a special product of the bacteria or virus (antigen) is introduced into the body, often by injection, but occasionally by mouth, which stimulates the human body to manufacture its own protective antibodies. Immunity produced in this way is always more satisfactory as it lasts a long time. *Its only drawback is that it often takes two to three months for the human body to build up such immunity.*

Passive immunity is used when an animal, such as an ox, has first been actively immunised and has itself manufactured antibodies which are then used to protect man. The great value of this method is that it gives immediate immunity, but this is very transient and rarely lasts longer than about four to six weeks. It is, however, very useful either to treat a patient suffering from the disease, such as diphtheria antitoxin, or to give a temporary immunity to a person who has been in close contact with the disease and who may be incubating it. A disadvantage is that the patient may easily be sensitised to the protein of the animal and suffer from serum sickness.

A more satisfactory passive immunity is obtained by using immunoglobulin, the active constituent of human blood which contains the antibodies although the immunity is still transient.

In preventive medicine, greater use is made of active immunisation than passive immunisation.

Active immunisation

The dangers of communicable disease arise in two main ways.

- By a *direct invasion process* of a certain part of the body. Examples include inflammation of the lung in whooping cough, of the small intestine in typhoid or of part of the central nervous system in encephalitis.
- By the bacteria producing a very powerful *poison* (toxin), either as it grows in the body or after the bacteria has grown in food. Examples include diphtheria, tetanus or toxin food poisoning.

Diseases caused by direct invasion are usually prevented by using an antigen which consists of either the dead bacteria or viruses concerned (typhoid prevented by Typhoid Parathyphoid A & B Vaccine (TAB), or whooping cough by whooping cough vaccine), or else by a modified or changed live bacteria such as Bacillus Calmette-Guérin (BCG) in tuberculosis, or live virus as in Sabin vaccine in poliomyelitis. In the latter two cases, the live bacteria or virus has been changed (undergone a mutation) which results in the modified bacteria or virus being unable to produce the real disease in the human, but it can still produce a modified reaction which will then be followed by an immunity.

Some quite startling successes have been achieved by immunisation. Diphtheria is probably the best example. In the ten years before immunisation started in 1943, approximately 50 000 cases occurred each year. This meant that about one person in ten might ordinarily have been expected to suffer from diphtheria at some time during life. After immunisation was introduced, the incidence fell rapidly. This improvement has continued and in 1988 one case was traced. Immunisation has virtually eradicated the disease.

Although other diseases have not diminished so dramatically, there has been a similar improvement in poliomyelitis which has now become very rare (one paralytic case reported in 1988).

It is important to realise that people inherit different amounts of natural immunity. A few fortunate persons have a remarkable natural immunity while many others have little or none. When all people are immunised their natural immunity is added to very considerably. This means that, after immunisation, there will still be considerable variation in the amount of immunity in any group which has just been immunised. Over a period of years, protection will gradually wear off. Obviously the person who had very little natural immunity will have any acquired immunity lowered more quickly in this way, to a level where an attack of the disease will not be averted.

This is the reason why, after immunisation, it is never possible to guarantee complete protection in everyone. Most diseases are usually avoided in 90% of people by immunisation. Those who do develop an attack after immunisation usually develop a much milder one.

Active immunisation schedule for a child

Age	Immunisation
Birth	BCG vaccine (for Asian babies and for babies whose parents have tuberculosis)
2 months	Triple immunisation (diphtheria, whooping cough and tetanus) plus oral poliomyelitis
3 months	Triple immunisation (diphtheria, whooping cough and tetanus) plus oral poliomyelitis
4 months	Triple immunisation (diphtheria, whooping cough and tetanus) plus oral poliomyelitis
12–18 months (usually before 15 months)	Measles, mumps and rubella (MMR)*
By 5 years (around school entry)	Booster: diphtheria, tetanus and poliomyelitis (oral or inactivated vaccine)
11–13 years	(Girls only) rubella (german measles) if the girl has not already received MMR
11–13 years	BCG vaccine (to protect against tuberculosis)
15 years (or school leaver)	Booster: tetanus and poliomyelitis (oral or inactivated vaccine)

*If MMR is refused measles only vaccine can be given at 15 months or, in an epidemic, at six months then repeated at two years.

Triple immunisation against diphtheria, whooping cough and tetanus

These immunisations are combined for convenience. They are given first to the young baby at two months because of the importance of avoiding whooping cough early in life when it can be a dangerous disease.

The diphtheria and tetanus portions of this immunisation are toxoids protecting against the powerful toxins in both diseases. It is impracticable to inject toxin for it has many dangers. If, however, formalin is added to toxin, its chemical composition is changed and the resultant toxoid is quite harmless, but fortunately it will act as an efficient antigen and produce a good immunity.

The whooping cough portion of the immunisation is a true vaccine – it is a mixture of killed whooping cough bacteria. Injection of such vaccine leads to a good immunity for four to five years. This means that immunisation will postpone the danger of an attack of whooping cough until after the age of five years, so avoiding the dangerous attacks which occur in very young children.

Whooping cough vaccine should not be given to children with a personal or family history of convulsions, cerebral irritation in the neonatal period, epilepsy or any other disorder of the central nervous system.

The diphtheria immunisation requires a booster dose periodically and this is given when the child is aged five years and 15 years.

Tetanus immunisation is boosted by inoculations at five and 15 years and afterwards when injury occurs and there is therefore a danger of developing tetanus.

It is most important to realise that all three doses of the primary immunisation at two months, three months and four months must be given to ensure complete protection. The first of these injections is followed immediately by hardly any protection – the first dose seems to prepare the body's mechanism for producing antibodies. The second dose is followed immediately by a fair protection, but *it is the third dose which produces the most lasting protection*. For this reason, mothers must make certain that their children have all three doses. A system of computerisation of all immunisation records helps to remind parents of the need for further immunisations in their children.

Poliomyelitis

This disease was a serious threat until widespread immunisation was introduced in the early 1960s. Since then only occasional cases have been reported in the United Kingdom. The continued absence of this disease in any epidemic form is due to the success of poliomyelitis vaccination.

Originally dead inactivated (Salk) vaccine was used but in 1962 this was superseded by Sabin oral vaccine which has the following advantages:

— it is easier to administer – by mouth rather than injection;
— it produces an immunity not only to a clinical attack of poliomyelitis, but also to a carrier state in the intestine;
— it can be given to close contacts to reduce the danger of an epidemic; and
— it is free from dangers of allergic reactions.

There are three types of poliomyelitis virus – types I, II and III – *and all three must be included in any vaccine*. The mechanism of protection in the oral vaccine is that after each dose the small intestine is seeded with one of the particular types of virus which then grows rapidly and colonises the intestine. This is followed by a marked immunity to that type of virus.

Once the intestine has been seeded by a virus of a particular type, it cannot be colonised again with the same type, so the second dose leads to colonisation of one of the other types and the third dose with colonisation and protection against all three types. *It is essential that three doses are given to ensure complete protection.* The vaccine is given conveniently on a lump of sugar (three drops) or in a sugar solution. Care should be taken to store it in a refrigerator to maintain its potency.

Measles

Immunisation against measles is carried out using live vaccines (Scharz strain) given by a single injection at the age of one year or shortly afterwards. This usually produces a satisfactory immunity. No child suffering from active tuberculosis or with an allergic history should be immunised against measles. (See below for combined measles, mumps and rubella immunisation.)

Combined measles, mumps and rubella (MMR)

In late 1988, a combined measles/mumps/rubella (MMR) vaccine was introduced into the United Kingdom with the intention of immunising all children (both boys and girls) between the ages of one and two years. The decision to include mumps immunisation for the first time was aimed at preventing two very unpleasant complications of mumps – meningitis and, in boys, orchitis.

MMR is a freeze-dried preparation which has to be stored between 2°C and 8°C and protected from light. The dose is 0.5 ml to be given by the intramuscular or deep subcutaneous route. For parents who refuse MMR immunisation for their children, the ordinary measles immunisation is recommended (see above). It is hoped that all children not previously immunised will receive MMR when they start school (unless there is a contraindication). MMR immunisation should always be given even if there is a previous history of measles, mumps or rubella. Mild reactions may occur after a week (as with measles vaccination) and a mild parotid swelling may occur after two weeks but such children are not infectious.

Rubella (german measles)

Vaccination against rubella should be given to girls aged 11–13 years who have not received MMR at 15 months of age, or when starting school, to avoid any danger of infection during early pregnancy. A single dose of freeze-dried, live attenuated virus of the Cendehill strain is used.

Routine vaccination of adult women is not recommended as it is uncertain whether the strain of virus can reach or harm the fetus. It is most important that a woman is not pregnant at the time of vaccination and does not become pregnant for at least two months after immunisation. If vaccination is requested, a screening serological test should first be carried out by the Public Health Laboratory Service and vaccination should only be offered to those who are sero-negative (approximately 10%).

Tuberculosis

Immunisation against tuberculosis is undertaken using a live vaccine of the Bacillus Calmette-Guérin (BCG) type. This strain of bacteria is named after the two Frenchmen who first developed it at the beginning of the century. It is a modified or attenuated strain of tubercle bacillus which has lost its power to cause the disease in man but can produce a small trivial skin lesion after injection. This local skin infection later leads to an immunity against tuberculosis.

BCG immunisation is only used on people who have no skin sensitivity to tuberculin as shown by the tuberculin test. Four main groups of people are immunised against tuberculosis.

- Close contacts (e.g. other members of the family) of a case of tuberculosis. This group includes the new-born baby of parents, either of whom has had tuberculosis in the past and babies of recently arrived Asian families.
- Schoolchildren aged 10–13 years, who are tuberculin negative. This represents approximately 5% of schoolchildren. With the parents' consent, all children aged 12 years are given a skin test at school. Those who are tuberculin negative are then vaccinated with BCG.
- People who, in their occupation, are liable to run a greater risk of infection from the disease – examples include nurses and doctors in training. It is usual to give a tuberculin test to all new nursing and medical students and to give BCG vaccination to any who are negative. With the increase of routine BCG vaccination to schoolchildren aged 12 years, fewer and fewer nursing and medical students need BCG vaccination on entry.
- Children of certain immigrants in whose communities there is a high incidence of tuberculosis (especially those from Pakistan, Bangladesh, India and Africa).

After vaccination with BCG, a small skin lesion develops which may suppurate for some weeks and may not clear up until a few months after vaccination. This is quite normal and all that is required is a dry dressing to cover the lesion. Sometimes BCG vaccination is followed by an axillary adenitis. This is rare and usually clears up without complications.

Rabies

As rabies is widespread on the Continent, there is currently considerable concern regarding the danger of the disease spreading to the United Kingdom, however this danger has been limited by the Rabies Act 1974. Rabies can be prevented by early active immunisation, immediately after contact with a rabid animal, however the course of injections is long and painful.

Human diploid cell vaccine should be used and the course consists of 14 daily injections into the abdominal wall with a booster dose 10 days later and a final booster 20 days after that.

For people at special risk (handling animals that may be rabid) two immunisations of duck embryo vaccine are given 4–6 weeks apart. Booster doses are given six months later and then every three years.

Anthrax

Immunisation against anthrax has now been introduced for all workers at risk. Three doses of killed vaccine is used with second and third injections after six and then 20 weeks. A single booster injection is given annually.

Hepatitis B

Hepatitis B is spread by blood, saliva, semen and vaginal secretions and can be prevented by prior immunisation. The following persons (including many health staff) should be considered at high risk and be given protective vaccination. Three doses are required, the second after one month and the third after six months.

Persons at highest risk include the following:

— staff working in renal dialysis units;
— people working in units that deal with known carriers of hepatitis B;
— personnel working in haemophiliac or blood transfusion units;
— personnel in laboratories;
— nurses, medical and dental students;
— renal dialysis patients who, when travelling abroad, receive haemodialysis outside the United Kingdom.

Other individuals who may *from time to time be at high risk* include:

— those working in institutions for the mentally handicapped;
— health staff working in areas of the world where there is a known high prevalence of hepatitis B;
— non-immune sexual contacts of hepatitis B carriers;
— active male homosexuals;

— parental drug users;
— mentally handicapped persons entering a residential institution for mentally handicapped individuals.

Passive immunisation

Reference has already been made to the use of tetanus antitoxin which can be used to prevent attacks of those diseases in a person who has not been immunised but who is at risk. In diphtheria only, antitoxin is a valuable therapeutic agent in the early stages of the disease.

A very useful form of passive immunisation is an extract from *human blood immunoglobulin* which contains the antibodies of infectious diseases. Immunoglobulin, to be of any value in active immunisation, must have been separated from the blood of a person who has suffered from the disease. Examples of the use of immunoglobulin to prevent disease are given below.

Rubella (german measles)

This is a minor communicable disease and immunoglobulin is only ever used to prevent an attack in the case of a woman who is in the early stage of pregnancy. This is because an attack of rubella during the first three months of pregnancy will often result in either a miscarriage or the birth of a congenitally malformed child.

For this reason, if any woman in the first three months of pregnancy is known to have been in contact with a case of rubella and has never suffered from the disease, or has not previously been actively immunised against rubella (see pages 52–3) she should at once be given 2.0 g of immunoglobulin. This will protect her for about six to eight weeks, which is long enough to avoid the danger of any birth complication.

There is only a danger of congenital malformations in the child from an attack of german measles in the first three/four months of pregnancy. An attack later in pregnancy is harmless and, therefore, there is no need to immunise a woman contact at that stage.

Measles

Immunoglobulin is occasionally used to prevent an infant or young child (who has not previously been immunised actively against the disease) catching measles because of the special dangers in individual cases, especially when measles occurs within a paediatric ward which contains a number of unprotected ill children. The sudden complication of an attack of measles would be undesirable for it might prove dangerous in an already ill and debilitated child, such as a child with leukaemia. To prevent this, the other children within the ward are immunised with immunoglobulin (collected from people who have suffered from measles) and this immediately gives them an immunity for about six weeks. The usual dose in a child under two years is 0.4 g and 0.75 g in older children. In such circumstances, this is a valuable preventive health measure.

In addition, in certain circumstances human specific immunoglobulin is available. These preparations have a high antibody content, having been prepared from sufferers of recent infections or immunisations. The following are available.

- *Hepatitis B virus immunoglobulin* This is available to protect individuals at special risk after injuries from surgical needles (needlestick injuries) or bites from an infected person or for babies born to hepatitis B positive mothers.

- *Anti-tetanus immunoglobulin* This was made available through the regional transfusion centres and is used to prevent tetanus in patients who have seriously contaminated wounds.

- *Anti-rabies immunoglobulin* This is available for the post-exposure treatment of persons who are manifestly sensitive to equine antiserum as shown by a skin test.

- *Anti-varicella immunoglobulin* This is mainly used for children with leukaemia who are on immunosuppressive therapy and who have been in contact with chickenpox.

Other information regarding immunisations

Consent to immunisations

As legally an injection is an assault on the person, it is necessary to obtain the written consent from a parent or guardian before immunising any child or young person under the age of 16 years. Consent is not required in adults.

With oral immunisation, consent is not so important although in the case of children it is usual to obtain the consent of the parent. This can conveniently be obtained by circulating letters from school. Recently there has been a move to obtain consent to cover all immunisations necessary for a child, and this practice is likely to spread as it is a much simpler arrangement.

Adverse reactions to immunisations

Severe reactions to immunisations are rare but when they do occur they are a contraindication to further immunisations. About a third of children may have mild reactions about 7–10 days after immunisation and about 10% of girls may have mild joint pains after rubella immunisation.

Severe anaphylactic reactions, although very rare, can be very dramatic and the correct treatment should always be at hand in a specially prepared pack. Emergency treatment includes the following.

(*i*)   The patient should be placed on his or her left side.
(*ii*) Insert an airway if the person is unconscious.
(*iii*) Give adrenaline 1/1000 intramuscularly (see Table 6.1 for dosage).
(*iv*) Give oxygen and send for a doctor.
(*v*)   If necessary, start cardiopulmonary resuscitation. A dose of 100 mg hydrocortisone may be given by intravenous injection. Repeat the adrenaline if necessary up to a maximum of three doses.

Table 6.1 Dosage of adrenaline 1/1000 for use in anaphylaxis.

Age	Dosage
Less than 1 year	0.05 ml
1 year	0.1 ml
2 years	0.2 ml
3–4 years	0.3 ml
5 years	0.4 ml
6–10 years	0.5 ml

Immunisation for people travelling outside this country

There are three diseases for which immunisations are given as protection – typhoid fever, yellow fever and cholera.

Typhoid fever Typhoid and paratyphoid fevers can be prevented by giving a course of Typhoid Paratyphoid ABC vaccine (TAB) which is a suspension of killed bacteria.

Two doses are given at not less than ten day intervals but not more than two months. Booster doses should be given every two years.

TAB immunisation should be given to all persons who are going to travel in countries in which primitive water supplies are used. These include all tropical countries, North Africa and country areas of Italy, Spain and Greece. It is also a wise precaution if camping in Europe.

It is usual to suffer from a mild reaction after TAB inoculations – the patient complains of headache and has a slight pyrexia for a few hours.

Yellow fever Yellow fever is a serious tropical virus disease which is limited to a narrow band of country in mid-Africa and central South America. An effective immunisation is given by injection of a live attenuated virus. Very stringent storage conditions are essential for this vaccine which is freeze dried. For this reason, special centres have been set up in this country to give yellow fever vaccination and it can only be given at such centres.

Immunisation is only necessary for persons visiting those parts of Africa or South America where the disease occurs. For all such travellers, immunisation against yellow fever is compulsory.

Cholera   Immunisation against cholera is only necessary for travellers who are visiting certain parts of the Indian subcontinent or other far eastern countries in which cholera occurs.

The immunisation is by means of a vaccine (a suspension of killed cholera bacteria) and consists of two inoculations with at least two weeks in between each dose. Moderately severe reactions may follow this inoculation.

Vaccination has proved relatively ineffective against the El Tor strain.

Arrangements for giving immunisations

Immunisations for children can be given either

— by the family general practitioner at his or her own surgery; or
— at district health authority child health clinics when mothers attend with babies.

There is no special advantage in the immunisation being undertaken at child health centres, and general practitioners often arrange a special weekly time at their surgeries for immunisations so that mothers may then bring their children there for immunisation without having to mix with ill persons attending ordinary surgery sessions. The doctors have to give immunisations free as part of their service but are paid a small fee for the record card of each completed immunisation or vaccination.

7   Prevention of communicable diseases

Methods of prevention have been more highly developed in those diseases which are communicable or infectious (which can be passed from person to person or from animal to person) than in other illnesses.

Seventy years ago, it was felt that isolation was likely to be the most valuable single factor, and strict isolation of the patient and his or her contacts (quarantine) was widely practised. With more and more information as to the exact methods by which these diseases spread, it was realised that isolation is of little value in many communicable diseases.

The role of the infectious disease hospital has completely changed in the last sixty years. When isolation was considered to be essential, large infectious disease hospitals were built, often in out-of-the-way districts, so that the isolation of the patients treated in them could be more complete. Today, the main reason for arranging admission to such hospitals or wards is not isolation, but because the patient needs hospital treatment as adequate treatment cannot be provided at home.

In the case of viral haemorrhagic diseases, complete isolation in a specially designated hospital unit is still essential.

Dangers of treating communicable diseases in ordinary wards

It is very undesirable to treat any case of communicable disease in an ordinary ward or even in a side ward of an ordinary ward in a general hospital. Treatment of the patient can quite easily be carried out in an ordinary ward but the danger is that the infection may spread to other patients (cross infection).

Because of this difficulty, modern hospital practice is to have small single bedded disease units – say two wards each containing 12 single rooms attached to a large central hospital. It is also helpful to have such units attached to a large paediatric hospital. Any sudden infection in a child already in the hospital can then be treated in the communicable disease unit without interrupting the treatment of the main condition, as the same consultant paediatrician can continue to be in charge.

Methods of spread of communicable disease

Before the methods of prevention for individual diseases can be discussed, it is necessary to study generally the methods of spread of communicable disease in the United Kingdom. There are three main groups.

- *Airborne or droplet infection*
  - *Streptococcal infections*, e.g. scarlet fever, erysipelas, puerperal fever, tonsillitis
  - *Staphylococcal infections*, e.g. pemphigus neonatorum
  - *Pneumonococcal infections*, e.g. pneumonia
  - *Diphtheria*
  - *Meningitis*
  - *Tuberculosis*
  - *Common childhood infectious diseases*, e.g. measles, whooping cough, mumps, rubella

- *Faecal-borne: gastro-intestinal infections*
  - *Typhoid* and *paratyphoid fever*
  - *Food poisoning*
  - *Dysentery*
  - *Infantile gastro-enteritis*
  - *Poliomyelitis*
  - *Infective hepatitis*

- *Direct spread by contact*
  - From animals, e.g. *anthrax*
  - From milk, e.g. *undulant fever*, *brucellosis*
  - From rats, e.g. *leptospirosis*
  - From rabid dogs and other infected animals, e.g. *rabies*
  - From humans, *sexually transmitted disease*, e.g. *syphilis, gonorrhoea, AIDS, hepatitis B*

As will have been seen from Chapter 6 immunisation plays an important rôle in preventing many airborne and faecal-borne diseases.

Epidemiological investigation is the second method by which communicable diseases are prevented and their spread controlled. Epidemiology is the study of all factors which affect disease – the cause of the illness and all the conditions associated with its incidence. A full investigation is undertaken in all cases so that, as far as possible, the exact method of spread of the disease in the patient can be traced. If this is possible, it will often prevent further cases for some person may be infectious without showing any symptoms at all. Such a person is a *carrier*.

Before any investigation can be started, it is, of course, essential to know where all cases have occurred. For this reason, the majority of communicable diseases are compulsorily *notifiable* – they must be reported immediately on diagnosis to the District Medical Officer. A small fee is paid to the doctor for each notification.

Sexually transmitted diseases have never been made notifiable in the United Kingdom because it is feared that, if they were made so, it would result in concealment of infections and inadequate treatment. Certainly those countries which have introduced notification of sexually transmitted diseases have a higher level of these diseases.

The following is a complete list of notifiable diseases

Anthrax
Cholera
Diphtheria
Dysentery (amoebic or bacillary)
Encephalitis (acute)
Food poisoning
Lassa fever
Leprosy
Leptospirosis
Malaria
Marburg disease
Measles
Meningitis
Meningococcal septicaemia
Mumps

Ophthalmia neonatorum
Plague
Poliomyelitis (acute)
Rabies
Relapsing fever
Rubella
Scarlet fever
Tetanus
Tuberculosis
Typhoid or paratyphoid
Typhus
Viral haemorrhagic fever
Viral hepatitis
Whooping cough
Yellow fever

The following communicable diseases are NOT notifiable

AIDS
Chickenpox
Common cold
Influenza

Pneumonia
Sexually transmitted
    diseases

Method of investigation

A very careful history should always be taken from the patient and close contacts. Any link between the patient and other cases of the disease is carefully investigated. If the disease is one not normally present in the United Kingdom, such as malaria or typhoid, any link with someone who has recently travelled abroad is followed up. In a gastro-intestinal infection such as food poisoning or typhoid, which is usually the result of a food contamination, a complete history is taken of the food eaten.

In any communicable disease, there is a latent period between infection and the first symptoms and signs of the disease, called the *incubation period*. Thus a person infected with typhoid will show no abnormal signs until 14 days later when the early symptoms of illness first appear.

A knowledge of the likely incubation period is important for it allows the questioning in collecting the history to be concentrated where it is most likely to be helpful, i.e. at the start of the incubation period (when the patient became infected). When the first symptoms of typhoid appear it is necessary to go very carefully over the patient's movements 14 days previously to find out how infection may have been contracted. This includes finding out what food and drink may have been consumed.

Incubation periods are never easy to remember and can vary in the same disease. They can be conveniently divided into four groups.

Very short incubation periods   2 hours–18 hours

Staphylococcal toxin food poisoning
Salmonella food poisoning
Clostridium perfringens toxin food poisoning

Short incubation periods   2 to 7 days

Streptococcal infections, e.g. scarlet fever, puerperal infection, erysipelas, tonsillitis, Staphylococcal airborne infections, e.g. pemphigus neonatorum
Pneumonia
Diphtheria
Influenza
Meningitis
Dysentery
Infantile gastro-enteritis
Paratyphoid
Anthrax
Gonorrhoea

Long incubation periods   10 to 21 days

Lassa fever	(usually 10 days)
Marburg disease	(usually 10 days)
Chickenpox	(usually 17–21 days)
Rubella	(usually 17–20 days)
Measles	(usually 12 days)
Whooping cough	(usually 14 days)
Mumps	(usually 17–20 days)
Typhoid	(usually 14 days)
Poliomyelitis	(usually 11–14 days)
Syphilis	(usually 18–21 days)
Infective hepatitis	(usually 18–45 days)
Rabies	(usually 10–42 days but occasionally up to 4 months)

Exceptionally long incubation period

AIDS   (very variable but more than 2 years and may
                               be as long as 7–8 years)

Bacteriological or *virological* investigations are very important in
communicable diseases. They aim at confirming the diagnosis and
discovering which close contacts are also infected (carriers).

In airborne bacterial diseases, nose and throat swabs can be taken.
In tuberculosis, sputum tests, both by direct examination and culture,
should be carried out on patients.

*In the faecal-borne diseases, specimens of faeces or rectal swabs of
patients and contacts should always be examined.* In most outbreaks, it
is usual to find some contacts who are infected without symptoms
(carriers). In many cases the carrier state may only last a short time
but, if the carrier works with foodstuffs, further infections may easily
occur.

Blood examinations are also carried out. In the early stages of
typhoid fever a positive blood culture will be found, allowing a
completely accurate diagnosis to be made earlier than by any other
method.

In virus disease, virus isolations may be possible, e.g. influenza and
poliomyelitis. Another method is to examine the blood very early in
the illness and then about six weeks later when a significant rise in
antibodies will be noted. This test can be used for a retrospective
diagnosis in such cases. Because of the longer time taken with virus
isolation and these blood examinations, they are less helpful in investigations than with the bacterial diseases.

Carriers

A carrier is someone who is infected with a disease which is excreting
bacteria or virus causing the disease without suffering from any
symptoms. Carriers may be nasal, throat, faecal or urinary and are of
two kinds.

Convalescent carriers People who have had the disease but who, in
their convalescence, still excrete the bacteria. An example is a patient
who has had typhoid, is now better, but who still has typhoid bacteria
in the faeces. Such people are usually temporary carriers, harbouring
the bacteria for only a few weeks, but a few become permanent
carriers, and intermittently carry bacteria in their faeces all their life
(chronic typhoid carrier).

Symptomless carriers These are people who have never had any
illness or any symptoms but who are carriers. In such cases, infection
produces a sub-clinical attack without symptoms, and the carrier state

follows. An example is given by typhoid, which shows all types of carriers, or poliomyelitis. Symptomless carriers can also be either temporary or permanent.

Types of carriers

Anatomically, carriers can be divided into the following groups.

- *Nasal carriers*, e.g. streptococci, diphtheria, staphylococci.
- *Throat carriers*, e.g. diphtheria, meningococci, streptococci.
- *Faecal carriers*, e.g. typhoid, poliomyelitis, dysentery.
- *Urinary carriers*, e.g. typhoid.

A chronic typhoid faecal carrier excretes typhoid bacilli in the faeces intermittently. Usually the faeces are positive for two weeks then negative for three to five weeks and then positive again. Because of this, repeated faecal examinations in typhoid are necessary otherwise a chronic carrier could be missed because the examination was carried out during a period when no bacteria were being excreted.

Special screening tests

X-rays form an important part of the investigation in an outbreak of tuberculosis.

Detailed methods of preventing communicable diseases

Airborne infections

Streptococcal infections

These include such varied diseases as scarlet fever, erysipelas, puerperal pelvic infection, tonsillitis, cellulitis and septicaemia. The usual method of infection is from either a case or unsuspected case, or from a nasal or throat carrier. It is also important to realise that the same type of streptococcus may cause scarlet fever in one patient, tonsillitis in another and even puerperal pelvic infection if a woman recently confined is infected. A careful search should always be made to discover any infections and, among very close contacts, a search for nasal carriers by examining bacteriologically nasal swabs is always worthwhile. Throat swabs are less useful.

In special problems such as the avoidance of puerperal infections, very great care must be taken to ensure that aseptic conditions are always maintained during and after confinement. *No midwife with a nasal or throat infection should ever be allowed to attend a mother in her confinement.* The midwife in such circumstances must remain off duty until better and until bacteriological examinations of her nose and throat are normal. If an unexpected streptococcal puerperal infection occurs, the nasal and throat swabs of all who attended the birth must be examined to make certain that none of them is a carrier.

Some of the most dangerous infections that can follow surgical operations are streptococcal infections. The stringent preventive measures taken in all surgical theatres to ensure aseptic conditions, including preparation of patient's skin and theatre aseptic techniques, are all examples of preventive measures to reduce the chance of streptococcal infections.

In certain serious accidents, it may be impossible to prevent infection gaining access into a patient's tissues. In such cases, prophylactic treatment with chemotherapy and antibiotics is started as a further preventive measure.

Staphylococcal infections

Some of the most dangerous neo-natal cross infections in the nursery units of maternity hospitals are caused by penicillin-resistant staphylococci (pemphigus neonatorum). Preventive measures include the following.

— Early recognition to enable the case to be promptly removed from the unit.
— Strict barrier nursing techniques after the first case has been diagnosed.
— Early discharge of mothers and babies so that time for cross infection is kept as short as possible.
— In those outbreaks which are not immediately controlled, the stopping of new admissions so that the chain of infection is closed.

Diphtheria

Immediately a case of diphtheria is diagnosed and removed to hospital, an investigation is started to discover the source of the infection. Nasal and throat swabs of close contacts (members of family and class mates) should be taken. Other members of the family are excluded from school until bacteriological tests are completed and also other members of the family are excluded from work if there is a risk of spread, for example a food handler.

Daily visits should be paid to the family by a health visitor or environmental health officer to check that no one has developed an illness as it is not only important to prevent the disease but to diagnose it early, when treatment is so much more effective. Other children in the family and close contacts should be given a booster immunisation and those who have never been immunised should be given their first immunising dose.

If any of the contacts is found to be a carrier, *a virulence test* must be carried out on the diphtheria bacteria isolated. A minority of these are avirulent, i.e. incapable of producing diphtheria. No carrier should be implicated as a possible source of infection until he or she has been confirmed to be carrying virulent diphtheria bacteria.

Any contacts who develop early suspicious signs should be given immediately a protecting dose of diphtheria antitoxin. An early small dose of such antitoxin is of great importance in reducing the severity of attack. The main method of preventing diphtheria is to see that as many young children as possible are fully immunised against the disease. Although it is hoped that the percentage of young children immunised will exceed 90%, it is essential that it never falls below 70% for, below this figure, there is a risk of an outbreak of diphtheria.

Tuberculosis

A total of 4022 cases of respiratory tuberculosis occurred in England and Wales in 1988 (2392 in men and 1630 in women). This ratio of 59.48% male to 40.52% female cases has been fairly constant over the last few years in the United Kingdom. In addition, 62.3% of the male cases were over the age of 45 years. In 1988, 478 persons died from tuberculosis emphasising that this disease is still a problem in the United Kingdom.

Tuberculosis is usually diagnosed and treated by the chest physician at the chest clinic which is a specialised outpatient department. In some districts specially trained health visitors called *tuberculosis visitors* carry out the preventive health work with patients in conjunction with the chest physician. Most of this work involves home visiting.

The majority of cases of tuberculosis today are caused by direct infection from one human being to another by droplet (airborne) infection. The control and prevention of tuberculosis depends on tracing the infection, taking steps to reduce the chance of infection, and immunisation of those at risk.

Tracing of infection   Tuberculosis does not spread like measles by chance, short-lived contact, but follows fairly long and continued repetitive contact such as that which occurs among the members of the same household, classroom or office. When any new case occurs, it is essential to search for the cause of the infection among close contacts.

Arrangements are made to examine all members of the same family and household or members of the same office or classroom. In all instances, 'examination' must include a chest X-ray of all adults over the age of 15 years and, for children under this age, a tuberculin skin test and an X-ray for any found to be positive. It is most important that every effort is made to make certain that *every close contact* is examined. This is because the cause of the infection could be in someone who may have slight symptoms but may be afraid to have an X-ray. Because of the preponderance of tuberculosis infection today in men over the age of 45, particular attention must always be paid to X-raying them. It is important to realise that a person may have a heavily infected sputum and be a most likely cause of infection and yet be able to carry on a normal life. Therefore, the absence of any symptoms should never be used as an excuse to dispense with an X-ray.

Steps to reduce the chance of infection

Sputum disposal   Every patient must be taught how to dispose safely of any sputum. Although it is hoped that in every patient the disease will be rendered quiescent, it is just possible that they may develop a transitory positive sputum from time to time and it is most important that, if this does occur, disposal of sputum is carried out carefully.

Expectoration of sputum should always be into a plastic sputum bottle containing a small amount of sterilising fluid. This sterilises the sputum after 20 minutes and also reduces its viscous and sticky nature, making disposal easier. The contents of each sputum bottle should be washed down a toilet and *never brought into the kitchen*. Each sputum bottle should have a plastic screw top (not metal as the sterilising solution reacts with metal).

Housing   Overcrowded housing and sleeping accommodation pro-duces conditions favouring the spread of this disease. No patient should ever sleep in the same room as another member of the family. The one exception is where the patient is a married person; in this case the couple can share the same room but should have twin beds. It is most important that *no parent who has had tuberculosis should ever sleep in the same room as a child*. Equally, no child with tuberculosis should share a room with other children.

If the house of the patient is not large enough to allow the patient to have a separate bedroom, *immediate rehousing is essential* to avoid infection spreading through the family. Most local authorities have special priority housing schemes which enable patients to be rapidly rehoused before further infection occurs.

Occupation   No person who has tuberculosis should be employed in an occupation in which there is a chance of spreading the disease if a relapse occurs. This means *work should not be undertaken in the food trade or in close association with young children under the age of 12 years*, such as teaching or nursery nursing. Consequently, no person is allowed to enter training to be a teacher unless he or she has a clear chest X-ray. Periodic check-ups for teachers are also encouraged.

Likewise all staff employed in children's homes or nurseries should always be X-rayed before commencing their employment. It is illegal for a person with open tuberculosis to be employed in the food trade.

Follow-up Careful follow-up of all patients must be carried out for five years after infection. This follow-up should be both at a chest clinic and by home visits to ensure that social factors at home have not deteriorated. If this occurs, a relapse in health is more likely.

In follow-ups, careful note is made of the level of nutrition for it is known that if this is defective a relapse is more likely to occur.

It is wise for home visits to be paid at least *once in six months* even when the patient is quiescent. In women patients, this will ensure that any pregnancy will be known to the tuberculosis visitor before full term.

Pregnancy in a patient whose tuberculosis is controlled is likely to do no harm but it is essential that everything is done to help the mother meet this extra challenge. Delivery should take place in hospital and arrangements should be made for her to have a prolonged convalescence after delivery. The baby must be vaccinated immediately with BCG. If the problem is known early in pregnancy, before six months, it is usually possible to make satisfactory arrangements for the care of the baby and family. But if the problem is only discovered in the puer-perium, the mother may ignore the convalescent period to look after her family and baby, and in this way, risk permanent damage to her health and, perhaps, spread of infection in her family.

Immunisation of those at risk The ingestion of live virulent tubercle bacilli by anyone may, or may not, result in a recognisable clinical infection of tuberculosis. In many instances, the individual has sufficient resistance to prevent a clinical infection occurring. In all cases, however, a skin sensitivity develops.

If later a minute quantity of old tuberculin is injected into the skin of such a person, a sharp reaction or flare occurs. This is called a Mantoux positive skin test or tuberculin positive test. It means that, at some time in the past, the person has been in contact with live tubercle bacilli. All such individuals should be X-rayed, as occasionally a latent infection will be found. If no disease is discovered it can be assumed that there is enough immunity to resist infection. In this way, the tuberculin test, although one of hypersensitivity, can be used as an indicator of immunity. A negative tuberculin test occurs in people with no special sensitivity. All newborn babies are tuberculin negative, and the change to positive only occurs after subsequent infection.

Immunisation using BCG vaccination should be offered to all negative reactors in the following groups:

— all family contacts of cases;
— all medical students and nurses;
— all schoolchildren aged 10–13 years;
— children of immigrants in whose communities there is a high incidence of tuberculosis irrespective of their age (this is particularly important in Asian immigrants).

Measles, mumps and rubella (german measles)

The prevention of these diseases rests mainly with successful immunisation. The new combined measles/mumps/rubella (MMR) vaccination (see page 103) should succeed in preventing the greatest hazards of these diseases (dangerous complications which, even if rare, are responsible for a few deaths or residual handicaps in children). In the case of rubella, early immunisation of children should eventually prevent the complications (miscarriage or the development of congenital abnormalities in the infant) which can follow if a pregnant woman develops rubella during the first three months of pregnancy.

Passive immunisation is occasionally used where an attack would be more dangerous than usual (see page 111).

Acute meningitis and encephalitis

Since 1985, there has been a marked increase in the number of cases of acute meningitis notified in the United Kingdom. During 1988 in England and Wales, 2987 cases of acute meningitis were notified – this compares with 1230 cases in 1984 (an increase of 143%).

Figure 7.1 illustrates in graphic form the increase for *Meningococcal meningitis*, the commonest bacterial acute meningitis.

There are many bacterial and viral causes of acute meningitis and encephalitis. The commonest bacterial causes identified by the Communicable Disease Surveillance Centre for England and Wales are *Neisseria meningitidis* (34.7%), *Haemophilus influenzae* (27.4%) and *Streptococcus pneumoniae* (15.6%). The remaining 22.3% include other streptococci, *Listeria monocytogenes* and *Escherichia*.

The viruses responsible for both meningitis and encephalitis also contain many different types but the commonest are echovirus (33.9%), mumps (20.7%) and Coxsackie A (16.2%). This complication of mumps has been one of the main reasons for the introduction of the new combined vaccine (MMR). This protects against measles, mumps and rubella and is given to all infants between 12–18 months of age (see page 106).

The prevention of meningitis and encephalitis is very difficult (apart from immunisation in mumps and measles) because for every clinical case found there are many subclinical infections (those without any

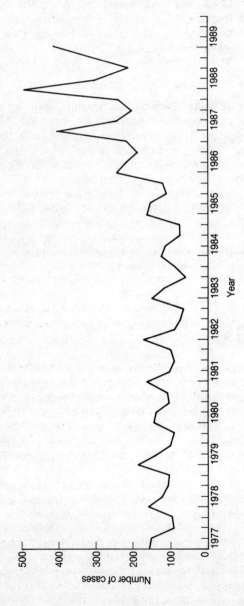

Fig. 7.1 Meningococcal meningitis, England and Wales, 1977–89. (From OPCS, Monitor MB2, 89/1.)

symptoms). Throughout the increase seen since 1985, there has been a concentration of cases in the Stroud area of Gloucestershire, although many other areas have shown an increase, including the conurbations of Birmingham, Bristol and Liverpool.

Early diagnosis is most important as many cases of acute meningitis respond well to antibiotic treatment and the patient fully recovers provided treatment is started early after the first symptoms.

Faecal-borne infections

Typhoid and paratyphoid fever

Typhoid fever can be spread by *water* and *food*. Paratyphoid fever is spread by food.

Prevention   The prevention of typhoid and paratyphoid depends on:

— full immediate investigation of cases to discover the cause;
— control of chronic carriers;
— food control including sampling at docks, pasteurisation of milk supplies and ice cream, prohibition of infected shell-fish;
— environmental hygiene;
— immunisation of holiday visitors to certain countries where the risk of infection is high e.g. Yugoslavia, Africa and country areas of Italy and Spain.

In both diseases, infection is introduced into water or food by another human being who is either suffering from the disease or is a carrier.

Most infections result from carriers. The majority of typhoid cases traced in England and Wales are contracted abroad. For instance, in 1988, 174 infections were traced and of these at least 117 were contracted abroad. Any person who is a carrier and who handles food of any description or who is employed by water supply departments can be dangerous.

For this reason, whenever a case of typhoid fever occurs, a complete investigation must be carried out immediately to find the cause of infection. A careful history is taken to find out what food was eaten by the victim and close contacts at the time of infection. This means inquiry at the start of the incubation period, 14 days before the first symptoms in typhoid, and seven days in paratyphoid fever.

Immediate stool examinations must be carried out on all close contacts and especially on all kitchen personnel. If a carrier is discovered, the typhoid bacteria must be identified and typed by *phage typing*. It is possible to divide typhoid and paratyphoid bacilli into a number of different types. These are then compared with the type causing the outbreak. If the types are dissimilar, then the carrier could *not* have caused the outbreak. If the type is the same, the carrier *could* have been responsible. The discovery of a carrier of the same type does not prove the cause and further investigations must be undertaken.

The large typhoid outbreaks of the past were mainly water-borne due to water supplies being infected. In the United Kingdom, the Croydon outbreak of 1937 involving 290 persons was the last large water-borne outbreak. This outbreak was caused by a urinary carrier among the workmen carelessly contaminating a deep well which formed part of Croydon's water supplies.

Careful methods of sewage disposal and purification and sterilisation of water supplies which are universal in the United Kingdom have reduced the likelihood of any further water-borne outbreaks.

But every case must be carefully investigated to ensure that the cause is found. Omitting to do this could lead to a serious spread as was seen in the disastrous Zermatt water-borne outbreak of typhoid fever in 1963 resulting in 434 cases.

Food supplies may be infected by carriers. For this reason all known cases of typhoid or paratyphoid are very carefully followed up with fortnightly stool examinations for at least six months or longer to make certain that they do not become chronic carriers. About 5% of all typhoid cases become chronic carriers and intermittently excrete typhoid bacilli, usually in their stools but occasionally in their urine. Animals are not a source of typhoid although some paratyphoid cases have been traced to infection in cows.

Once a chronic carrier is diagnosed, a careful check is kept on the occupation undertaken and other members of the family. No chronic typhoid or paratyphoid carrier is allowed to be employed in the food trade or to work in a kitchen or place where infection could be passed on. Members of the family of a carrier must be protected periodically by immunisation with TAB vaccine.

In 1945 a serious outbreak of typhoid fever was caused in Aberystwyth in Wales by home-made ice cream being infected by a chronic carrier. Now, by law, all ice cream must be pasteurised, a heat process which kills any typhoid bacilli present.

In 1964 an extensive outbreak of typhoid fever occurred in Aberdeen. Over 400 cases occurred with five deaths. The most probable cause was a can of corned beef which contained typhoid bacillus. It is thought that the typhoid bacillus gained entry to the can after it had been sterilised. This probably occurred by the tin being cooled by contaminated unchlorinated river water.

To prevent any possible recurrences, *it is essential that all water used for cooling in any canning process should be pure chlorinated water.*

Safety of nursing staff   TAB immunisation should be given to all nursing staff looking after typhoid patients to protect them from the dangers of cross infection. Cases of typhoid should always be treated in communicable disease hospitals or units.

Food poisoning

The main causes of food poisoning are:

- *Chemical causes*: e.g. tin, antimony;
- *Bacterial toxin food poisoning*
  - *Staphylococcal* toxin;
  - *Clostridium perfringens* toxin;
- *Salmonellosis*.

Incidence There has been a very rapid increase in food poisoning since 1981. In England and Wales in 1988, 39 713 cases of food poisoning were traced by the Public Health Laboratory Service. This represents a four times increase in food poisoning from 1981 to 1988. The majority were caused by *Salmonellosis*.

All cases of food poisoning must be immediately and fully investigated to discover, if possible, the cause. This investigation, if successful, will normally suggest ways and means of avoiding a recurrence.

Chemical food poisoning is only likely to occur when completely unsuitable containers (such as those made from galvanised iron) are used in which to cook foods.

Staphylococcal toxin food poisoning results when foodstuffs are infected with certain strains of *Staphylococcus aureus* and are then stored in warm conditions enabling the bacteria to multiply within the food. This produces an enterotoxin, a poison which acts upon the stomach. An interval of at least 12 hours must occur between infection of the food and its being eaten to allow sufficient toxin to be produced to lead to food poisoning.

Staphylococci usually contaminate foods from either a skin or nasal lesion in a food handler. They do, however, also attack the skin of animals and, in the cow, may lead to a staphylococcal infection of the udder with subsequent contamination of the milk.

Once staphylococcal food poisoning toxin has been produced in any foodstuff, it is very difficult to destroy by heat as it is heat stabile. This means that even boiling a foodstuff already contaminated with the toxin would only destroy a very small and insignificant amount of that toxin.

As staphylococci are usually present in the noses of 10% of people, this food poisoning can best be avoided by ensuring that all foods are:

- either eaten within an hour or two of preparation; or,
- if kept, are always stored in cool, refrigerated conditions which

are too cold for bacterial multiplication (toxins are produced only by bacterial multiplication); and
— prepared under the cleanest conditions possible. This means that a high degree of personal hygiene is important. Hands must be frequently washed and habits avoided which would encourage transfer of staphylococci from the nose and mouth of the food handler to foodstuffs.

Great care must be taken to prevent any food handler who has an acute or chronic skin infection, infected cut, boil or paronychia from handling food. Legal regulations recommend all infected cuts must be covered with waterproof dressings to avoid contaminating foodstuffs. It is even more satisfactory to exclude from food handling any person so infected.

Clostridium perfringens (Cl. welchii) toxin food poisoning is less severe than staphylococcal toxin poisoning but is much commoner. The toxin, which is also heat-stabile, is produced by multiplication of *Clostridium perfringens*, a spore-bearing anaerobic bacterium which can also cause gas gangrene. The spores of this bacteria are widespread, in soil and often in faeces. However, being an anaerobic bacterium, it will only multiply in the absence of oxygen. For this reason, it mainly produces food poisoning in meats or in stews and soups made by long standing low temperature simmering.

Prevention   Spores of *Clostridium perfringens* are found in many meats and therefore inevitably will gain access to kitchens. Infections with this type of food poisoning will only be avoided if the following rules are strictly observed.

— Avoid precooking of meats.
— Avoid storing any food between 49°C and 10°C for more than three hours.
— If meats have to be precooked, it is essential that they are rapidly cooled and maintained below 10°C in a domestic refrigerator.
— Care must always be taken when gutting animals such as rabbits to avoid contamination of the flesh with faeces from the intestine (which will be likely to contain large quantities of spores of *Clostridium perfringens*).

Salmonellosis

Salmonellosis is the commonest type of food poisoning being responsible for approximately 63% of all cases. It is an infective gastro-enteritis in which the small intestine is attacked by one of the salmonella bacteria producing an inflammation. There are over 1000 serotypes but the commonest found in the United Kingdom are

S.̇ *typhimurium* (35.8%), S. *enteritidis* (32.8%) and S. *virchow* (7.0%).

Method of spread   There are six main sources of salmonellosis.

- Human cases and carriers.
- Domestic animals and rodents.
- Eggs of ducks and hens.
- Pigs.
- Chickens.
- Untreated raw milk.

Any one of these sources may lead to contamination of food but *fortunately a very heavy infection is necessary to lead to a salmonella food poisoning*. This means that usually there has been *infection* with salmonella bacteria and *incorrect storage of the food*, e.g. the foodstuff has been stored for more than 12 hours at normal room temperatures and not refrigerated – this allows rapid bacterial multiplication which will not occur at cold refrigerated temperatures. In addition it is wise to avoid duck eggs even in cooking, as they often have a high level of infection.

Whenever an outbreak of salmonella food poisoning occurs, a complete investigation must take place to find if possible the cause of the infection.

A particular search for faecal carriers should always be made among all kitchen personnel and all should have their stools bacteriologically examined. If any carrier is found, it must not be assumed that he or she is necessarily the cause, for such a carrier may also have been infected in the outbreak. All carriers must stop handling food immediately and not do so again until they have been cleared. The carrier state usually lasts only a few weeks and it is unusual for it to become chronic.

Any foodstuff which is precooked and then stored for a lengthy period before consumption, such as cooked and prepared meats, may be dangerous if storage has been faulty and the food has become infected. Naturally infected foods can also cause trouble. For example, serious outbreaks of food poisoning have been traced to heavily contaminated eggs and coconut products imported from abroad but fortunately an effective heat treatment has been devised.

Prevention   It will be seen that all salmonella food poisoning can best be avoided by the following measures.

- Extreme care being taken in preparation of food, and with per-sonal hygiene among food handlers. This reduces the chances of a carrier accidentally contaminating any food.
- All food prepared being eaten immediately. Any left over food should be thrown away. In this respect, it is most undesirable to

prepare a sweet today for lunch tomorrow, unless it is stored in a refrigerator.

- Where food, such as meat pies, is stored for any length of time, it must be stored at low temperature, below 4°C, preferably in a refrigerator.
- Gamma radiation from a cobalt-60 source is being used to destroy salmonellae in frozen whole egg, coconut, imported meats and animal feeding stuffs.
- Pasteurisation of liquid milk. Only 3% of the population in the United Kingdom now drink untreated raw milk but in all reported cases of salmonella food poisoning 6.9% are associated with the consumption of such milk.
- Avoidance of eating raw or lightly boiled eggs.
- Ensuring that any frozen chickens are completely defrosted before cooking.
- Never storing cooked meats next to fresh meats.

Listeriosis

During the last two to three years, there has been increasing concern about the spread of Listeria infections. These are bacterial infections caused by *Listeria monocytogenes*, an aerobic bacteria which is very common in soil, animals and poultry and which, in certain circumstances, can cause disease in humans.

Transmission of Listeria infections is mainly by foodstuffs and particularly by those where the preparation does not involve a long cooking or heating process. Unlike most bacteria which can cause food poisoning, Listeria bacteria can increase slowly at refrigerated temperatures. Another difference is that three groups of the population are at special risk:

— pregnant women;
— their newborn infants; and
— adults who are receiving immunosuppressive treatment.

Listeria monocytogenes is widely present in nature – surveys have shown up to 29% of healthy persons carry the bacteria in their stools. There is a seasonal incidence with the disease being more common in early summer.

Types of listeriosis

During pregnancy   When the disease attacks pregnant women, it usually shows two or more febrile episodes – the woman has some or all of the following symptoms: headache, general malaise, pharyngitis, conjunctivitis, diarrhoea, abdominal or low back pain. Occasionally the febrile attack may be misdiagnosed as pyelonephritis. Blood culture at this stage is usually positive. If ampicillin is given promptly, the fever quickly subsides but the woman may get relapses. The second episode usually follows later in pregnancy when a 'flu-like illness with a low pyrexia develops. This is often followed by the birth of a premature baby who may also be infected (see below). It is thought that this secondary episode is probably caused by a re-infection from the placenta.

The mother usually recovers completely, but the outlook for the infant is often very serious or fatal.

Neonatal infections   Two methods of infection occur:

— haematogenous transplacental transmission; and
— intrapartum infection as the newborn child traverses the birth canal.

In pregnant women with listeriosis, bacteria are often present in the vagina. About 70 perinatal infections occur each year in the United Kingdom. In newborn infants, two forms of the disease are seen:

— a septicaemia within two days of the birth, the premature baby is particularly likely to show respiratory distress and rashes may occasionally also be seen;
— a meningo-encephalitis may develop after the fifth day following the birth.

Occasionally, a slowly developing hydrocephalus may also follow.

Up to a third of infected babies are stillborn. Provided prompt treatment is given with ampicillin, approximately 50% mortality can be expected in the remainder. With late or no treatment the mortality is likely to reach 90%. Provided any surviving infant was at least of 36 weeks gestation when born, sequelae are most unlikely.

Disease in adults other than pregnant women   Central nervous system infections are the most likely forms of listeriosis seen in adults other than pregnant women. Fever of a low grade is usually present and focal neurological signs may develop such as cranial nerve palsies or hemiparesis. Occasionally there is a progressive loss of consciousness eventually leading to coma.

In immunosuppressed adults who develop any form of meningitis, infections with listeriosis are among the commonest causes. Treatment is ideally with ampicillin and this should be continued for at least one week after all fever has subsided. The prognosis for adult forms of listeriosis is usually good provided treatment is started promptly.

Dysentery

The bacterial dysentery caused by *Shigella sonnei* (often called Sonne dysentery) is the commonest form of dysentery in the United Kingdom. It is usually a mild, short-lived gastro-enteritis which is only serious in young babies or debilitated elderly persons. In 1988, 3692 cases were notified (at least 20% were contracted abroad).

Sonne dysentery is spread by direct contamination from person to person. In a closed community, such as a ward or nursery, it spreads slowly at first but, as soon as a substantial proportion of persons are infected, it spreads more quickly.

The best way to avoid outbreaks is:

— to diagnose dysentery early; and
— to isolate all cases and carriers.

This is especially important in day nurseries and hospital wards. All cases of diarrhoea must be *bacteriologically examined* (stool specimens) to make certain that any early cases are identified – there is always a proportion of symptomless carriers among close contacts but usually they are carriers for only two to three weeks.

By careful investigation and isolation of cases and carriers, serious outbreaks will usually be avoided. If, however, a widespread outbreak has been allowed to develop, isolation will achieve little. The aim should, therefore, always be to diagnose the first cases. This can only be done if stools of all patients who develop any diarrhoea, however mild or transient, are routinely submitted for bacteriological examination.

Infantile gastro-enteritis

This is a general term used for any severe gastro-enteritis in young infants. The exact cause of some outbreaks is often uncertain but in others infection has been traced to certain pathogenic strains of *Escherichia coli* including 0 26, 0 55, 0 111, 0 125, 0 126, 0 127, 0 128 and 0 229. Many enteroviruses (echovirus and Coxsackie B virus) have also been identified as causes.

The virus responsible for many attacks of infantile gasto-enteritis can be identified by use of the electron microscope. Serologically the virus, which unfortunately has been given many different names including reovirus-like agents, orbivirus, rotavirus and duovirus, is related to the virus of calf diarrhoea. As soon as the problems of culturing this virus *in vitro* are overcome it is hoped it will be possible to develop a prophylactic vaccine.

Prevention These attacks can best be prevented by complete investigation when they occur and by arranging for all young infants to spend as little time as possible in hospital or residential nursery units. There is no doubt that many attacks result from cross infection – infection spreading rapidly from infant to infant in a ward. It is therefore most important that any infant with diarrhoea *is isolated immediately* and that *no child with a history of diarrhoea is ever admitted to a clean infants' ward* but straight into the *isolation unit*.

Once infection has occurred, especially the serious type of gastro-enteritis that occasionally attacks the nursery unit of a maternity ward, new admissions should be stopped and the ward emptied as soon as possible by discharging mothers and babies home early. In this way, the chance of widespread infection is reduced.

Attempts to control the spread of infantile gastro-enteritis by strict barrier nursing nearly always fail, probably because of the intensity of infection and the rôle infected dusts play in spreading the disease.

Encouragement of breast feeding can do much to reduce the incidence of infantile gastro-enteritis and every effort should be made to keep breast feeding going if the infant develops an illness. If the baby must enter hospital his mother should also be admitted so that breast feeding may be maintained.

Poliomyelitis

The success of the mass immunisation programme which started over 30 years ago means that poliomyelitis is now a rare disease, with only a few cases occurring each year – three in 1986, three in 1987 and two in 1988. Provided that the immunisation of infants using oral vaccine is continued at a high rate (see page 107) its virtual disappearance is likely to continue. (Oral vaccine is now used but originally, from 1959–61, poliomyelitis vaccination was by injection which was also effective but not so long lasting.) The extra precautions that should be taken should a case occur are described below.

Poliomyelitis has the most well-defined seasonal incidence of any known communicable disease. Outbreaks in the United Kingdom always occur in late summer and early autumn, in August, September or October, hence there is only a serious risk of epidemic spread in these months.

Poliomyelitis is a faecal-borne disease, spread by direct contact from person to person usually living in the same household. Although infected, the majority of close contacts show no symptoms and only rarely does clinical poliomyelitis result.

When a case of poliomyelitis occurs, it is therefore important that, as far as possible, the members of the same household are segregated from the general population. Child contacts should certainly be kept away from school for at least three weeks. By isolating the family as far as possible, the chance of spreading infection is reduced.

In addition, as soon as any case occurs, immediate immunisation using oral poliomyelitis vaccine should be given to

— all contacts at home, work or school; and
— all people living within an approximate radius of a quarter of a mile from the patient.

This not only serves to boost their immunity but also blocks the entrance of 'wild' or epidemic virus into their intestines and thus helps to reduce the chance of further infection.

Household contacts should be placed under surveillance for three weeks. They should be visited by a health visitor daily to check their temperature and whether they have any symptoms. If any abnormality is noted, then the contact should be put to bed immediately and kept as quiet as possible. This is important because *violent exercise in the patient showing the earliest signs of poliomyelitis can result in a severe attack*. As a further precaution, no close contact of a case of poliomyelitis should be allowed to indulge in strenuous exercise for three weeks. Close family contacts should, therefore, not go on walking tours or any similar activities at this time.

Restrictions among the general population regarding swimming baths are probably useless in preventing the spread of poliomyelitis. However, swimming is a fairly active form of exercise and should be avoided for three weeks among close family contacts.

As already explained the most valuable preventive measure against poliomyelitis is to make certain that as high a proportion as possible of people under 40 years of age are completely immunised against the disease using oral Sabin vaccine.

Cholera

Although classic cholera last appeared in epidemic form in the United Kingdom in 1866, recently there have been a number of outbreaks in westernised countries from the new El Tor strains. Occasional cases are notified in the United Kingdom and invariably these cases are persons who have acquired their infection abroad. Seven cases were notified in 1985, nine in 1986 and three in 1987.

Air travel facilitates the spread of this disease which has a short incubation period of two to three days.

Contamination of water supplies is the classic method of spread but flies can also be responsible if sewage disposal methods are crude. Direct spread from food handlers who are carriers is also a possibility.

El Tor cholera remains in the stools for at least 14 days and occasionally for up to three months.

Prevention   This mainly depends on purification of water supplies and safe disposal of sewage. In epidemics, water and milk must be boiled (unless already pasteurised) and careful segregation of all patients arranged with terminal and concurrent disinfection.

Active immunisation should be arranged for those at special risk (doctors and nurses) and for travellers to countries where the disease is epidemic. Immunisation provides about 50% protection for a short period and revaccination is advisable every six months. Results, however, have been disappointing against the El Tor type of cholera.

Direct spread – from animals

Anthrax

Anthrax is a rare disease (none in 1987, two cases in 1988) and is usually caught by direct spread from the hide, wool or bones of animals. It is only seen in people whose occupations bring them into contact with animals and animal products. The main groups of people at risk include dockers handling hides, who occasionally develop anthrax, and wool sorters.

Prevention   This depends on the following measures.

— Special treatment of wool imports to kill any anthrax spores at a number of centres close to the mills.
— Protective clothing being worn by persons handling hides and bones.
— Immunisation against anthrax for all associated workers (see page 110).

As a further safeguard, the dangers of anthrax are explained to all those working in occupations in which there is a danger of contracting the disease. Diagrams of early symptoms are prominently displayed so that if anyone develops the skin lesions of anthrax, it is more likely to be recognised and diagnosed early. All such workers also carry a special card to show to their general practitioners so that the doctor knows of the special risk of contracting anthrax which their occupation carries.

The early diagnosis is most important as modern treatment can quickly cut short an attack of anthrax.

Leptospirosis

Leptospirosis, caused by *Leptospira icterohaemorrhagiae*, is primarily a disease of rats (36 human cases were notified in 1988). Infections in man result from the skin being infected by water contaminated with rat urine and usually only occur among abattoir or sewage workers who are most likely to come into close contact with rats. All such workers should be warned of the dangers of infection and of the importance of a high standard of hygiene. It is especially important that they avoid contaminating skin with water which may have been infected by rat's urine. It is especially dangerous to walk barefoot in such places.

Rabies (hydrophobia)

At present in the United Kingdom considerable concern is being shown about the dangers and problems of rabies because of the increase of this disease on the continent. Many different wild animals can be infected (including foxes, otters and rodents) but the vast majority of cases in wild animals have been traced to foxes (about 90–94% in European countries). In fact an epizootic (an animal epidemic) in foxes has spread during the last 15 years to France from Germany, Switzerland, Austria, Denmark and Belgium. An interesting campaign of oral vaccination of wild animals in six countries of Europe was started in 1986 (see Fig. 11.6, Chapter 11, page 198). About 75% of all animal outbreaks on the continent have occurred among wild animals and the remainder among domestic animals. Dogs are most commonly affected in this group but cats and bovines are also infected.

Prevention   The virus of rabies is in the saliva of rabid animals. After a bite from a rabid animal, the virus spreads in humans to the central nervous system producing the characteristic symptoms. The disease is very dangerous with a high mortality and anyone who has been bitten by a rabid animal must be immunised (see page 110). The incubation period is usually about two to six weeks but in a few cases may be much longer.

Rabies Act 1974   Under this Act, there is a compulsory six months quarantine period for all animals entering the country. Effective precautions must also be taken against the transmission of the disease within quarantine kennels. All dogs and cats entering quarantine must be vaccinated on entry with a proved potency-tested inactivated vaccine; they must also be revaccinated after one month in quarantine to extend immunity.

Dogs and cats are allowed to enter Britain only at a limited number of ports. Animals landed illegally may be destroyed on landing and the Act provides severe penalties, including up to one year's imprisonment for offences against the orders under the Act.

Further orders provide for a wider range of measures to control any outbreak of rabies in Britain. These include destruction of foxes, controls on the movement of domestic pets and their vaccination, the seizure of strays and the banning of hunting, and cat and dog shows.

Prophylactic vaccination against rabies (see page 110) should be offered to all persons who are at risk in their work, including:

— those employed at quarantine kennels;
— those working in quarantine premises in zoos;
— agents who are authorised to carry such animals;
— those working in search and acclimatisation centres where primates and other imported mammals are housed;
— those working in ports regularly importing animals.

Booster immunisation should be given every two to three years.

Legionnaire's disease

This is a serious respiratory disease which first appeared in Spain and America in the 1970s. Since then a number of outbreaks have been traced in the United Kingdom – the worst of these was an outbreak in 1985 when 101 cases occurred at Stafford District Hospital (there were 28 deaths). A further outbreak of 60 cases was traced at the British Broadcasting Corporation (BBC) headquarters in London in 1988.

Method of spread   The disease is caused by a bacteria *Legionella pneumophilia* and, so far, 14 serogroups of this organism have been identified. The bacteria is found in natural and artificial water supplies. It is an airborne infection and domestic hot water systems, jacuzzis, showers, industrial water-based coolants and water-cooled air-conditioning systems have all caused outbreaks.

The prevention of Legionnaire's disease depends on the design and operation of hot water systems, and especially those which may lead to the entry of contaminated airborne particles into a ventilation system from a cooling tower (this was the mechanism found to be responsible for the Stafford outbreak).

Cooling towers require regular cleaning and treatment with biocides and also hot water systems should use calorifiers to ensure storage temperatures remain above 50°C.

8 AIDS, sexually transmitted diseases and viral hepatitis

Acquired immune deficiency syndrome (AIDS)

AIDS is caused by infection with a long acting virus, human immunodeficiency virus (HIV), which prevents the human immune system from functioning properly. The disease probably first appeared in Africa but soon spread to America and can now be found in most countries of the world. The first clinical cases were described in Los Angeles in 1981.

AIDS represents the most serious threat this century in the field of communicable diseases because of its unique features. The virus renders the body susceptible to attacks from other infecting agents – bacteria, viruses, worm and protozoal infections – by virtually destroying the body's normal immune systems. This also means that the usual range of protective immunisations are not effective in preventing common infectious diseases. Certain unusual cancers are also found in some patients with AIDS.

The disease develops in two stages. Firstly, the original infection with HIV. Specific symptoms are usually absent at this stage so that the diagnosis can only be made by blood tests which demonstrate a rising level of antibodies to HIV (seroconversion).

At a much later stage (often years later) clinical AIDS may develop. As AIDS is still a relatively new disease, it is not yet possible to be certain as to what proportion of those infected with HIV will eventually develop clinical AIDS. The usual time interval between the original infection with HIV and the subsequent development of clinical AIDS is also not yet known, although it has been demonstrated in America that the interval may be as long as seven or eight years. Future observations alone will answer the questions with certainty and it may well be at least another 10–15 years before the answers are known.

Clinical AIDS

The disease presents in two main forms, infections and unusual forms of cancer.

Infections The infections, called opportunistic infections, are usually harmless to man but, because the body's immune system has been seriously damaged by earlier invasion with HIV, they now become recognisable and dangerous diseases. The inability of the body to respond in the normal way by producing an increasing immunity to infection can lead to the death of the patient. The infections include the following.

— Various helminth and protozoal infections with, for example, toxoplasmosis or *Pneumocystis carinii* which both cause pneumonia, strongyloidosis which causes pneumonia or can affect the central nervous system, and cryptosporidiosis which presents with diarrhoea.
— Various fungal infections, for example aspergillosis and candidiasis which both affect the oesophagus and lungs, cryptococcosis which affects mainly meninges but also bones, lungs and genito-urinary tract, and histoplasmosis which affects lungs, spleen, liver and gastro-intestinal tract.
— Many unusual or atypical bacterial infections, for example atypical mycoplasmosis.
— Certain fairly common viral infections which usually cause trivial attacks in normal persons (e.g. herpes simplex) can be very serious in the AIDS patient. Life threatening disseminated herpes simplex can develop.

Unusual forms of cancer These include the following.

— Kaposi's sarcoma which presents as a flat or raised reddish-purple lesion on any part of the skin or hard palate.
— Cerebral lymphoma.
— Non-Hodgkin's lymphoma.
— Lymphoreticular malignancy which starts more than three months after an opportunistic infection.

Methods of spread of HIV

There are three main ways HIV (and therefore AIDS) can be spread.

● *By sexual intercourse* HIV virus is commonly found in seminal and vaginal secretions of those infected. This means both homosexual and heterosexual persons are at risk if one partner is infected.
● *By blood to blood contamination* i.e. by blood transfusion when the donor blood is infected by HIV. Tragically a number of haemophiliac patients in the United Kingdom have been infected in this way. *All blood and blood products used for transfusion, whether collected in this country or imported, are now heat treated and therefore safe.* However there are still many countries in the

world (particularly Africa) where blood transfusion is a hazardous procedure. 'At risk' individuals who may require a blood transfusion periodically should avoid such travel. Nurses, particularly those working in casualty departments, should *realise the potential danger of contact with the blood of any patient and surgical gloves should always be worn when treating people who have been involved in traffic accidents and other patients who are bleeding*. Staff in renal dialysis units must also take similar precautions.

Many intravenous drug abusers have been infected with HIV by sharing syringes. Minute amounts of blood are often left in the needle or syringe and can quite easily lead to person to person spread if the earlier user has the virus circulating in their bloodstream. As will be explained later in this chapter (page 149), such careless use of syringes is also a common method of spread of viral hepatitis (particularly viral B hepatitis). New sterile syringes are essential for all injections (including any therapeutic ones). Home sterilisation, carried out by boiling glass syringes and needles, has also been shown to be unsafe, particularly with viral infections.

- *By the maternal-fetal route*, either by infection during pregnancy via the placenta, by infection of the baby during birth by contact with an infected mother's vaginal secretions or blood, or later via breast milk.

Types of persons found to have clinical AIDS

AIDS has not been made a notifiable disease for the same reasons that sexually transmitted diseases are not notifiable – if they had been made notifiable there would be a danger of concealment which could lead to more spread of these diseases. The diagnosis of HIV infection involves the laboratory services and this is why the Communicable Diseases Surveillance Centre in England and Wales and the Communicable Disease Unit in Scotland undertake the task of collecting data of both HIV infection and of any patients who later develop clinical AIDS (see Table 8.1).

When interpreting these figures, which clearly indicate likely methods of spread, great care must be taken. These are clinical cases and as the period of time between infection with HIV and the development of AIDS is usually many years, Table 8.1 represents not only the earliest infections in the outbreak (before the actual methods of spread were fully understood) but before there was known widespread dissemination of HIV throughout the world. It would be a mistake to believe that AIDS will in the future continue to be mainly a disease of practising homosexual men.

A more balanced picture of the likely proportion of types of cases is given by Table 8.2 which indicates the types of persons already found to be infected with HIV in the United Kingdom. Note that of the 7557

Table 8.1 Cases of AIDS in the United Kingdom by patient characteristics (cumulative totals to the end of June 1990). (Prepared from direct voluntary confidential reports by clinicians to the PHLS Communicable Disease Surveillance Centre and the Communicable Diseases (Scotland) Unit.)

Type of patient	Men	Women	Total	Deaths
Homosexual or bisexual	2734	0	2734	1481
Intravenous drug abuser	90	27	117	51
Homosexual and drug abuser	50	0	50	24
Haemophiliac	204	3	207	137
Recipient of blood:				
Abroad	12	16	28	21
UK	15	9	24	18
Heterosexual				
Partner with above risk factors	9	20	29	15
Others:				
With known risk abroad	104	47	151	70
With no evidence of exposure abroad	11	10	21	8
Child of at risk or infected parent	10	15	25	15
Other or undetermined	41	6	47	29
Totals	3280	153	3433	1869

HIV positive cases identified up to September 1987, 44.7% were homosexual men, 15.7% drug abusers and 0.6% in a combination of these two groups. This means that at least 39% belonged to other groups. Almost certainly many individuals other than homosexual men and intravenous drug abusers will increasingly be at risk of developing AIDS in the future.

Table 8.2 Patient characteristics of the 7557 HIV positive cases reported in the United Kingdom to end of September 1987. (Prepared from information supplied to PHLS Communicable Diseases Surveillance Centre and the Communicable Diseases (Scotland) Unit.)

Patient groups	Males	Females	Unknown	Total	%
Homosexuals	3381	—	0	3381	44.7
Intravenous drug abusers	760	400	24	1184	15.7
Homosexuals and drug users	45	—	0	45	0.6
Haemophiliacs	1056	4	1	1061	14.0
Blood recipients	41	28	1	70	1.0
Heterosexual contacts	150	164	8	322	4.3
Child of HIV positive mother	25	21	28	74	1.0
Others/several risks/no information	1204	88	128	1420	18.7
Total	6662	705	190	7557	100.0

Symptoms of AIDS patients

The signs and symptoms of persons developing clinical AIDS depend on the type of complication which develops as a result of the damage to the immune mechanism of the body. The following are the six most likely symptoms seen.

- Continuous and intermittent fever with a body temperature of more than 38°C.
- Loss of weight – more than 10%.
- Persistent swollen lymph glands (larger than 1 cm).
- Intermittent and/or continuous diarrhoea.
- Increasing tiredness and fatigue which begins to have the effect of reducing activity.
- Night sweats.

Laboratory investigations often show the following abnormalities:

— anaemia;
— leucopenia;
— lymphopenia;
— thrombocytopenia;
— raised gamma globulins.

Prevention of AIDS – importance of health education

The only certain way to avoid AIDS is to understand fully the mechanisms of infection with HIV and then to avoid running the known risks. This entails improving the health education of the whole population. An important starting point in any campaign is to ensure that all health professionals completely understand that the risk is NOT confined to small groups such as homosexual men or drug abusers but is far wider – anyone can be at risk if they ignore the dangers of spread of infection. Far too many members of the public do not realise the potential dangers facing everyone.

Nurses and other health staff should act as health educators to their patients whenever the opportunity occurs. The importance of nurses always wearing gloves when dealing with any patient where contact with blood is likely has already been stressed.

In 1986, the Government mounted a widespread health education campaign aimed at teaching the general public the dangers of AIDS and its methods of spread. Over £20 million was spent on all forms of publicity and an explanatory leaflet was delivered to every household. As with all large scale health education campaigns, the effectiveness of the message very much depends on supplementation later by health staff in their day to day contact with patients and their families. It is particularly important to teach young persons at school and in further education the true dangers of AIDS and how these can be avoided.

The following are the practical steps to be taken to avoid AIDS:

- *The need to limit sexual contacts* The greater the numbers of sexual partners, the greater will be the chance of infection with HIV. This cannot be overemphasised – even if all the other preventive steps are taken (use of condoms etc.) – no prevention is better than a monogamous heterosexual relationship (one sexual partner of the other sex for life is the ideal) or celibacy. It is important to realise that any sexual heterosexual contact could be dangerous if either partner is HIV positive and this fact is not known by the other partner or is concealed from them. The same is true of homosexual relationships where anal or oral sex represents the main dangers.

- The use of a condom in any casual sexual contact is essential for the safety of both partners. The object of using a condom is to prevent the partner from coming into contact with seminal or vaginal fluids. Oral sex should also be avoided. The Government campaign not only stressed the value of condoms but helped to make condoms more widely available. Travellers should always take stocks with them as condoms purchased in some countries may be unreliable.

- Realising that there is a greater risk of infection in any homosexual relationship mainly because there is a higher proportion of homosexual men already infected with HIV.

- Recognising there is a special danger of contamination from any used syringe. The only certain way to avoid this danger is always to use a new sterile disposable syringe for each injection. After use, the disposable syringe should always be carefully destroyed (to ensure it cannot be used again). 'Home sterilisation' of glass syringes has been shown to be inadequate as far as the destruction of viruses is concerned. There is much debate regarding the suggestion that known intravenous drug abusers should be provided with free sterile disposable syringes (as is the practice in the Netherlands and Edinburgh) and certainly this would reduce the danger of HIV infection in such individuals.

Sexually transmitted diseases (STDs)

Sexually transmitted diseases spread by sexual intercourse – one partner infecting the other. There are three common STDs; non-specific genital infection, gonorrhoea and syphilis. In addition, genital warts, candidiasis (thrush), genital herpes, trichomoniasis vaginalis and pubic lice are also sexually transmitted. As explained below (see page 149) certain viral hepatitis infections can also be spread by sexual

Table 8.3 New cases of common sexually transmitted diseases seen at National Health Service genito-urinary medicine clinics in England, 1986. (From Health and Personal Social Service Statistics, 1988.)

	Males	Females	Total
Non specific genital infection	106751	51545	158296
Cases of gonorrhoea	24450	16255	40705
Cases of syphilis	1387	545	1932
Genital warts	40253	26815	67068
Candidiasis (thrush)	11535	51573	63108
Genital herpes	9983	8817	18800
Trichomoniasis	923	13118	14041
Pubic lice	6508	2825	9333

intercourse. Table 8.3 gives the new cases of sexually transmitted diseases recorded in England in 1986.

Non-specific genital infections

In men, this usually presents as a urethritis (urethral discharge) but, in women, over 90% are symptom free – a few later develop a urethritis or pelvic genital infection. The incubation period is 10–28 days. In approximately 70% of cases, *Chlamydia trachomatis* can be isolated and, in the remainder, the cause is usually not found. In women, it is the commonest cause of pelvic inflammatory disease and subsequent infertility. Occasionally arthritis can develop as a late complication. Tetracycline is mainly used to treat non-specific genital infection.

Gonorrhoea

Gonorrhoea has an incubation period of three to ten days (usually five). In men, the first symptoms are a urethral discharge with some pain on micturition. In women, about 60% have no symptoms and the remainder a vaginal discharge.

Treatment is with penicillin but, increasingly, patients are also treated with tetracycline to clear up any co-existing non-specific genital infection.

In both *non-specific genital infection* and in *gonorrhoea, follow up should always be undertaken after three weeks to assess treatment and after three months to make certain that a double infection with syphilis has not occurred.* The initial treatment with antibiotics may suppress the development of the characteristic primary chancre.

Syphilis

This is potentially the most dangerous STD but, fortunately, treatment with penicillin in the primary stage (usually about three weeks after infection) or in the secondary stage (after about eight weeks) will prevent the very serious complications from developing later. Treatment early in the pregnancy of a woman infected with syphilis will also prevent any danger of congenital syphilis in her child.

Initially, after an incubation period of 9–90 days (usually 21 days), a painless ulcerated sore (chancre) develops at the site of the infection. Confirmation of diagnosis is by bacteriological examination identifying the presence of the spirochete *Treponema pallidum*.

Other STDs

The other conditions mentioned in Table 8.3 are usually mild but, in the case of genital herpes, may be confused with cystitis. Candidiasis (thrush) is a fungal infection leading to an intense irritating white creamy discharge. Treatment with pessaries containing nystatin, clotrimazole, miconazole or econazole is usually very effective. Trichomoniasis also causes a vaginal discharge which is treated with metronidazole; the male partner should also be treated at the same time. Pubic lice are, to a less extent, genital infections being spread from body to body – they are not strictly sexually transmitted although are seen mostly in clinics dealing with STD cases.

Prevention of sexually transmitted disease

The prevention of sexually transmitted disease depends on:

— complete and efficient diagnosis and treatment of all cases;
— the searching out of suspected cases; and
— avoidance of casual or promiscuous sexual intercourse.

- Diagnosis, especially of gonorrhoea, is not simple in the female, and an infected woman can remain so for a lengthy period without necessarily realising she is infected. In doubtful cases, hospital out-patient attendance is desirable so that bacteriological smears may be taken and blood tests examined.
- Whenever a case of sexually transmitted disease is diagnosed, a careful history should be taken and arrangements made for the cohabiting partner to be medically examined as soon as possible. To carry out this contact tracing, specially trained nurses and social workers are attached to all sexually transmitted disease departments. Their task is to trace the cohabiting partner wherever possible and persuade him or her to come to the clinic for a full examination.

- Better education is needed, so that all persons realise that only by self control and avoidance of casual sexual intercourse will such diseases be avoided. It is especially important to realise that, *without bacteriological tests, it is impossible even for a doctor to exclude the possibility of such disease in any person.* This should be explained to all who may otherwise be misled into believing they can tell when a contact is, or is not, infected.

During the past few years, there has been a change in the pattern of sexually transmitted diseases in the UK. There has been an increase in the number of non-specific genital infections, genital herpetic infection and candidosis.

There was also a slight rise in the numbers of new cases of early syphilis but the total number of cases of gonorrhoea has fallen from 59 028 in 1977 to 41 705 in 1986 (England). There has however been a disturbing increase in the penicillin-related gonococci identified – mostly from infections imported into the United Kingdom. The number of cases of syphilis has fallen from 2854 in 1979 to 1930 in 1986.

Viral hepatitis

The generic name 'infective jaundice' covers a number of cases of hepatitis caused by viruses. In about 54% of these, hepatitis A virus is responsible, 13% by hepatitis B and the remainder by a virus called non A/non B or by hepatitis C or by viruses which, as yet, have not been identified. Cases of 'infective jaundice' are notifiable and, during 1988, 5063 cases were reported in England and Wales (3190 hepatitis A, 390 hepatitis B, 363 hepatitis non A/non B and 1120 other viruses).

Hepatitis A

This type of hepatitis has an incubation period usually between three and five weeks. It is spread by the faecal–oral route and usually follows person to person contact. Many food-borne epidemics have been reported and, during the incubation period, there is a heavy excretion of virus in the stools and careless personal hygiene amongst food handlers is often responsible for the spread of infection at this time. *Hepatitis A is rarely sexually transmitted but this mode of spread can occur after oral–anal contact, usually in homosexual men.*

Hepatitis A does not result in liver failure and complete recovery is normal although it may be many weeks before the patient feels really well again. A vaccine against hepatitis A is being developed but is not yet in general use. Passive immunisation using immunoglobulin can be given to close contacts and has been used to control hepatitis A outbreaks in nursery schools and homes for the mentally handicapped.

Hepatitis B

An earlier name for this type of hepatitis was 'serum hepatitis' mainly because one of the usual ways of spreading this disease is through contaminated blood. It is however now known that hepatitis B can also be spread by other infected body fluids such as semen, vaginal secretions, saliva and breast milk.

Infection with blood products can occur by way of the following.

* Accidental inoculation of health staff during surgical or dental operations or when assisting with renal dialysis.
* First aid help during traffic and other accidents especially when there is haemorrhage. Clean rubber gloves should always be worn in such instances and, as has been stressed previously, it is good practice for all nurses to have a pair of rubber gloves in their car.
* Needles and syringes shared by intravenous drug abusers. As already explained the one safe method is always to use a new disposable sterile needle and syringe for each injection.
* Tattooing and ear piercing. Cases have occasionally been traced to this source.

It is important to realise that carriers (showing no symptoms) are not uncommon – about 5–10% of individuals who are infected with hepatitis B virus develop into life long carriers. In the United Kingdom the carrier rate is only 0.1%, but in Africa and the Far East up to 20% of the indigenous population are carriers making the chance of infection by the various routes mentioned above much more common.

Hepatitis B has similar clinical features to other forms of hepatitis – fever, headache and fatigue with jaundice. Complete recovery does occur in most patients, but a small proportion (5–10%) develop liver damage (cirrhosis or liver failure) and primary cancer of the liver may result. A reliable vaccine has now been developed against hepatitis B (see Chapter 6, page 110).

Non A/Non B hepatitis

This is becoming the commonest form of hepatitis in many countries of the world following blood transfusion. The long term consequences can be very serious and chronic liver damage (with the risk of liver failure later) has been reported in as many as 50% of cases. Both short and long incubation periods have been seen in this form of hepatitis.

9 Prevention of non-communicable diseases

With non-communicable disease, the greatest barrier to prevention is that so little is known about the causes of disease. Research into the causation is continually being carried out and the factors connected with the incidence of such diseases are slowly being unravelled. It is, however, a very complicated study as there is a multiplicity of factors involved. Even in diseases whose cause is as yet hardly understood, wide differences exist between the various social classes as shown on page 46, suggesting that the living conditions of the various social classes may increase or diminish the dangers of developing such diseases.

Sometimes important factors only come to light by a steady increase in a disease leading to greater and greater research which finally finds an important causative factor. An example of this is given by cancer of the lung, the increase of which has been shown to be connected with increased cigarette smoking. But as yet, research even in this instance has not discovered all the chemical factors in cigarette smoke which produce this carcinogenic effect. Another example is bladder cancer. Epidemiological studies have shown that there was a higher incidence of bladder cancer among workers in the dyestuffs industry and indicated three aromatic amines, α-naphthylamine, β-naphthylamine and benzidine as potent carcinogens. Also it was found that antioxidants made from α- and β-naphthylamines were used frequently in rubber and cable industries. Since the use of α- and β-naphthylamines was banned, bladder cancers in men who entered the industries after this ban have fallen although those employed before the ban still show a marked excess.

Prevention of non-communicable diseases can always be considered from three aspects.

- Complete prevention of the disease ever occurring in any individual (*primary prevention*).
- Early detection of disease in a person who has no symptoms (*secondary prevention*) – this is the same as screening.
- Prevention of complications from a disease already existing before the effects have produced disability or handicap (*tertiary prevention*). Unless correct treatment is carried out for a chronic disease

such as diabetes mellitus, asthma or hypertensive disease, many long term complications and disabilities may occur.

Ischaemic heart disease

The incidence of ischaemic heart disease increased markedly from 1960 to 1980 but has been fairly steady since. Much research has been carried out throughout the world to discover what causes this condition. Although much has yet to be discovered it is clear that considerable differences in the incidence of ischaemic heart disease occur throughout the world (see Table 9.1).

Table 9.1 Deaths from ischaemic heart disease in various countries per 100000 population (both sexes), 1986 (unless otherwise indicated). (From World Health Annual Statistics.)

Japan	49.5	Austria	257.8
Hong Kong	52.9	Germany (Federal)	265.4
Spain	111.1	New Zealand	270.4
Portugal	121.7	Netherlands	284.5
France*	155.4	Australia*	290.0
Israel	187.2	Ireland**	382.1
Canada	213.8	England and Wales	427.8
USA**	237.1	Scotland	547.7

*1984
**1985

The reasons for these differences are not completely known. The latest views are that a number of factors are probably important. These include the following:

— high blood lipid levels (especially if accompanied by low intake of fibre in the diet);
— hypertension;
— cigarette smoking;
— genetic factors;
— physical inactivity;
— increase in body weight;
— diabetes;
— nervous stress;
— the sex of the individual (particularly in attacks in younger persons).

A short, heavier person is more prone to an early attack than a tall thin person. Regular exercise seems to have some protective effect and farmers and others leading active lives have a lower incidence than sedentary workers. There is certainly an endocrine factor which is probably responsible for the higher rate in younger men. Under the age of 45, the disease is eight times commoner in men than in women. After the menopause the rate in women increases until by the age of 70 it is equal to that of men.

Prevention   At present, there is no agreement about the exact steps which should be taken to avoid ischaemic heart disease. Some suggest that it would be wise to do a routine blood cholesterol test on all men aged 30 and that, in those in whom a raised level was found, a diet should be commenced in which animal fats are replaced by vegetable fats. Also, care should be taken to avoid becoming overweight. However, many physicians feel that to do this would only worry many patients unduly and, in the end, more harm could be caused.

Further research is necessary to try and find the most important causes. Until this has been achieved, there is no doubt that the following simple rules are helpful and likely to reduce ischaemic heart disease.

— Avoid overweight at all costs.
— Constant exercise, such as walking should be encouraged – daily exercise is probably much more useful than sudden bursts of exercise.
— Do not smoke cigarettes. However, if anyone stops smoking, these risks will fall to the level of the non-smoker within a few months.
— Ensure that the diet contains plenty of fibre.

For anyone who has already had an attack of ischaemic heart disease these simple rules are even more important, as well as taking small daily doses of aspirin.

The cancers

The true causative nature of cancers is, as yet, unknown. There are, however, many associated factors now recognised which are known to predispose to the development of cancers – most of these are connected with some chronic recurring form of irritation. It is known that various skin cancers can be caused by irritation from oils and sunlight and cancers of the tongue by the irritation of a clay pipe. It is likely that the association between cigarette smoking and lung cancer, and between atmospheric pollution and lung cancer, is of this nature. A clear connection has also been demonstrated between the development of liver cancers and exposure to monomeric vinyl chloride. The greatest dangers have been traced to men who open and clean the autoclave where vinyl chloride is polymerised. Another causative factor in primary liver cancers is chronic hepatitis particularly after infection with viral non A/non B hepatitis.

Most cancers show their highest incidence in Social Class V and their lowest in Social Class I (see Fig. 9.1). The exception is cancer of the

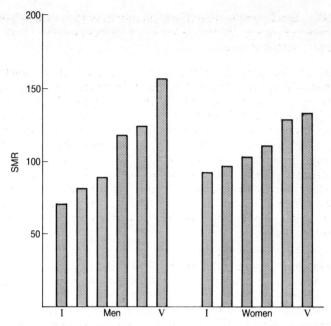

Fig. 9.1 Mortality from malignant neoplasms by social class in men and women aged 20–64 years, England and Wales, 1979–80. (From *Occupational Mortality*, OPCS, 1987.)

breast in women but it is not known why this cancer differs in this respect.

Prevention of cancers depends on many factors.

— Removal of the irritating cause such as stopping smoking, or the avoidance of excessive sunbathing, especially in fair-skinned people.
— Protection from radiation especially for persons likely to be exposed in their jobs, e.g. radiographers, some nurses and some scientists.
— Early recognition and radical treatment of a precancerous condition (this is the basis of cervical screening in cancer of the cervix uteri – see below).

International cancer mortality

There are marked variations in the cancer mortality in different countries of the world (see Table 9.2). Many of these differences are too great to be explained by varying degrees of diagnosis and treatment. Exceptionally low death rates for cancer of the lung and breast occur in Japan but the rate of cancer of the stomach is high. When the

Table 9.2   Cancer death rates in different countries per 100000 population, 1986 (unless otherwise indicated). (From World Health Statistics, 1988.)

Site	USA	Austria*	France	Netherlands	UK*	Australia	Japan
Stomach							
Males	7.2	29.3	16.0	19.5	23.2	10.9	50.6
Females	4.4	24.9	10.6	12.6	14.8	6.3	29.3
Lung							
Males	72.5	67.2	64.4	104.6	102.0	54.4	38.7
Females	32.7	18.6	8.6	13.7	40.7	16.8	13.9
Breast							
Female	32.8	42.1	33.6	41.3	52.4	27.2	8.5
Cervix uteri	3.7	5.8	3.1	4.2	7.3	4.4	2.9
Leukaemia							
Males	8.1	7.3	9.6	7.4	7.7	7.3	5.6
Females	6.3	7.0	7.4	6.0	6.5	5.5	3.7

*1987

cancer rates for Japanese who emigrate to the USA are studied, the rates quickly approximate to the American levels suggesting that the main factors may be environmental (including diet) rather than genetic.

Cancer of the cervix uteri

Cancer of the cervix uteri was responsible for the deaths of 1942 women in 1988 in England and Wales but this death rate has been falling. Table 2.12 (page 46) shows the marked variation in the various social classes. Repetitive damage to the cervix uteri is a predisposing cause to this cancer and this is one of the reasons for a higher rate in Social Class V women who generally have larger families than women from Social Class I or II.

Prevention   There is a widely used screening test (exfoliative cytology) which can detect a precancerous condition in the cervix. The technique of the test is simple. A vaginal speculum is passed and a direct smear is obtained from the cervix and examined histologically. If there are abnormal mitotic changes in the nuclei of the epithelial cells removed, a complete gynaecological examination should be carried out to ascertain whether a pre-cancerous lesion exists. If these investigations confirm a pre-cancerous condition, it is then usual to operate and remove the cervix (or complete uterus) before a dangerous invasive cancer develops or, in early cases, to use specialised laser treatment.

Such smears are collected by general practitioners or at a special clinic. Regular testing in this way should be carried out on all women once every 3–5 years. The ideal is every three years but once every five years is adequate *provided there is no delay in the re-testing*. The three year programme allows more time to follow up any women who fail to return promptly. It is in Social Class V that most of these difficulties are seen and the relatively small number of women in Social Class V who have regular smear tests is thought to be a contributory factor for the very high mortality rate of cancer of the cervix in this group (see Table 2.12, page 46).

Cancer of the lung

The increase in cancer of the lung from 1950–80 was most dramatic. It is always difficult when comparing the incidence of any disease over a number of years to assess how much better diagnosis may be responsible – in other words, how much of the increase is apparent and not real. However, if the incidence of cancer of the lung is examined in England and Wales over the last 33 years, 1947–88, it is possible to ignore this diagnostic factor as, by 1947, widespread use of radiology and bronchoscopy was taking place in the diagnosis of lung lesions, and it is safe to assume the degree of diagnosis was similar. In this period of 41 years, the number of deaths from cancer of the lung has increased 3.8 times from 9204 in 1947 to 35 302 in 1988.

This increase is serious especially as cancer of the lung is difficult to treat effectively and usually results in the patient's death within 1½ to 2 years of diagnosis in all but 5% of cases. As cancer of the lung is easily the commonest cancer, prevention of lung cancer is one of the most serious problems facing medicine today.

There are marked differences between the incidence of the disease in various countries (see Table 9.3). However, it will be noted that in all countries cancer of the lung is commoner in men, and that the Netherlands and United Kingdom are in the unenviable position of having the worst figures.

Much research in various parts of the world has been carried out to investigate the factors associated with this great increase in cancer of the lung. All the various surveys in different countries have shown that

Table 9.3 Mortality from cancer of the lung per 100000 population, in various countries, 1986 or 1987. (From World Health Annual Statistics, 1988.)

Country	Males	Females
Japan	38.7	13.9
Australia	54.2	16.8
France	64.4	8.6
Austria	67.2	18.6
USA	72.5	32.7
United Kingdom	102.0	40.7
Netherlands	104.6	13.7

more lung cancer patients are smokers of cigarettes than are the controls in the experiments. It has also been shown clearly that death rates from lung cancer increase steeply as consumption of cigarettes increases. Heavy cigarette smokers have thirty times the death rate of non-smokers.

The Royal College of Physicians has studied the problem and clearly states that 'cigarette smoking is an important cause of lung cancer. If the habit ceased, the number of deaths caused by this disease should fall steeply in the course of time'.

Research in America has also shown that there are highly abnormal cells in the sputum of heavy smokers – cells which are showing many abnormal changes and may be pre-cancerous. The interesting and encouraging feature is that, if smoking stops, then, within a short space of time, there is a diminution in the number of such cells in the sputum and finally they disappear altogether. This suggests that to give up smoking is to reduce the chance of developing cancer of the lung – a repeated finding reported from all surveys.

Although the mortality from cancer of the lung cases is at an all time high level (in 1989, 34 581 people died from this cause in England and Wales) the mortality in men is falling (a drop of 11.6% from 1982 to 1989) whereas in women over the same period, the deaths increased by 16.5% (see Table 9.4). This difference is also reflected in the latest smoking trends in children – a survey carried out by OPCS in 1986 showed that 12% of girls aged 11–15 smoked regularly compared with 7% of boys (in Scotland the figures were 14% and 10% respectively). Among 16–19 year olds the figures are roughly equal at 30%.

Table 9.4 Deaths from cancer of the lung, England and Wales, 1981–9. (From DH 4 Series OPCS Monitors.)

	1981	1982	1985	1988	1989
Males	26297	25962	25994	24671	23821
Females	8430	8870	9798	10631	10760

If the problem of cancer of the lung is to be significantly reduced, it is most important that young women realise the increased risks smoking involves – otherwise although mortality in men seems likely to continue to fall gradually, the increase of smoking in women may well counterbalance this effect with the result that the overall mortality may remain at similar levels. Professional women working in the health services have a particular responsibility; if they do not smoke (or give it up if they have started), the example which they provide to their patients and to the public with whom they are constantly in contact is bound to be of value in ensuring the effectiveness of any health education programme. The Royal College of Physicians has suggested seven courses of action.

— More education of the public and especially schoolchildren concerning hazards of smoking.
— More effective restrictions on the sale of tobacco to children.
— Restriction of tobacco advertising.
— Wider restriction of smoking in public places.
— An increase of tax on cigarettes, perhaps with adjustment of the tax on pipe and cigar tobaccos.
— Informing purchasers of the tar and nicotine content of the smoke of cigarettes.
— Investigating the value of anti-smoking clinics to help those who find difficulty in giving up smoking.

Cancer of the breast

Cancer of the breast is an important cause of death in women. Table 2.12 (page 46) shows a small inverse curve among the social classes with the highest figures in Social Class I. There is, however, a much wider range between the mortality in different countries as shown in Table 9.5.

Table 9.5 Cancer of the breast (female) death rate per 100000 population, 1986/87. (From World Health Annual Statistics, 1988.)

Japan*	Australia*	USA*	France*	Netherlands*	Austria**	UK**
8.5	27.2	32.8	33.6	41.3	42.1	52.4

*1986; **1987

Breast feeding is common in Japan and this fact may be partly responsible for the low death rate there. The high rate in the United Kingdom emphasises the need to prevent this disease as far as possible. The Standardised Mortality Ratio (1980 = 100) shows mortality is still rising steadily – by 1986 the SMR was 110. A recent study has shown that prolonged use of oral contraceptive pills from an early age (in the teens or early twenties) makes the occurrence of breast cancer before the age of 36 more likely. What is now being studied in a further research project is whether this risk will be maintained for older women in their late thirties or forties. Previous research has found that women who start using the pill in their mid twenties or thirties do not face an increased risk. The modern low dose pill which contains 50 microgrammes or less of oestrogen is safer than the pills containing higher doses. The reduction in mortality from cancer of the breast is linked with early diagnosis. The type of cancer is also an important factor – the most rapidly spreading types being those which occur in pregnancy and lactation. Much cancer education today is directed towards explaining how important it is for women to palpate their breasts regularly (when taking a bath is usually most convenient) and to report to their doctor at once if any form of lump is discovered, so that an investigation can be made immediately. Note that the survival rate seven years after treatment is 43.6% and there is evidence that the earlier treatment is started, the better the results.

Mammography

The Forrest report published in 1986 pointed out that all studies had shown the value of mammography, particularly for women over the age of 50 years. This test uses single mediolateral oblique X-rays of the breast and enables very early diagnosis of cancer of the breast to be made. Many District Health Authorities are at present planning to introduce mammography as a screening test for cancer of the breast during the next three years. In the UK all women between the ages of 50 and 64 years are to be invited for screening by mammography by March 1993. Screening for older women (over 64 years of age) will be provided on request every three years.

It is particularly important to follow up very carefully (using mammography) any woman who has already had one cancer of the breast as research studies have shown there is a 4–6 fold risk of a primary cancer developing in the opposite breast.

Cancer of the stomach

In England and Wales the fourth commonest cancer is that of the stomach – in 1989, 9062 people (5465 men and 3597 women) died from cancer of the stomach. Deaths from this cancer have been falling steadily – there has been a fall of 11.3% from 1982 to 1989. It is interesting to note the following with regard to cancer of the stomach.

- There is a well-marked variation in the social classes rising steadily from an SMR of 50 for Class I to 158 for Class V (see Fig. 9.2).
- There is a well-marked geographical association with the highest rates in the rural areas of North Wales.
- There is an association between chronic gastric irritation (chronic gastritis or a previous gastric ulcer) and the subsequent development of a cancer. Also those with pernicious anaemia have three times the incidence of the general population.
- Genetic factors may be significant. Persons with blood group A have a 20% greater incidence.
- Diet may play a part. The high Austrian incidence may be connected with the highly spiced foods eaten in that country.

Cancer of the colon

Cancer of the colon is the second commonest cause of death from cancer, after cancer of the lung in men and cancer of the breast in

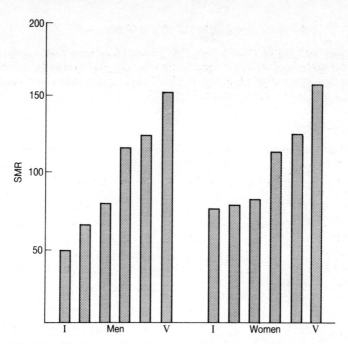

Fig. 9.2 Mortality from cancer of the stomach by social class in men and women aged 20–64 years, England and Wales, 1979–80, 1982–83. (From *Occupational Mortality*, OPCS, 1987.)

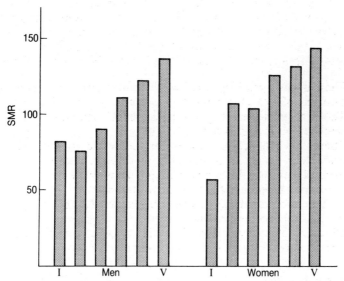

Fig. 9.3 Mortality from cancer of the bladder by social class in men and women aged 20–64 years, England and Wales, 1979–80, 1982–83. (From *Occupational Mortality*, OPCS, 1987.)

women. In 1989 in England and Wales, 5282 men and 6344 women died from this condition. Studies in Nottingham in England have shown that screening a general practice population for occult blood in the stools enables the diagnosis to be made at an early (and treatable) stage.

Cancer of the bladder

More cases of cancer of the bladder occur in men than women – a ratio of 2 to 1. In 1989 in England and Wales 3177 deaths due to cancer of the bladder occurred in men and 1575 in women. Many different causes have been identified, including the following.

- Smoking has been shown to be an important factor.
- Occupation (reference has already been made to the incidence of cancer of the bladder in the rubber and cable industries due to the exposure of workers to benzidine and naphthylamine based derivatives).
- Infestation of the bladder by *Schistoma haematobium*. This is a common cause of cancer of the bladder in Egypt and Tanzania.

There is a marked social class gradient in this cancer (see Fig. 9.3).

Bronchitis

In the last 20 years there has been a remarkable drop in the number of deaths from bronchitis in England and Wales, and this trend is still continuing (see Table 9.6). This fall represents a drop of 50.1% in men and 29.7% in women. This probably reflects the greater reduction in the numbers of men now smoking, while the proportion of women who have stopped smoking has fallen to a lesser extent.

The social class gradient is very marked in both sexes (see Fig. 9.4).

Hypertensive disease

Hypertensive disease has shown the greatest fall in mortality of any disease during the period 1961–87 and the fall still continues (see Table 9.7). The reason for the large and continuing fall is undoubtedly the success of treatment with anti-hypertensive drugs which lower the blood pressure without curing the cause of the hypertension. However, as the main hazards of hypertension are the physical damage to blood vessels that prolonged high pressure produces, this treatment is very effective provided it is continued for the rest of the patient's life. This is an important health education point that all nurses should emphasise to hypertensive patients.

Table 9.6 Deaths from bronchitis, England and Wales, 1981–88. (From OPCS Monitors, DH 2 Series.)

	Males	Females
1981	13482	5651
1988	6666	3971

Table 9.7 Deaths from hypertensive disease per 100000 population, England and Wales, 1961–87. (From various OPCS Monitors, DH 2 Series.)

Years	Males	Females
1961	31.7	40.5
1966	21.6	27.5
1971	17.6	20.4
1976	14.2	16.8
1980	10.6	12.0
1986	7.5	9.1
1987	6.7	8.2

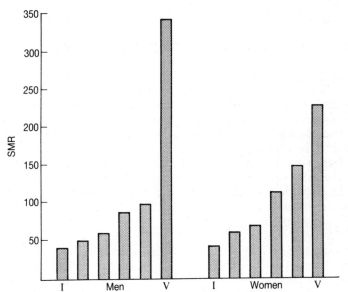

Fig. 9.4 Mortality from bronchitis by social class in men and women aged 20–64 years, England and Wales, 1979–80, 1982–83. (From *Occupational Mortality*, OPCS, 1987.)

Peptic ulceration

Peptic ulceration shows a marked variation in mortality between the social classes (see Fig. 9.5). There are other marked epidemiological

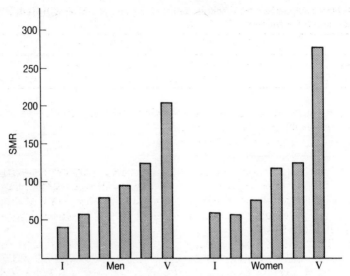

Fig. 9.5 Mortality from peptic ulceration by social class in men and women aged 20–64 years, England and Wales, 1979–80, 1982–83. (From *Occupational Mortality*, OPCS, 1987.)

differences between gastric and duodenal ulceration. Gastric ulcers are four times commoner in men than in women. Duodenal ulceration is more often associated with mental stress – there is a particular increase in the incidence of duodenal ulcer in professional persons such as doctors and lawyers who accept a considerable degree of personal responsibility.

There is often a strong association with the occupational regime followed by patients suffering from peptic ulcers. Those whose occupations do not allow them to have regular meals, such as long-distance drivers, can often trace relapses in the ulcer history to periods when irregular meals were usual.

The prevention of recurrence of peptic ulcers depends as much on being able to regulate, as far as possible, the life of the patient so that irregular meals and worry are avoided, as on the medical treatment of the condition.

Deaths from both gastric ulcer and duodenal ulcer are falling in both men and women.

Diabetes

Diabetes is commoner in women than in men (ratio approximately 4:3). During the 1980s, and particularly from 1983–87, the mortality from diabetes increased dramatically in both sexes (see Table 9.8),

Table 9.8 Deaths from diabetes mellitus, England and Wales, 1980–87. (From various OPCS Monitors, DH 2 Series.)

	1980	1982	1983	1984	1985	1987	1988
Men	1993	1979	1955	2687	3156	3327	3380
Women	2788	2555	2561	3682	4296	4310	4492

although deaths remained fairly static in 1987 and 1988. The cause of the increase up to 1987 is not clear.

The disease is really of two types.

- The more serious diabetes seen in younger persons in which there is a strong heredity factor. In studies of such diabetes it has been shown that if one twin develops the disease the chance of the other also developing diabetes is five times greater in identical twins than in other twins.
- The 'adult' type of diabetes which is a much milder disease usually controllable by diet. There is a higher incidence of adult diabetes in overweight persons. In the 1939–45 war, less adult diabetes occurred and this was probably connected with less overnutrition due to food rationing. The avoidance of obesity is therefore an important preventive feature of adult diabetes (see below).

Another aspect of diabetes where tertiary prevention is possible is to ensure that treatment prescribed is properly carried out by arranging for a health visitor or diabetes specialist nurse to visit all diabetic patients regularly. If the health visitor is attached to the diabetic clinic or general practice, he or she will be able to get to know the treatment prescribed for each patient. By visiting regularly he or she can check whether the treatment is understood and is being followed and whether any early complications, such as peripheral skin lesions are present.

Adverse social conditions in the home can have a disastrous effect on the treatment of diabetes and this visiting can reduce difficulties at home. It also allows the physician treating the disease a means of discovering, at an early stage, any problems which the patient may have in treating him or herself at home.

Obesity

Marked overweight is associated with an increased tendency to develop the following diseases:

— diabetes;
— ischaemic heart disease and heart failure;
— degenerative arthritis in weight bearing joints (hips and knees).

As the obesity increases, the expectation of life of the individual falls – it has been estimated that the expectation of life decreases by 1% for every 1 lb weight above normal. Because of this clear association, much illness can be prevented by reducing the weight of persons who are excessively overweight. In particular, it is most important that the tendency towards overweight is checked early in adult life and *especially in the age group 35 to 50 years*. The aim should always be to keep the weight below average.

Three distinct types of obesity are given below.

- *'Hibernators'* Overweight persons who have adapted to low-energy diets so that dieting produces less and less effect. Such patients can now have their metabolic rate (and therefore their rate of weight loss) returned to normal under carefully controlled conditions in a metabolic ward.
- *'Compulsive eaters'* These form a large and well-recognised group whose obesity is entirely due to their continuously ingesting much larger quantities than they need. Any method which reduces the food intake of such patients will reduce their weight. Various strictly controlled dieting methods can be used but often fail eventually because of the tendency of such people to over-eat later. A novel and simple method is to fit such patients with a dental splint which forces them to stick to a milk-based diet. This has proved a satisfactory method for it prevents any return to uncontrolled eating at the end of any dietary regime.
- *'Small' fat people* The energy requirements of these people are very small because they have so little lean tissue. Such obese patients, who fortunately are a small group, are very difficult to treat and the condition may prove intractable once it has become firmly established.

Treatment for overweight

An important initial stage is to ensure that the individual is properly motivated i.e. is determined to lose weight. Once that has been established, the aims should be as given below.

- To lose weight gradually – if a loss of 1 lb per week can be achieved and, if this can be kept up, nearly four stone (25 kg) can be lost in a year.
- To understand as much as possible about calories in food and drinks. Simple calorie guides (booklets) are useful as they educate the individual and especially demonstrate which foods should be avoided.
- To aim at taking approximately 1100–1300 calories a day for only eight weeks at a time and then have a break for two weeks before

returning to the restricted calorie regime. If this is done, the 'hibernator' syndrome is unlikely to develop.

- To remember to count the calories of everything which passes the lips – food and drink and especially alcohol (most alcoholic drinks contain at least 100 calories).
- To have three simple meals a day and to avoid snacks between meals.
- To take plenty of fibre, i.e. fruit, green vegetables and salads. Some of these contain very low amounts of calories and are extremely useful in making up bulk in foods without adding much to the calories consumed.
- To take most calories early in the day rather than later in the evening – avoid very small breakfasts and snack lunches and wherever possible have light evening meals.
- If unsuccessful to try many different approaches – some individuals are helped by a group (e.g. Weightwatchers) but this is only likely to be of lasting value when it becomes a constant feature.
- To avoid crash diets or any special efforts (such as 'health farms'). What is required is constant control of intake of food and drinks.

Epilepsy

The problems created by epilepsy include the following.

— To find an effective treatment which will control the fits.
— To help the patient to overcome the social disadvantages which too often follow epilepsy.
— Treatment must be continuous and always calls for much care and patience to ensure that the best combination of drugs is found.
— Unfortunately many stigmas are attached to the patient with epilepsy, mainly due to ignorance on the part of the public who mistakenly believe that it causes dangerous behaviour. Many patients find it essential to conceal their disease.

Often, much illness and many problems can be prevented by special care being taken in the rehabilitation of people with epilepsy. The question of stigma must never be ignored. By the better understanding, which follows social after-care and preventive work, it is often possible to prevent someone who suffers from epilepsy from losing their job, and thus to add stability to life.

Much still needs to be done both individually with patients and collectively to educate the general public as to the true nature of this disease. Reference has already been made in Chapter 5 to the educational problems in epilepsy (see pages 101–2).

Diseases connected with occupation

A number of diseases are caused by contact with various poisons, irritants and dusts. The prevention of such industrial diseases is the responsibility of the occupational health services.

Strict standards are laid down regarding the uses of all dangerous chemicals, solvents and gases in industry which could lead to illness. These include the following.

— Dangerous metals, e.g. lead, phosphorous, mercury, arsenic, manganese, antimony, cadmium, chromium, nickel, copper, aluminium.
— Oils, pitch and tar.
— Dangerous gases, e.g. ammonia, benzol, carbon dioxide, carbon monoxide, carbon tetrachloride, chlorine, nitrous fumes, petrol, phosgene, sulphur dioxide, sulphuretted hydrogen, trichlorethylene.
— Dangerous solvents.
— Radiation hazards in industry.

Safety measures in industry come under the HM Superintending Inspector of Factories to whom all poisoning accidents must be reported. A full investigation is always carried out and wide publicity given to any important preventive method recommended.

Illnesses from industrial poisons vary greatly, from blood disorders to cancers of the skin and to occupational dermatitis. In some instances, such as workers who are continuously working with lead, regular routine blood tests must be carried out to make certain that no hidden changes are occurring in the blood which could be a sign of cumulative poisoning.

Some industrial dermatitis can be avoided by all workers having a medical examination *before* they start to work on hazardous jobs. In this way, it is possible to prevent certain susceptible people ever running these risks. This has been very useful in ensuring that persons with a previous or family history of dermatitis are never employed in a process in which dermatitis is a hazard.

Prevention of dust diseases

The chronic inhalation of certain dusts eventually leads to the development of pathological lesions in the lungs. The most dangerous dusts are those containing minute particles of *silica* or *asbestos dusts*.

The term *pneumoconiosis* is used to describe diseases caused by these dusts. The industries in which dusts are hazards include a section of the coal-mining industry where extraction of coal includes mining in areas where silica dust occurs. The level of pneumoconiosis (especially silicosis) was very high from some mines before preventive health measures were introduced. *Silicosis* is a fibrotic lung disease in which the lung tissue is slowly destroyed and replaced by fibrosis. Emphysema with loss of vital capacity follows, leading eventually to complete invalidism. Tuberculosis is a common complication.

Strict preventive measures now include the following.

— Regular medical examinations, including X-ray, of all people employed in any occupation in which pneumoconiosis is a risk.
— Immediate suspension from work of anyone found to be suffering from pneumoconiosis, including the earliest radiological signs, or from tuberculosis, together with the payment of a special financial benefit.

As well as these medical examinations, dust diseases can be prevented by undertaking the following measures.

— Replacement of a dangerous dust with a harmless one. An example is replacement of sandstone wheels for grinding metals by carborundum. Of course, this replacement is not possible in mining.
— Dust suppression by good general ventilation, by exhaust ventilation over the process, or by introducing a wet process in which dusts are kept to the minimum.
— Personal protection of the workforce by the wearing of masks. This is usually only possible for short spells. General reliance should never be placed on workers wearing protective masks.

The inhalation of asbestos dust over a period of years leads to *asbestosis*. This disease is rather similar to silicosis, although tuberculosis is a rare complication. However, the *risk of cancer of the lung is greatly increased in asbestosis* and has been estimated to be at least ten times that of the general population.

The various preventive measures mentioned above have greatly reduced the risk of developing pneumoconiosis. They also reduce the seriousness of the condition if it occurs by removing the individual from the dusty occupation as soon as the earliest abnormal signs are discovered on X-ray.

Prevention of accidents

Increased attention has been paid recently to all forms of accidents both at work, in the home and on the road.

Traffic accidents

In England and Wales in 1987, 4754 persons (3319 men and 1435 women) were killed in accidents on the roads. This represents a 9.3% fall from the 1982 figures – the year before the compulsory seat belt legislation. Although there was a marked fall'in injuries and deaths of drivers and front seat passengers in the period 1983–87 (demonstrating the effectiveness of such preventive measures) the greater use of motor vehicles has restricted the fall.

Industrial accidents

About 550 persons are killed every year at work. There are many contributory factors in occupational accidents, all of which are preventable. Accidents at work can be prevented by adhering to the following practices.

— Careful selection and training of personnel in the factory. Certain people are found to be 'accident prone' – that is, they are very liable to have accidents. Such people can sometimes be recognised early and steps taken to see that they are not placed in positions of danger.
— Complete investigation of all accidents. This is undertaken by the Chief Inspector of Factories who publishes an illustrated booklet every quarter where the causes of accidents are analysed so that the reasons for the accidents can be pointed out, and similar catastrophes avoided.
— Good working conditions – good lighting, intelligent use of colours in factories, proper guarding of all machinery.
— Good discipline among employees including the wearing of protective clothing. In the United Kingdom there has been great resistance to protective clothing – for instance, the wearing of steel helmets on building-sites. However, there are now signs that more protective clothing is being worn – certainly it can be decisive in preventing injury in the event of an accident.

Home accidents

Reference has already been made, in Chapter 4, to the importance of preventing home accidents among children. There is a great deal of social class differential in accident mortality among children aged 1–14 years, as well as a consistently higher level in boys compared with girls at all ages as shown by Table 9.9.

The other age group which is particularly liable to home accidents is those over the age of 75 years. Falls and falling objects are the main cause of such accidents. The extra dangers which this age group

Table 9.9 Fatal accidents in childhood by sex and social class (1–14 years), England and Wales, 1979–80, 1982–3. Rates per 100000 population. (From Occupational Mortality, OPCS, 1979–80, 1982–83.)

| | Social Class | | | | | | | Ratio |
	I	II	IIIN	IIIM	IV	V	All	V/I
Boys	24.6	36.1	41.9	55.2	63.9	118.1	56.3	4.8
Girls	16.9	17.1	19.6	21.9	33.1	61.4	26.8	3.6

Table 9.10 Deaths from home accidents, England and Wales, 1988. (From OPCS Monitors, DH4, 88/5, 89/1, 89/2.)

Age group	Males	Females
0–14	134	79
15–44	461	157
45–64	324	204
65–74	257	279
75+	690	1647

experience are clearly shown in Table 9.10 which gives the details of home accidents for England and Wales in 1988. It is important to note the higher number of deaths in women over the age of 75 years than in men. This is connected not only with the larger number of women compared with men at that age but with the fact that the rate of accidents rises sharply in the eighties and nineties. These accidents can be prevented by the following measures.

— Good lighting, especially on staircases, landings and passages.
— Renewal of faulty equipment – worn carpets, broken stair rods, carpets not properly secured, trailing wires from electrical equipment, loose floor boards.
— Ensuring that visual defects in the elderly are corrected by suitable spectacles.
— Better understanding by old people of the dangers of home accidents – more effective health education in this respect would help.

Prevention of mental illness

The exact cause of most mental illness is not yet fully understood. However, a great deal is already known about some of the most important factors related to its development. These include the following.

• *Intrinsic* factors connected with the individual and particularly associated with

— heredity factors
— developmental factors.

- *Extrinsic* factors to do with the individual's occupation, home and life surroundings.

- *Intrinsic* factors are complicated. Hereditary factors are more of an inherited predisposition to develop mental illness than being born with an illness. The predisposition may never result in illness and the likelihood of illness developing even in someone with a predisposition depends more on stages in the individual's life and environmental (extrinsic) factors.

  The most likely times for mental illness to develop in any individual are puberty, pregnancy, the menopause, late middle age and retirement. Mental illness is the commonest cause of days lost from work in women but only the fourth commonest in man.

- *Extrinsic* or environmental factors are even more complicated as each person continuously selects different features from the environment. The more unsatisfactory and insecure the surroundings of anyone, the more likely it is that mental illness will develop but each person will react differently if placed in the same surroundings.

  Once a mental illness has started, the longer the illness goes on, the more likely it is to be permanent, regardless of the detailed circumstances associated with its commencement. It is, therefore, important to try and diagnose even the very early signs of mental illness – in say a child – for early diagnosis will help treatment.

  Many 'functional' disorders are due to bad social effects in childhood, or too rigid or ill-judged moral or cultural standards, or rejection by a parent. Many such problems are met by social workers, health visitors and school nurses in their ordinary work. More and more arrangements are being made to introduce preventive psychiatry into child care services, and many authorities have introduced psychiatrists into the routine work of the child health clinic and in work in community homes with disturbed deprived children.

  It is impossible to protect any person from all mental or physical trauma in life – in fact, attempts to do this may very well encourage mental breakdown. It is, however, always possible to alter an environment in one way or another and this may help to avoid an impending illness.

  The occupation and work which a person does has an important effect on mental stability. Much illness can be averted by employment suitable for the person. Careful medical and psychological testing before people are placed in various occupations can help to avoid subsequent mental illness.

  Training schemes, as described in Chapter 17, for mentally

handicapped persons are invaluable in helping them to be rehabilitated. Great care must always be taken with the placement of children with severe emotional or behavioural disorders in industry when they leave school.

Finally, it is most important that sensible, true and balanced advice is always given. Health education programmes should always be aware of the dangers of wrong advice which may be handed down from parents and grandparents. Many needless fears can be caused in this way and these, in a person predisposed to mental illness, may be the spark which starts off an illness.

10 The rôle of the nurse in prevention of ill-health: with special reference to health education

Types of prevention

There are three types of prevention – primary, secondary and tertiary – and nurses play an important part in all, especially those nurses who work in the community, in primary health care teams in general practice, or in close association with them.

- *Primary prevention* is the complete avoidance of disease. This includes persuading families and individuals to take advantage of *prophylactic measures*, such as *immunisation*, against certain diseases. Many immunisations are given to infants and young children but a number are also given to adults who may be in a hazardous situation because of their occupation or who need protection against diseases endemic to a country to which they intend to travel. *Health education* is an important part of primary prevention, for example in persuading people to avoid certain habits, such as smoking, which are known to damage health. The illnesses which may be caused by such habits often occur many years later. Fluoridation of water supplies and the use of toothpastes containing fluorides are further examples of primary prevention.
- *Secondary prevention* (often called '*screening*') is aimed at detecting the very earliest signs of disease before any symptoms are apparent. Many such tests are carried out on infants and toddlers (e.g. tests to discover congenital dislocation of the hip, phenylketonurea, and hypothyroidism). Nurses play a crucial role in all of these, mainly in carrying out the tests, ensuring that the correct treatment is undertaken and in subsequent counselling. Once the problem has been discovered immediate treatment can be given and this usually prevents the disease developing its potentially damaging effects.

  Screening is also important in adults. For example the detection of early hypertension (raised blood pressure) in adults enables effective treatment to be commenced before any permanent damage has been done. Provided that this treatment is continued for the remainder of the individual's life the serious stage of the disease and its sequelae may never be reached. Cervical cytology is another example of secondary prevention.

● *Tertiary prevention* is concerned with persons already suffering from some chronic disease. It *aims to prevent serious complications developing* by treating the disease in such a way that permanent handicaps do not result, hence preventing much disability. In many of these diseases complications develop insiduously over years and their prevention calls for much careful painstaking work. An essential feature of tertiary prevention is to *ensure that patients understand a great deal about their condition* and how it can damage health or produce disability. Much of this health education is undertaken by nurses working in association with primary health care teams. The success or failure of tertiary prevention usually means the difference between the patient eventually being able to lead a reasonably normal life or becoming an invalid. Hence tertiary prevention is crucial to the quality of life of such patients.

As the proportion of very elderly persons in the community increases (see page 312), the need for successful tertiary prevention, and the importance of the role of many nurses working in the community, will become even greater.

Health education

All three forms of prevention depend on being able to convince parents, children and adults that it is important to prevent diseases or to mitigate their effects. The practice of health education involves persuading individuals to make the right choice and is a continuing process throughout all stages of life. In the end, the success of health education will depend on the person concerned making balanced decisions based on logic, rejecting what is obviously unwise and choosing what is sensible. In many instances the choice is not clear cut. Most people will have to modify and change what they choose to do a number of times during their lifetime as evidence accumulates suggesting that a particular habit or practice is more hazardous to health than was previously thought. People, both children and adults, should be encouraged to adopt a flexible approach, and it is important that any professional involved in health education never adopts an authoritarian attitude. Advice that is too rigid and has to be modified as new facts emerge is likely to alienate many people and will undermine their future confidence. At the same time, the health professional should guide and lead and, in so doing, take some responsibility for the individual's health.

Health education falls into three main categories.

- Individual health education
- Group health education
- Mass media health education.

In most cases the final decision made by any individual depends on features from all three categories of education, but particularly individual and mass media health education. In many instances advertising (or persuasion) in the mass media can be said to prepare the individual to make some decision or to take some action, for example choose one type of food rather than another, accept advice to change a potentially dangerous habit such as smoking, or to use condoms because of the danger of HIV infection and AIDS. Individuals may seek expert advice before deciding that a suggested change in lifestyle is justified. In health matters it is likely that advice may be sought from the nurse working in the community (health visitor, district nurse or practice nurse) or a nurse who happens to be a neighbour or friend. Although the advice may be sought in an unofficial or casual way, the effectiveness of the reply and the advice given may well be crucial to the individual's final decision. Hence *the rôle of nurses is very important in practical prevention of ill-health*, whether it be primary, secondary or tertiary prevention.

This chapter provides details of the various preventive procedures commonly used in the community and associated with primary health care. In practice, much primary and secondary prevention is carried out continuously and simultaneously and these two forms are discussed together. Subdivisions have been made into prevention in (*i*) infants and children; (*ii*) young adults (aged 18 to 25 years); (*iii*) adults (aged 26 to 64 years) and (*iv*) elderly persons. However it must be emphasised that health education for the prevention of any disease and the promotion of well-being should be exercised for all persons in whatever age group whenever appropriate.

Primary and secondary prevention

Infants and children

Infants and children provide one of the best opportunities to prevent many diseases and in this respect the rôle of the health visitor is crucial (their rôle in child health care has already been described in Chapter 4). The practice nurse may assist the health visitor but it is usually the latter who initiates most preventive measures through constant *individual health education*. Regular home visits, beginning immediately following the birth, enable the health visitor to assess accurately many important relevant details and to offer practical advice on, for example, *infant feeding problems* and the *prevention of accidents* in the home.

All forms of *immunisation* described in Chapter 6 are excellent examples of primary prevention. The way that many health visitors are able to achieve a greater than 90% immunisation rate in infants is by becoming the friend and adviser of the mother.

The health visitor is also in a position to be able to carry out a series of *screening tests* in the home, for example tests to exclude congenital dislocation of the hip, phenylketonuria and hypothyroidism (see pages 74–5). Follow-up examinations are usually carried out at special child clinics held at the health centre (or other clinic).

Child clinics provide an excellent opportunity for *group health education*, with small groups of mothers (say 5–8) being encouraged to participate in discussion of a particular subject with the health visitor. Visual aids, including short video films and overhead projection slides, may be useful here. Group health education is valuable as it helps people realise that others may be experiencing similar problems to themselves – a realisation which can be very reassuring. Often the health education and learning process continue in further discussions outside the group.

Mass media health education, through leaflets, booklets and posters, can also influence those attending health centres and child health clinics. Once interest has been aroused, by far the most influential mass media health education comes from the radio and television. However the impact of such information is greater when there is an opportunity to discuss the topic further with a health care professional, such as the health visitor or practice nurse. The combination of mass media and individual health education is very effective – mass media health education raises the interest in a subject, but it is usually individual health education that is the more decisive.

Social pressures within any group can also become powerful influences towards change. For example, when it is generally accepted by a group of mothers that smoking by an expectant mother is detrimental to the health of the baby, the mother who continues to smoke is likely to feel under considerably more pressure to give up the habit.

Occasionally a natural opportunity presents itself to a group to discuss a subject in more detail. A sudden cot death may become the centre of interest and discussion, or a serious case of child abuse (physical or sexual) which has been widely reported in the press may provide the health visitor with the opportunity to raise the subject and to get the group to discuss it together. Advice given at this time is likely to make a big impression and can be extremely valuable in health education. This indicates how health education can become a continuous process involving many people in their ordinary lives.

Another technique which health visitors (and practice nurses) may find useful is to identify special 'at risk' groups of infants in whom the level of certain congenital deformities is likely to be higher than normal (see pp. 76–77). Most general practices keep records of their families and patients (age/sex registers) and the use of computers in keeping these records is increasing.

Computerised records are invaluable in providing health visitors, practice nurses and school nurses with much information which could help in the prevention of health problems. For example recall and check of immunisations and follow-up visits, records of any previous accidents in the family (multiple accidents occur in some families indicating special hazards in that home), child abuse problems and analysis of other useful and relevant data. It is known, for instance, that general child mortality is twice as high in Social Class V than in Social Classes I and II so a record of the social class of each patient in the age/sex register would be useful.

Young adults (aged 18 to 25 years)

Independence is very precious in early adult life and most young adults are eager to demonstrate that they are now making their own decisions. It is also a time of much questioning of accepted rules and customs. *Mass media health education* can have a marked effect at this stage of life provided it is subtle and not authoritarian – an authoritarian approach can be counterproductive, especially with this age group. Many social habits, which can have an important effect on later health, are determined at this age. Smoking and alcohol may be experimented with and the outcome, whether the young adult persists to become a permanent smoker or heavy drinker, may well be determined. There is usually little contact with the health services for those aged 18–25 years unless some physiological event like pregnancy occurs. At the same time most young persons are eager to learn more about health and its problems and many will be reading widely.

This is the time when sexual behaviour is becoming very important and there will be opportunities for *individual health education* especially in further education, university or in work situations. Great concern is being expressed at present on the spread of AIDS and its potential threat to future generations. It is most important that young adults fully understand the facts (see Chapter 8). A certain amount of 'trial and error' is bound to take place, hence it is essential to stress the value of condoms (providing a physical barrier to infection) and that casual sexual contacts should be avoided thereby reducing the risk of HIV infection. If the message is presented in a clear lucid way, it is more likely that young people will adopt sensible sexual behaviour, i.e. one monogamous sexual relationship.

An especially important time for health care professionals to practise health education is when pregnancy occurs for the first time. This is discussed further in the next section although it is recognised that such education is just as important for and applicable to young adults who are about to embark on parenthood. However, in at least 25% of young persons a first pregnancy will occur when the partners are unmarried, although a proportion will marry before the child is born. Abortion is an option that may well be considered and the nurse often has a difficult task in giving balanced advice on the subject. The nurse must always be very careful to *respect the confidentiality of any information received*. Whether or not parents are involved must be left to the young person. Unless confidentiality is always absolute, a person's confidence in health professionals may be destroyed and the potential to help in the future may be lost.

Adults (aged 26 to 64 years)

As mentioned previously, health education should be a continuous process. Many of the points discussed below may well be applicable when providing health care, including health education, to young adults.

To many people, marriage and setting up a new home together is a crucial step in their lives. Usually both partners bring to their new life principles and habits learnt in their parental homes. In the first months and years many of the essentials of their future life together are determined – their sexual life, the pattern of their day-to-day routine, including diet and nutrition, habits such as smoking or alcohol consumption, their recreation, sport and exercise, their holidays and general attitude to life. Their first experience of illness together and their reaction to it will also be important. Pregnancy is another challenge for it forms an essential part of the maturation process of any marriage. It will inevitably lead to many reappraisals by the couple and many changes in the pattern of their life together.

Increasingly health care professionals are realising that the *first pregnancy, and particularly the antenatal period, is an ideal time for health education*. Once any couple realise that the future health and well being of their expected child is largely in their own hands, health education is likely to be very effective. It is important to involve, and not to isolate, the father-to-be both in the preparation for and in the birth itself.

Screening by amniocentesis has already been described in Chapter 3 (see page 56) and is increasingly being used to identify possible problems in the infant, such as an open neural tube defect (spina bifida), Down's syndrome (this is especially important for mothers over 35 years of age and for those who have already given birth to a child with Down's syndrome or have a family history of such children), and Duchenne muscular dystrophy. In families that are known to have had a case of Duchenne muscular dystrophy 50% of all boys born will, on average, be affected, hence a knowledge of the sex of the child is important. The same is true of haemophilia. All health care professionals should be knowledgeable about these tests so that they can give sound advice to anyone who wishes to discuss this type of screening.

Most expectant mothers are very keen to do anything which will give their expected baby the best possible chance in life. Many will be prepared to give up smoking – partners should also be encouraged to do so. Many sacrifices have to be made for anyone to become a caring parent and the attitudes of both parents during the pregnancy may be the starting point of a sounder and happier relationship, or the opposite. There may be ignorance regarding the subject of sex in the antenatal period and this should be discussed with both parents to avoid any unnecessary decisions which may lead to resentment and/or guilt.

Much importance is placed on the *nutrition* of the mother during the antenatal period (see also page 55) and on the feeding of the baby. This provides an excellent opportunity for health education into what is essential not only for the baby and mother but for all the family in the future. The value of protein intake, vitamins (taken both in natural foods or as a supplement), calcium (it is in these early years of life that this is so essential if a disease like osteoporosis is to be prevented later), fibre intake, fluid consumption and not too much salt in foods – all these should be considered. A real attempt should always be made to explain why certain parts of our diet are so important, for example why fibre is required for the healthy function of the colon and therefore for the avoidance of diseases such as diverticulitis.

Many women begin to put on excess weight during their first pregnancy or in the following couple of years. The *avoidance of obesity* is one of the more essential preventive lessons which should be learnt at this stage of life. Explanations should stress that all individuals are different in the way they burn up calories – some will rarely put on excessive weight whilst others will rapidly do so even if taking the same diets. A reappraisal of the type of food eaten is of value after pregnancy. Every effort should be made to encourage anyone who has a tendency to overweight to learn how foods vary greatly in their calorie content. A simple booklet purchased from all newsagents under such titles as *Your greatest guide to calories* can be invaluable. Anyone who uses such a guide will quickly realise what type of foods contain large amounts of calories and therefore should be avoided.

Obesity (see also pages 163–5) is a constant threat to some people and the problem of overweight can easily get out of hand, especially in the 35 to 50 years age group. Any information learnt earlier can therefore be very useful. It is never too early to emphasise that gross overweight is associated with a considerable reduction in life expectancy – such individuals will always be heavily penalised in life assurance premiums.

The experience of an expectant mother having her blood pressure taken on every antenatal visit may well raise the question of the *value of regular blood pressure checks* later in life. It is a wise precaution for everyone to have their blood pressure checked every 2–3 years – the practice nurse should be able to arrange this. Early hypertensive disease (see page 160) often produces no symptoms and it is always an advantage to identify such disease early so that effective treatment to lower the blood pressure to normal levels can be started.

Osteoporosis is a disease which mainly affects elderly women. The early preventive measures include ensuring the child and young adult have an adequate intake of calcium (milk etc.). Increasing evidence suggests that hormone replacement therapy at the time of the menopause will markedly reduce the incidence of osteoporosis in later life. An increasing proportion of general practitioners are now giving hormone replacement therapy routinely at the menopause and the health visitor or practice nurse should be able to trace such women from the age–sex register and arrange for such treatment. At the same time women who are at special risk of osteoporosis could be identified. Women who are at special risk include those who have a thin physique, have an early menopause, drink excessive coffee, take alcohol regularly, smoke cigarettes, have taken steroids in the past and those whose lifestyle is sedentary or who are relatively immobile.

Occasionally there is a need for special *immunisations* for adults. These include travellers to certain countries (see Chapter 6, page 113) and protection of certain persons at special risk (see Chapter 6, page 110). An example is given by hepatitis B. As this at risk group includes those professionals who may accidentally come into contact with blood (doctors and nurses, those working on renal dialysis units or in blood transfusion units or laboratories) the practice nurse should check on any patients in the practice who fall into these groups and ensure that they are protected. This includes doctors and nurses working in the practice. Checks should also be made on any passive immunisations which may be desirable for patients (see Chapter 6, pages 111–2).

Secondary prevention (or screening) in adults is particularly useful for cancer of the cervix, breast cancer and cancer of the colon (see Chapter 9). The use of computerised records and the inclusion of social class on the age/sex register, as mentioned previously (see page 176), can assist in screening. For instance, the value of cervical cytology (see page 154) is greatest in Social Class V as it is known that mortality is highest in that class (see Table 2.12, page 46). To be able to ensure that all women in Social Class V in any practice have a cervical cytology test would be a great advantage and make the prevention of cancer of the cervix much more effective.

Tests for glaucoma are available free to any adult over 40 years of age with a history of glaucoma in the family.

Health visitors and practice nurses are often involved with screening tests and it is important that they understand the criteria which makes the tests acceptable and effective. The criteria include the following.

- The disease being searched for should always be one which has potentially serious consequences (either life threatening or may lead to a handicap).
- The test should be
  - simple to carry out and unequivocable in interpretation,
  - objective and not subjective,
  - completely safe and not produce fear or apprehension.
- All screening tests must be accompanied by counselling so that the person undergoing the test fully understands the nature of the test, and in the event of it being POSITIVE, THAT TREATMENT MUST BE STARTED IMMEDIATELY.

Elderly persons

All three forms of prevention of ill-health – primary, secondary and tertiary – are of great importance in elderly people. Changes in a person's state of health may occur gradually, especially in their seventies and eighties, and it is useful if the health care professionals can identify these changes as it is then possible to prevent serious deterioration and permanent handicap (tertiary prevention). Some examples of particular health problems in this age group are given below.

Eyesight   As serious impaired sight and blindness are mainly found in this age group (see page 331) an *eye test should be carried out every two years*. Early recognition and treatment for conditions such as *cataract* are important and simple questioning by health visitors, district nurses and practice nurses can often identify those at greatest risk. Two signs suggest that an elderly person may be developing a cataract. Firstly the individual begins to notice that it is easier to see in a dimly lit room (in dim light the iris opens more and allows the clearer part of the lens to transmit more light). Secondly, the individual finds that it is necessary to have his or her glasses changed more frequently. Regular eye tests are important and can help avoid accidents – failing sight is often a contributory cause of falls in elderly persons. Arrangements may need to be made for such tests, especially for very old people living alone. Where necessary someone may have to take the patient to see an optician who will always test not only the eyesight but the tension in the eye (for glaucoma).

Deafness   Deafness is more common in people over the age of 60 years. If failing hearing is suspected a full audiometric test should be carried out. If hearing loss is confirmed and a hearing aid fitted. It is very important to explain that treatment with a hearing aid is usually very disappointing at first. Hearing is normally lost differentially – appreciation of high notes (the consonants in speech) are lost to a greater degree than the low notes (the vowels in speech). The hearing aid, being an amplifier, magnifies all sound equally so the high notes can now be heard but seem to be drowned by the low ones. This is confusing and often leads to the hearing aid being discarded as useless. If only the elderly person would persist with the hearing aid, after some weeks the brain will adjust and the recognition of speech improve significantly. Unless properly treated deafness always has serious consequences as it leads to social isolation.

Foot problems   Minor foot problems are very common in the elderly and can result in considerable limitation of mobility. If discovered early and treated effectively independence can often be maintained. Lack of mobility results not only in isolation but often nutritional difficulties follow as the elderly person finds it impossible to travel far to all types of shops. The incidence of osteoporosis is more likely in immobile elderly women with the danger that even minor accidents may result in fractures.

Nutritional problems   Nutritional problems become much more common in those over the age of 75 years. Health visitors, district nurses and practice nurses should realise that these problems may be occurring, especially in those whose partner has recently died. Many nutritional problems are caused by the survivor (usually the widow) settling for snack meals (e.g. tea and toast) once the discipline of preparing proper balanced meals has eased now that the person is living alone. A simple explanation usually helps as once the elderly person realises that a balanced diet with adequate protein, vegetables and fruit is still important a return to normal eating habits usually follows.

Accidents in the home   For those people over the age of 80 years accidents in the home (mostly falls) are a particular hazard (see page 326). Many are caused by a combination of poor eyesight and bad lighting and advice from health professionals working in the community or in hospital can often help avoid such accidents. The ability to balance in the dark (by the use of the semicircular canals in the inner ear) begins to deteriorate quite quickly in most people once the age of 80 years has been passed and it is therefore essential that a good light is always used if the person has to get up at night.

Confusional states   Two main types of confusional states occur in elderly persons – acute confusional states and Alzheimer's disease.
    If *acute confusional states* are diagnosed correctly and effectively

treated the outlook is usually good and the patient often recovers completely. Many such states are precipitated by chest infections. As dehydration may also be an important contributory cause, an elderly person with a chest infection must be encouraged to drink plenty of fluids. Acute confusional states are also more likely to occur in patients on certain medications (e.g. tranquillisers, β-blockers, cimetidine, anticholinergics and levadopa) or in persons with conditions which often lead to hypoxia (some parts of the body not getting enough oxygen), such as heart failure, respiratory difficulties or anaemias. It is important that nurses point out these possible problems to those caring for such patients, or to the patient him or herself where appropriate.

Acute confusional states start suddenly and the patient is nearly always anxious. This is an important difference from *Alzheimer's disease* where there is a more gradual onset and anxiety is nearly always absent – in fact there seems to be a complete lack of insight or understanding, on the part of the sufferers, as to what is happening and they do not realise that their ability to comprehend common features of life is disappearing.

The ability to recognise and differentiate the two conditions can help in reassuring any relatives who often assume that all confusional states in elderly persons are the beginning of Alzheimer's disease. Confusion caused by illness other than Alzheimer's disease, or by some treatments for other diseases, can, once recognised, usually be easily corrected, although the individual may still have to cope with the underlying condition. Equally the correct diagnosis of Alzheimer's disease in an elderly person defines the most likely future problems and dangers. Any such patient who happens to be living alone is at very special risk and, eventually, full-time care in a psychogeriatric unit or nursing home will be necessary.

Hypothermia Hypothermia in elderly people can be avoided by health education and by careful observations, especially by nurses involved with the care and treatment of such people in their own home. At greatest risk are those who are:

— living alone;
— relatively immobile;
— ill or recently have been ill.

Many elderly people at the greatest risk of hypothermia have a seriously diminished sense of cold and do not feel uncomfortable when sitting in a room which is too cold. Another contributory factor is that a number of elderly people believe that, for good health, it is essential to sleep in a bedroom with the window open, even in the coldest weather in winter. Such habits are often difficult to change but occasionally the opportunity to point out the dangers of cold rooms occurs much earlier in life (when individuals are looking after their own young children). Health education at such a time can do much to disperse this wrong idea and can prevent the danger of hypothermia in the parent later in life.

Tertiary prevention

Tertiary prevention (the prevention of serious complications following chronic illness) is mainly possible in adults and occurs especially in those over the age of 65 years. Many types of patients respond to tertiary prevention including those with the following diseases:

— ischaemic heart disease and peripheral vascular disease;
— hypertensive disease;
— asthma and bronchitis;
— diabetes mellitus;
— many forms of arthritis;
— stroke patients;
— very painful chronic disease;
— accident cases.

The prevention of permanent handicap, leading to a sharp reduction in the quality of life, is most important. To be completely successful *tertiary prevention should form part of a continuous process*, beginning shortly after the commencement of the illness. Tertiary prevention is often synonymous with rehabilitation, which is mainly concerned with ensuring that the patient recovers his or her full function. This often involves considerable improvisations which, in many instances, are to do with mobility. No one can lead a normal life if their mobility becomes seriously restricted. Lack of mobility usually leads, quite rapidly, to social isolation which, in turn, increases the person's handicap.

In teaching those struggling with chronic painful debilitating diseases, such as rheumatoid arthritis or the results of a stroke, to lead useful and reasonably normal lives, the most influential health workers are those in constant contact with the patient and family. This is often the nurse working in the community. Close relatives and friends of the patient may also need help in understanding that *overprotection should be avoided if independence is not to be lost*. 'Respite care' may also be needed for those caring continuously for a patient. Health education should be supplemented with help from community agencies which encourage patients (adult and elderly) to remain actively independent. For example attendance at a day centre, run by either the health or the social services, can help in ensuring that the patient is not over-protected and allows contact with others who may be far more handicapped. Such contact can provide encouragement to the potentially disabled person who sees how much has been achieved by some enterprising individuals, who may be coping with far worse handicaps than themselves.

One of the most serious difficulties which must first be overcome is that of inertia. Too often the patient and relatives feel that all is lost and that it is a waste of time attempting to carry on any normal life. Tertiary prevention will only be successful if such a negative reaction is overcome. Many approaches will usually be needed. Day centres aim not only at getting patients out of the home and mixing with many people but also at motivating individuals and discovering what is most likely to interest them.

Importance of anticipation of future problems   The secret of successful tertiary prevention lies in being able to anticipate future difficulties, not only in the medical and nursing fields but in the environmental and social ones. Housing can be crucial and being in the correct type of accommodation can make all the difference. For anyone with a handicapping illness, especially if it is progressive in which eventually mobility will become a serious problem, it is vital for the nurse to realise that it almost certainly will be necessary for the person to avoid stairs and steps. Adaptations to the ground floor may be possible so that the patient can stay in his or her present home. Patients should seek help from the local social service department and especially their community occupational therapists (see Chapter 16). In illnesses like multiple sclerosis in which patients may gradually lose their mobility, anticipation of such difficulties before they actually occur does much to prevent further handicap and often enables individuals to lead a reasonably normal life because total mobility is lost only towards the end of their illness.

Financial benefits

An understanding of the various financial benefits which are available, particularly the *attendance allowance*, the *mobility allowance* and *invalid care allowance*, is important (see Chapter 16, pages 275–6). Such information should be an essential part of health education and can be quite crucial in preventing further rapid deterioration of the patient and their family. All nurses should know about the scope of such financial help although the minutiae of claiming them can be left to social workers and others working in the welfare benefits field. It should be realised that the potential value of such financial help is often completely negated by ignorance in many people who do not realise that *these benefits are designed to help everyone who is seriously disabled irrespective of their financial means*. The proportion of those applying for allowances such as the attendance allowance is always much lower than the incidence of such seriously disabled people in society. It is up to all in the health and social service fields to increase the 'take up' of this most valuable financial help. Although the allowances cannot compensate for a serious handicap, they can make life much more comfortable for the patient and relatives.

Organisation of health education

The Secretary of State for Health has overall responsibility for the policy and development of health education. Centrally, many functions are delegated to the *Health Education Authority*. Locally, the District Health Authority, through its District Medical Officer, is responsible for health education and the distribution of health education material.

In addition to the rôle of health care professionals already described in this chapter, the following professional staff also have an important rôle in health education.

- *Health education officers*   Over half of all health authorities employ such staff. Many of these officers have had training in a nursing, health visiting or teaching field. Their main function is the organisation and promotion of health education by:
  — training staff to carry out group or individual health education;
  — collecting and distributing suitable material and information;
  — assessing and evaluating the impact of the health education undertaken.
- *General practitioners* have many opportunities for health education especially as the majority of patients have great faith in their doctor's advice. It is important that each doctor realises the opportunities of carrying out health education at all times during his or her practice.
- *Teachers* also have a widespread influence on the lives of their pupils. School life always plays an important part in health education, as any success with children moulds the attitudes of future generations. If children learn how best to avoid disease and maintain good health at school, they are most likely to ensure their own children benefit in the same way.
- *Social workers* are also involved, especially when dealing with children, physically and mentally handicapped persons and those of retirement age.

It will be understood from this list that *health education is a multidisciplinary task* and that the rôle of the professional health education officer is mainly to help others to play a useful part.

The Health Education Authority

The Health Education Authority is the national body set up to organise health education with an annual budget which comes as a direct grant from the Department of Health, the Scottish Home and Health Department, the Welsh Office and the Department of Health, Northern Ireland. The main functions of the Health Education Council include the following.

— To advise on priorities for health education.
— To advise and carry out national or local campaigns in co-operation with health authorities or local authorities.
— To produce information and publicity material and to publish articles of interest to those engaged in health education.
— To sponsor and undertake research including epidemiological and statistical research, cost benefit analysis and evaluation.
— To act as the national centre of expertise in health education.
— To encourage and promote training in health education work.
— To cooperate with local education authorities in schools, colleges and polytechnics.
— To maintain contact with and advise various national voluntary bodies engaged in specialised aspects of health education work.

Voluntary bodies and commercial organisations

Many different voluntary bodies are involved nationally in health education especially in the field of accident prevention e.g. the Royal Society for the Prevention of Accidents (ROSPA), and in cancer education. Commercial organisations mainly prepare visual aid material for use in health education – films, videotapes, filmstrips, slides. Although this material may be self-advertising as well as having a health educational content, much of this commercial advertising is discreetly carried out and the material can be very useful.

11   The world's health problems – the work of the World Health Organisation (WHO)

The control of international health has become increasingly important in a world in which the rate of travel from one country to another is becoming progressively faster. The international controlling body for health in the world is the World Health Organisation (WHO) which was set up from the work of an expert committee of the Economic and Social Council of the United Nations in 1946. By 1989, there were 166 member states in WHO including all the major powers in the world. The headquarters of WHO is at Geneva but there are six regions (see Fig. 11.1):

— Africa with headquarters at Brazzaville;
— Americas with headquarters at Washington DC;
— East Mediterranean with headquarters at Alexandria, Egypt;
— Europe with headquarters at Copenhagen;
— SE Asia with headquarters at New Delhi;
— West Pacific with headquarters at Manila, Philippines.

Each region has its own Regional Advisory Committee on medical research but there is a single coordinating Global Advisory Committee.

Although WHO is concerned with all problems of health, it has always paid particular attention to the value of preventive medicine and has always played an important rôle in stimulating and assisting in developing the preventive medical services of the under-developed countries. The principle that has been constantly followed by WHO is that 'health is now a world responsibility . . . for health, like peace, is one and indivisible'.

A WHO Executive Board meets twice a year in Geneva and a World Health Assembly meets annually. Examples of successful cooperation among member states include the recent eradication of smallpox from the world. In 1978 the World Health Assembly accepted as a new universal aim the theme 'Health for all by Year 2000'.

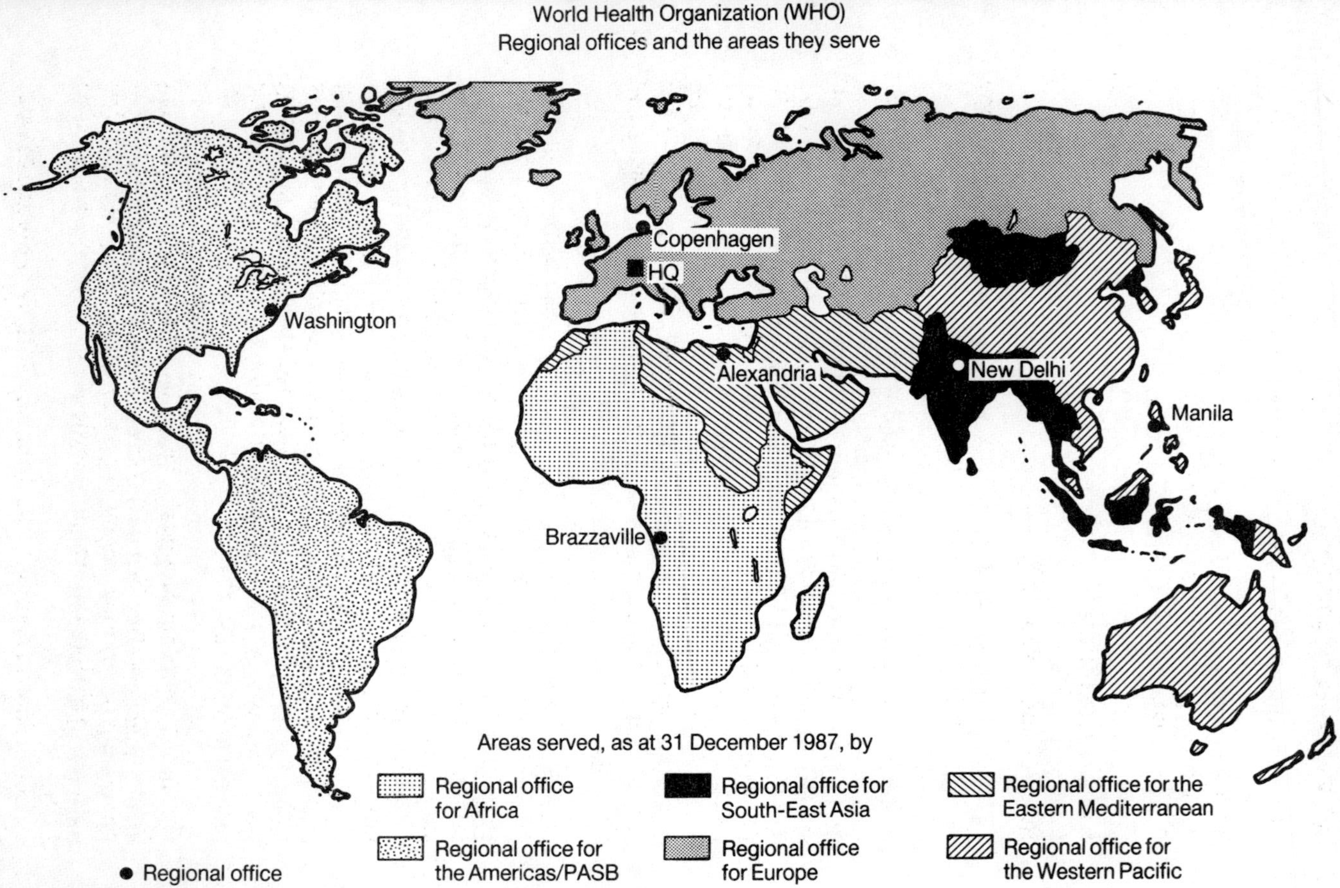

World Health Organization (WHO)
Regional offices and the areas they serve

Manila

New Delhi

Copenhagen

HQ

Alexandria

Brazzaville

Washington

• Regional office

Areas served, as at 31 December 1987, by

Regional office for Africa

Regional office for the Americas/PASB

Regional office for South-East Asia

Regional office for Europe

Regional office for the Eastern Mediterranean

Regional office for the Western Pacific

Fig. 11.1   The six regions of the World Health Organisation (WHO).

Work undertaken by WHO

The work undertaken by WHO falls under three headings.

- Health promotion and care.
- Disease prevention and control.
- Information and teaching.

Health promotion and care

Research and promotion

A great deal of research is carried out, with the help and support of the WHO, in many countries of the world.

General health protection and promotion

Women, health and development   WHO has recently been very much concerned with the increased participation of women in the decision making processes and policy and with the development of health programmes especially in the maternity, child welfare and family planning fields. Studies have been undertaken in Ghana, Mali and Mexico to see how best *women can be used as providers of health care and in the promotion of environmental health*. In Europe, WHO has recently supported studies into emotional aspects of pregnancy and childbirth.

Nutrition   WHO has helped to integrate nutritional priorities in primary health care and guidelines have been published for the training of community health workers in this subject. In 1986 WHO established a breast feeding data bank as part of a global nutritional surveillance programme. This helps to coordinate the results of over 1000 surveys and studies into breast feeding in 126 countries over the last 26 years.

Obesity amongst children and adults has, in the past, mainly been reported from developed countries. However obesity has recently been reported from all WHO regions, including rural developing countries, and WHO is supporting studies into the causes of this overweight at all ages and in all areas.

Oral health (including fluorides)   The WHO global data bank set up a few years ago has reported an increasing tendency for dental caries to be found in developing countries while now a lower prevalence has been reported from developed countries. This is clearly seen in Table 11.1.

The addition of fluoride to diet to prevent teeth decay began 45 years

Table 11.1 Population-weighted mean numbers of decayed, missing or filled teeth per person at 12 years of age, 1980–86. (From *The Work of WHO*, 1986–87, Biennial Report of the Director General of WHO.)

	Developing countries	Developed countries	All countries
1980	1.63	4.53	2.43
1984	2.53	3.88	2.87
1986	2.16	3.82	2.58

ago and WHO has recently been monitoring the results. In the USA 65% of the population is now receiving main water supplies to which fluoride has been added and the results have been dramatic, particularly in cities where the caries rate has decreased markedly.

In the developing countries of South America only 45% of the population have access to main water supplies. Here the addition of fluoride to table salt has been tried extensively with excellent results in the reduction of tooth decay and caries. In Switzerland and France there is widespread use of fluoride toothpastes and WHO has reported good results with far fewer caries.

Accident prevention   Studies have been initiated by WHO into various national safety policies. Two collaborative centres have been set up by WHO – one in Amsterdam, Holland for domestic safety and one in Atlanta, Georgia, USA for injury prevention. In Europe, WHO has continued to cooperate with studies on alcohol and safety in Greece, Hungary, Spain and Yugoslavia.

Protection and promotion of the health of specific population groups

Maternal and child health, including family planning   The main work has concentrated on five subjects – maternal and new born infant care, child health, growth and development, adolescent health and health aspects of family planning (including infertility).

The 'district team problem-solving approach' in maternal and child care health, which was first tried out in 1986 in Malaysia has been a success and, with the help of WHO, has been used in a number of developing countries. An international conference promoted by WHO and held in Nairobi in 1987 stressed the need to give a *high priority to the reduction of maternal mortality especially in developing countries*.

In the field of the care of the new born, studies designed to improve the recognition of small infants who are at high risk have been supported by WHO. Chest circumference measurement (rather than weight) in small infants has been shown to be very reliable at identifying infants likely to be at high risk.

Family planning has been widely supported by WHO since its inception and during 1986 and 1987 WHO provided technical support (directly or indirectly) to 126 family planning projects in 91 countries. The integrated approach towards family planning adopted by WHO includes the prevention of infertility. Studies coordinated by WHO in four countries showed that properly trained primary health care staff equipped with appropriate algorithms (guidelines on step-by-step procedures) and adequate drugs could contribute significantly to the prevention of infertility.

Human reproduction research   Included in the current research being supported and coordinated by WHO is a study of the efficacy of fertility regulatory methods currently being used by 300 000 couples in the world and the evaluation of the short and long-term safety of such methods.

Workers' health   There are three main approaches being used at present by WHO.

— To ensure broader coverage (mainly through primary health care) of the working population.
— To develop innovative guidelines for the protection and promotion of health of people at work with special attention to vulnerable groups.
— To expand the network of WHO coordinating centres for the study of workers' health.

Health of the elderly   Much data on the health of the elderly is collected by WHO. Guidance is given to member states on what best to do for various socio-economic groups of elderly people in order to maintain the well-being of these persons. Fifty participants from all WHO regions attended the last Annual WHO International Course on Epidemiology of Ageing held in London and were trained in methods for developing national policies and programmes.

Protection and promotion of mental health

Psychosocial factors in the promotion of mental health and human development   A recent review in all WHO regions showed an increasing awareness of the importance of mental health issues. Mental health in adolescence is of particular concern since all adolescents are at high risk of psychosocial problems at a time when life-long patterns of behaviour are being established. Pilot work is at present being undertaken in all WHO regions on this topic.

Mental health of the elderly is another high priority area. A special subject under study is the impact of bereavement on the health of elderly people and an evaluation of the value of psychosocial support at such a time.

Prevention and control of alcohol and drug abuse   Many drug abuse control programmes have been initiated by WHO. Recently guidelines have been prepared to identify high risk populations who are likely to abuse drugs. In Europe, AIDS among drug abusers was the subject studied at a special consultative meeting held in Stockholm in 1986. Drug related problems in adolescence were particularly considered.

Prevention and treatment of mental and neurological disorders   Subjects recently studied by WHO, or with their support and/or collaboration, include the following.

— Alzheimer's disease and the epidemiology of senile dementia.
— A large comparative study of the incidence, manifestations and course of schizophrenia.
— Morbidity studies into neurological disorders.
— Research relating to epilepsy.
— Research relating to the consequences of strokes.
— The protection of the rights of mentally ill people.
— Research and development of services for mentally handicapped persons in the Western Pacific Region.

Promotion of environmental health

The promotion of environmental health is particularly important in most developing countries where basic needs such as a safe clean water supply are often completely lacking. There is nearly always also a lack of proper sanitation. Figure 11.2 illustrates the global levels of water supply for urban and rural districts of the world, and Fig. 11.3 the sanitation position in urban and rural districts in the world. Note that in both rural and urban districts of the world, there is a vast difference between the level of provision of services.

Food safety is still an important top priority for all countries of the world including the developed ones and WHO continues to be active in organising training seminars.

Disease prevention and control

This section of the work of WHO has always been very highly developed.

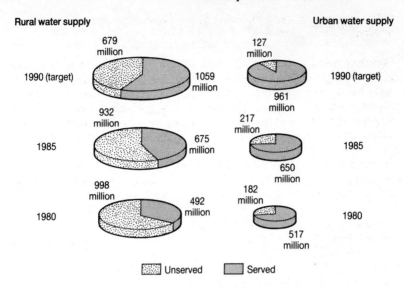

Fig. 11.2 Water supply: global levels of service coverage. (From *The Work of WHO*, 1986–87, Biennial Report of the Director General of WHO.)

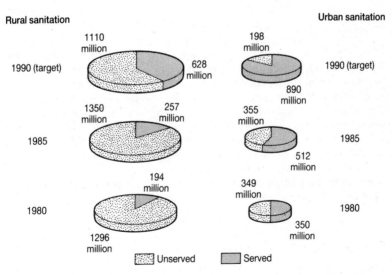

Fig. 11.3 Sanitation: global levels of service coverage. (From *The Work of WHO*, 1986–87, Biennial Report of the Director General of WHO.)

Reporting service run by the World Health Organization on the world-wide incidence of serious infectious disease

The WHO publishes a weekly bulletin on the world-wide incidence of serious infectious diseases and particularly on plague, yellow fever, cholera, typhus and relapsing fever. This bulletin contains exact details of numbers of such cases and the cities and ports in which they have occurred throughout the world. It also records brief details of other unusually large epidemics (such as influenza and AIDS) which may be occurring in different parts of the world. It notes any changes made locally by a country in its immunisation or vaccination requirements so that those advising travellers are kept informed. These bulletins are invaluable as a reliable up-to-date record of the incidence of serious infection and are of the utmost importance to medical officers at all large ports and airports.

A daily epidemiological radio-telegraphic bulletin is broadcast by the World Health Organization from Geneva, Saigon, Keelung and Manila, and once or twice a week broadcasts from Tokyo, Hongkong, Singapore, Karachi, Madras and Mauritius.

Other important diseases which are considered by the WHO are discussed below.

Immunisation   Recently there has been a remarkable increase in the percentage of children protected from various diseases by immunisation. By the end of 1988, WHO estimated that 50% of the children of the world have been immunised. This compares with a level of 5% in 1978. Much of this dramatic advance has occurred because of the emphasis which WHO has placed upon immunisation. WHO has persuaded many countries to invest heavily in this form of prevention. Figure 11.4 and Table 11.2 show the percentage of children under the age of one year who are immunised against tuberculosis, diphtheria, pertussis, tetanus and measles and of pregnant women immunised against tetanus in each WHO region.

WHO estimates that in the developing countries (excluding China)

Table 11.2   Percentage of immunisation coverage (July 1987). (From *The Work of WHO*, 1986–87, Biennial report of the Director General of WHO.)

	Children under one year of age			Pregnant women	
	BCG	Diphtheria-pertussis-tetanus third dose	Poliomyelitis third dose	Measles	Tetanus
	%	%	%	%	%
1983	27	28	22	13	11
1984	50	46	47	38	11
1985	47	46	48	42	12
1986	49	53	55	45	15

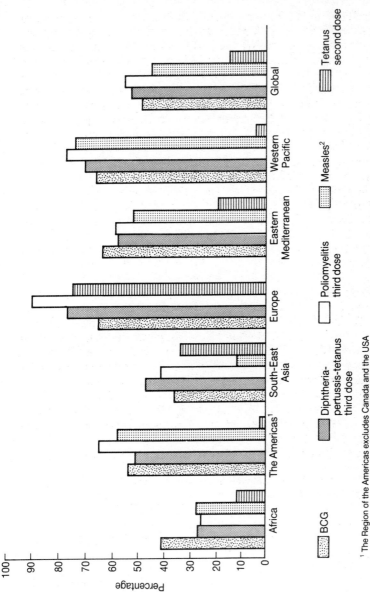

Fig. 11.4 Estimated percentage of children under one year of age immunised against tuberculosis, diphtheria, pertussis, tetanus, poliomyelitis and measles and of pregnant women immunised against tetanus by WHO region (July 1987). (From *The Work of WHO*, 1986–87, Biennial Report of the Director General of WHO.)

*immunisation is preventing more than one million deaths a year from
either measles, neonatal tetanus or pertussis and over 175 000 cases of
poliomyelitis.* However, almost *250 000 cases of poliomyelitis* and *over
three million deaths a year* are attributed to either *measles, neonatal
tetanus or pertussis* so although big improvements have already occurred, there is plenty of room for further advances.

Malaria   The control of malaria has always been one of the main aims
of WHO since its formation 45 years ago. The latest world malaria
situation is summarised below.

About 100 million clinical cases of malaria occur each year and the
total number of persons infected is about 250 million. Of the total
world population of 4818 million, 1327 million (28%) live in areas
which have been free from malaria since the late 1940s. About 768
million (16%) live in areas where malaria has been eradicated; 2318
million (48%) live in areas where measures directed against the
transmission of malaria are carried out. The remaining 8% of the
world's population (405 million persons) live in areas – mainly in
tropical Africa – where, owing to lack of antimalarial measures,
prevalence remains virtually unchanged.

WHO has been associated with much research dealing with the
spread of malaria. As *Plasmodium falciparum* (the organism which
causes malaria) continues to show resistance to chloroquine (the drug
used to treat and prevent malaria), new antimalarial compounds are
being sought and some are at an advanced stage of development.
WHO is undertaking research in the development of a vaccine, using
genetic engineering methods to produce antigens from different life-
cycle stages of the malarial parasite. These vaccines are now being
tried out on volunteers.

Diarrhoeal diseases   WHO has given a high degree of priority to
efforts to control diarrhoeal diseases in developing countries. In the
African Region of WHO 39 countries have formulated plans of
operation and in 33 of them programmes have now started. Much
training has already been undertaken with the help of WHO and, since
September 1983, more than 10 000 participants have attended training
seminars.

The control of diarrhoeal diseases, especially in developing
countries, has been based on *oral hydration salt therapy* which is
simple, cheap and effective. The development of these programmes is
clearly shown in Fig. 11.5 which shows the 1986/87 situation and the
targets for 1989. One of the most encouraging signs is the large
increase which has already been achieved in the production of oral
rehydration salts in the countries which use them extensively.

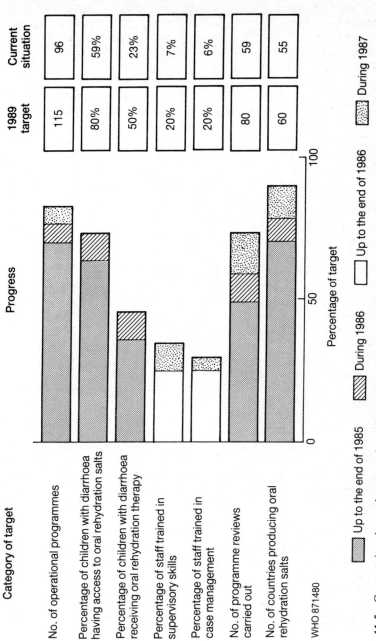

Category of target

No. of operational programmes

Percentage of children with diarrhoea having access to oral rehydration salts

Percentage of children with diarrhoea receiving oral rehydration therapy

Percentage of staff trained in supervisory skills

Percentage of staff trained in case management

No. of programme reviews carried out

No. of countries producing oral rehydration salts

WHO 871480

Progress

Percentage of target

	1989 target	Current situation
	115	96
	80%	59%
	50%	23%
	20%	7%
	20%	6%
	80	59
	60	55

Up to the end of 1985   During 1986   Up to the end of 1986   During 1987

Fig. 11.5   Current situation and progress in achieving the 1989 targets of the WHO Diarrhoeal Diseases Control Programme.

Tuberculosis   In the industrialised countries the incidence of tuberculosis continues to decrease at an annual rate of over 10%. In these countries (excluding USSR) about 250 000 new cases are reported annually with 18 000 deaths. The majority of the cases with active disease now occur in the older age groups and most of them are the result of endogenous reactivation of old infections.

In the developing countries, the annual risk of infection shows a decline of at least 50% since the 1960s when comprehensive community based control programmes were first introduced. The main reason as to why this rate of decline cannot be accelerated is the shortage of financial resources.

Tuberculosis is now often seen as an early manifestation of AIDS. Depending on the prevalence of infection, an incidence as high as 60% has been observed in people with AIDS. An interesting feature of tuberculosis in people with AIDS is that tuberculous bacteraemia (Bacillus tuberculosis circulating in the blood) is considerably more common resulting in a variety of extrapulmonary forms of the disease, from lymphatic involvement to intracranial manifestations.

Zoonoses   WHO has always given high priority to the prevention of the zoonoses (diseases which are spread through animals). Of particular interest are rabies, echinococcus, leptospirosis and the major food-borne diseases related to animals and animal products such as salmonellosis and brucellosis.

Much research is being carried out and encouraged by WHO into rabies prevention through vaccination of susceptible animals. Studies in dogs have shown that 80–90% of the dog population is accessible for vaccination and therefore a mass vaccination programme would be a possibility. Encouraging results on the *oral immunisation of wild animals* in Europe against rabies have been reported at a WHO workshop held in 1986. Foxes (the main reservoir of infection in Europe) and badgers have been successfully vaccinated by placing oral vaccine in a bait. Six countries (Austria, Belgium, France, Federal Republic of Germany, Luxembourg and Switzerland) are at present carrying out a large scale effort at wildlife vaccination to form a rabies-free area (see Fig. 11.6).

Sexually transmitted diseases   WHO has always been prominent in publishing practical guidelines for programmes to control sexually transmitted diseases. An expert standing Committee of WHO gives advice. With the mounting evidence that sexually transmitted diseases are important in the transmission of human immunodeficiency virus (HIV), WHO has emphasised the importance of early and effective management of all cases and their partners.

Fig. 11.6 Areas of Europe where oral rabies vaccination has been introduced. (From *The Work of WHO*, 1986–87, Biennial Report of the Director General of WHO.)

AIDS   The various problems of AIDS and its epidemiology, diagnosis and treatment have been discussed in detail in Chapter 8. WHO has been very active in developing a global AIDS strategy. The first step in this strategy is to *prevent human immunodeficiency virus (HIV) dissemination* which is *spread through the behaviour and actions of individuals*, i.e. through sexual intercourse and self-injection, particularly if shared syringes are used. (As mentioned in Chapter 8, early in the AIDS epidemic a number of haemophiliac patients contracted HIV infection from contaminated blood extracts which had been imported from the USA. All blood and blood products used in the UK are now subject to heat treatment which removes this risk.) The most effective way to prevent the spread of HIV infection is to ensure that everyone knows how the spread occurs and can therefore modify their behaviour to keep any risk as low as possible. *Widespread health education is essential* to ensure that all individuals (whether uninfected or infected with HIV) realise that they have a clear responsibility not to put themselves or others at risk.

Early in the pandemic (a world-wide epidemic) WHO realised that information and teaching will only be totally effective if those whose lifestyles place them in a 'high risk' group for contracting HIV infection (homosexuals and drug abusers using injections) are reached and influenced by the health education.

WHO has also stressed how important it is that those who are infected with HIV are not excluded from contact with others and are not segregated or discriminated against. A recent World Health Assembly directed WHO to 'stress to Member States and all others concerned, *the dangers to the health of everyone of discriminating action against and stigmatisation of HIV infected people and persons with AIDS* and members of a population group'. The Assembly went on to urge countries 'to protect the human rights and dignity of HIV infected persons and people with AIDS and of population groups (i.e. homosexuals and drug abusers) and to avoid discriminating action against and stigmatisation of them in the provision of services, employment and travel'.

WHO further emphasised this view by pointing out that *discrimination may also actually represent a threat to health*. Many countries have accepted this point and are actively working to prevent discrimination by undertaking various health education programmes. Figure 11.7 is an example of an excellent poster prepared in the USA to help reduce and avoid any possible discrimination towards HIV infected children.

Another important aspect of the WHO programme on AIDS has been to stress the *global features of the disease* – infection has quickly assumed world wide proportions and has spread quickly in both developing and developed countries (i.e. it has become a world-wide epidemic). It cannot be prevented by attempting to segregate people or to exclude certain groups from travelling – any attempt to control AIDS by any form of quarantine is bound to fail.

WHO also has pointed out that AIDS is not only a health problem but has *very important social, educational and behavioural facets*. Guidelines have been issued on health promotion, epidemiological surveillance and forecasting. Sensitive issues such as AIDS in prisons, breast feeding and HIV infection, the importance of the safety of blood transfusions and heat treatment of blood products and the immunisation of HIV infected infants and young children have been tackled. The importance of periodic reassessment of epidemiological, social and behavioural factors as the pandemic develops has also been emphasised.

Blindness   The number of countries who have a national blindness prevention programme (most of which were set up with the help of WHO) increased from 40 to 50 in 1986/87. All such programmes have been designed to have a primary health care approach. Much of the work of preventing blindness is initially carried out by local health workers who have been trained in simple eye-care procedures. In rural

I HAVE AiDS
PLease hug me

I can't make you sick

AIDS HOT LINE FOR KIDS
CENTER FOR ATTITUDINAL HEALING
19 MAIN ST., TIBURON, CA 94920, (415) 435-5022

Fig. 11.7 An American poster urges people not to discriminate against people with AIDS.

areas of many developing countries it is difficult for any patient to obtain specialist help, mainly because of the difficulties of travel and the shortage of specialist ophthalmic staff.

Communicable eye diseases, especially trachoma caused by a virus infection, are a major cause of blindness in many countries, although they are slowly being brought under control. In contrast, *cataract has become the universal major cause of the loss of sight* and the greater longevity of people in all countries has become a contributory factor. In many developing countries there is an ever increasing back-log of unoperated cases.

WHO assists by arranging training programmes and has promoted research on the epidemiology of cataract and on the various risk factors. The primary eye-care poster which was so successfully developed by WHO is now printed in 12 languages and continues to be very useful. Another helpful development has been the setting up of small-scale workshops for the production and assembly of cheap standardised spectacles.

Cancer   WHO plays a unique role in cancer prevention. Most national health programmes concentrate on the early detection and treatment of cancers whereas *WHO has specialised its work on the epidemiology of cancer*. This is done in two ways. Firstly by the collection and publication of data about cancer in all countries of the world; many of the tables quoted in Chapter 9 comparing international differences in cancer mortality are examples of this data collection by WHO. Secondly, by the work of WHO with the International Agency for Research on Cancer (IRAC). The IRAC was established in Lyon in France in 1963 and is an autonomous body within the framework of WHO. Five nations contributed to its foundation but 14 countries now participate in the control and financing of its activities. The IRAC systematically collects and analyses data on cancer from all parts of the world. Its work has confirmed that there are enormous differences in cancer occurrence in different geographical areas of the world and among different ethnic and religious groups in the same area.

The commonest cancer in women is either breast or cervical cancer (uterus), except in USSR where cancer of the stomach heads the list. In men, the top ranking cancer varies in different regions and includes lung, liver, bladder, lymphoma, stomach, mouth/larynx and prostate. Lung cancer is mainly a male cancer in developed countries but it is now also increasing rapidly in women.

The IRAC has found that *80% of cancers are linked to environment and life styles*. The problem is made more difficult to analyse accurately because there are usually a multitude of factors affecting incidence, and one risk factor may be magnified by the presence of another. An example is given by cancer of the larynx – a recent study in South Western Europe has confirmed that alcohol and smoking are implicated and that when both habits are combined the risk is significantly higher than for either alone. Many different potential cancer causing factors have been identified by the IRAC – environmental ones from sun to diet (and this includes different methods of preserving food), tobacco consumption, occupation especially when associated with the breathing of mineral fibres or dusts or exposure to certain chemicals, air and water pollution and inadequate hygiene.

Oesophageal cancer is an example of a cancer which varies greatly in different geographical zones. A high incidence is found in what is called the *oesophageal cancer belt*, described by Sharon Whelan in an article in *World Health*, June 1989. This belt stretches from the shore of the Caspian Sea in Northern Iran through the Southern republics of the USSR to Western China; in this area the incidence rates of cancer of the oesophagus are 200 times higher than in the rest of the world. The likely explanation is that it is probably due to a combination of dark tobacco and distilled alcoholic drinks in Brittany in France, and to opium products on the Caspian shores. The incidence of oesophageal cancer is also high in parts of Eastern South America and in part of Northern France.

Another very interesting cancer incidence is primary cancer of the liver – three quarters of the reported cases (250 000 cases per year) occur in the developing countries. The areas of highest incidence are sub-Saharan Africa, East and South-East Asia as far west as Burma and Melanesia. There seems to be a *close correlation between the high incidence of primary liver cancer and the prevalence of chronic carriers of hepatitis B*. A study has begun in Gambia to evaluate the effectiveness of hepatitis B virus vaccination in preventing chronic liver disease and primary liver cancer in a population at high risk.

By acting as a disseminator of information and by supporting promising research, WHO plays an important role in the prevention of cancer throughout the world. As all cancers tend to affect middle aged and elderly persons, it is clear that many developing countries will see an increase in cancers as the expectation of life of their communities lengthens and more and more of the population reach the ages when cancer is most likely to occur.

Other work of WHO in the field of disease prevention and control
WHO is also active in the study of and research upon tropical diseases and leprosy as well as cardiovascular diseases and other non-communicable diseases.

Special demographic problems faced by WHO

Many authors have commented upon the rapid growth of the world's population and some countries have taken steps aimed at reducing the number of children born. However an even more significant trend is that, *especially in developing countries of the world, the number of people surviving to old age is rising sharply*. Dr Kalache, in an article in *World Health*, March 1989, pointed out that, although earlier in this century the majority of elderly people were living in the developed countries of the world, since the 1980s the balance has changed and now most of the world's elderly are living in developing countries. It is estimated that, by the beginning of the 21st century, *three quarters of the total elderly population in the world will be living in developing countries*. As recently as 1975 only 3.8% of persons living in developing countries were aged 65 or over. By the year 2025, it is expected that this proportion will have risen to 7.5% and that a further doubling will

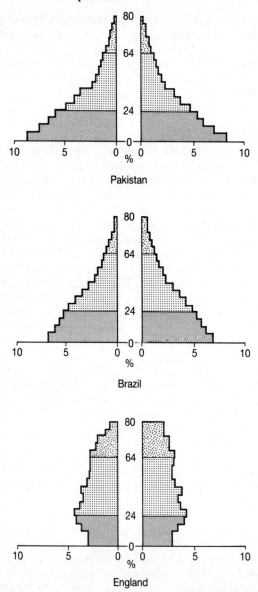

Fig. 11.8 Changing age structure of a population as a country becomes more developed. (From *World Health*, March 1989.)

take place by the year 2050. These dramatic predictions emphasise the medical, social and economic problems which will inevitably follow. Not only will there be many health care problems but the change will mean that the pyramid of the existing population structure will diminish and that the work force will also fall, although it will still have to support the whole community (see Fig. 11.8).

Mortality in developed countries

WHO publishes very detailed vital statistics about the health of the 33 most developed countries of the world, including the whole of Europe and USSR, Australia, New Zealand, Canada, Israel, Japan and USA. The total population of these countries amounts to 1000 million persons.

The overall expectation of life (from birth) averages out for all people at 73.7 years but there are wide variations. In Japan the birth life expectancy is 79.1 years while in East Europe it is 70–71 years. There is a clear and constant difference between the sexes, with women always having a longer life expectancy. The average life expectancy for women is 77.2 and 70.1 for men. There are four countries where the birth expectancy for women exceeds 80 years – Japan (82.1 years) with France, Sweden and Switzerland making up the quartet. Japan also reports the longest life expectancy for men (75.9 years).

The commonest cause of death in these countries is heart disease (3.3 million or 30% of all deaths), cancer 1.9 million (17.3%), strokes 1.5 million (13.6%), respiratory diseases 0.9 million (8.2%) and violent deaths 0.75 million (6.8%) of which 170 000 were the result of car accidents and 130 000 the result of suicides.

Extrapolating the results from studies carried out in USA, a total of *1.5 million deaths a year are caused by smoking* in these developed countries as a whole. Most of these deaths occur under the age of 65 years, a finding which invalidates the theory that most deaths attributed to smoking occur among the elderly.

Health for All by the Year 2000

This historic concept and principle was laid down at a WHO meeting at Alma-Ata in 1978. The position 10 years later was assessed at a meeting of 22 senior health experts at Riga in 1988. The WHO's total commitment to the principles of Health for All by Year 2000 (HFA) was renewed and it was recommended that, in order to accelerate progress towards that goal, countries should take the action as outlined in Table 11.3. (See pages 206/7)

Table 11.3 Action recommended by the World Health Organisation in order to attain the goal of Health for All by Year 2000 (HFA).

1. **Maintain HFA as a permanent goal of all nations up to and beyond the year 2000**
   Reaffirm Health for All as a permanent objective of all nations, as stressed in the Alma-Ata Declaration, and establish a process for examining the longer term challenges to Health for All that will extend into the 21st century.

2. **Renew and strengthen HFA strategies**
   Each country should continue to monitor its own health problems and develop its own health strategies in the spirit of Health for All. This will reveal its most pressing health problems and identify the most seriously underserved and vulnerable populations. Programmes should be directed towards those populations in the spirit of equity, inviting their active participation in the development and implementation of the strategies.

3. **Intensify social and political action for HFA**
   Intensify social and political actions necessary to support shifts in policy and allocation of resources required to progress toward Health for All, including the involvement of other sectors, non-governmental organisations, communities and other interested groups. Seek mechanisms for promoting new partnerships for health among them and with governments.

4. **Develop and mobilise leadership**
   Give strong emphasis in every country to developing and stimulating the interest in HFA.

5. **Enable the people to share in decision-making and action for health**
   Empower people by providing information, technical support, and decision-making possibilities, so as to enable them to share in the opportunities and responsibilities for action in the interest of their own health. Give special attention to the rôle of women in health and development.

6. **Make intersectoral collaboration a force for HFA**
   Support the creation of sustained intersectoral collaboration for health by incorporating health objectives into sectoral policies and activating potential mechanisms at all levels.

7. **Strengthen district health systems based on PHC**
   Strengthen district health systems based on primary health care, as a key action point for focusing national policies, resources and local concerns on the most pressing health needs and underserved people.

8. **Plan, prepare and support health manpower for HFA**
   Change educational and training programmes for health personnel emphasising relevance to health services' requirements by locating learning experiences in functioning health systems based on primary health care. Provide strong moral and resource support for personnel, particularly those working in remote or difficult circumstances.

9. **Ensure development and rational use of science and appropriate technology**
   Emphasise the applications of science and appropriate technology to the critical health problems that threaten populations in all parts of the world,

and strengthen research capacities of Third World countries, with emphasis on research aimed at improving the health of the most deprived people.

10. **Overcome problems that continue to resist solution**
    Establish priority programmes aimed at overcoming serious problems where underdevelopment or disturbances of development are major contributing factors and progress has been very limited, such as: high infant, child and maternal mortality rates; substance abuse, such as tobacco and alcohol; and the imbalance between population growth and environmental and socio-economic resources. Develop improved approaches through primary health care emphasising intersectoral action.

12 Nutrition and environmental health

Nutrition

Nutrition and public health are inseparable, as a well-balanced and adequate food supply is essential for complete health. A balanced diet must contain adequate protein, essential vitamins, certain mineral salts and plenty of fibre as this has a protective action against colonic diseases and ischaemic heart disease. As the Western world has developed foods rich in animal proteins, more fat has been eaten and carbohydrates rich in sugar have become popular. However there is mounting evidence that such a diet is not ideal and the marked increase in ischaemic heart disease, certain colonic diseases and obesity over the last three decades has been connected with this trend. At present, there is a move towards diets in which dairy fats are reduced and foods rich in fibre are increased. Nutritional problems are (*i*) worldwide; (*ii*) national; and (*iii*) individual.

Worldwide problems

The task of providing an adequate food supply for the rapidly increasing world population is one of its major social problems. *Protein malnutrition* is one of the main public health hazards in developing countries. As food supplies are increased, a further complication is that this improvement in nutrition leads to an increase in population which, in turn, makes heavier demands upon the food supply. Indications show that food supplies are not keeping pace with the increase in world population. The solution lies both in controlling the growth of the world's population and in increasing its food supply by various improvements in agriculture, pest control and research to discover more suitable crops and animal stocks.

The national problem

The national nutritional problems of the United Kingdom are complex, but for many years a national nutritional policy has been accepted which ensures that the following conditions are met.

- All essential foodstuffs should be available to the whole population at reasonable cost, and present in variety.
- Certain priority foods should be provided for certain sections of the community. Examples include vitamins and subsidised dried milks for mothers and young infants, free school meals for children whose families are in need, and subsidised meals on wheels and lunch clubs for elderly people.
- Standards of milk production are controlled nationally – areas are designated where all herds must be free from tuberculosis; a Brucellosis Incentive Scheme is in operation and regulations introduced for the pasteurisation of milk supplies and other products (e.g. ice cream).
- Minimum standards are maintained for many foodstuffs and constant sampling ensures that these are reached.
- Many foods are fortified to guarantee adequate supplies of vitamins.
- Adulteration of foodstuffs is prevented by extensive legislation on such aspects as food preservatives or additives.
- Foodstuffs must be free from disease and this is achieved by meat and food inspection both at ports and at abattoirs and markets.
- Food handlers must be clean and must not contaminate the food – food hygiene.
- Continuous health education is carried out to teach the public about nutrition.

The individual problem

The individual nutritional problems are directly related to the type, amount and variety of foodstuffs consumed. Foods must supply the energy needs of the body in the form of calories and the proteins necessary for growth and tissue replacement; hence the correct proportion of proteins, carbohydrates and fats must be present in the diet which should also contain adequate amounts of vitamins, minerals and fibre.

Components for an adequate diet

Proteins   Proteins may be of animal or vegetable origin. The best are obtained from milk, egg, meats, fish, kidney or liver, for such foods contain large amounts of essential amino acids. The amount of protein required varies – a child uses about one-third of his or her protein requirements for growth, but an adult requires relatively little for replacement of tissue. Generally, it is accepted that an adult requires a minimum of 70 g of protein daily, although this amount may often be exceeded. Unlike fats and carbohydrates, proteins cannot be stored in the human body. In adults it is possible to obtain large quantities of proteins from vegetable sources, but for children, a high proportion of proteins should be of animal origin.

Fats Fats are a concentrated form of energy and some are vehicles for the fat-soluble vitamins A and D. Fats are easily stored and form the main reserve of energy. The main sources of fat are butter, eggs, cream, cheese and fatty meats. Apart from herring, salmon and trout, there is very little fat in fish.

Carbohydrates These are the starches and sugars – bread, potatoes, cane sugar, glucose. They are the cheapest form of food and the body can metabolise them rapidly to produce energy. As family income diminishes, so the amount of carbohydrate in the diet increases. Roughly half the energy requirements of the body are obtained from carbohydrates. Fats and carbohydrates are to some extent inter-changeable, the latter being necessary for the proper metabolism of fats. Carbohydrates are stored in concentrated form, glycogen, in the liver and muscles and this can be rapidly broken down into glucose to provide energy in an emergency.

Mineral salts Many different mineral salts are needed by the body including those given below.
Calcium is required for ossification, clotting of the blood and for regulating muscular contraction, especially of the heart muscle. The best sources of calcium are milk and cheese. Most vegetables and fruits contain satisfactory amounts. Note that meat, fish, sugars, fats and highly milled cereals are deficient in calcium. It is most important that the growing child has good supplies of calcium. If any child's intake of calcium is too low, osteoporosis, especially in females, is more likely to develop later in life (after the age of 65 years).
Phosphorus is also required for ossification and for the proper metabolism of fat. With the exception of butter and sugar, most foods are excellent sources of phosphorus.
Iron is required to form the haemoglobin of the blood. Only a few foods – egg yolk, liver, whole grains, beans, kale and some fruits – are satisfactory sources of iron. It is absent in butter and present in only very small quantities in milk.
Iodine is necessary for the proper functioning of the thyroid gland and for preventing goitre. Fish, milk, and leaf vegetables are good sources.
In addition, potassium, copper, magnesium, manganese, zinc, boron, fluorine, selenium, molybdenum are also required in minute traces. The function of many of these is obscure and they are often referred to as 'trace elements'.

Fibre Fibre is the cellulose element in food and, in general, is not absorbed, being excreted in the stools (it forms the main bulk of bowel motions). Fibre is valuable for two reasons. Firstly it contains certain chemicals which are absorbed and which are very useful in fat metabolism. Provided that plenty of fibre is eaten, fats from dairy products are unlikely to increase the chance of ischaemic heart disease. Secondly, fibre is necessary for the satisfactory health of the large bowel (colon). In Third World countries where people have to take large quantities of fibre to obtain their proteins, diseases such as diverticulitis are unknown.

Fibre occurs naturally in salads, most vegetables (especially in their skins), fruit and wholemeal flour and brown bread. Many breakfast cereals are fortified with fibre in the form of bran.

Vitamins These are organic compounds whose presence in small quantities is necessary for correct growth and health. Many different vitamins have been isolated but the most important are fat-soluble vitamins and water-soluble vitamins.

Fat-soluble vitamins These include vitamins A, D and K.

Vitamin A is present in many animal fats in liver, eggs, fish-liver oils, and is introduced into most butters and margarines. The yellow plant pigment carotene, which is found in green vegetables and carrots, is transformed into vitamin A by the body. Vitamin A deficiency causes a degeneration of surface epithelium which can lead to *night blindness* due to a deficiency of visual purple, *xerophthalmia* which is a drying and thickening of the cornea and later to *keratomalacia* which is a softening and inflammation of the cornea leading to opacity and blindness, and to *hyperkeratosis* of the skin. These conditions are rarely seen in the United Kingdom but are common in the Middle East.

Vitamin D is the vitamin which controls the deposition of calcium and phosphorus in bones. The best natural sources of vitamin D are cod and halibut liver oils, but the vitamin can be produced by the action of ultraviolet rays upon ergosterol. Vitamin D deficiency in infants leads to *rickets* and in adults to *osteomalacia*, a disease where, due to inadequate utilisation of calcium, there is a softening of the bones. This condition is endemic in underdeveloped countries and may affect pregnant and lactating women. It is extremely rare in European countries. Rickets has been largely eliminated from this country by the introduction of vitamin D fortification of margarine and butter and by ensuring that all babies are given vitamin drops.

Vitamin K is necessary for maintaining the prothrombin level of the blood and therefore for promoting clotting. It is synthesised by bacteria in the intestinal tract and also is present in many vegetables (spinach, cauliflower, cabbage, kale). Vitamin K deficiency is seen as a hypoprothrombinaemia in haemorrhagic disease of the newborn produced by a deficiency of intestinal synthesis of the vitamin.

Water-soluble vitamins   These include the *vitamin B complex* which contains at least four important factors – vitamin B_1 (thiamine), vitamin B_2 (riboflavine), nicotinic acid, and vitamin B_{12} (cyanocobalamin) – and *vitamin C.*

Vitamin B_1 (thiamine) is present in whole grain cereals and acute deficiency (*beri-beri*) is found in tropical countries. There are two forms, dry beri-beri characterised by a polyneuritis and wet beri-beri with cardiac failure. In the United Kingdom, *thiamine deficiency is usually seen in chronic alcoholics* who are taking a high carbohydrate diet with a very low intake of the vitamin. The symptoms usually are those of a peripheral neuritis.

Vitamin B_2 (riboflavine) is found in milk, eggs, liver and kidney. Deficiency of this vitamin shows itself as a dermatitis of the seborrhoeic type affecting the skin around the nose, mouth and ears. There may also be a sore tongue, an angular stomatis and vascularisation of the cornea which may eventually lead to a corneal opacity.

Nicotinic acid is found naturally in whole grain cereals excluding maize. Deficiency produces the clinical syndrome of *pellagra* seen in the maize-eating communities of eastern Europe and Asia. In the United Kingdom nicotinic acid deficiency is occasionally seen in conjunction with chronic alcoholism.

Vitamin B_{12} is found in whole grain cereals. A deficiency causes pernicious anaemia as, in the absence of Castle's intrinsic factor from the gastric secretion, vitamin B_{12} in the diet is not absorbed.

Vitamin C (ascorbic acid) is present in green vegetables, fresh fruit, oranges, tomatoes and blackcurrants. Note that *milk, including human milk, is a very poor source*. Deficiency leads to scurvy in which bleeding occurs in mucous membranes. Today, in the United Kingdom, *vitamin C deficiency is occasionally seen in old people living on their own* because often they neglect their diet, especially during the winter. Spontaneous haemorrhages appear, teeth may become loose and skin purpura may be present. Preventive measures include arranging a varied diet containing plenty of fresh vegetables and fruit. Because of the deficiency of this vitamin in milk *it is essential to give all babies, whether breast or bottle fed, vitamin C additives*. Convenient forms include orange juice or rose hip syrup.

Calorie requirements of the diet   Every diet must contain a minimum quantity of protein (preferably first-class proteins) and a balance of carbohydrates and fats to give sufficient calories as well as adequate mineral salts and vitamins.

The calorie requirement of the body varies in men and women depending upon the energy needed for the performance of heavy work and to maintain body temperature, especially in cold climates. As a rough guide, a minimum daily calorie requirement for a person at rest is approximately 1400 to 1550 calories. For light work about 2000 to 2750 calories are needed and for heavy work approximately 3000 calories. In pregnancy, women usually require about 2500 calories daily and this must be increased to approximately 3000 calories during lactation.

About 300 calories come from the 70 g of protein in the diet. The balance is made up from both fats and carbohydrates and it is always best to ensure a balance of these in varied foods. In old age, calorie requirements are less.

Food control

Many diseases that affect animals can also attack humans. The prevention of such illnesses depends on the care and control of food production and on the various inspections taking place to avoid contaminated food ever being eaten by humans.

Food inspection at ports

As much of the food in the United Kingdom is imported from abroad, careful inspection is made of all food arriving at the port of importation. Each consignment is inspected and sampled and can be imported only if the *port health staff* are satisfied as to its high standard.

All meat imported has to have a special certificate of purity from the country of origin and, in addition, is carefully examined by *meat inspectors*. If any disease is found, the complete carcase is given a very careful further examination. If the disease is only local, and the diseased portion can be completely removed, this is done. But, if the disease is widespread, the whole carcase is condemned and either has to be re-exported or destroyed, or stained and sent for animal food-stuff after complete sterilisation. Certain meats are *prohibited meats* and cannot be imported. These include the following.

— Scrap meat which cannot be identified.
— Meat comprising parts of the wall of the thorax or abdomen from which any part of pleura or peritoneum has been detached.
— Meat, except mutton and lamb, from which a lymphatic gland has been removed.
— The head of an animal without a submaxillary gland.

Tinned goods are sampled and examined and a small sample is sent to a bacteriologist for a full and complete bacteriological examination to check on the sterility of the product. If the results are unsatisfactory, the whole consignment can be condemned and not allowed to be imported.

All types of foodstuffs are examined in the same careful way.

Meat inspection

Continuous meat inspection is undertaken on all meat produced and eaten in the United Kingdom. After slaughter in the abattoir a systematic and careful inspection of all carcases is undertaken by specially trained inspectors. If any disease is found, it is dealt with in the same way as already described in port meat inspection.

Forty years ago *tuberculosis* was common in cattle in the United Kingdom. Although it is now rarely seen, it is still important to take steps to avoid meat infected with tuberculosis from ever coming into a kitchen. If this occurs infection is very likely as working surfaces, such as tables, will soon become contaminated. The pathogenic bacteria in the meat might be destroyed by heat in the cooking, but other foodstuffs would rapidly be infected via the contaminated working surfaces. The Aberdeen typhoid epidemic of 1964 was probably spread in this way – from a contaminated counter in a cooked meat department of a supermarket. For this reason, contaminated meat is only allowed to be used for animal foodstuffs provided it is sterilised and thoroughly stained with a dye to make such meat easily recognisable.

There are also a number of infectious conditions in animals which lead to the condemnation of the meat including various forms of *salmonellosis*, *septicaemia*, *anthrax*, *pyaemia* and *actinomycosis*.

Prevention of disease by control of milk supplies

Milk is a very important and essential part of our food supplies and forms the basis of all infant feeding. Milk supplies have always been particularly liable to lead to the spread of infectious disease for the following reasons.

— The cow may suffer from two diseases which can be passed on to humans via her milk – *tuberculosis* and *brucellosis*.
— Milk supplies may be contaminated in the process of collecting and distributing milk. In the past, before modern clean methods of milk distribution were perfected, epidemics traced to such causes included *typhoid*, *paratyphoid*, *diphtheria*, *scarlet fever* and other *streptococcal infections*, *food poisoning*, *dysentery*, *gastroenteritis* and *brucellosis*.

It is now extremely rare for infection of any kind to be traced to milk. This improvement has resulted from two factors.

— A successful nationwide campaign to eradicate tuberculosis and other diseases from all dairy herds.
— The large scale pasteurisation of milk supplies and the use of other heat treatment methods (see below).

Pasteurisation of milk means the subjection of the milk to heat treatment for a specified time so that any live pathogenic or disease-producing bacteria are killed. The usual process of pasteurisation is the *High Temperature Short Time process* in which milk is retained at a temperature of not less than 71.5°C (161°F) for 15 seconds and then immediately cooled to a temperature of not more than 10°C (50°F). Immediately after pasteurisation the milk is bottled by machine and sealed so that no further chance of contamination can occur. Thus the milk is delivered to the householder completely safe and free from infection.

Sterilised milk is milk which has been filtered and homogenised, and then maintained at a temperature of not less than 100°C (212°F) for such a period as to comply with the turbidity test. In practice, after filtering and homogenising, the milk is poured into bottles and heated to 108°C (227°F) for 10–12 minutes.

Ultra-heat-treated (UHT) milk has been retained at a temperature of not less than 132°C (270°F) for a period of not less than one second, and then immediately placed in sterile containers in which it is supplied to the consumer.

As a further precaution, any person working in a dairy shop who develops a communicable disease must notify the local 'proper officer' who is generally the District Medical Officer or another specially designated community physician. The 'proper officer' can prohibit the sale of milk if it is likely to cause disease, until it has been heat-treated.

The 'proper officer' can also prohibit any person who is an open infectious case of tuberculosis from working in a dairy or milking cows on a farm.

Sampling to prevent adulteration of milk and food supplies

The possible adulteration of food supplies is very carefully guarded against by the continuous sampling of all foodstuffs. At the beginning of the century, there was widespread adulteration of food in the United Kingdom and this led to disease due both to dangerous additives to food and the lowering of nutritional value of some foods which were diluted in this way.

The adding of water to milk is fortunately easily detected by a test on the freezing point of milk – the adulterated milk has a higher freezing point. Sampling of milk supplies goes on all the time and very heavy penalties are given to the rare offenders.

Only very limited preservatives are allowed to be added to certain foods. As preservatives could mask staleness of food and encourage incorrect food storage, making food poisoning attacks more likely, it is illegal to add preservatives to the majority of foods, including all milk products. Examples of foods to which limited preservatives may be added are sausages, jams, and pickles.

Environmental health inspectors carry out sampling which, of course, is always without warning, on shops and stores selling food, drugs and drink. Samples are tested for purity and for any evidence of adulteration. This constant vigilance has resulted in a very high standard being maintained in all food products, and cases of adulteration are very rare. Recently a few instances have been traced where items of food, particularly baby foods, have been intentionally adulterated with items like glass in a vindictive attempt to damage the reputation of major international firms. All parents should carefully examine baby foods and their packaging and immediately report anything suspicious.

Special precautions for special foodstuffs

Certain foodstuffs, for example shell-fish and ice cream, are particularly liable to contamination which may result in disease in humans, and special precautions are necessary to avoid this.

Shell-fish   Many shell-fish are eaten raw. For this reason, special precautions must be taken to ensure that shell-fish do not become contaminated with pathogenic bacteria. Unfortunately shell-fish often contain *typhoid* and *paratyphoid bacilli* if they have been collected from a sea-shore or sea which is grossly contaminated with sewage. A number of outbreaks of typhoid fever have been caused in this way.

Many parts of the sea-shore around the United Kingdom are polluted as crude sewage is often emptied into river mouths. Special regulations are enforced, preventing the collection of shell-fish from dangerously polluted beaches. Shell-fish can be purified by immersion in specially prepared tanks for two to three weeks. This is carried out commercially in certain places to make certain that no danger of spreading typhoid exists.

Ice cream   Ice cream is particularly liable to spread infection because, although bacteria will not multiply at the low temperatures necessary for ice cream, the bacteria present in ice cream will be preserved at such temperatures. This means that a disease like *typhoid fever*, which can easily be spread by a tiny infecting dose, could be spread widely by ice cream which has become contaminated with typhoid bacilli. This is what happened in the Aberystwyth ice cream typhoid outbreak in 1945 when over 100 cases of typhoid occurred.

To prevent any possible recurrence, all *ice cream must, by law, now be pasteurised* and then cooled and left at a temperature not above 9.3°C (45°F) until frozen. This compulsory pasteurisation has prevented the danger of further epidemics of typhoid.

Special preventive measures relating to food handlers

Under various Food Hygiene Regulations special precautions must be taken by all food handlers in shops and stalls to avoid spreading disease. These include the following precautions.

- All steps must be taken to avoid food becoming contaminated – food must be covered and protected from flies and contact with the public.
- No open food – that is food not in a tin or jar – must be placed lower than 18 inches (45 cm) from the ground.
- Anybody handling food must keep his or her person and clothes clean.
- Any open cut or abrasion must be covered by a waterproof dressing to avoid staphylococcal lesions in whitlows, boils, etc. from contaminating food and causing food poisoning.
- All food handlers must refrain from spitting and smoking.
- All wrapping paper must be clean – newspapers are not allowed except for uncooked vegetables.
- Any food handler who becomes aware that he or she is suffering from *typhoid* or *paratyphoid fever*, *salmonella* infection, *dysentery* or *staphylococcal* infection, must notify the 'proper officer', the District Medical Officer or another specially designated community physician.

In addition there are widespread regulations about food premises, all designed to reduce the chance of infection. These include regulations about the provisions of washing facilities with hot and cold water, and working surfaces to prevent accumulation of bacteria in cracks on unsuitable types of surfaces. Standards are also laid down for the construction of premises and the temperature at which foods may be stored.

Further regulations concern many aspects of the transport and handling of foodstuffs. All such regulations are designed to prevent the spread of disease.

Housing and town planning

The house a person lives in has an important influence upon that individual's life and well-being. It also has a significant effect upon health.

A satisfactory house must reach certain physical standards, such as being free from dampness, being well lighted and ventilated, having a proper water system including hot water system and bath, an adequate internal toilet, sinks and proper drainage system, adequate means for preparing, storing and cooking food. These physical standards are invariably found in modern houses, but many older houses, especially in industrial areas, lack some of them.

The house must also be suitable for the family living there – not only must it be large enough, but it should be sited in an attractive way not being too close to other houses, and form an integral part of a group of houses or area. No family living in an inadequate house will be able to enjoy life completely. Nor will all the families of a large area be able to live properly unless all the necessary community services – shops, churches, schools, doctors' houses, health centres and hospitals, community centres, cinemas, etc. – are present. In communities such as a country town which has developed over many years, often centuries, all such facilities will usually be present, having been added to the community gradually.

It is in the area which has developed quickly in which so many of these facilities are missing. Examples include 'slum' areas and some new housing estates.

- 'Slum' areas in industrial towns, built in the last century when the absence of transport led factory owners to crowd together in small areas too many badly built houses which are now deteriorating, now provide overcrowded, unpleasant, damp and unhealthy homes.
- Many new housing estates contain sound houses, but all too often the necessary community facilities are absent. Hundreds of houses may be built without all the essential community services, such as shops, being provided.

It is now known that it is best to plan a whole neighbourhood unit in all urban development. Since 1948 new towns and housing areas have always attempted to follow the neighbourhood unit plan. Developments should not be too large, and a neighbourhood unit for about 10 000 persons is considered ideal. Within such a development not only should the necessary houses be built but essential services such as shops, schools, churches, community centres, library, police station, clinics, health centres etc. should be provided.

Effects of bad housing on health

Although slum clearance – the demolition of unsuitable houses – has been going on since the 1920s, there still remain many poor houses in the large cities and industrial towns. What effect does such poor housing have upon the health of those living in it?

It is not difficult to demonstrate that the health of people living in slum areas is inferior to those living in good areas. There is a greater amount of communicable disease present and, when the children develop the usual childhood diseases, there is a higher incidence of complications. Overcrowding, which is usually present in slums, and poor housing and living conditions leads to a greater spread of communicable diseases. Unsuitable housing makes the individual *more liable* to disease, as the incidence of infection is more likely, rather than actually producing disease.

The majority of poor houses are damp – either from defective roofs or gutters allowing rain water to enter the house, or by rising dampness percolating upwards from the ground, due to the absence of a damp-proof course. Damp living conditions lead to an exacerbation of various *rheumatic problems* so commonly found later in life, a *higher child mortality*, and a greater incidence of serious chest conditions such as *acute bronchitis*. Such conditions also aggravate *chronic bronchitis* in the elderly. Dampness always has a most *depressing effect* on the occupants of the home, who see their efforts at redecoration ruined, and leads to much unhappiness and aggravation of minor mental and emotional disorders.

The overcrowding effect of poor housing has a stultifying effect upon the proper development of the family. No family can hope to reach its full potential in such conditions and families give up because the effort to overcome the difficulties becomes too great. The extra strain of looking after a mentally handicapped child in such conditions is tremendous and is often so difficult that the child may have to be admitted to hospital although he or she could have stayed happily at home had the house been more suitable. Poor housing cannot be said to be a cause of mental illness but it certainly is a contributory factor and has a very bad and often disastrous effect on the mentally ill person living there. Even after the acute state of the mental illness has passed, unsatisfactory home conditions can retard recovery.

The *level of accidents* both in children and old persons is much higher in those living in poor houses. This is due to bad lighting and steep unsuitable stairs which predispose to accidents resulting from falls. Overcrowding is also associated with an increased number of scalds and burns.

Poor housing conditions not only predispose the individual to attacks of some diseases but may also be an important factor in the *correct management of illness*. A patient with angina of effort or a chronic cardiac condition must be able to avoid stairs. In a modern house, it is usually possible to arrange this by turning a downstairs room into a temporary bedroom and this works quite well, especially if there is a downstairs lavatory. But in the slum house, this would be impossible and the management of such a case is made difficult. Either the patient would have to climb steep stairs or stay permanently upstairs; there is also the complication that in the slum house there is not usually an inside lavatory.

The management of various forms of malignant disease is made very difficult in slum houses. A case of a person with a colostomy, for instance, will produce many extra problems in the absence of a bathroom, internal lavatory and proper washing facilities.

Local authorities realise the importance of doing all they can to provide good houses. It is usual for the housing authority to give special priority for urgent housing for really important medical reasons, so that the effect of poor housing on health can be minimised. Tuberculosis infection can be prevented by the rapid rehousing of a patient's family if they are living in an overcrowded slum house.

Methods of dealing with unsatisfactory houses

Unsatisfactory houses can be dealt with in a number of ways.

— Slight defects can be put right by serving an abatement notice on the owner.
— Individual unfit houses can be demolished or repaired.
— Houses or parts of houses may be closed.
— Large Clearance Areas can be defined. This is the usual method used for large scale slum clearance. The Department of the Environment holds a local inquiry where the council has to provide public evidence of unfitness of houses and where owners can bring their own evidence.
— Houses in multiple occupation can be controlled.
— Special measures can be used to improve houses.

All these methods are used by the environmental health inspectors who are responsible for this work.

Atmospheric pollution and health

Although the control of atmospheric pollution has improved markedly in recent years many large cities and towns, especially those in industrial areas, had, in the past, their atmosphere constantly polluted by smoke and other fumes in the air. It is known that the health of the people living in such areas was affected by this atmospheric contamination.

Atmospheric pollution is probably a small factor in the production of lung cancer, for it is known that the level of lung cancer is higher in industrial areas than in country areas. It is a minor problem compared with cigarette smoking, but it is a factor.

However, the most serious danger to health occurs in those unfortunate people who have some degree of *chronic bronchitis*. Many of these are elderly and their respiratory and cardiac function is impaired. The British climate, with its damp misty winter days, always tends to make such patients worse but really serious medical problems arise when atmospheric pollution in the form of a smoky fog (smog) occurs.

To such patients even minor pollution increases their symptoms while a major fog, lasting a few days, often brings them very near complete collapse. For instance, in the historic smog of London in December 1952, it is estimated that just under 4000 patients with chronic bronchitis died. The inhalation of smoky particles and/or sulphur gases commonly present in industrial areas both play a part in aggravating the chronic bronchitic's condition.

Living in an atmosphere that is always dirty has a most depressing effect upon people and adds greatly to their daily problems. Since the Clean Air Act came into force in 1956, local authorities have progressed towards the ideal of clearing the atmosphere of all pollution. It was hoped to achieve this by two means.

- Preventing the building of any new factory plant unless its means of producing heat or power are completely smokeless. Prior approval of all such plans must be given by local authorities before any building construction can start.
- Introducing smoke control areas in which it is an offence to produce any smoke at all or to burn ordinary coal. Before any part of a town can be made such an area, all the houses must have cooking and heating methods which are smokeless. This may mean replacing old grates with modern ones capable of burning smokeless fuel. A more satisfactory method is to change to other forms of power such as oil, gas or electricity.

Control of water supplies

In the United Kingdom the control of water supplies, their purification and cleanliness has been so reliable that one hardly considers that this is an important health safeguard. The disastrous epidemic of typhoid in Zermatt, in Switzerland, in 1963 provides a reminder of the dangers which face any population which ignores stringent high safety standards.

There are two bacterial diseases spread by water – *typhoid fever* and *cholera*. Cholera is a disease, seen mainly in the East, which can spread because of grossly inadequate water and sewage systems. Its epidemic spread today in this country is virtually impossible.

However typhoid fever could quite easily be spread by water unless constant care is taken to ensure that the purification of water is complete. This entails the following measures:

- storage of water in reservoirs;
- filtration of water;
- sterilisation of water using chlorine to make certain that any bacteria not removed by filtration are killed.

In addition, great care is always needed to make certain that no employee in a water works contaminates the supply. In particular, *it is essential to make certain that no typhoid carriers are ever employed in a water works*. Careful medical tests including agglutination blood tests are carried out on all such employees to reduce the chance of a carrier not being detected among the staff of the water works. The last serious water-borne outbreak of typhoid fever in this country was in Croydon in 1937 when 290 cases of typhoid fever occurred. It was caused by a urinary carrier contaminating the water supply while he assisted in work on a deep well forming part of Croydon's water supply.

Very high standards are maintained in the water supplies in this country and further large scale outbreaks of water-borne typhoid are most unlikely to occur. The most vulnerable supplies are probably some country ones especially during the crowded holiday months of July and August. Constant sampling of all water supplies is an extra safeguard for such sampling will immediately show if the purity of the water supply has suddenly deteriorated.

Skin contact with water contaminated with rats' urine can lead to the development of Leptospirosis (see pages 137–8).

The freedom of infection from water supplies in this country is no guide to the hazards of many foreign countries. *Many cases of typhoid occur each year in travellers who have visited the Indian sub-continent, Italy, Spain and North Africa* especially when these visitors have stayed in remote country areas or have taken camping holidays. If such a holiday is planned, it is essential either to (*i*) *sterilise all water* with a simple camp sterilisation outfit; or (*ii*) be *protected with a course of TAB inoculation* before starting. This protects against typhoid fever and paratyphoid fever (see page 128).

Fluoridation of water supplies

It is known that the variation in dental caries found in different areas is connected with the content of natural fluoride in the water consumed by the people of that area (see page 91).

In localities where the natural fluoride content of the water supply is low, fluoride can be added to the water supply to bring the level to about one part of fluoride per million parts of water. This has been done in many parts of the world and has always been followed by a substantial reduction in the amount of dental caries in the children in that area. After pilot trials, the Department of Health has advised that all water supplies should have fluoride added to them where the natural supply of fluoride is deficient. It is known that if this is done, there should be a reduction of at least 60% in the dental caries. A number of areas (about 7% of England and Wales) have already introduced artificial fluoridation. Unfortunately ill-informed persons have campaigned very forcibly against fluoridation on the grounds that it is 'mass medication' and an intrusion into their individual liberty.

This attitude is very difficult to understand when it is realised that chlorine is added to all water supplies for safety. There is ample evidence that fluoridation would be a valuable preventive medical factor and would undoubtedly result in far less pain and suffering in children from dental caries. It is to be hoped that this public reaction will not be allowed to interfere with what is a most valuable preventive dental service.

13   The structure of the social services

The 'social services' in the United Kingdom cover many different types of service but mainly fall into three well-defined groups.

- Social services provided by *local authority social services departments* – by the metropolitan districts in the large conurbations or by the London boroughs in London and by the county councils in the rest of England and Wales (see Fig. 13.2, page 235). These services include a wide range of statutory, community and residential services for children, physically disabled, mentally disabled, homeless and elderly people. The hospital social work services are also provided by local authorities although such work is entirely undertaken within a hospital setting.

  These types of social services are described in Chapters 14 to 19. Centrally, these services are the responsibility of the Secretary of State for Health and the Department of Health.

- The *probation and aftercare service* which is attached to the courts and works mainly with adult offenders who, as part of their sentence, are placed on probation. In addition, much of the aftercare work for discharged prisoners is undertaken by this service. Note that much of the court aftercare work of juvenile offenders (delinquent children) is carried out by local authority social services (see Chapter 14).

  The probation service is quite separate from the local authority social services and, like the Prison Service, is centrally the responsibility of the Home Secretary and the Home Office.

- *Voluntary bodies*   There are many well established voluntary bodies providing social services of all kinds both on a national and local basis. They include specialist bodies working with children, such as the National Society for Prevention of Cruelty to Children (NSPCC), Barnardo's, National Children's Homes, the Family Welfare Association, and groups dealing with the elderly, such as Age Concern. The Women's Royal Voluntary Service covers a wide range of voluntary help while the Family Service Units provide assistance to problem families. There are many specialist voluntary bodies working in the field of the disabled including the Central Council for the Disabled and the British Council for the

Rehabilitation of the Disabled. Locally, Councils of Social Service and Rural Community Councils undertake a coordinating rôle in respect of many small voluntary bodies or local branches of the large national bodies.

Many of these voluntary bodies are providing services which could also be undertaken by Social Service Departments and it is therefore essential that very close working arrangements are made. In many instances, some of the finance necessary for their function is provided by the Social Services Committee of the Local Authority.

Nationally the government department which is mainly responsible for voluntary bodies is the Department of Health, and in some instances this department encourages voluntary work in the social services by providing small grants to voluntary bodies especially in respect of experimental schemes. Examples of such grants recently made include financial help to reduce and prevent alcohol abuse.

A further example of voluntary work in the social services is the Citizens' Advice Bureaux. These were first developed in the 1939–45 war to help with various queries about rationing, missing relatives, etc. Their rôle has been widened recently to include consumer protection, the provision of legal advice and the explanation of various pension rights. They are particularly valuable in helping families who may be unwilling to seek help from statutory services (such as a Social Services Department) because they may feel aggrieved for some reason – they may have been evicted for rent arrears or generally are resentful of the way they have been treated in the past by local authorities and other statutory services. For this reason many local authority Social Services Committees give financial grants to the Citizens' Advice Bureaux to enable them to help clients who otherwise would be unlikely to seek help. Centrally there is a National Association of Citizens' Advice Bureaux linked to local bureaux by a regional committee.

Central Government control of local authority social services

In England the main government department concerned with the administration of local authority social services is the Department of Health. The Minister in charge is the Secretary of State for Health, a member of the Cabinet who is also responsible for the health services (see page 1). The advantage of having the same Minister (Secretary of State for Health) and the same government department (Department of Health) for the social services and the health services is that, in many instances such as disability, mental disorders or old age, families need help from both services and this arrangement assists coordination.

The rôle of the Department of Health in social services is similar to that described for the health services (see pages 3–4). The Department is primarily concerned in assisting the development of social services in three main ways.

- *Advisory*   From time to time important advisory memoranda on various social services are issued by the Department of Health. These deal with every aspect of the services including the planning of various residential establishments. Recent examples include advisory memoranda on community services for the elderly and mentally handicapped and child abuse.
- *Policy and planning*   Policy and planning of the social services is an essential function of the Department of Health as it helps to provide a balanced service in the community. An excellent example is in the case of the services for mentally ill persons who are currently cared for in mental hospitals. In future it is hoped that many of these people will be discharged into the community *but this will be possible only if a parallel increase is provided in all forms of community social services*, including a marked increase in the day centre and hostel provision by local authority social services departments.
  The central structure of the Department of Health is organised to ensure the integration of planning between the social and health services. A central planning division has been set up alongside a central regional division so that in both the social and health services professional officers are working closely with their linked administrative officers.
- *Financial*   This is another important indirect method of control of the social services. Special extra financial allocation is made by the government (acting on the advice of the Secretary of State) in the revenue support grant (paid by the government to local authorities) so that certain social services can be developed.
  Revenue (or costs of running day-to-day services) is financed by
  —   the revenue support grant from the government; and
  —   the local community charge.
  The *revenue support grant* is the large block grant of money paid from the government to local authorities to assist them with their services (it represents approximately 60% of all local government expenditure). It includes a 'population' element and a 'needs' element which reflect the social problems and social services provided by that authority. The actual division of the block grant is made by each local authority (who therefore decides how much will be spent on social services, education, roads, environmental health etc.). However, the larger the rate support grant, the greater the likelihood of social services being developed locally.

Special investigations in the field of social services

The Department of Health arranges for special research investigations to be undertaken in the field of social services. The Secretary of State can, through Parliament, appoint special expert committees to look into certain aspects and to report back. An example was the Inquiry set up in 1987, presided over by Lord Justice Butler-Schloss to examine the allegations of child sexual abuse in Cleveland.

Rôle of other government departments in social services

Although the main government department dealing with social services is the Department of Health, other departments, particularly the Home Office and the Department of Employment, do have certain powers.

The *Home Office* is the main department dealing with the problems of law and order in the United Kingdom and has been active in the encouragement of *community development*. This attempts to improve the social conditions of people by encouraging them to participate more in the running of their own affairs. The Home Office has set up a number of interesting seven-year experimental community development projects in some cities, including Liverpool and Coventry, which could have a very important effect on future social service development.

The *probation service*, run in conjunction with Clerks of the Magistrates, is controlled centrally by the Home Office and a close link must be maintained between Probation and Social Services Departments especially in relation to the problems and care of delinquent children.

Until 1982, the Home Office also had an important function in social services in the *Urban Programme* (which includes the former Inner Areas Partnership). This is a special form of financial aid (both capital and revenue) given to certain projects to encourage new developments, mainly in the large cities and urban areas where there is an urgent need to develop social services. Under the Urban Programme the government provides 75% and the local authority 25% of the cost. Urban aid covers projects by both local authorities and voluntary bodies, although in the latter instance the appropriate local authority has to pay 25% of the cost of each project. This help usually lasts from one to five years. Examples of urban aid projects approved in the last three years include many new day nurseries, day care centres for the elderly, residential units for children and various schemes for the physically and mentally handicapped.

The *Department of Employment* is mainly concerned with the special employment problems of the handicapped. Its officers include the Disablement Resettlement Officers (see page 277) and the Blind Persons Resettlement Officers. Both work very closely with the social services.

Community care

To extend various forms of community care for physically handicapped, mentally ill and handicapped and elderly persons has been a
priority of various governments in the United Kingdom for the past
10–15 years. In 1986 Sir Roy Griffiths, on behalf of the Secretary of
State for Health and Social Services, began a review of all forms of
community care and his report entitled *Community Care: Agenda for
Action* was published in March 1988. After a period of consultation the
Secretary of State reported to the House of Commons in July 1989,
indicating that the government intended to implement the majority of
the Griffiths Report.

The Griffiths Report made a distinction between health and social
care. The Secretary of State supported this view and proposed that all
health care should remain the responsibility of the existing health
services. The existing community health services will continue to play
an essential part in meeting the medical and nursing needs of people
outside hospital. In future, however, *important changes are being
proposed in the way in which non-health care is provided* and, when
necessary, funded at public expense. It is planned that *local authority
social service departments should act as the main coordinating body for
all forms of social care in the community*. A new funding structure is
suggested for all those seeking help from public funds and, in future,
there will be a single budget handled by the local authority who will
assume responsibility for the care elements of public support for
people in *private and voluntary residential care and in nursing homes*.
This will mean that the Department of Social Security will cease paying
for those at present in private homes – this change will not apply to all
those at present in such homes but will do so for those entering such
homes from a date to be announced.

Each local authority is asked to make plans which will be inspected
by the Social Services Inspectorate at the Department of Health. The
local authorities, through their Social Services Departments and in
collaboration with others including doctors and other caring professions, will be responsible for assessing any individual's needs,
designing suitable care arrangements and securing their delivery. It is
not intended that local authorities will provide all the services directly
themselves and they should make the *maximum possible use of the
voluntary, not-for-profit and commercial sectors* so as to widen the
individual's choice and to increase flexibility and innovation. In particular, the Department of Health is urging local authorities' social
service departments to *act in an 'enabling' and not just in a 'providing'
capacity*. Local authorities will be expected to develop better services
for people at home and to make greater use of independent providers.

Resources are going to be transferred to local authorities to enable
them to undertake the extra functions but *the government has not*

agreed with the Griffiths Report recommendation that specific grants should be paid to provide 'a significant proportion of the whole of the cost of the programme'. The one exception is that *specific grants will be payable for severely mentally ill people discharged from hospital for social care in the community*. The new specific grant will be created in order to encourage local authorities to arrange the care of such persons in line with health authority plans and objectives. This specific grant will be paid by health authorities on the basis of plans and targets put to them by relevant local authorities.

A further part of the Griffiths Report recommended that local authorities be asked *to establish inspection and registration units*, at arms length from the management of their own services, which would be responsible for checking on standards in their own homes and to involve independent outsiders in these arrangements. The government has accepted this recommendation.

Finally, the Secretary of State for Health emphasised that general practitioners will be expected to ensure that social service departments are aware of their patients' needs for social care, as recommended in the Griffiths Report.

A White Paper was published in late 1989 giving further details of how the government intended to implement the proposals of the Griffiths Report. In July 1990 the Secretary of State for Social Services made a statement in the House of Commons indicating that the government is altering the dates of implementation of the changes in community care. It was originally envisaged that the changes would be implemented in April 1991; however, due to the large public expenditure involved, the changes are now to be phased in three stages.

Phase 1   April 1991   The following new procedures and grants will be established.

— New inspection units in local authorities plus the establishment of a complaints procedure.
— New specific grants for mentally ill people. This grant will be at the rate of 70% and will support total expenditure of £30 million.
— New specific grants for local funding of voluntary bodies providing a service for drug and alcohol abusers. This grant will also be at the rate of 70% and will support an expenditure of £2 million.
— The present specific grants for the training of social services staff will be increased by £7.5 million to support a total expenditure of £35.5 million.

Phase 2   April 1992   The planning of the community arrangements will be completely implemented both for local authorities and health authorities. The remaining development work will proceed.

Phase 3   April 1993   The new benefit arrangements will be fully implemented. Until that time present arrangements for direct payment by the Department of Social Security will continue. The proposals for the preservation of benefit rights for those already residing in private and voluntary homes will be implemented from 1 April 1993.

Local authority social services

Structure

Each major local authority must have a Social Services Committee to control its social services (the full list of these is given below), and must appoint a Director of Social Services who is the chief officer in charge of the Department of Social Services which administers all the services.

Local authority social services are run by the County Councils in England and Wales, by the Metropolitan District Councils within the large conurbations of the West Midlands, Merseyside, Greater Manchester, West Yorkshire, South Yorkshire, and Tyneside, and by the London Boroughs in London. In Scotland the departments are called Social Work Departments and are controlled by the Regional local authorities. In Northern Ireland a unified structure, which is outside local political control, deals with the social services and all the health services. There are four Boards set up to administer the social and health services (see Chapter 1, page 17).

Types of social services provided by the Social Services Committees

The following is a summary of services provided by each Social Services Committee.

- *Care of the elderly*   This includes both field work services carried out within the community, and residential care (see Chapter 18).
- *Care of the physically handicapped*   Blind, deaf and dumb, hard of hearing, spastic, epileptic, paraplegics and other disabled persons (see Chapter 16).
- *Social work advice to the homeless*   (see Chapter 19).

The main legislation covering the above services includes the National Assistance Act 1948 and the Chronically Sick and Disabled Persons Act, 1970.

- *All child care services*   Including child care protection, child care supervision, acceptance of parental responsibility for children committed into the care of the local authority, control of various residential units for children, admission units, reception centres, residential nurseries, children's homes, control of community homes with education on the premises and classifying centres (formerly approved schools and remand homes) and certain services for adoption. Much of the preventive work in child abuse cases is organised under the child care services (see Chapter 15). The legislation for these services is consolidated into the Child Care Act 1980 but is now being revised by the Children Act 1989.

- *Social work and family casework dealing with the mentally disordered* Including the provision of social workers (formerly mental welfare officers), adult training centres, workshops and residential accommodation (hostels) for the mentally disordered.
- *Day care for children under five years of age* Including provision of day nurseries and the supervision of private nurseries and child minders.
- *Provision of home helps*
- *Care of unsupported mothers* Including residential care.
- *Hospital social workers* Provision of social work services for hospital patients.
- Work in the field of drug and alcohol abuse (see Chapter 19).

Organisation of social services departments

There are many different forms of organisation in social services departments. However, most have Area (or District) teams of social workers (see below).

The chief officer is the *Director of Social Services*, next is the Deputy Director of Social Services, and usually Assistant Directors are in charge of the other sections. Each Area (or District) is usually under the control of an Area (or District) social services officer. A typical arrangement is shown in Fig. 13.1. It will be noted that there are at least five main parts to the headquarters of a social services department:

— that dealing with residential services;
— that dealing with field work services;
— that providing facilities for training;
— that dealing with hospital social work;
— that dealing with administration.

Full details of the various types of residential and field work services are given on the pages mentioned below. These include the following.

Residential services
— Elderly (see pages 333–4)
— Children (see pages 246–7)

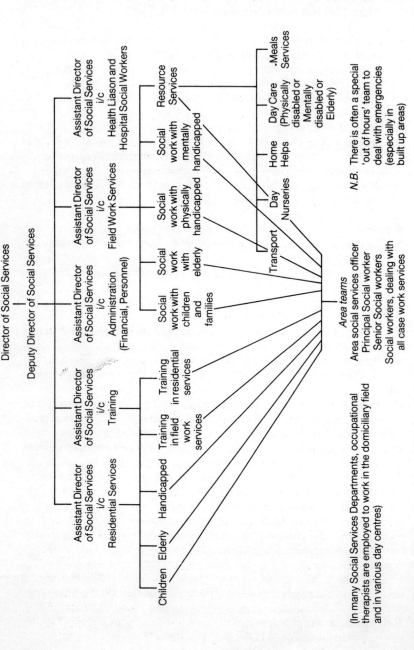

Fig. 13.1 The structure of a typical Social Services Department.

Director of Social Services

Deputy Director of Social Services

Assistant Director of Social Services i/c Residential Services

Assistant Director of Social Services i/c Training

Assistant Director of Social Services i/c Administration (Financial, Personnel)

Assistant Director of Social Services i/c Field Work Services

Assistant Director of Social Services i/c Health Liason and Hospital Social Workers

Children Elderly Handicapped

Training in field work services Training in residential services

Social work with children and families

Social work with elderly

Social work with physically handicapped

Social work with mentally handicapped

Resource Services

Transport Day Nurseries Home Helps Day Care (Physically disabled or Mentally disabled or Elderly) Meals Services

Area teams
Area social services officer
Principal Social worker
Senior Social workers
Social workers, dealing with all case work services

(In many Social Services Departments, occupational therapists are employed to work in the domiciliary field and in various day centres)

N.B. There is often a special 'out of hours' team to deal with emergencies (especially in built up areas)

— Physically handicapped (disabled) (see page 280)
— Mentally disordered (see pages 298–9; 309)

Field work services
— Family and child care (see pages 000–0)
— Disabled (see page 277)
— Mentally disordered (see pages 297; 305)
— Elderly (see pages 313–4)
— Transport (see page 279)
— Home helps (see pages 336–7)
— Meals services – meals-on-wheels or luncheon clubs (see page 320)
— Day nursery provision (see pages 237–8)
— Homeless families (see pages 338–40)
— Adoption services (see pages 249–251)

Training
— Induction training for new entrants
— In-service training for existing staff
— Professional training (field work, social work training) usually by two-year full-time courses
— Practical training – receiving students from full-time courses who are doing practical field work placements
— Training for residential staff (in both children's units and in old people's homes)
— Senior post-graduate training for qualified staff including training in management.

The standards of training of social workers is the responsibility of the *Central Council for Education and Training in Social Work* (CCETSW). This Council is responsible for promotion of training in all fields of social work. Social work training is currently undergoing change, with the introduction of a new Diploma in Social Work (DipSW) which will eventually replace the existing Certificate of Qualification in Social Work (CQSW) and the Certificate in Social Service (CSS), although the latter two will continue to be recognised as professional qualifications. Much of this training is carried out in cooperation with universities, polytechnics and commercial colleges run by local education authorities. Each social service department should have a training unit plus training officers.

Hospital social work deals with the various social problems of patients in hospital. Medical casework is undertaken to help the patient and family to adjust to the illness. Other forms of help and assistance are given with convalescence etc. (see pages 340–1).

Area social services teams

A very important part of each social services department is the area social services team. By arranging for all the casework for family and clients to be undertaken by such coordinated teams of social workers, it is hoped that problems will be considered as a whole rather than in a fragmented way and that this will lead to a *family social service* dealing with all types of social problem in the family whether this presents as a problem in a child, a disabled person, an old person or a mentally disordered individual. The teams are made up of social workers, of whom some specialise in child care, others in mental illness or handicap, in care of the elderly or the physically handicapped.

The population size of areas varies from about 40 000 to 100 000 depending on the district and its social problems. An ideal area will have from ten to thirty social workers mainly working in groups of five or six under the leadership of a senior social worker. Each team deals with the problems of *clients* (the term used for persons referred to the social services department).

Close coordination must be maintained with other workers – health visitors, district/community nurses, medical social workers, doctors, teachers, psychiatric social workers, educational welfare officers, community workers, youth leaders, general practitioners and the many voluntary bodies helping in the district. Usually each Area social work team controls the allocation of:

— home helps;
— meals-on-wheels;
— day nursery places;
— vacancies in old persons' homes;
— places in residential accommodation for children;
— telephones.

The key individual in each team is the *Area Social Services Officer* and any nurse working in the area who comes across a difficult social problem should refer the case to this officer.

Liaison between the health and social services

Many of the social services in local authorities represent the main supporting services within the community for persons recovering from illness or suffering from some chronic disabling condition. Many of the necessary aids, gadgets or adaptations for the handicapped which are so essential for the successful rehabilitation of many disabling conditions (e.g. arthritis, paraplegia, multiple sclerosis, spasticity) are supplied by social services departments. The closest liaison between the two services must therefore be developed and maintained.

On the health side a community physician is usually appointed with responsibility for liaison – sometimes called a Specialist in Community Medicine (Social Services) – and on the social services side a senior officer is appointed (usually an Assistant Director of Social Services) to take charge of the hospital social work service and to be responsible for integration.

Local arrangements should be made to assist day to day co-operation. Social workers should visit health centres and group

Fig. 13.2 Social Services Authorities, England.

practices from time to time so that they can meet not only the general practitioners, but the health visitors, district/community nurses and school nurses working from the centre.

There should also be working links created between social workers and the hospital services especially through the medical social workers at all hospitals and particularly at geriatric and mental hospitals.

The locally designated community physician responsible for co-ordination acts as medical adviser to the social services department and consequently becomes acquainted with all the medical problems of the department. It is particularly important that *health visitors work closely with social workers* for many of the problems they deal with are also important to the social services department and vice versa. Both health visitors and social workers find themselves working with 'problem families', but each dealing with different aspects – the health visitor from the preventive health point of view and the social worker dealing with the social difficulties (this is particularly important in preventing child abuse (see pages 257–9)). The closer that the two groups of officers can work together, the better the results. Case conferences to consider difficult individual cases may be arranged between such workers, with other officers working with the families invited, especially those from the education or housing departments. Although the social services department is responsible for the organisation of social services within each local authority, cooperation with many different services is needed including those providing health care, education, housing, probation, police and voluntary services. It is only by improving the arrangements between so many different services that the best possible result will be obtained for each family.

A map of the Social Services Authorities in England is given in Fig. 13.2, on the previous page.

14   Care of children in need

All local authorities, through their Social Services Committees and departments, have special responsibilities for providing child care services for supervising and looking after children and young persons under the age of 18 years. In much of this work the social services department is attempting to find the *best possible alternative arrangement for care of the child in the absence of the parents* – either because the parents have abandoned the child, the child is an orphan, or because the parents have been found incapable of looking after the child properly. Every attempt is made in trying to settle the child in a suitable family placement in order to provide the child with as normal a home as possible. For this reason, large institutional homes are no longer used.

Special help is given to parents who, because of social reasons, cannot look after their children during the daytime. Most of this help is given in *day nurseries* or *day care centres*, *playgroups* or with a *child minder*.

Day nurseries and day care centres

Day nurseries are provided by Social Service Departments to help care for young children when this care cannot be provided at home due to *social circumstances*. Such reasons would include sudden illness of the mother leading to her admission to hospital, an unmarried mother who has to go out to work to support her family, or a widower or widow with a small child.

Under the Children Act 1989, the duties of local authorities have been extended and they must now provide day care and supervised activities for preschool children and for school aged children outside school hours and in the holidays *for children in need*. Such children are defined in the Act as 'children who need services to secure a reasonable standard of health and development' and includes children who are disabled. In future all social service departments, together with the local authority education department, must publish a review of these services every three years.

Day nurseries look after children from a few weeks old up to the age of five years when they can go to school. In some cases, the need for care is temporary while an acute social crisis occurs in the family. It is usual for about 50 children to be looked after in each nursery. 'Family groups' are set up in each nursery so that about ten children are looked after together covering an age range from six months to five years. Babies under six months of age are looked after separately.

Each nursery has a trained matron and deputy matron plus a number of trained nursery nurses. The staff are responsible for all aspects of care of the children including their health which must be carefully supervised. Special attention is paid to ensure that:

— every child is fit when admitted;
— every child is fully immunised; and that
— any case of communicable disease is immediately investigated.

Dysentery or gastro-enteritis can be particularly serious if they spread in a day nursery (see pages 134–5) and any child with diarrhoea must be sent home until all bacteriological tests are normal.

Day nurseries are being increasingly used for young handicapped children (with various disabling conditions e.g. spina bifida) to help with their development. It is best if such children are looked after in ordinary day nurseries rather than being segregated in a special nursery. Where a day nursery has a number of handicapped children it will be necessary to employ larger numbers of staff. *Nursery Nurses* qualify after a two year course and by gaining the certificate of the Nursery Nurses Examination Board.

Private day nurseries, playgroups and child minders

Many private day nurseries, playgroups and child minders look after children and each Local Authority, through its Social Services Committee, is responsible for ensuring that proper standards of staff, fire precautions and accommodation are provided. Each such unit must be registered with the Local Authority and inspected from time to time to check that the correct standards are being maintained. All people caring for more than one child in their own home, whether for profit or not, *must be registered with the local authority*.

Child care services

These services primarily look after children who need care and protection because of the neglect, abandonment or inability of the parents to cope due to some sudden emergency (illness, separation, etc.) or exposure to moral danger. The Children Act 1989, which comes into operation in late 1991, identifies the type of children (called children in need) for whom the local authorities' child care services are designed. A child is considered to be in need if any of the following situations arise.

- If the child is unlikely to achieve or maintain, or have the opportunity of achieving or maintaining, a reasonable standard of health or development without the provision of the services of the local authority.
- If the health or development of the child is likely to be significantly impaired, or further impaired, without the provision of such services for the child.
- If the child is disabled.

The Children Act 1989 defines a child as disabled 'if he or she is blind, deaf or dumb, or suffers from a mental disorder of any kind or is substantially or permanently handicapped by illness, injury or congenital deformity or such other disability as may be prescribed'.

In all cases the first consideration is *the need to safeguard and promote the welfare of the child*. Every social services department must investigate fully each case which comes to their knowledge. Social workers undertake this inquiry.

The Children Act 1989 simplified existing child care legislation in the United Kingdom and has introduced some very important changes. The basis of the Act is the principle that children generally are best looked after within the family with both parents playing a full part and, if possible, without resort to legal proceedings. This principle is expressed in the Act by the following.

- A new concept of *'parental responsibility'* (replacing 'parental rights').
- The ability of unmarried fathers to share that responsibility by agreement with the mother.
- Local authorities now have a duty to give support for children and their families.
- Local authorities now have a duty to return a child who is being looked after by them to his or her family unless this is against the child's interests.
- For a child who is looked after, away from home, by the local authorities they now have a duty to ensure contact between the child and his or her parents whenever possible.

Parental responsibility

In the past, child care law spoke of 'parental rights' where a child taken into care had the parental rights transferred to the local authority. The Children Act 1989 abolishes this arrangement. In the future, whenever a child is taken into care permanently, the local authority will accept parental responsibility. All decisions about parental authority must be made by the courts (Magistrate, County or High Courts, depending on the complexity of the case). It is not possible, as formerly, for a local authority to assume parental responsibility as this question must be determined by the Court. This allows maximum opportunity for decisions to be challenged, questioned and properly discussed.

General parental responsibility will be conferred on both parents if they are married and on the mother if not. A father who is not married to the child's mother may acquire parental responsibility if the mother agrees. If both parents are in agreement, this can be done by a simple agreement and without going to Court.

Children away from home

When the local authority has to arrange for a child to live away from home (for any period) because the natural parents are unable to look after him or her properly or need respite, it is preferable that *voluntary arrangements* be made. In such instances, the parents retain their parental responsiblity and act as partners with the local authority or with those caring for their child. The parents should participate in the child's care and in decisions made, and they should also retain contact so that the child can return to them as soon as possible.

All administrative measures to exercise compulsion on a child being looked after, whether to limit contact with a parent or to prevent the parent recovering the child, are abolished by the Children Act 1989. The Act also now recognises that a *child's racial origin, culture and language are important factors* to be taken into consideration by the local authority looking after the child.

Every local authority must prepare the child for the time he or she leaves school until the age of 21 years. A *complaints procedure* must be introduced by every local authority and must contain an independent element.

The child's interests are paramount

This overriding principle which has been an important bench mark in all child care since 1976 has been further strengthened by the Children Act 1989, which contains a check-list of matters to be considered in all Court proceedings. Heading this list is the fact that the Court must have regard to the child's wishes and feelings. With the Court's permission, a child may seek a Court Order about his or her future.

In local authority proceedings, such as the application for a care order, the child is always to be a party to the proceedings. Generally the Court will appoint a '*guardian ad litem*' and it will always be the guardian's duty to represent the child in these proceedings and to safeguard the child's interests. The child will also be entitled to separate legal representation.

Court Orders

The Children Act 1989 gives power to a Court to make the following orders.

Care Orders and Supervision Orders – to determine parental responsibility. The sole ground for a Care Order is one of 'harm' or 'likely harm' to the child.

Residence Orders – to decide with whom the child will live.

Contact Orders – to decide what form of contact the child is to have with other people.

Specific Issue Orders – to deal with any other particular matter in relation to the child.

Prohibited Steps Orders – to prohibit anything being done in relation to the child, for example to ensure that a parental responsibility order by the Court is carried out.

Further Court Orders can be made regarding the protection of the child (see below), Education (see page 243) and Family Assistance (see page 244).

Protection of children

The Children Act 1989 gives wide powers to Courts to intervene to protect children at risk of harm within the family, provided the child is suffering or is likely to suffer significant harm because of a lack of reasonable parental care or because he or she is beyond parental control. In such cases the Court can do the following.

- Order the assessment of a child where there is real suspicion of harm (*Child Assessment Order*).
- Order the removal or retention of a child in an emergency (*Emergency Protection Order*).
- Order that a child be put under local authority care or supervision pending a full investigation and hearing of the proceedings (*Interim Care and Supervision Orders*).
- Make *Private Law Orders* altering the arrangements about with whom the child lives, regulating his or her contact with other people, determining any particular matter relating to his or her upbringing and prohibiting any particular step being taken.

Note that the Act defines the test of reasonable parental care as 'that care which a reasonable parent would provide for the child concerned'.

It is important to realise that a standard of care which would be reasonable for a normal healthy child *may not be reasonable if the child has particular social needs* because, say, he or she has *brittle bones*, is *asthmatic*, or *mentally disabled*.

Child Assessment Order

If an assessment of a child is needed to decide whether significant harm is likely and *it is clear there is not an emergency* an application can be made by the local authority for a Child Assessment Order which lasts up to seven days. The main difference between this order and many others is that it does not convey parental responsibility to the holder. It is hoped that this order will be helpful where there is concern about the child, but the parents and carers are uncooperative and an application for a care or supervision order would not be appropriate.

Emergency Protection Order

This order has replaced the Place of Safety Order and is used where there is reasonable cause to believe the child is likely to suffer significant harm unless

— removed from where he or she is to another place; or
— kept where he or she is.

An Emergency Protection Order is also used where it is impossible to carry out full enquiries because the parents unreasonably withhold access to the child and there is reasonable cause to believe that access is required as a matter of urgency.

Emergency Protection Orders are mainly used in serious suspected or proved cases of child abuse. The practical application of this order is discussed fully in Chapter 15 (see page 262).

Private Law Orders

In disputes between parents a Private Law Order to protect the child may be sought by a parent or others who have some legal responsibility for the child.

Age limit

In all cases where parental responsibility has been transferred to a local authority, this *ceases when the young person reaches the age of 18 years*.

Further powers of Courts

The Children Act 1989 gives power to a Court to make an Education Supervision Order when a child of school age is not being properly educated. This means that, in future, a care order cannot be made in such cases.

Child care provisions

Local authority accommodation

A local authority must provide accommodation for a child in need in their area who requires it as a result of any of the following.

- There being no person who has parental responsibility for the child.
- The child is lost or has been abandoned.
- The person who has been caring for the child being prevented (whether permanently or not, and for whatever reason) from providing the child with suitable accommodation or care.

The range of options which a local authority can use includes the following.

- A family placement with a family, relative or another suitable person. Under previous child care law this was usually referred to as 'boarding out'.
- Placement in a community, voluntary or registered children's home.
- Other appropriate arrangements, for example for older young persons hostels for semi-independent living or arrangements for rented accommodation.

In many instances the local authority looks after the child for quite a short time during a family crisis (perhaps a few weeks). The most appropriate method of care is used – family placement or the child stays in a small home or even an admission unit if the period is very short. Children rarely suffer from any deprivation in such cases and it is usual for other members of the family either to remain with the child or to visit regularly. If the crisis lasts some months then the aim of the local authority is to attempt to keep the family together, preferably in a family placement.

Care Order

When a Court passes a Care Order the parental responsibility is transferred to the local authority. Such cases are the more serious ones involving grave neglect, abandonment or moral danger to the child. Once parental authority has been transferred the only way that the natural parents can reclaim their child is by petitioning the same Court which made the original Order to revoke it. The Court must then decide whether the parents are now responsible enough to justify returning the child to their care. If the Court decides they are not, the child remains in the care of the authority; if the Court decides they are responsible enough, the parents will have the child returned to them.

Preventive social and rehabilitation work with children

Increasing emphasis is being laid on the importance of *preventive work* in child care. This depends upon the social services taking action early enough to enable them to prevent a child coming into care or appearing before a Court.

There is a great deal of evidence that everything must be done to *avoid family breakdown*. As this will be made more likely if the family gets into debt and is made homeless, there is power for the Social Services Committee to make financial payments to prevent a child coming into care. These may even include the payment of rent arrears. Much of this financial help is concentrated on ways which are likely to prevent child delinquency – holiday adventure schemes or clubs, etc.

The social services department and its social workers should also do all in their power to try to *rehabilitate* each child in its care so that the child may eventually return to the family.

Family Assistance Orders

Under the Children Act 1989, a Court may make a *Family Assistance Order* in family proceedings. This enables a social worker or probation officer to be made available to give advice and assistance and, where appropriate, befriend the person named in the order – this may be the child, a parent or guardian of the child or any person with whom the child lives. Before such an order may be made, each person named in it must give his or her consent. Such an order may last up to six months and is designed to give expert advice to families, especially in separation and divorce cases.

Types and methods of child care

The needs of every child should be carefully assessed on admission into care and each child should be placed according to that assessment.

The aim in child care is to look after every child in the way which is best suited to his or her needs. Supervision is always carried out by trained social workers and *each case must be reviewed every six months*.

The ideal is to care for each child in conditions and environment as near normal as possible.

It is usual for a child to go to an *Admission Unit* where any special needs are carefully assessed. There are five main ways in which a child can be looked after.

- *A family placement* The child lives with a family just as if the child was in his or her own home. This is an ideal arrangement and is used wherever possible, particularly in long stay cases. The person with whom the child lives is called a local authority *foster parent* and such people are very carefully chosen to ensure the right type of person is used. All children in a family placement must be visited regularly and at least once every six weeks by social workers from the social services department. The frequency of such visiting is very carefully controlled by the Department of Health.
- *A family group home* Placement of a child in such a home, containing four to six children of different ages, is the next best type of care wherever family placement is not possible. It aims to look after the child in small units where life can be very similar to that in any large family. These homes are scattered throughout a community and made inconspicuous so that the child's living conditions can be kept as near normal as possible.
- *A small children's home* Children who do not seem suitable for either family placement or life in a family group home may be cared for in small children's homes, containing from twelve to eighteen children. Many of the children living in these homes later progress to other forms of care. A certain amount of assessment can be undertaken in such homes and an unstable child often settles well.
- *In a child's own home under supervision* This arrangement is often used during the rehabilitation of children to see if they can now settle back into their own home.
- *A children's home run by a voluntary body* Examples include Barnado's and the National Children's Home.

Need for continuous review

In all instances it is most important *to review each child's progress regularly* and to attempt *to rehabilitate that child* so that eventually it may be possible to return that child home.

With the disturbed child who has had a difficult home background, this may mean many different stages have to be passed through. Such a child may go to a reception centre, small children's home, family placement, a short trial back at home (which may or may not succeed) and much patience is always needed. The eventual success or failure will only be seen when that child becomes an adult; the constant aim is to help children to develop and mature so that they grow into responsible, mature and happy adults.

Community homes

All types of children's homes and the former remand homes and approved schools are now called community homes. Some of these have education provided on the premises (see below).

Special residential units

The larger local authorities social services departments usually provide five special residential units – an admission unit; a residential nursery; a reception centre; a community home with education on the premises for children on remand or for assessment (former remand homes); and a community home with education on the premises for treatment (former approved schools).

Admission unit

The admission unit is the place into which all urgent cases are admitted. The number of children looked after varies, but many look after 45–50 children. Children needing short-term care, especially if the emergency is likely to be short lived, are often cared for in admission units but others are carefully assessed in the admission unit to decide which type of care is best suited to the child. Once this has been decided the child goes on to the appropriate care which may be either residential nursery, reception centre, family placement or admission to a family group or small children's home.

Residential nursery

Small children under the age of five years and babies may be looked after in a residential nursery immediately following admission. Many of the short-term care cases will stay there while in care, but some of the older children may later leave for family placement or other forms of child care.

During the past few years, more and more social service departments have been closing their residential nurseries and relying on using a carefully selected panel of foster parents to look after babies in care. It has been found that such an arrangement is best for it enables a one-to-one relationship to be established between the foster parent and infant.

Reception centre

Some children need a longer period of assessment or may have difficulty in settling down and these are looked after at a reception centre. Some of these children are maladjusted and the regime of the centre allows a longer and more expert assessment of the child to be undertaken.

Community homes with education on the premises (CHEs)

Separate community homes are run by the larger social services departments *for children on remand or for assessment or for treatment*. Originally their main function was to accommodate children on remand for some serious offence while full investigations (especially psychiatric) took place. Today the most important function undertaken is *the assessment of each child* who is committed to the care of the local authority by a Court (because of conviction on some serious offence).

Many children who pass through such community homes are maladjusted or disturbed having come from an unsatisfactory home. It is, therefore, important to have staff in charge who are trained in dealing with such children and each community home should make arrangements for a psychiatrist to be available to help.

Entry into such a community home used to follow the decision of a juvenile court sentencing the child. Now the decision in such a case is usually made by a case conference of social workers of a social services department after assessment at a suitable assessment centre which indicates that a stay in such a community home could be beneficial for the child.

Education for children in care

In all community homes with education on the premises, including admission units and reception centres, the local education authority may run one or two classes at each centre which the children can attend or the teachers may be employed by the social services department.

Once the child is transferred to other types of care – family placement, family group or small children's home – the children attend *normal schools in the community* and, if this is still practicable, the same school that they attended before coming into care.

Juvenile proceedings

Following the Children Act, care orders may no longer be imposed as a sentence in criminal proceedings. The fact that a child has committed an offence may be evidence that he or she is suffering, or is likely to suffer, significant harm so a local authority may apply for a care or supervision order in respect of the child. 'Harm' includes behavioural or social development. Supervision orders may still be made in criminal proceedings and these often include a residential requirement for a child or young person to live in the local authority accommodation provided for up to six months.

Intermediate treatment

A juvenile court can place a child on a supervision order and attach to it an order for the child to attend a local scheme of intermediate treatment. The principle underlying intermediate treatment is that wherever possible it is better to keep the young offender within the family and community and to attempt to resolve problems away from the situation in which they arose. At the same time intermediate treatment aims at the following.

— Providing a more realistic method of working with the young offender than removing him or her from home.
— Avoiding the side effects of institutionalisation which so often may follow placing the young person in a residential home.
— Avoiding some of the difficulties of reintegration into the community when the child has been admitted to a residential home.

Increasingly intermediate treatment is chosen as an alternative to admitting a child to a community home with education on the premises (CHE). It is usual to arrange that the young person on intermediate treatment undertakes useful tasks such as car maintenance in the hope that energies will be channelled into the development of skills. A short period of residential care (not longer than a few weeks) may be arranged and wherever possible this is linked to the other programme of help to the young person.

Probation orders

Probation orders for young persons under 17 years have been replaced by *supervision orders* which may be made in both criminal and care proceedings. These supervision orders are now administered by social services departments.

Borstals

The Borstal system of training was introduced in 1908. The aim is to provide training for offenders from 15–21 years of age and the sentence is in two parts: (*i*) a period of training in a Borstal establishment (run by the Home Office), minimum six months, maximum two years; (*ii*) a period of supervision up to a further two years. Social service departments are not responsible for the Borstal system which comes under the Home Office and the Probation service.

Adoption services

Every Social Service Authority (County Councils, Metropolitan Districts and London Boroughs) must establish and maintain an adoption service. This should be done in conjunction with its other social services for children and with the other approved societies in its area. In future therefore all Social Services Committees will be in charge of an adoption service.

The responsibility for approval and registration of adoption societies in England and Wales is that of the Secretary of State for Health. It is hoped that this will ensure uniformly good standards of adoption practice throughout the country.

The legal status of an adopted child will, in future, be exactly similar to that of a child born to the adopters.

Unless the child is related to the adopters or has been placed with them by a High Court order or an adoption agency, an adoption order cannot be made unless the child has had his home with the applicants for at least 12 months.

The following are some of the more important requirements for adoption.

- A legal adoption is by an adoption order granted by a Court of law.
- Persons who may adopt include the mother or father of the child and either can only *singly* adopt if (*a*) the other parent is dead or cannot be found or (*b*) there is some other reason justifying the exclusion of the other natural parent.
- A married couple may adopt where each has attained the age of 21 years (this is the sole exception to the general rule that an adoption order shall only be made to one person).
- An adoption order may be made on the application of one person where he or she is 21 years of age or over and is
  — not married; or
  — the spouses have separated and are living apart and the separation is likely to be permanent; or
  — the spouse is, by reason of ill-health (physical or mental), incapable of making an application to adopt.
- Normally a male person cannot singly adopt a female child.
- A child who has been married cannot be adopted.
- An adoption order may contain such terms and conditions as the Court thinks fit.
- The *court hearings must be in private.*
- The child must have been in the care of the applicant for at least three consecutive months.

- The applicant must notify the local authority if the adoption has not been arranged through an adoption society.
- The persons whose consent is necessary must fully understand the nature of consent. Parental consent to adoption may be dispensed with where a parent cannot be found or is incapable of giving agreement or where a child has been seriously ill-treated.
- The adoption must be in the best interests of the child.
- The adoption must not be arranged for reward.
- Social workers must visit prospective applicants during the three month period.
- Cohabiting couples cannot jointly adopt a child.
- If the parents agree to the adoption the Court appoints a *Reporting Officer* who visits the parties and reports back to the Court. Where there is no agreement, the Court appoints *Guardian ad litem* who is an officer who safeguards the interests of the child on behalf of the Court.
- *Parental consent to adoption* is now given *before an adoption order is made*. This procedure relinquishes and frees the child for adoption. It allows the parent to give early consent and can, in this way, be less traumatic.
- *Foster parents and others who have looked after the child continuously for five years can apply to adopt the child without any fear that the child can be removed before the Court hearing*. This enables foster parents who have satisfactorily cared for a child for five years to apply for adoption without being worried that the local authority or natural parent can remove the child from their care.
- Adoptions may be arranged only through an adoption society unless the person wishing to adopt the child is a close relative of the child.

Health considerations

It is important for health care professionals to realise that there are important health considerations relating both to the child who is to be adopted and to the adopting parents. The adopting parents should know all about the general health of the child and of any defects of sight, hearing, speech or mental handicap. Serological tests for syphilis and HIV infection should be carried out. In the same way, the adopting person should be in *good general health and be suitable temperamentally and psychologically to care for a child* and have a good family history. Circumstances which should also be considered include mental illness, mental handicap, epilepsy, tuberculosis and any other serious chronic diseases.

Access to birth records

Adopted persons over the age of 18 years now have a legal right to information about their birth records. The local authority social services departments and adoption agencies have a duty to provide *counselling*. People adopted after 12 November 1975 must be given an opportunity to see a counsellor but need not do so; those adopted before 12 November 1975 must see a counsellor before being given the information that they seek.

15 Child abuse

Since the late 1960s, increasing interest has centred upon child abuse and much research and investigation has taken place into this subject. Child abuse can occur as neglect, physical abuse, sexual abuse or emotional abuse (see page 254 for further details). In addition, as explained on page 254, a fifth form, 'grave concern' is now used where there is a significant risk of any of the above-mentioned forms of child abuse. Of these, the two main forms of abuse are:

- *physical abuse*, the deliberate physical injury to a child; and
- *sexual abuse* where a young child is sexually interfered with in the home surroundings. Although the majority of child sexual abusers are men or youths, and often a male relative (father, step-father, cohabitor, elder brother), occasionally a woman is involved, either as the abuser or in consenting to or arranging for the abuse to take place.

Both child physical and sexual abuse are now known to have existed for a long time but it is only in the last two decades that the degree of abuse has been appreciated. In the case of child sexual abuse, the controversy in Cleveland in 1987 when no fewer than 464 cases of alleged child sexual abuse were reported in a population of approximately 550 000 over a few months highlighted the problem. Widespread investigations followed, including an Inquiry set up by the Secretary of State and presided over by Lord Justice Butler-Schloss. The recommendations of this Inquiry and the subsequent advice from the Department of Health have now emphasised many important facts and principles about both child sexual abuse and child physical abuse, its recognition and diagnosis and its treatment. At the same time, the Department of Health issued an important booklet entitled *Working Together* which is essentially a guide to arrangements for inter-agency cooperation to protect children from both forms of abuse. In this chapter the important essentials of the recommendations of the Butler-Schloss Inquiry and the Department of Health's advice are fully described.

There are some striking similarities as well as differences between the two forms of child abuse. The *similarities* between child physical abuse and child sexual abuse include the following.

- Both physical and sexual abuse are found in *all types of families and social classes*. Although cases are commoner in certain social groups in society, many instances of child abuse will be missed if it is assumed the cases never, or very rarely, occur in those families usually described as the 'pillars of society'. Such judgements should never be used for professionals must realise that instances of both child physical abuse and child sexual abuse do occur throughout the whole strata of society.
- Both conditions *usually start gradually and are progressive*. This means that unless the child abuse is recognised early and properly treated, not only will the abuse get worse but other children in the family may also be abused. (Indeed, children born into the family in the future may eventually be affected.)
- *Child abuse can become self generating*. The child who has been abused may later become an abuser when he or she becomes a parent. This characteristic is often seen in child physical abuse but, as yet, not enough research has been undertaken to see to what extent this pattern may also occur in child sexual abuse. However because all human beings are so much influenced by their earliest experiences in life, it should never be assumed that a person who is known to have been sexually abused as a child will never become a sexual abuser as an adult.

The *differences* between child physical abuse and child sexual abuse are most *obvious when the effects on the child are studied*.

- In any case of *child physical abuse, progressive injury* to the child is likely to occur and therefore a proportion are in acute danger. Hence delay over diagnosis and effective treatment can lead to severe injury and even death in some children. Therefore, in the investigation and treatment of child physical abuse, *the safeguarding of the child is paramount at all times but particularly early in the development of the syndrome*. For this reason short term separation of the child from the family to allow the fullest investigation to take place is still justified in serious cases.
- In most cases of *child sexual abuse* the damage to the child is primarily *emotional*. All suspected cases must be fully investigated but there is never the degree of urgency to protect the child by immediate separation from the family as there is in serious cases of child physical abuse. Indeed routine removal of the sexually abuse child from the family may increase the child's emotional difficulties. In Cleveland in 1987 it was the routine removal of so many

children from their families following suspected sexual abuse that produced so many disturbing factors. The suspicion of child sexual abuse is a very emotive accusation which can easily destroy marriages and family life, particularly if accompanied by the removal of the child, even if the suspicion is later shown to have been unfounded.

Recognition of child abuse (physical and sexual)

The Department of Health's publication *Working Together* defines and classifies child abuse into the following five categories.

- *Neglect*   The persistent or severe neglect of a child (for example by exposure to any kind of danger, including cold and starvation) which results in severe impairment of the child's health or development, including non-organic failure to thrive.
- *Physical abuse*   Physical injury to a child, including deliberate poisoning, where there is a definite knowledge or reasonable suspicion, that the injury was inflicted or knowingly not prevented.
- *Sexual abuse*   The involvement of dependent, developmentally immature children and adolescents in sexual activities they do not fully comprehend, to which they are unable to give informed consent, or that violate the social taboos of family rôles.
- *Emotional abuse*   The severe adverse effect on the behaviour and emotional development of a child caused by persistent ill-treatment or rejection. All abuse involves some emotional ill-treatment. This category should be used where it is the main or sole form of abuse.
- *Grave concern*   Children whose situations do not currently fit the above categories, but where social and medical assessments indicate that they are at significant risk of abuse. These could include cases where another child in the household has been harmed or the household contains a known abuser.

The distribution of the five categories of child abuse in England and Wales in 1988 is shown in Fig. 15.1. Note that grave concern is the highest category (37%), followed by physical abuse (28%), sexual abuse (15%), neglect (13%) and emotional abuse (4%).

Stages of work in child abuse cases

Three are three main stages in the management of the individual case of child abuse (physical or sexual) – (*i*) recognition and investigation; (*ii*) assessment and planning; and (*iii*) treatment and review.

Percentages

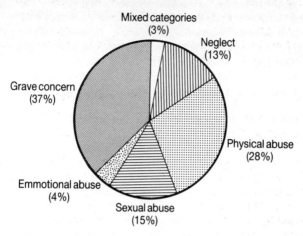

Fig. 15.1 Children on child protection registers by reason, England and Wales, 1988. Total numbers, 40 900. (From *Social Trends*, 1990.)

Recognition and investigation

The diagnostic signs of physical child abuse are described on pages 260–2, and of child sexual abuses on pages 264–6.

In both forms of child abuse, once any professional suspects that child abuse is occurring, it is essential *to refer this concern to either the social services department, police or National Society for the Prevention of Cruelty to Children (NSPCC)*. Whenever any person *alleges child abuse a full investigation must be undertaken and every allegation must be considered serious unless proved otherwise*. Once the facts have been identified, the question 'Is the child still in danger?' must be asked. If this appears to be so, an *Emergency Protection Order* must be obtained immediately from a Court (see page 242). It is essential to act urgently in the worst cases of physical child abuse for any procrastination can be disastrous.

Once the child is not in immediate danger (either because the child has been removed from the household under an Emergency Protection Order or because of the nature of the case), the next step in all cases is to call a *case conference*. This should be set up immediately (within 24 hours), either by the social services department or by the NSPCC in those areas where this body acts as the main specialist for child abuse. Any professional can request such a conference. Every case conference should include those already concerned with the case – the paediatrician, the family doctor, the social worker, the health visitor, the police, a teacher from the school (if the child or a brother or sister is still at school), the NSPCC inspector and, if relevant, the probation officer. *Parents should also be invited, where practicable*, to attend part, or if appropriate, the whole of case conferences unless, in the view of the Chairman of the conference, their presence will preclude a full and proper consideration of the child's interests. *Parents should be informed of the outcome of a case conference as soon as is practicable* and this information should be confirmed in writing.

The case conference decides whether the case is child abuse and determines the next action. In any case conference it is *most important that all such decisions are made jointly and not by any individual professional*. It has often been shown that the only way to ensure the wisest decision is made is to do so after the sharing of all the information and facts. In the past, many mistakes have been made by failing to follow this principle.

Once the case conference has decided that there is a case of child abuse (either physical or sexual) the name and address of the child and family must be entered on the *local Child Protection Register* (see page 258) and the parent informed in writing that this action has been taken.

Assessment and planning

Once any child has been identified as having been abused and his or her name entered on the Child Protection Register, then either the *social service department or the NSPCC should be responsible for all future child care*.

The next stage is to appoint a *Key Worker*, who has three main functions:

(*i*)   to carry out all aspects of care for the child and family;

(*ii*)   to prepare a multidisciplinary plan for the child and family, including a comprehensive social and medical assessment, and short term and long term objectives; and

(*iii*)   to act as the leading professional for all inter-agency work. The Key Worker should indicate exactly what the role of other agencies should be (each agency should confirm their acceptance of their appointed tasks). Once this plan has been drawn up and accepted, it should be recorded in the notes of the case conference.

Treatment and review

The treatment of physical child abuse is different from sexual child abuse and these are therefore described separately (see pages 262–3 and pages 264–6).

Child protection duties of social services departments of local authorities

The Children Act 1989 makes it clear that, to ensure that children will be protected, the local authority (through its social service department) is under a duty to investigate fully in the following circumstances.

- Where they have reasonable cause to suspect that a child who lives or is found in their area is suffering or is likely to suffer significant harm.
- Where they have obtained an emergency protection order in respect of a child.
- Where they are informed that a child who lives or is found in their area is subject to an emergency protection order or is in police protection.
- Where a Court in family proceedings directs them to investigate a child's circumstances.
- Where a local education authority notifies them that a child is persistently failing to comply with directions given under an Education Supervision Order.

The aim of the investigation should be to establish whether the local authority needs to exercise any of its powers under the Children Act 1989 with respect to the child.

Inter-agency coordination in child abuse

If child abuse is to be effectively reduced, it is essential that coordination between the social services, health services, education services, police services and voluntary services (especially the NSPCC) is made efficient in all districts. Two features have evolved to assist in this coordination – Area Child Protection Committees and Child Protection Registers.

Area Child Protection Committees

In each district, an Area Child Protection Committee has been set up on the advice and direction of the Department of Health. The main function of the Area Child Protection Committee (formerly called the Area Review Committee) is to act as a policy forming body to ensure that the arrangements for dealing with both forms of child abuse (physical and sexual) are satisfactory.

Each Area Child Protection Committee should include representatives of the appropriate Local Authority (especially the Director of Social Services, who usually acts as the Convenor and Secretary, and the Director of Education), the Health Services (especially paediatric and other consultants, the District Medical Officer, the District Nursing Officer, plus the specialists in community medicine dealing with social services and child health) and a senior police officer, senior inspector of the NSPCC and a representative of the Chief Probation Officer. Area Child Protection Committees should meet regularly (four times per year) and should undertake the following duties.

— Review local practice and procedure for dealing with such cases with special reference to inter-agency guidelines to be followed.
— Ensure that immediate hospital admission for children at risk is accepted.
— Approve written instructions defining the exact duties and responsibilities of professional staff in connection with non-accidental injury.
— Provide education and training programmes for staff in the health and social services.
— Review the work of case conferences.
— Inquire into the circumstances of cases which appear to have gone wrong and from which lessons could be learned.
— Ensure that procedures are in operation to safeguard continuity of care between neighbouring areas and in those instances when families move to another area.
— Agree arrangements for the operation of the Child Protection Register.

Child Protection Registers

A central register of information is essential in each district to ensure there is an effective means of recording and sharing information about child abuse. The register is usually maintained by the social service department but, in those few districts where the NSPCC acts as specialists for child abuse, the latter would organise the register. The following information is always recorded.

— Identification of the child and family and details of any other children in the household (names and addresses etc.).
— The nature of the child abuse.
— The Key Worker and core group. In addition, a record of the general practitioner, the health visitor, name of the child's school, details of the original referral, investigations and treatment plans and review and date of deregistration (if applicable) would also be maintained.

The register is absolutely confidential – queries are always dealt with by the 'ring back principle'. There should be arrangements to share information between neighbouring authorities. A most important feature of registers is that they should be *readily accessible at all times*. It should be possible to consult the register on a 14 hour basis so that doctors, nurses, social workers in the community can obtain information which is reliable and up to date. The ability of a doctor in a casualty department or a health visitor or social worker in the community to seek out information from such a register could be vital to an early and effective diagnosis of physical child abuse. Notes of all referrals to the register are made and, where two separate enquiries are made within 18 months, the two professionals concerned are informed so that they can contact each other in order to discuss the circumstances.

Note that the discovery that a child or family is already on the Register does not prove that the present incident is child abuse, but does call for extra special care and vigilance.

Urgent protection of children at risk

In a proportion of cases of child abuse it is essential to ensure that the child in question is protected from further abuse. This is more often necessary in child physical abuse whilst the early investigations take place but is also important in cases of child sexual abuse where the child is being intimidated or assaulted.

The Children Act 1989 introduced the *Emergency Protection Order* which must be obtained from a Court, and lasts for not more than eight days, although in certain circumstances it can be extended for a further seven days. The Order directs that the child must either be moved (to a safe place such as a hospital or children's home) or detained (this would cover the child who is already in hospital and who is likely to suffer if he or she is returned home). There is a right of appeal to the Court for the order to be discharged after 72 hours and there are also new powers for obtaining a medical or psychiatric examination. Subject to Court direction, the person responsible under the order for the child must allow reasonable contact with the child by specified persons.

There is a legal duty on the local authority to investigate the child's circumstances where the child has been made subject to an Emergency Protection Order. Under the Children Act 1989, the Court is given power to *assist in the discovery of children who may be in need of emergency protection by ordering disclosure of information and by issuing warrants (to authorise entry to search the premises)*. It also provides for cases where there may be another child on the premises to be covered by an Emergency Protection Order.

A further safeguard for children in urgent need of protection is given in the Children Act 1989. This allows *a child to be taken into police protection for up to 72 hours* where a constable believes that the child might otherwise suffer significant harm. The constable must ensure that the case is inquired into by an officer who has been designated for this purpose by the chief officer of the police area.

Child physical abuse

Child physical abuse is the deliberate injury of a child, usually by parents, step-parents or cohabitors. Formerly this abuse was called non-accidental injury and originally baby battering until it was recognised that it can occur to children of all ages, although the majority of serious cases occur to children under the age of eight years.

Many different factors are known to accompany child physical abuse. In some of the worst cases criminal neglect by parents and others may be connected with other forms of antisocial behaviour – assaults, drunkenness, frustration, bad living conditions. There is a higher proportion of cases in single parent families, many of whom inevitably have to accept unsatisfactory and overcrowded living conditions where unsympathetic neighbours or landlords are constantly complaining about babies and infants who seem to be crying a great deal.

There is certainly a *greater proportion of child physical abuse by parents who*:

(i)   *themselves were physically abused as a child*;
(ii) *are very young and under the age of 20 years* (such parents often have to face very unsatisfactory living conditions and poverty, and may also be immature and much less tolerant of the problems which all young children inevitably produce); and
(iii) *are suffering from some psychiatric illness*, which may be characterised by their inability to cope with everyday problems, and especially those of infants and young children.

Diagnosis and early recognition

Child physical abuse can present itself in many ways but usually starts by one or both parents, a step-parent or cohabitor slapping, hitting, punching or severely shaking the child, causing bruises and occasionally more serious injuries. The following conditions may be seen.

- Minor bruises which show that the child has been gripped tightly or shaken.
- Minor injuries (especially facial bruises) probably caused by slapping or hitting the child. The type of injury is usually similar, 70% being soft tissue injuries to the head and face. There may be 'finger bruising' in which the outlines of the fingers which slapped the child are clearly seen within the bruised area. Such bruising tends to pick out the bony prominences. In many cases, the lips are thick

and bruised and there is a torn upper lip frenum. Ribs are frequently bruised or broken and X-rays often indicate that these injuries have been caused in the past. Occasionally small burns may be present.

- An unexplained failure of the child to thrive.
- Unusual behaviour by the parents. This may take many different forms – over-anxiety and frequent attendance with the child at clinics or surgeries, plausible explanations of an injury which does not fit the case, or unnatural lack of concern for the child's condition.

Repetitive and progressive abuse

Child physical abuse is repetitive and progressive. Many cases show similar characteristics; stress of various kinds is common including poverty (in one survey 80% of abusers were in receipt of income support), unemployment (many fathers batter their children when engaged in maternal tasks), overcrowding and unsatisfactory housing conditions and many have unstable marriages. Another interesting finding is that the parents are often very young (about four years below the national average). Studies have shown that teenage parents are less tolerant and have a low tolerance towards the baby's crying. A high proportion of the women involved are pregnant at the time.

A proportion of parents shown to be responsible for child abuse are mentally disturbed or inadequate emotionally. It is interesting that the 'innocent' parent (usually the mother) does not do more to protect her child; the most likely explanation is that she has never learnt how to stick up for herself and for her children. Certainly many of the parents involved never received any affection when they were children and consequently find it very difficult to relate as a normal parent does towards their child.

Any additional stress will tend to precipitate problems – moving house often results in much loneliness and resentment and battering is then more likely.

Early diagnosis of child abuse depends upon the alertness of many professional staff including general practitioners, paediatricians, health visitors, district nurses, midwives, social workers and the staff of many voluntary organisations including the NSPCC. Because injury to the child is always a dominant feature, all those working in casualty or accident departments of hospitals should be especially vigilant. Once there is a reasonable degree of suspicion of physical child abuse, the child should at once be admitted to a hospital (or very occasionally a children's home) for diagnosis and for the child's own safety. In many instances, an Emergency Protection Order will be obtained from a court (this can most easily be arranged by the Social Services Department) but the child may be just 'provided with accommodation'. In all cases an immediate case conference should be arranged (see page 255).

In those instances in which the professional worker does not feel that the suspicions are firm enough to arrange immediate admission to a hospital, it is still advisable to hold a case conference to decide on the next action. *If suspicion is very slight*, in every instance the nurse should, at least, undertake the following:

— consult the family doctor;
— discuss the details of the case with a senior colleague;
— make a record of such consultations and discussions;
— make enquiries to find out if the child and family are on the Child Protection Register.

Treatment and rehabilitation

Most cases of child physical abuse will initially be in the care of the paediatrician who will be responsible for the assessment and treatment of the case in hospital. Assessment should include both physical and psychiatric investigations. Skeletal surveys should be undertaken in doubtful cases. Case conferences will continue to be held and should indicate the most likely methods of treatment. These should vary considerably in different cases and may include the following.

● Receiving the child into *statutory care* by the local authority (by Court Order). In the very worst cases there will also be prosecution of the parents.
● Providing the child with accommodation. This may be risky in some cases because parents may suddenly remove the child from hospital or the children's home. Therefore, in all cases where this is done the Social Services Department must always be prepared to seek an urgent Emergency Protection Order if that need arises.
● Arranging for the child to remain under supervision in the home by a Supervision Order obtained from a court.
● Returning the child home with planned help to the parents.

In all instances the aim is to ensure that the short and long-term interests of the child are met as far as possible. It is important to realise that, although there are a number of serious cases of intentional injury and neglect that can only be properly treated by permanent removal of the child from the parents, the majority of cases are quite different. In these the physical child abuse has been caused by many other factors – bad living conditions, unemployment, poverty, threat of eviction (especially if babies cry repeatedly) and by minor psychiatric illnesses. *These parents urgently require help and if this can be satisfactorily given they may be assisted to develop into perfectly satisfactory parents and families*. However, the causative factors *must* be discovered. In many instances, the temporary provision of residential care (in a residential nursery or children's home) may be required to enable the parent to be treated.

Day care

Many people who have been found to ill-treat their children are young and often very isolated and lonely. In a number of instances the mother herself had an unhappy childhood or was brought up in a broken home.

A very useful method of helping is to admit the child to a day nursery or play group and then to arrange for the mother to help in the group. In this way, the mother is assisted to make new friends and to obtain the support she needs. Indirectly she will be taught to improve her relationship with her own child from the example of care she will see in the nursery or play group.

More and more social services departments are now developing day care which can be extended to older children in the same family who come along to the unit after school.

Many girls' schools now arrange for senior girls to help periodically in play groups and day nurseries, and thus to learn more about the methods of care of young children. This is particularly important because the incidence of child abuse is highest in teenage mothers.

Some local authorities have arranged to deal with many cases in nurseries close to a paediatric department which makes the development of special working arrangements between the health and social services departments easier.

Periodic review of long-term cases

Some of the most difficult problems are found in long-term cases. It is absolutely essential that periodic reviews of such cases are undertaken. These must involve the many professional workers who would normally be concerned with the care of that child and especially general practitioners, teachers, school nurses, health visitors, education welfare officers, social workers (including those working in child guidance) as well as those working with voluntary agencies in that area. In all older children (and some of the worst cases of child abuse occur in older children) it is most important that the *levels of communication between teaching staff* and others concerned with the child in school and *health visitors* and *social workers* are always good.

The statutory duty to protect and care for all children who are in need is that of the Director of Social Services and his or her staff, or the NSPCC in those few areas where this organisation acts as specialists in child abuse for the whole area. Unless there is an effective network of information between all staff working in education, health and social services, action by the social services department may be delayed until it is too late to prevent further injury. For this reason, long-term cases should never be written off until a case conference agrees that no further risk remains. Unless this multidisciplinary team approach is always used, mistakes of the past will be repeated.

In any serious case of doubt, a doctor or nurse should always arrange immediate hospital admission for the child to enable more detailed investigations to be undertaken. In cases of difficulty, the problem should always be reported by telephone to the Director of Social Services or Area Social Services Officer (see page 231).

Child sexual abuse

Although child sexual abuse has always existed, detailed studies have only recently been undertaken. The incidence in the Cleveland controversy was an alleged 464 cases in a population of 550 000 (a rate of 84 per 100 000). Not all of these were proven cases. In Liverpool, a city with a population of 490 000, studies have been going on since 1980 and these indicate that 13% of the 600–700 case conferences held each year were child sexual abuse cases. Such an incidence would be of the order 15.9 per 100 000 and this is probably more realistic than the Cleveland figures.

Child sexual abuse is an extremely emotive subject and it is never easy to involve the parents in any investigation without risking complete destruction of their own personal relationships. In physical child abuse any parent may inadvertently raise suspicion by natural discipline of a child, but to introduce a sexual element in the affection given by a parent or other adult to a child of either sex is to suggest something which most parents would find offensive. Certainly there is no doubt that most people feel greater abhorrence towards anyone who has been found to sexually abuse a child compared with physical abuse instances, especially if the physical abuse has been of a minor nature or if there are extenuating circumstances.

Diagnosis and recognition

Diagnosis of child sexual abuse is always difficult. It mainly depends on the professional being aware that there is a possibility of sexual abuse, especially in certain circumstances. Apart from the few cases where a child unequivocally alleges sexual abuse in the clearest terms, the diagnosis is rarely clear cut and is usually only reached after a lengthy period of assessment. Even where a child has made an unambiguous accusation, this is often later retracted when the seriousness of the disclosure is realised.

There is no simple test to confirm child sexual abuse except when semen is found or blood from a different group than that of the child. Very careful assessment, observation and investigation by many different professionals is needed. A multidisciplinary approach is most important to ensure a balance between over-enthusiasm and zeal and failure to act in time. Doctors, social workers, nurses, health visitors, teachers and the police all have a part to play.

The starting point in the diagnosis of child sexual abuse should be the raising of suspicion that it may be occurring. It is helpful to consider three types of suspicion – serious, moderate and mild.

Serious suspicion should be raised in the following instance.

— When the child makes clear verbal allegations of sexual abuse. If the allegation is spontaneous, it would be most unusual for it to be a fabrication.

Moderate suspicion is justified in the following instances.

— If the child makes an allegation of sexual abuse in ambiguous terms (so that it is not clear precisely what occurred).
— If a child is sexually provocative to adults or discloses detailed knowledge of sexual matters in conversation, fantasy or drawings or appears preoccupied with sexual fantasies and behaviour.
— If a child responds to questioning by describing sexual abuse but has not made a spontaneous allegation.
— If a child shows a specific fear of a father, step-father or sexually mature older brother.
— If a child is living in cramped circumstances and the mother is known to be a prostitute – but it should be noted that a particular family setting should never, on its own, be grounds for serious suspicion.

Mild suspicion should be aroused in the following instances.

— If a child shows behavioural or emotional disturbance for which no other cause can be found.
— If a child shows unexplained changes in behaviour.
— If a child makes a suicide attempt.
— If a child runs away from home when there is no obvious cause.
— If there is an unusually close relationship between the father or step-father and the child and, at the same time, there is marital discord in the home.

The test of reflex anal dilatation has been considered to indicate sexual abuse. However, the Butler-Schloss report clearly states that *there is no proof of a direct link between reflex anal dilatation and the diagnosis of sexual abuse*, although its presence does raise the level of suspicion.

Management and treatment

Unlike child physical abuse, child sexual abuse does not necessarily call for an immediate emergency response or for the removal of the child from the household. The *one exception is where the child is liable to assault or intimidation – then care away from the home must be provided promptly.*

Much support and counselling is needed for the parents and family and a specialist social worker skilled in this rôle can be invaluable. It may well be that, initially, it would be best for the abuser to leave the family home, at least for a period while further investigations take place. Obviously all treatment must ensure that the interests of the child be given priority. But one crucial question must be asked: *Should treatment also strive to keep the family together?* The answer will depend on individual circumstances and the flexibility of the family's attitudes. It is also always important to endeavour to find out the views of the child.

Many different patterns of treatment are at present being tried and no doubt the best alternative will eventually evolve. In many instances, the solution may turn out to be very individual with a variety of solutions being tried. The abuser may be required to live away from home but still be able to support and have access to the family. On the other hand, the split between the parents may be complete. Whether it is worthwhile attempting to reconcile the parents must depend on their attitude. Expert advice and counselling will always be most important. The Butler-Schloss Inquiry suggested that *specialist assessment teams* could be set up with advantage. These would include a social worker, a doctor and a specialist police officer working together. This team would carry out the initial assessment and then indicate which course of action would be most likely to be in the best interests of the child.

It is clear that, at present, there is little expertise in dealing with child sexual abuse in either the social, health or police services. The model of treatment for physical child abuse is clearly not appropriate to many cases of child sexual abuse. The development of successful forms of treatment will be most likely to occur if prejudice and revulsion are not allowed to cloud the issue. What is needed is the evolution of a series of models of treatment (mainly by trial and error) until some are shown to have the best chance of success. *The test of success must be in the long term results – when a child who is known to have been sexually abused grows up into a normal loving caring adult and parent with good personal relationships, happy with his or her own family and children.*

16   Care and rehabilitation of disabled people

The Department of Health is centrally responsible for the community social services for disabled or physically handicapped people.

Locally each major local authority (County Council, Metropolitan District Council or London Borough) is responsible through its Social Services Committee. The chief officer in charge of these services is the Director of Social Services (see page 231).

In addition, there are large numbers of national and local voluntary bodies working for the handicapped; examples include the Royal National Institute for the Blind, the Royal Association for Disability and Rehabilitation (RADAR), the National Spastics Society, the national Multiple Sclerosis Society, and various Deaf and Dumb Associations. Most local authorities give monetary grants to help such voluntary bodies.

Relationships between health services and social services

Medical, nursing and social services all attempt to help the handicapped in different ways. Doctors and nurses carry out the physical treatment of the handicapped in hospitals or in the community while the social services are more concerned with rehabilitation and with helping them to lead an active life and to overcome their social problems or difficulties. It will follow from this that nurses and social workers must work closely together if the best results are to be obtained. The fact that the local areas of operation for each are roughly the same geographical size helps to ensure that the closest liaison can usually be achieved.

Generally social services concentrate upon aids to normal life within the community – housing, adaptations to houses, employment, special workshops, transport, various aids and gadgets, handicraft centres, social centres and clubs and holidays. For these reasons, most social services provided by local authorities are in the community while many medical and nursing services are in the hospital or outpatient departments. District and community nurses, health visitors and general practitioners also are actively engaged in helping many handicapped people in their own homes. It is *most important that the social worker links up with these medical and nursing services*; this is best done by social workers visiting hospitals and general practitioners to ensure that a continuous working arrangement is maintained at all times. The eventual success with any individual handicapped person is closely connected with the degree of such cooperation between doctors, nurses and social workers. Eventually it is hoped that social workers will work closely with primary health care teams.

Legislation

Disabled Persons (Employment) Acts, 1944 and 1958

These Acts are designed to help all disabled people. A *'disabled person'* is defined as one *'who on account of injury, disease or congenital deformity, is substantially handicapped from obtaining or keeping employment'*. Every employer who employs twenty or more people must, under the above-mentioned Acts employ a *minimum of 3% of disabled persons* among his staff. The names of all disabled persons are held on a register.

Although the wide definition of disabled people has reduced the effectiveness of this Act, it has helped to increase the opportunities for employment of handicapped people.

Chronically Sick and Disabled Persons Act, 1970

The Chronically Sick and Disabled Persons Act, 1970 gives many special responsibilities to local authorities in respect of those who are substantially and permanently handicapped (including those who are mentally handicapped). The main duties of local authorities include the following.

- *Information* Local authorities must ensure (*i*) that they are adequately informed of the numbers and needs of the handicapped so that they can properly plan and develop their services, and (*ii*) that the handicapped and their families know what help is available to them by general publicity and personal explanations.
- *Provision of services* Local authorities, when satisfied that certain services are necessary to the handicapped person, can provide the following services:
  - practical assistance in the home;
  - radio, television, library or similar recreational facilities in the home;
  - recreational facilities outside the home and assistance in taking advantage of educational facilities;
  - travelling facilities for handicapped persons;
  - assistance in carrying out adaptations to the home;

— facilitating the taking of holidays;
— meals at home or elsewhere;
— a telephone and any special equipment necessary for its use.
- *Housing*   Every local authority must have regard to the special needs of the disabled and any new houses planned must show that special provision is made for them. This clearly gives housing authorities a duty to plan and provide special housing accommodation for handicapped people.
- *Premises open to the public*   There are a series of requirements for public buildings. These deal specially with the following facilities for the disabled.
    — Providing means of access to and within the buildings and in the parking facilities and sanitary conveniences. Such provision must be considered before planning permission is given.
    — Need for a local authority to provide public sanitary conveniences.
    — Need for anyone providing sanitary conveniences in premises open to the public for accommodation, refreshment or entertainment, to make provision, as far as is practicable, for the disabled.
    — Adequate sign-posting for the above provisions from outside.
    — Need to provide facilities for access, parking, and sanitary conveniences suitable for the disabled as far as is practicable at school, university and other educational buildings.

In addition, there are special clauses about Advisory Committees for the handicapped either nationally or locally and these insist that members of *such committees must include persons with experience of work for the disabled and people who are themselves disabled.*

Many local authorities have provided excellent services (especially telephones) for the handicapped, but some have been slow to assist. As some of the more progressive local authorities provide these extra services free and others make charges, there is unfortunately a varying standard of service for handicapped people throughout the United Kingdom.

National Assistance Act, 1948, Section 29

This gives the local authorities the responsibility of providing a further wide range of social services for handicapped people including home training, occupational therapy and many other domiciliary services.

Disabled Persons (Services, Consultation and Representation) Act 1986

This Act aims at improving the effectiveness of services for mentally and physically disabled persons by introducing an 'advocacy' service. When disabled people cannot represent themselves because of their disability, an 'advocate' or representative is appointed to act on their behalf.

Much of the Act is concerned with improving the effectiveness of Section 2 of the Chronically Sick and Disabled Persons Act 1970 (see above) by way of the following.

— Ensuring that any help for the disabled person is coordinated properly.
— Requiring the *local authority to assess the needs of every disabled person when requested to do so*.
— Insisting that the *results of such an assessment are given in a written statement*, including explanations of the various decisions of the local authority.
— Ensuring that the *local social service department gives the disabled person all proper help* (including 'interpretation assistance' for a deaf and dumb person) and *considers every case on its merits*.

In addition, the Act includes important provisions to help disabled young people in the difficult transfer period immediately after leaving school.

The Act also ensures that every social service department must periodically publish general information about the services it provides for disabled persons under the 1970 Act.

Incidence of disability

Four important surveys were carried out in Great Britain from 1985 to 1988 by the Office of Population, Census and Surveys. The first report was published in 1988. After an initial postal screening of 100 000 persons, 14 308 individuals living in private households and 3833 living in residential establishments were selected. All individuals were further studied either by postal enquiries or by full personal interviews. This survey focused on 13 different types of disability: locomotion; reaching and stretching; dexterity; personal care; continence; seeing; hearing; communication; behaviour; intellectual function; consciousness; eating, drinking and digesting; and disfigurement.

Most adults in the survey were found to have more than one disability. The three commonest disabilities were in *locomotion, hearing* and *personal care*. Among those living in private households musculo-skeletal complaints, especially arthritis, were the most com-

Table 16.1 Estimates of numbers of disabled adults by severity (thousands), Great Britain, 1985–88. (Frrom survey carried out by OPCS, 1985–88.)

Severity category	In private households (thousands)	In establishments	Total population of disabled adults
10	102	108	210
9	285	80	365
8	338	58	396
7	447	39	486
6	511	34	545
5	679	29	708
4	676	27	703
3	732	19	751
2	824	16	840
1	1186	13	1199
Total	5780	423	6203

monly found. Ear complaints, eye complaints and diseases of the circulatory system were also often mentioned. For those living in residential establishments, mental complaints, especially senile dementia, were most commonly found followed by arthritis and strokes.

The severity of the 13 types of disability was divided into 10 categories with category 1 the least severe and category 10 the most severe. From the results of the survey estimates were calculated of the likely numbers of disabled persons in Great Britain. These are given in Table 16.1. Note that it is estimated that there are *6.2 million disabled persons in Great Britain* of whom 422 000 (7%) live in some form of residential establishment. Almost 14% of adults living in private households have at least one disability. The greatest number are in category 1 and from then onwards there is a gradual fall in the numbers as the severity of the disability increases. When those disabled persons living in establishments are analysed, the opposite is found – the largest numbers are in the most severe categories: no less than 188 000 (44.5%) are in the two most severe categories (9 and 10). Altogether there were 210 000 individuals found suffering from the most severe category 10, of which just under a half live in private households.

Disability and age

One of the most striking findings of this survey was the way the rate of disability rises with age (see Fig. 16.1). Note that the rate of disability accelerates after the age of 50 years and rises very steeply after age 70 years. Almost *70% of disabled persons were aged 60 years and over* and almost a half were aged 70 and over. Among those living in residential establishments the proportion of very elderly disabled residents was very high – half were aged 80 years and over.

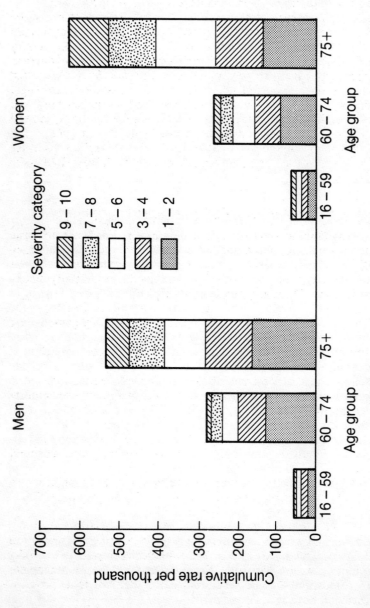

Fig. 16.1 Estimates of prevalence of disability among adults by age and severity category for men and women. (From OPCS, Survey, 1985–88.)

There was also a connection between the most severe categories of disability and age – 4% of adults with the severest categories 9 and 10 were aged 70 years and over, 41% were aged 80 years and over.

Another interesting feature was that there were consistently *more disabled women than men*. This is partly due to the fact that women live, on average, six years longer than men. However the *rate of disability* (which allows for the differing numbers of men and women in the population) is *higher for women than men and this indicates that elderly women are more likely to be disabled than men of the same age*.

Comparisons of disability for different regions in England and Wales, standardised for differences in their age distributions, showed that the highest rates of disability were in the North (Wales and Yorkshire and Humberside), while the Southern regions (Greater London area, South East, East Anglia and the South West) had lower than average rates.

General principles for helping disabled people

In the rehabilitation of all handicapped people there are certain basic principles which are important. No social service can succeed if they are ignored, and it is essential to understand them, for they carry the secret of success and can quite simply be modified for every handicapped person. There are four main principles.

- The problems of every handicapped person are *highly individual and personal*.
- The best solution for any handicapped person is that which is *as near normal as possible*.
- A large amount of *improvisation* will probably be necessary.
- *Great determination and singleness of purpose* is usually essential for success.

- *An individual approach*   The difficulties of any handicapped person vary with each individual. This is because the problems depend on:
    — The age of the person – there is a very high incidence of disability in persons over the age of 75 years (see page 271).
    — The nature and extent of the handicap.
    — The reaction of the disabled person to the handicap.
  Thus, many blind people are able to hold down an important job whilst others who are blind may be unable to carry out successfully quite a simple occupation. The handicap is the same, complete blindness, but the end result and size of the individual problem varies greatly.

  The reaction of handicapped people to these *difficulties depends very much on the attitude of those who have tried to help in the early and crucial stages*. A correct approach and attitude of mind here are essential. What is wanted is an understanding, which very often means something quite different from ineffective and maybe sentimental sympathy. Often the best approach is a fairly tough one which promises the handicapped person little but many hard struggles and disappointments.

For these reasons, individual visiting and assessment are always a most important first step in rehabilitation. As the social background of the handicapped person – their home and their family – plays a significant part in overcoming the handicap, it is important that assessment includes these.

● *Maintaining normality*   There is a very simple rule to follow in determining what any handicapped person should attempt to do. *The best solution is always the one which is as near normal as possible*.

This basic principle applies to all aspects of work with handicapped people including education and occupation. A person with no handicap usually works in an industry or in an office and is not in any way protected. This is also the best solution for any handicapped person.

If difficulties are found in suggesting the next stage in rehabilitation, a useful indicator is given by considering what occupation the person would be following if he or she was not handicapped. The aim should always be for the rehabilitation process to progress towards this goal.

The constant hope given by successfully reaching various stages in rehabilitation will do much to counteract any attitude of self pity in the handicapped person which must be avoided at all cost.

● *Improvisation*   Just as the problems of each handicapped person differ, so will the solutions. Hence, an ability to improvise in overcoming the inevitable and unexpected difficulties is most important. Those working with handicapped people cannot afford to be narrow minded, too set in their ways or hidebound by convention. All the most successful are resilient and often unconventional people to whom improvisation comes naturally.

● *Determination*   It is always easy to find an excuse for failure when dealing with handicapped people. Therefore, to succeed, it is important to *concentrate solely upon success*, however remote this might seem to be. If possible, the handicapped person and those immediately around him or her, should be fired with an enthusiasm to succeed irrespective of the difficulties and inevitable disappointments ahead. *A complete singleness of purpose should be encouraged* and this often helps to overcome difficulties.

Main groups of disabled

The main groups of disablement for which local authorities provide social services include the following:

— blindness and partial sightedness;
— total deafness from birth, including the deaf and dumb;
— hardness of hearing, acquired deafness, usually late in life;
— congenital disabilities, spina bifida or spastic diplegia;
— paraplegia and hemiplegia;
— various paralytic diseases (e.g. multiple sclerosis, muscular dystrophy, poliomyelitis);
— strokes;
— serious arthritic conditions – rheumatoid arthritis, spondylitis, severe osteoarthritis;
— epilepsy;
— accident cases.

Special financial help available to seriously disabled people

Attendance allowance

Attendance allowance is an allowance for adults and children aged two years and over who are severely disabled physically or mentally and have needed a lot of looking after for six months or more. There are two rates, the higher rate for those who require attendance both by day and night and a lower rate for those who need attendance either by day or night. The allowance is NOT payable if the disabled person is living in accommodation provided by a local authority or is receiving free in-patient treatment in a National Health Service hospital.

A kidney patient on dialysis is paid the allowance if dialysis takes place at home, but not if it is carried out in hospital for more than four weeks.

Mobility allowance

The mobility allowance is a cash benefit which is payable to seriously disabled persons aged 5–65 years to help them become more mobile. Anyone of 65 years of age in receipt of a mobility allowance may continue to receive it until 80 years of age. New applicants, however cannot qualify after the age of 65 years. It is additional to any other social security benefit, is taxable but for married women is considered as part of her 'earned income' and therefore usually is exempt from tax.

To qualify, the applicant must live within the United Kingdom and have resided there for at least 12 months within the preceding 18 months and the following special medical conditions must be satisfied.

(*i*)   The person must be unable or virtually unable to walk because of physical disablement; *and*

(*ii*)   the inability to walk must be likely to persist for at least 12 months from the time the claim is made; *and*

(*iii*)   the person's condition must be such that he or she can benefit from time to time from increased facilities for mobility.

The mobility allowance is paid to more than one person who qualifies living in the same household. It is intended to aid mobility but may be used for any purpose – helping to pay for the family car, hiring taxis, taking a holiday etc. In the case of an adult receiving the allowance on behalf of a child, that person then has to sign an undertaking to apply the allowance for the benefit of the disabled child.

Motability

This is the name of a voluntary organisation formed on the initiative of the government to assist disabled persons to get maximum value for money in using their mobility allowance to acquire a car. Two schemes are available: a leasing scheme; and a hire purchase scheme.

In the first, a new car is leased for 3–4 years in return for surrendering the mobility allowance for this period and, in most cases, also paying a 'once and for all' advance rental. Full details of both schemes can be obtained from RADAR, Mortimer Street, London W1.

Exemption from vehicle excise duty (VED)

All recipients of the mobility allowance are exempt from the VED. This also applies to *those who qualify but are over the age limit* to receive the mobility allowance.

Invalid Care Allowance

This is a weekly cash benefit for people under pension age (16–64 years for a man, 16–59 years for a woman) who spend at least 35 hours a week looking after someone who is receiving either an Attendance Allowance or a Constant Attendance Allowance (following an industrial accident or as a result of an industrial disease). If the individual has children or supports another adult, extra benefit is payable. In 1989 the Invalid Care Allowance was £26.20 per week.

Social services available for disabled people

The following are the social services provided by local authority social services departments and voluntary bodies working with them.

Social worker support and assessment

Social workers are available to assess and advise the handicapped at home. Initially each handicapped person is registered and his or her needs carefully assessed and catalogued. Social workers are usually attached to area social work teams (see page 234) and include specialists trained to work with the blind and who can teach Braille, and to work with the deaf and dumb using sign and finger language.

Social workers work closely with other community workers such as health visitors, district nurses and general practitioners. Special services such as meals-on-wheels and home helps can be arranged by the social worker.

Employment for disabled people

There are two main ways in which disabled people can be employed full time: (*i*) in ordinary or 'open' industry; (*ii*) in special sheltered employment.

'Open' industry refers to ordinary occupations where each handicapped person works with and under exactly the same conditions as a person with no handicap. Full wages are paid without any subsidy.

This is always the best solution, but is, unfortunately, only possible for a proportion of the employable handicapped. The success of placing a handicapped person in open industry will depend on the employment opportunities of the area and the efforts of the social services department and Disablement Resettlement Officers (DROs) of the Department of Employment to find openings in local industries. It should be possible to place many intelligent well trained disabled persons in most industries. With the blind, special *Blind Persons Resettlement Officers* are employed to assist finding places in industry for the handicapped (see page 285).

Sheltered employment is subsidised employment (full-time) arranged either in a special workshop or in a home workers scheme (details for the blind on pages 285–6). The Department of Employment runs special Remploy workshops for handicapped people and some local authorities run their own workshops. There are also many voluntary bodies who run sheltered workshops usually with financial help from local authorities.

Industrial therapy services

Many local authorities run industrial therapy services and, in this way, assist the handicapped with their rehabilitation. Reference is made later to such services provided for mentally handicapped people (see pages 307–8) and similar services are made available to the physically handicapped. The aim of these services is mainly to train and prepare physically disabled individuals for full-time work.

Handicraft centres

Handicraft centres are also provided by local authorities for disabled people and are usually staffed by handicraft instructors. The main aim of such centres is to assist those who are disabled to enjoy recreational facilities although complete rehabilitation towards eventual full-time employment may not be possible.

Occupational therapy services

Most local authority social services departments employ occupational therapists. These may be on a *domiciliary basis* where the occupational therapist calls on each handicapped person at home from time to time, or the services may be provided at *special rehabilitation centres*. In such cases the handicapped persons are often brought to the centre by special transport.

The concept of the work of occupational therapists has changed and much more emphasis is now placed on *teaching disabled people to live with their handicaps* rather than instruction in craft work. In this way they are helped to overcome their muscular difficulties by the use of various aids or machines including knitting and fretsaw machines, various looms and treadle lathes. A number of crafts are also taught at such centres.

Occupational therapists also train patients in special training kitchens and these are especially useful to the handicapped housewife to help her become more independent. Various aids and gadgets are tested out in these kitchens so that later the correct aid can be fitted in the handicapped person's own kitchen.

Attendance at such centres may be on a full-time or part-time basis. As well as the training undertaken at each centre, the *social value of handicapped people meeting each other and becoming less isolated is also important.*

Much chronic invalidism can be caused by the disabled person becoming more and more withdrawn as he or she stays permanently at home meeting only close friends or family. If the handicapped person is brought to a rehabilitation or handicraft centre, his or her confidence is helped by meeting other people and seeing what can be achieved, and further deterioration can be prevented. Domiciliary occupational therapy services are also provided by many health authorities.

Aids centres

Permanent aids centres containing a wide range of equipment suitable for the disabled have been established in London by the Disabled Living Foundation and by some local authorities including Liverpool, Newcastle and Birmingham. These aids centres set out to enable disabled people and their families to see for themselves the range of equipment available. It is usual to staff such units with experienced occupational therapists and to run the centre on an appointment system as it usually takes 1½ to 2 hours to demonstrate all the equipment available.

Disabled people and their families wishing to visit such centres should contact either the Disabled Living Foundation, 346 Kensington High Street, London W8, or the local Directors of Social Services.

Transport

Mobility for handicapped people is very important. Individual problems depend very much on the type of handicap. Various adaptations can be made to cars so that they can be safely driven by hand controls only.

Individual transport   Individual transport for severely disabled people is the responsibility of the government. Until 1976, direct provision of adapted cars or three-wheelers (Invacars) was the main method. But *direct provision, through the Artificial Limb and Appliance Service, is now available only to war pensioners and very special cases.* All other severely handicapped persons use the mobility allowance (see page 275). The production of Invacars has ended but those who have such a vehicle can continue to use them. Anyone using an Invacar may transfer to the mobility allowance without medical examination or age limit. Local authorities provide the run-in, drive and base for the garage which is erected by the Department of Health.

Local authorities often provide *temporary wheelchairs* on loan to help those who have a transient need – less than six months. In permanent cases, after this period, the Artificial Limb and Appliance Service should provide the wheelchair.

Group transport   Local authority social services departments provide various vehicles, personnel carriers, mini-buses, etc., to carry the handicapped from their homes to various centres. Many of these vehicles are fitted with hydraulic lifts so that wheelchairs with their occupants can easily be loaded and unloaded.

The success of many of the activities and services provided by local authorities (various centres and clubs, etc.) depends to a large extent on the efficiency of transport services for handicapped people which must be adequate to meet the needs of the area.

Holidays and outings

Many voluntary bodies and local authorities arrange special holiday schemes for disabled persons. These have become more and more ambitious in recent years and include holidays abroad, with arrangements made as regards transport and all holiday activities. Special staff go with the handicapped group which usually contains many severely handicapped people in wheel chairs.

Some local authorities also help handicapped people by subsidising ordinary holidays arranged by the disabled person him or herself with a small monetary grant. This enables the disabled person to arrange a more expensive type of holiday (for example, to stay at a hotel with a lift).

Emphasis today is on the *provision of normal holidays* in which the non-handicapped members of the family can share with the disabled individual. There are, however, a number of special holidays arranged for handicapped people and some local authorities have special seaside holiday homes for the disabled.

Social centres and clubs

Many voluntary bodies run special social centres and clubs for handicapped people. Local authorities usually give financial support to such centres or provide a central club which voluntary bodies may use at no cost. Transport can be provided by the local authority.

Housing for disabled people

The design of the home occupied by the individual disabled person is very important. Many adaptations are needed to enable a severely handicapped person to live normally – larger doors, no steps, large bathrooms and toilets and special fitments.

It may be possible to *adapt the home* or to introduce special aids (see below). But with the most severely handicapped, for example the paraplegic, it is usually easier and cheaper for the local housing authority to *build specially designed bungalows* which incorporate such adaptations.

In the case of an individual who suffers a paraplegia following an accident and who is consequently admitted to a regional hospital spinal centre, *it is most important that the housing requirements are considered shortly after admission* and not left until just before the patient is discharged home. Most patients will remain in such hospitals for at least six months and it is essential to ensure that the local authority has all this time to solve the housing difficulties which often are considerable. Certain adaptations may be needed at the patient's home or even rehousing, either of which may take months to achieve.

Minor adaptations, aids and gadgets

Under the Chronically Sick and Disabled Persons Act, 1970, local authorities help by providing (usually at no cost) minor adaptations including the following.

— *Ramps* or *handrails*. In 1986 in England 60 000 adaptations were made to private dwellings each costing £150 or more. Also 144 000 adaptations were undertaken for handicapped persons in local authority dwellings.
— *Hoists* in bedrooms and bathrooms for those paralysed in the legs so that they can become more independent and mobile.
— *Modifications to table implements*; knives, forks, spoons, to make them more easily used by people whose grip is weak or whose hands are deformed.
— Various *kitchen fitments for handicapped people*. These include many gadgets for one-handed people or those who only have power in one hand, and other aids for those whose balance is poor (e.g. slings to be fitted to sinks to allow such people to stand supported by the sling).
— *Kitchen management and planning* is most important. The height of various working surfaces and the design of kitchen furniture are examples. Many rehabilitation centres are fitted with model kitchens for handicapped people so that the occupational therapist can see which equipment best suits the handicapped person before steps are taken to fit out the handicapped person's own kitchen. Various kinds of cooking stoves can be tried in such demonstration kitchens.
— Various *personal aids in dressing* are all important so that the independence of the handicapped person is improved. In all this work, the aim is always to make the handicapped person as normal as possible and, in this respect, anything that engenders independence is valuable.

Other social services which are available include meals-on-wheels (see page 320) and home helps (see pages 336–7) for which charges are usually made.

Telephones

Under the Chronically Sick and Disabled Persons Act, 1970, most local authorities help by providing a telephone (and paying rent) for those who are severely handicapped and who live alone. Standards vary but most *local authorities give top priority to the handicapped living alone who cannot go outside even in fine weather*. Telephones are also provided for special medical cases. Any nurse coming across such a handicapped person who urgently requires a telephone should report the case to the local Director of Social Services.

Rehabilitation of disabled people

This is a joint enterprise involving the medical services, the Department of Employment and local authority social services departments and, in children and young persons, the education authority.

Rehabilitation usually starts in the hospital, in the rehabilitation or orthopaedic departments and then transfers to *rehabilitation centres* run by local authorities or special hospitals. Special transport usually brings the patient to the centre and makes it possible to extend more quickly the range of rehabilitation. At the centre, there are many and various machines and aids such as knitting machines, fretsaw machines, looms, as well as a training kitchen. There are also opportunities to follow many crafts.

The rehabilitation centre is usually open all day and people can attend for half a day or a full day. It is usual for the kitchen to be used by a handicapped person learning to cook, and in this way meals are prepared for themselves and others attending the centre.

One of the most valuable parts of the centre's regime is the *social life* provided, whereby handicapped people meet others. In many long and chronic illnesses or disabilities, there is a tendency for the patient to become more and more withdrawn and to stay permanently at home, meeting only family and close friends. Even when the physical disability improves, the individual very often continues to stay at home and this factor can make it difficult or impossible to rehabilitate the person back to an occupation. Attendance at the occupational therapy centre and travelling to it can greatly increase self-confidence and prevent permanent invalidism. Once a week at the centre, a social evening is arranged so that those attending the centre can relax together playing games, table tennis and dancing.

Rehabilitation from centre to workshops and industry

The aim of the occupational therapist is to transfer eventually the handicapped person either directly into open industry or to a special sheltered workshop. The latter are run by social service departments, various voluntary bodies supported by local authorities by financial grants and by the Department of Employment through the special Remploy factories (see page 277). These workshops are sited throughout the country and are designed to provide permanent work for severely disabled people.

Another very important link in the rehabilitation chain is the Employment Rehabilitation Centres run by the Department of Employment. These are designed to teach a handicapped person a new trade skill and are of great importance to those people who have had to learn a new job because the one for which they are trained is now unsuitable for them. An example would be a skilled miner who had a serious accident. Even though he may be left with only a minor degree of disability, it is obviously unwise for him to return to mining. Therefore, he is retained at such a centre and is given a new industrial skill. This is essential as it is the industrial skill of the person that usually determines whether he or she can be employed or not. The highest unemployment rate is always in the unskilled workers. If, therefore, in addition, there is a history of physical handicap, their chance of employment may be very slight. For this reason, *all handicapped people should be taught an industrial skilled occupation suitable* to their handicap, and the Centre is equipped to do this.

There must, at all times, be complete coordination between the occupational therapist and the Disablement Resettlement Officer.

Social services for the blind and visually handicapped (including partially sighted)

Registration

Proper registration of blind and partially sighted people is essential. Anyone who is thought to be blind is examined by a consultant ophthalmologist who carries out a complete visual examination and indicates the degree of lack of sight and the prognosis. Expert examination is important to make certain that further active treatment is not possible, and to obtain an accurate knowledge of the number of blind persons, their ages and requirements.

At present there are approximately 10 000–12 000 new cases of blindness are registered as blind in England and Wales. Of these 85% are aged 60 years and over – the problem of *blindness mainly occurs in late middle-aged and elderly persons*. There is a marked increased incidence of blindness in women compared with men. There is an even more marked tendency among the newly blinded to be elderly; only 8% of them are under 50 years of age and 81% are aged 65 years and over.

Because of the close association between blindness and old age, it must always be remembered that many of the problems discussed in Chapter 18 on the elderly may also present major difficulties for them.

Individual assessment

The problems facing any blind person vary greatly from individual to individual. The age at which blindness develops is a major factor. The child born blind has to learn to live the whole of life as a blind person – being educated as a blind person, employed as a blind person and face the difficulties of retirement and old age with the same handicap. Many elderly persons going blind over the age of 70 years have only the last years of their life to lead as blind people – education and employment never present any difficulties. Obviously in the intermediate age group, there are different problems.

The *personality*, *past training*, *intelligence* and the *home conditions* will all have a marked effect on either reducing or increasing the difficulties facing the blind person.

Each blind person must be carefully and individually assessed by expert social workers (usually called *home teachers for the blind*) whose task it is to unravel each problem and arrange for help. The attitude of the social worker can do a great deal to minimise the difficulties of each blind person.

With newly blinded adult people (rather than with aged newly blinded), assessment is never easy, for often the blindness has suddenly occurred leaving the person uncertain, full of self-pity and often bitter. Such newly blinded people should always be sent to a *special assessment centre* such as the one at Queen Elizabeth Homes of Recovery, Torquay, which is run by the Royal National Institute for the Blind. Here, under expert guidance, the person spends from four to six weeks while being assessed. Any self-pity is quickly lost and the individual soon realises that life as a blind person can still be full and interesting. After a visit to this home, most newly blinded people return to their own home with a new and essential spirit of hope. Any industrial training then becomes easier.

Even when the blind person has settled down well, the social worker should make periodic home visits and continue assessment in an unobtrusive manner. Only in this way is it possible to ensure that the wide social services available to blind people are properly used.

Employment

About 14% of the blind people in the United Kingdom are between the ages of 16 and 60 years, and it is in this group that the problem of employment occurs. Full time employment of blind people includes employment in 'open-industry'; or an occupation in sheltered employment, either in workshops or in home workers schemes.

Employment in 'open industry' The term 'open industry' is used to denote employment in an ordinary job (in industry or commerce) where the blind person works with, and is treated the same as, sighted people. No special arrangements are made as regards remuneration. There are many different types of occupations in which the intelligent, highly trained blind person can make a success, including a number of industrial processes such as capstan lathe operatives, telephone operators, piano tuners, etc.

The placing of blind people successfully in open industry depends on two important factors:

(*i*) having a helpful and sympathetic employer who is prepared to try out one or two blind people; and

(*ii*) being able to train the blind person not only before the job starts but actually while carrying it out.

In both respects, the work of the *Blind Persons Resettlement Officers* of the Department of Employment is invaluable. These officers include highly trained blind persons who arrange for the placement of blind people in industry. They liaise with the employers and find out what vacancies exist locally, in open industry, which would be suitable for a blind person. The Resettlement Officer then assesses the potential of the blind persons wishing to enter open industry and trains those selected. The officer then introduces each blind person to the new post and stays to help with the training. In this way, this officer is able to guide the blind person through the most difficult part of the job, the beginning, and help in the settling down period. Afterwards visits are paid to the factory from time to time to check how the blind person is doing. If any difficulties occur in the meantime, the employer can call upon the Blind Persons Resettlement Officer to help sort them out. There is no doubt that this service helps many blind people to find and retain employment in industry.

Following the general principle already mentioned, *the aim should always be to try and place as many blind people as possible in 'open industry'* – an employment solution which is normal. It is encouraging to note, in many areas, a steady increase in the proportion of blind people in open industry. In some instances the proportion of blind people in open industry is in excess of 65% of the blind people employed full-time.

Occupation in sheltered employment For those blind people who cannot, for some reason, manage to hold down a job in 'open industry', the next alternative is to try and place them in what is known as 'sheltered employment'. This is specially *subsidised full-time occupation* applicable to blind persons only.

If possible, the blind person needing sheltered employment should be sent to a *special workshop for the blind*. Here, after a period of training in a suitable occupation, he or she is employed in the workshop. There are many traditional trades for blind persons in workshops including basket making, rug making, brush making, chair caning, machine knitting. The blind person is employed at the workshop full time, just as in an ordinary factory. Specially trained sighted foremen assist in the finishing-off of articles, and arrange the marketing of the products.

Each blind worker receives the usual wage for the occupation although, because of the handicap, the worker might not have been able to earn this wage 'on piece rates'. The difference between what is actually earned and is paid is called '*augmentation*' and is paid by the local authority. Provided certain conditions are met, the Department of Employment will make a grant equal to 75% of the financial deficiency each year to the authority for each approved worker in sheltered employment. Certain capital grants are also available to voluntary bodies who provide satisfactory sheltered employment.

Home workers schemes are mainly found in rural areas and smaller towns where it is not possible to collect enough blind people together to form a sheltered workshop. Under the scheme the blind worker is provided with materials at home and makes a certain quota of goods which are later collected and marketed. Provided the individual averages a certain minimum output per week, *augmentation of wages* is paid as in the workshops. An example would be a blind person employed at home as a machine knitter; the knitting machine is provided by the local authority together with materials and orders.

Blind persons are employed in similar occupations in home workers schemes as in the workshops. Although many blind home workers schemes are excellent, they do not provide such a satisfactory solution as workshop schemes. In particular, it is often difficult to supervise the blind people satisfactorily and the blind persons themselves miss the company that they meet in a workshop. It is also more difficult for the blind person to concentrate on a high level of production – most homes contain too many distractions.

General social services for blind persons

- *Part-time occupations*   Some elderly blind people are keen to fill in a portion of their day by having a part-time occupation. This is usually arranged by the home teacher who helps organise any marketing assistance for articles produced. There are various arrangements to cope with this problem and many towns have a *disabled persons shop* which sells the products made in this way.

  Augmentation is never given to blind people working part-time as it is only intended to help and encourage those engaged in full-time work.

- **Learning to read** An important part of any social service for the blind is concerned with home tuition in reading. There are two forms of embossed type.
  - *Moon* Raised letters; easy to learn but a very slow and inefficient method of reading which, for this reason, is not often taught.
  - *Braille* This is the usual method of reading used by the blind. It is a complicated system of embossed dots arranged in a rectangular pattern. Braille is taught to all blind children and younger blinded adults, and to elderly persons who have both the ability and desire to learn. It takes an intelligent blind person at least six months fairly hard study to learn Braille and, for this reason, is beyond the ability of many elderly persons who go blind in later life. A useful indicator of the likelihood of an elderly person, who has recently developed blindness, learning Braille is given by finding out how much and what type of reading was undertaken before sight was lost. If the individual was an avid reader, it is always important to persevere with Braille. If, however, the blind person was a most casual reader of the simplest and widely illustrated newspapers, it is not likely that Braille will ever be learned. All persons recently blinded under the age of about 50 years, and all young persons should always be taught Braille.
- **Substitutes for reading** The Royal National Institute for the Blind have a large *library of recorded tapes of books* and will lend a standard tape recorder to each blind and partially sighted person wishing to take advantage of this service. The person borrows the tape recording of the required book, plays the tape and, in this way, can have a continuous and changing supply of books read aloud to him or her. Each local authority makes a contribution to the Royal National Institute for the Blind for each person in its area who is using this service.
- **Radios for the blind** The radio is a most useful service and greatly enjoyed by all blind people. There is a special voluntary society financed by the traditional appeal over the radio each Christmas Day, whose object is to ensure that every blind person is provided with a radio. Maintenance is arranged by local authorities.
- **Special aids** Special aids in the home are available for the blind. A good example is the special braille form of 'regulo' which can be fitted to gas stoves to help the blind person when cooking.
- **Provision of guide-dogs for the blind** A society exists which provides and trains special guide dogs which can be used by the blind. The selection and training of the dog and blind person is lengthy and costly and necessarily limits the number of blind people who can be helped in this way. Only a few breeds are suitable for training, for example, retrievers. The service is particularly valu-

288 Care and rehabilitation of disabled people

able for active blind people living alone. Local authorities meet the cost of training and provision of guide-dogs which is, today, usually in the region of £3000.

- **Holidays and hostels** The provision of special holiday homes for the blind is another general social function. Many of these are run by voluntary bodies, and local authorities assist by contributing and paying for the blind people from their area who use them. The holiday homes are specially adapted and make it possible for blind people to have a holiday of their own. The difficulties and dangers of going alone to ordinary hotels and boarding houses may prohibit blind people from taking holidays.

  There are a few specially designed permanent hostels for elderly blind people. But many more old people who are blind are looked after very satisfactorily in ordinary elderly persons hostels – perhaps two blind people in a hostel containing 40 sighted elderly persons – and in many ways the blind people seem to enjoy such hostels more.

  In 1989 approximately 53 000 handicapped people were sent on holiday in England and Wales with the help of social service departments.

- **Financial help** Although local authorities cannot help blind people by direct money grants, there are *special pension facilities* available to blind people. It is the responsibility of the social workers employed by local authorities to make certain that the blind people understand what these are.
  - For all blind persons aged 16 years and over, the income support rates are increased.
  - There are special income tax allowances for blind persons less any tax free disability payments.

- **Voting** A blind person has a right to vote by post in parliamentary and local elections or to have the ballot paper marked with the help of a sighted person.

- **Free postage** Free postage is allowed for a number of 'articles for the blind' including embossed literature, paper for embossing, and for recordings acting as an alternative to an embossed book.

- **Television licence** There is a reduction in the cost of any television licence.

Social services for other groups of disabled people

The social services described in detail above, provide a useful basis for a discussion of the services available to other handicapped persons. In all groups, it is always important to arrange for the following.

- As complete a system of *registration* as possible.
- *Individual assessment* by means of home visiting so that the

difficulties and problems of the handicapped person can be separately assessed in the surroundings of his or her own home.

Compared with the other social services described for blind people, there are many differences for other handicapped groups and these will now be discussed separately.

Social services for the deaf and dumb

The general term deaf and dumb describes people who are *born completely deaf* and who, in the past, *never developed any speech*, not because of a defect of voice production, but because normal speech is only learnt by copying what is heard – a process impossible in the congenitally deaf. With very modern methods of teaching, it is now possible to teach speech to most congenitally deaf children.

The problems of the group as a whole are mainly connected with the isolation from which they suffer. The need of most deaf and dumb people is, therefore, connected with arranging the following.

— Suitable *interpreter services* in obtaining a job or in sorting out any difficulty. Finding and keeping a suitable occupation is not usually a difficult problem for deaf and dumb people, provided they receive help, especially in interpretation from a trained social worker.
— *Clubs and recreational facilities.* Many deaf and dumb people use a mixture of sign and finger language by which they converse with each other. Because of this, they enjoy mixing with other deaf and dumb people rather than non-handicapped people with whom they often find it difficult to communicate.

Lip reading is also used to understand speech and many deaf and dumb people find television very enjoyable.

Most of the social services for deaf and dumb people are carried out by voluntary societies, many of which are connected with church bodies. There is an historical reason for their welfare which was originally started in the nineteenth century by the church, with the object of providing special church services which deaf and dumb people could follow. Today welfare services have developed widely to include all types of social services, but there are still special religious services held weekly for deaf and dumb people in many places.

Social services for the hard of hearing

People who develop deafness, having in the past enjoyed good hearing, are usually referred to as 'hard of hearing'. This term indicates that although deaf, such handicapped people have normal speech and listen either by lip reading or with the help of a hearing aid.

The greatest proportion of people who are hard of hearing are elderly, as deafness, like blindness, usually develops seriously in old age. It is important to ensure the following.

— That correct assessment of hearing is undertaken from time to time.
— That hearing aids are provided and are well maintained so that they are constantly helpful.

The assessment of hearing is usually carried out in an Ear, Nose and Throat department of a hospital, or in a special centre, such as those found in the school health service of large authorities. Hearing should always be tested by a pure tone audiometer. Coarse tests often used, such as listening to speech or the ticking of a watch, are of very limited value and of no use at all in assessing the degree of deafness to different frequencies of sound.

Probably there is no more neglected health aid than a *hearing aid*. The fitting of a hearing aid needs patience to ensure that it is fully understood by the deaf person. One of the problems is that, for most people, the loss of hearing is differential – the notes at high frequencies are lost to a greater degree than those at low frequencies. As the consonants in speech are in the high frequency range of sound and the vowels much lower, it is the consonants which are usually missed, rendering speech difficult to understand. When the hearing aid is fitted, it amplifies both high and low frequencies equally; hence the consonants can be heard but seem to be drowned by the vowels. This leads to many elderly people thinking the hearing aid is useless. The solution is to persist for weeks with the aid until the brain slowly adjusts and speech once again becomes intelligible.

Social services for paralytic conditions

These include both progressive conditions (multiple sclerosis, muscular dystrophies) and non-progressive states – usually the sequelae of accidents.

Many of these individuals need a variety of community services outlined on pages 277–82. Occupation should be possible for those whose mobility is maintained and especially for mild cases. Much of the social help this group requires is assistance with housing, transport and the fitting of various aids to enable them to live more normal lives within the community.

Paraplegia

Many of these cases result from accidents in which the spinal cord is permanently injured. The extent of the paralysis will depend upon the site of the injury – the lower the site the better the outlook and vice versa. All will be paralysed from the waist down, but if this is the main lesion (i.e. if the arms are unaffected) then up to 80% of patients should be able to lead reasonably normal lives and be able to follow an occupation. Such disabled people can, with the aid of suitable mechanised transport become quite mobile and will usually develop tremendous power in the arms to compensate and soon learn how to improvise.

Sporting facilities have always been an important part of the social facilities provided for paraplegics. This is because the strengthening of compensatory muscles is an essential part of training those with paraplegia to overcome their disability. Following the lead given by Stoke Mandeville Hospital both national and international sporting events are held each year culminating in the Paraplegic Olympics which are held in the same year as the Olympic Games. Many different sporting activities are suitable including archery, basket ball, etc. Some local authorities assist paraplegics by providing suitable premises and sports centres where these activities can take place.

Cerebral palsy (Spasticity)

Many spastic handicapped people need similar services to those with other paralytic or crippling diseases. Most of these conditions date from birth and, therefore, *suitable education and training facilities for the young adolescent are important.* Speech defects also pose special difficulties.

Recent work has emphasised that it is better to look after spastics in conjunction with other handicapped people. About 25% of spastics also suffer from epilepsy and, therefore, for this group the services outlined below may also be important.

Epilepsy

People with epilepsy present many problems not met with in other groups of handicapped people. This is not due to the unusual difficulties of treating epilepsy, but to the ill-informed and unfair attitude of the public generally.

Most people with epilepsy suffer from minor degrees of the illness and are well controlled and can quite satisfactorily be employed in most professions and occupations. In fact, there are many examples of people who have mild epilepsy, succeeding in most occupations. But the public have an unreasonable fear of people with this disease because, quite wrongly, they assume that the person with epilepsy may be dangerous. Some people even think the disease is some form of mental illness. All this adverse public reaction leads to many patients with epilepsy concealing the fact that they have had occasional epileptic seizures, because they fear that if it is known they have epilepsy, they may lose their jobs or find it difficult to find employment. The strain of concealing these facts is considerable, especially as a sudden unexpected attack of epilepsy at work, could, at any time, lead to discovery. For this reason, many patients in good posts live in constant fear of discovery and this often leads to the development of other difficulties including a minor anxiety state.

To help anyone with epilepsy, it is important to realise this difficult background and to try and arrange for the employer or prospective employer to know the full facts and that the epilepsy, if properly controlled, may be no hazard. It is usual for those with epilepsy to have some form of warning of an impending attack and, apart from avoiding one of the few dangerous occupations which are rarely sought after there are few jobs which are not suitable.

It is, however, essential that a constant and careful watch is kept on each person with epilepsy to make sure that the treatment received is controlling the disease.

The final success of any treatment depends on complete rehabilitation. Because of this, it is helpful to attach a specially trained health visitor or social worker to any hospital which treats serious epilepsy, so that all the social aspects of the illness – home, occupation, etc. – can be carefully investigated. In this way, much preventive work can be done and many problems can be avoided or corrected before they can have a serious effect.

Occasionally, it is necessary to admit to an epileptic colony a person whose epilepsy is uncontrollable or whose home is quite unsuitable. Most epileptic colonies are run by voluntary bodies and local authorities meet the cost. Although most people in colonies have to stay there permanently, every effort is made to rehabilitate them sufficiently to return to community life if at all possible.

Special medical assessment and treatment centres for epilepsy

Important special centres for medical assessment of difficult cases of epilepsy have been set up for children at Oxford (based on the Park Hospital for Children) and for adults at York and Chalfont (Bucks). Skilled assessment in difficult cases is essential and such units are just beginning to probe some of the complicated facets of epilepsy.

17   Care of mentally disordered people

Law relating to the mentally disordered

There are four main aims of the legislation concerning mentally disordered persons. These were brought up to date by the Mental Health Act 1983 and include the following.

- To remove whenever possible the stigma attached to mental illness.
- To bring mental illness and mental handicap under the same code of practice.
- To bring the medical treatment of mental illness and mental handicap on to the same basis as the treatment of physical illness.
- To develop as far as possible community social services for the mentally ill and handicapped.

- The *removal of stigma* attached to mental illness has never been easy as it is necessary to change the attitude of public opinion to mental disability. Due to ignorance as to its cause, many people feel ashamed, or have feelings of guilt, when a member of their family develops some form of mental illness.

  There is really no basis at all for such a reaction. Hardly any mental illness is hereditary. Mental illness is fairly common – each year 439 per 100 000 of the population are admitted to mental hospitals in England and one third of these are admitted for the first time. It has been estimated that one in 20 to 25 people are admitted to a mental hospital at some time in their life while probably double that number seek advice from their family doctor for an illness whose basis is primarily mental not physical. This means that few, if any, families do not contain some member who suffers from some form of mental illness.

  One of the most effective ways to help reduce stigma would be for all large district general hospitals to have mental health departments which would replace the isolated mental hospitals. This would mean that the reason for a patient's admission would not be so obvious – as it is when admitted to a mental hospital. It would also help to improve understanding between doctors and nurses treating physical and mental illnesses.

- *Mental disability* In *mental illness*, the main problem is some form of *mental instability*. Before the major reforms of the Mental Health Act 1959 it was treated quite separately from *mental handicap*, which is primarily a defect of the intellect in which *the intelligence of the person is seriously retarded*. From the aetiological aspect it is reasonable to consider them separately. However, in the individual case both factors often play a part. For example, in a case of mental handicap (in which the intelligence of the person is retarded) the prognosis will depend, to some extent, on the person's emotional stability. If this is quite normal, there is much more chance of successfully training the person to carry out some occupation and lead a reasonably normal life. However, if there is even a moderate degree of emotional instability, this may prove impossible.

  In the same way, an extremely clever person may be able to manage to live 'normally' even though he or she is extremely mentally unstable – their extreme intelligence enabling them to behave just within the bounds of the law for others will usually excuse their odd behaviour as being 'very eccentric'. If, however, the same individual happened to be dull and unintelligent (even if this fell short of mental handicap), social rejection and consequently serious problems are far more likely.

  The Mental Health Act 1983 deals with both forms of mental disability – mental illness and mental handicap.

- *Treatment of mental disability* Treatment of physical illness is designed to carry out a full investigation, to correct various pathological processes discovered and to restore the patient to full health. If this is not possible, the aim is to arrest development of the disease and to control problems. Treatment may take place at home by the family doctor, or the patient may be referred to hospital either as an out-patient or an in-patient for investigation and treatment. Once these are completed, the patient invariably returns home. Even in the case of a steadily developing disease with a fatal outlook, such as a malignant new growth, the patient is sent home and remains there as long as possible.

  The *treatment of all forms of mental disability* has the following important differences.

  (*i*)   There is usually a question of protecting both the patient and the community from the effects of the mental illness, for example the danger of suicide (a special problem is endogenous depression or, if there is any insomnia, in puerperal depression). Occasionally violent behaviour is noted (even criminal behaviour) which means that special arrangements have to be made to admit a few patients compulsorily and to retain them by compulsion in a mental hospital (*custodial care*).

(*ii*) Much mental illness and handicap is a long standing or chronic problem whereas in most physical diseases those persons admitted to hospital are either suffering from an acute attack or have been admitted to hospital for a series of investigations. As the cause of mental illness is often unknown, until recently few effective treatments were available.

Formerly, mental hospitals were almost entirely asylums, places where the inmates could safely be cared for rather than treated. Because of this, many who entered them remained there as in-patients for several years, and often for the rest of their lives. The introduction of tranquilliser drugs, better rehabilitation facilities and social services has changed all this. The aim today is to use hospital admission in mental disability mainly for the assessment and early treatment, and then to return the individual home for follow-up treatment and special social services after-care and rehabilitation. Occasionally it is still necessary to arrange an admission compulsorily, but it is hoped this will only occur only rarely. Wherever possible, the patient is encouraged to be admitted as an informal patient even if acutely mentally ill.

• The development of widespread *community social services* has made it possible for treatment to be continued while the person lives at home. If home conditions are not suitable, the individual may live in a *special hostel* provided either by the social services department or by a voluntary organisation. Such an arrangement is more normal and therefore to be preferred. Occasionally *boarding out* may be arranged with sympathetic persons who understand mental disability. Another excellent arrangement is to provide *sheltered flats* where two mentally handicapped people can live together quite independently.

Successful community care will only be possible if a wide range of supporting social services are available – *social workers* skilled in aftercare work, *hostels, adult training centres, special workshops, occupational therapy, clubs, job placement services* leading, if possible, to full-time employment being obtained in ordinary industry. Both the community social services (provided by social workers) and the community health services (general practitioners, district nurses, community psychiatric nurses, health visitors) must work very closely together so that all complement each other.

Compulsory hospital admissions

About 10% of mentally ill patients enter hospital compulsorily. In most of these persons, the reason for the admission is acute and serious. Under the Mental Health Act 1983, only persons who cannot be persuaded to enter hospital informally can be compulsorily admitted. Three types of compulsory admission are used.

- *Admission for observation in an emergency* (Section 4 of the Mental Health Act 1983)   This section is used for acute emergencies, *only lasts 72 hours* and requires either (*i*) an application by the nearest relative or by a specially trained social worker, or (*ii*) one medical recommendation. The applicant must examine the patient within 24 hours of making the application and the admission must be carried out within 24 hours of the medical examination.
- *Admission for assessment* (Section 2 of the Mental Health Act 1983)   Again the application can only be made by the nearest relative or by a specially trained social worker. Recommendations from two doctors are needed, one of whom must be approved as having specialist knowledge of the type of mental disorder from which the patient is suffering. Both doctors must examine the patient at the same time or within a period of seven days.

    Such a patient may be admitted and detained in hospital for a *period not exceeding 28 days*. There is an opportunity to appeal against detention under Section 2 of the Mental Health Act 1983 within the first 14 days of detention and then the case must be reviewed by a Mental Health Review Tribunal (see page 301).
- *Admission for treatment* (Section 3 of the Mental Health Act 1983)   This is the least common method of compulsory detention and is usually used for patients who have already been admitted to hospital under Section 2 but who need further detention in the interests of their own health or safety or with a view to the protection of other persons and who need to be kept in hospital for treatment. This method of admission and detention can be used for persons suffering from mental illness or from severe mental impairment or psychopathic disorder. However in the latter two instances, such patients may only be detained if they can benefit from treatment.

    Admission under Section 3 *lasts for six months and then for one year at a time. Any patient who has been compulsorily detained for three years without a Mental Health Review Tribunal must then be referred to the Mental Health Review Tribunal.*

Mental Health Act Commission

This Commission was set up in 1983. Its main responsibilities include the following.

— The exercise of general protective functions for detained patients.
— The visiting and interviewing of detained patients.
— Ensuring that patients are informed of their rights.
— Examining the lawfulness of detention.
— Investigating complaints.

Social services for the mentally ill

Role of local authorities

The social services departments of local authorities are responsible for developing widespread community social services for the mentally disordered (mentally ill and mentally handicapped). These fall mainly into three categories.

● Social work support provided by specially trained social workers.
● Day care facilities to help with the reintegration of anyone who has had mental illness or is mentally handicapped. These include social rehabilitation, occupational therapy, industrial therapy and work-shop provision.
● Residential facilities for those who have no satisfactory home to return to after their illness.

It is convenient to discuss social services for the mentally ill under the following headings.

● Prevention
● Housing
● Hostels
● Occupation
● General after-care
● Day care
● Hospital admissions.

Prevention of mental illness

Much preventive work in the mental health field is concerned with the *avoidance of further breakdown.*

In many instances, however, the *extrinsic factors* (see page 170) connected with the patient's environment especially at certain times of life, for example puberty, pregnancy, menopause, old age, *are the precipitating cause* of the start of the mental illness or a further breakdown.

Because of the extreme importance of the early years of life on the subsequent development of any person, it is most important to recognise early, if possible, *unusual signs of insecurity in a child*, as this is likely to indicate unsatisfactory home conditions. Most maternity and child health services today have a close link with a child psychiatrist and psychiatric social worker so that health visitors may discuss such cases and get help with their preventive work.

Social work support should be available to such a home at any time and the decision about who is best fitted to provide this should be made after joint discussion between doctors, health visitors, community psychiatric nurses and social workers. In the same way, close liaison should always be maintained between child guidance staff who are helping schoolchildren with emotional or behavioural disorders and social workers who may have to provide aftercare later.

Housing and conditions at home

Housing conditions which are unsatisfactory for the mental development of a child may be quite different from those precipitating physical illness. The home may be very well provided with the physical essentials of life, but the *important mental factor of stability, love and affection* may be missing. Some of the worst environments are those homes in which parental strife is continuous and unending, perhaps eventually leading to separation or divorce. For this reason the health visitor or social worker must pay particular attention to any home with such a background.

Even when early recognition of mental health problems has been made, it is never easy to change that home so that it becomes satisfactory. But it is always a great help to know the problem exists and it is usually possible to prevent the effects of the poor home conditions being very detrimental to the child.

The value of the right type of home is just as important for anyone who has had a mental illness and has been successfully treated in hospital. It may be better for such a person to go to a special hostel on discharge from hospital rather than return to an unsuitable home.

Small homes (hostels)

Homes can be of various types and are provided by either the social services department or by a voluntary body. The aim should always be to achieve *maximum integration between those living in them and the ordinary community*. This is easier if the hostels are small, accommodating 6–8 persons and if they are scattered throughout the area rather than built together. As far as possible, hostels should be like ordinary houses; they can be established successfully in the older larger house or by modifying two or three adjacent terraced houses together on a modern council estate. *Boarding out* can also be useful as an alternative to an unsuitable home provided sympathetic and understanding hosts can be found – because of this difficulty few successful boarding out schemes have yet been introduced by local authorities.

Occupation

A carefully chosen occupation can do much to prevent a person developing a mental illness or having a relapse, and is always an important factor in rehabilitation.

Many large industrial firms and HM Forces carefully examine all new entrants to assess as far as possible the type of personality, intelligence, aptitude and emotional stability, so that the individual can be fitted into the most suitable occupation. This is an important part of any occupational health service, for correct selection of occupation can avoid many breakdowns.

Having fitted the new entrant into a job, it is equally important that the worker is carefully watched in the early period of employment so that any signs of undue strain are recognised. This is also a valuable part of all student health services at Universities for it is known that serious mental illness in students can be avoided by ensuring early recognition of signs of stress.

A *Disablement Resettlement Officer* (DRO) (see page 277), a specially trained officer of the Department of Employment, will assist in finding employment for all handicapped people, including those who are mentally disabled. It is often difficult to find employment for persons who have had a mental illness. They may have lost their original job and there is usually a resistance among employers to re-employ them for fear they will again break down and perhaps dislocate their staff. It is important that any unavoidable delay should not depress the person who has just left a mental hospital. *Occupational therapy* at a special rehabilitation centre or attendance at a day centre should be provided as this will not only help in training the individual in physical skills (see below) but, perhaps more importantly, it will do much to *restore self-confidence* and get the person used to meeting others and prepared for normal working conditions.

Social workers assist the Disablement Resettlement Officer in trying to find suitable jobs for those recovering from mental illnesses. Some social services departments have found it useful to employ a full-time officer to do this task. Much of this work is slow, and in one year such an officer may only find employment for a few patients. Work is needed not only in finding jobs, but in meeting employers, and constantly helping to educate the public in the problems of mental illness. The successful placement of one such person may well lead to another post being found in the same firm.

General after-care

Most people who have had a mental illness will need long-term help and follow-up after-care, usually provided by the person's own family doctor, who often works closely with the social worker. All social aspects – home, family, occupation, etc. – play an important part in after-care and the social worker must ensure that close cooperation exists so that the person who has recovered from a mental breakdown is given every opportunity to return to normal life as quickly as possible.

Day care facilities for the mentally ill

Day care facilities play an increasingly important role in the rehabilitation of many former mental hospital patients. The centres should provide a wide opportunity for the individual to meet many different people and thus improve their social rehabilitation. Many such people lack confidence and their self-respect has been shaken by their illness. They need to gain confidence by demonstrating that they can manage quite well on their own (when they are away from their families). Daily attendance at such centres which are reached by a bus or train journey helps in regaining self-confidence.

The functions of such centres often overlap with those of day hospitals and sheltered employment. *Occupational therapy* should be available at day centres. As well as helping with the problems of readjusting to the demands of work, *cultural* and *educational activities* such as a study of art, music, drama or literature should also be provided at day centres. Those attending day centres should be encouraged to help in their daily running and organisation.

Hospital admission

Approximately 90% of all admissions to mental hospitals are made by the family doctor arranging for the patient to go into hospital informally (the same arrangement as for physical illness). The decision is made after discussion between the family doctor and the psychiatrist who will then look after and treat the patient in hospital.

Occasionally it is necessary to arrange compulsory admission of a mentally ill person, and detection in hospital for observation or as an urgent necessity (see page296).

Mental health review tribunals

There are many safeguards to make certain that no patient is retained in hospital compulsorily unless it is essential. Special Mental Health Review Tribunals, consisting of a senior lawyer as president, a psychiatrist and a lay member, are set up in each area to deal with requests for discharge from patients. After hearing the application the tribunal may direct the patient's discharge. It must do so if it is satisfied that any of the following conditions are met.

- That the patient is no longer suffering from mental illness, psychopathic disorder, mental impairment or severe mental impairment.
- That it is not in the interests of the patient's health or safety, nor for the protection of other persons, that the patient should continue to be detained.
- In the case of a psychopathic disorder that, if released, the patient would not be likely to act in a manner dangerous either to others or to him or herself.

Mentally handicapped people

Definitions

Mental handicap is a colloquial term in general use. It is not a legal term. The Mental Health Act 1983 introduced two new terms 'severe mental impairment' and 'mental impairment'. Both are similar but vary in degree. *Mental impairment* is defined as a state of arrested or incomplete development of the mind which includes significant impairment of intelligence and social functioning and *is associated with abnormally aggressive or seriously irresponsible conduct*.

Note that all people who are mentally impaired are also mentally handicapped but that only a small proportion of mentally handicapped people are also mentally impaired. *Mental impairment is a legal term and only persons who are mentally impaired can be dealt with under the Mental Health Act 1983*. The terms 'severe mental impairment' and 'mental impairment' in the Mental Health Act 1983 have replaced the terms 'severe mental subnormality' and 'mental subnormality' which should no longer be used.

There is a tendency to classify mentally handicapped people mainly according to their intellectual level, by means of intelligence tests (see pages 99–100). However, it is well known that intelligence tests often give unreliable results in people with such a handicap. The tests take no account of the individual as a whole – the personality, behaviour and skills – and the results can vary according to the motivation of the person being tested and the particular test used.

The basis for determining whether or not someone is mentally handicapped and what degree of handicap they have depends, therefore, on the following.

- An estimate of the person's intelligence.
- A social test to judge the ability of the individual to make use of intelligence (i.e. a test of performance). Generally children who are three years or more behind their average age group in school are probably mentally handicapped, unless there is another cause for their learning difficulties (e.g. deafness or prolonged absence from formal classwork because of physical illness).
- The emotional stability of the person. The majority of those who are mentally handicapped will need some type of special help from social services.

The range of mental handicap is wide. Some people are said to be in the 'borderline group'. Their intellect is very nearly what is considered normal, and they may have an IQ of between 70 and 85. Although they may have had a deprived background, difficulties at school and in finding employment, eventually they integrate well with society and do not need help from the social services. People who are only able to lead an independent life if given special support in their care and training are sometimes said to be mildly or moderately mentally handicapped. Their IQ is usually below about 65. People with profound (very severe) mental handicap (IQ below about 45) are unable to lead an independent life or to guard themselves against exploitation. They are sometimes said to have 'special needs' or to require 'special care'. They are usually multiply handicapped and may require nursing and physiotherapy. They often have a reduced life-span.

Incidence of mental handicap

In England and Wales approximately 60 000 severely mentally handicapped people of all ages are receiving day care services from local authority social services departments. About 63 000 severely mentally handicapped people are looked after in hospitals and residential accommodation but this number is steadily diminishing as more emphasis is laid on looking after as many as possible in the community.

Causes of mental handicap

Most mental handicap is present at birth and generally results from a mutation in which the individual is left with an incomplete development of the mind. Mentally handicapped people may belong to a recognised type such as Down's syndrome (previously called mongol-

ism because of the characteristic facial development reminiscent of
Mongol races) which is caused by a chromosome abnormality.

Occasionally mental handicap may follow severe birth injury – thus
approximately 48% of those with cerebral palsy have some degree of
mental handicap. Although there is a relationship between the degree
of spasticity and intelligence quotient, this is not invariable for *a few
very severely spastic individuals have normal intelligence quotients*.

Reference has already been made to the rare metabolic disease
phenylketonuria (see page 74), in which the child is born normal but
the defective metabolism soon results in a poisoning of the brain
leading to developmental delay within a few months. If phenylketonuria is diagnosed early – within six weeks of birth – and the child is fed
on a special diet, there is every hope that development will be normal.
It is for this reason that the blood of all babies is tested by the midwife
and health visitor on the tenth day and between four and six weeks of
life to make certain that every case is discovered (This test is repeated
between 4–6 weeks, *see* page 74). It is equally important to recognise
hypothyroidism by screening babies by a blood test.

Mental handicap occasionally develops following a *severe infection
of the brain or meninges*. For this reason, it is essential that no delay
ever occurs in diagnosing and treating such conditions.

Prevention of mental handicap

The opportunities to prevent handicap are increasing rapidly. The
following is a list of likely ways to avoid it.

- *Genetic counselling*   The aim in genetic counselling is to identify
  where there is a high risk of the transmission of hereditary disease
  leading to mental handicap. At present this is usually only possible
  after the birth of one affected child (unless there is a family history
  as in Huntington's chorea). In some cases it may be possible to
  estimate the risks of another handicapped child being born. If
  these are high because one parent is a carrier of an abnormality
  which is likely to show itself in other children, then the parents can
  seek family planning help to prevent conception of another child.

  It is possible to predict the chances of any parents having a
  Down's syndrome child. In a few instances there seems to be a
  family tendency to such births, shown by either a family history of
  such children or by the mother already having given birth to a
  Down's syndrome child. In such families genetic counselling is of
  considerable help. The incidence of Down's syndrome also progressively increases with the age of the mother (see Table 17.1).
- *Amniocentesis* (removal of a small quantity of amniotic fluid)
  Chromosome abnormalities can be detected at 16 weeks, in time to
  enable a termination of pregnancy to be carried out if investi-

gations show that the fetus is abnormal. This is advised routinely for pregnant women aged 35 years and over and for anyone who has already had a Down's syndrome baby (see also p. 57).

- *Immunisation of girls against rubella*   Immunisation between the ages of 11–14 years will prevent rubella infection which in the first three months of pregnancy may lead to brain damage in the fetus. Since 1988, all young children are offered MMR immunisation before the age of 15 months (see page 108).
- *Use of anti-D-immunoglobulin* to prevent haemolytic disease of new born (see pages 53–54).
- *Expert care in labour* to reduce the risk of hypoxia and brain damage to the infant.
- *Intensive care during neonatal period* for babies of low birth weight.
- *Screening* to prevent phenylketonuria (see page 74) and other metabolic diseases.
- *Earlier completion of families* will reduce the chance of a mentally handicapped child being born. The effect of this is shown by the increased chances of a Down's syndrome child being born to the older woman (see Table 17.1).

Table 17.1   Incidence of Down's syndrome by age of mother. (From Hook and Chambers, 1977.)

Mother's age	Risk	Mother's age	Risk	Mother's age	Risk
20	1/1923	30	1/885	40	1/109
21	1/1695	31	1/826	41	1/85
22	1/1538	32	1/725	42	1/67
23	1/1408	33	1/592	43	1/53
24	1/1299	34	1/465	44	1/41
25	1/1205	35	1/365	45	1/32
26	1/1124	36	1/287	46	1/25
27	1/1053	37	1/225	47	1/20
28	1/990	38	1/177	48	1/16
29	1/935	39	1/139	49	1/12

Social services for mentally handicapped people

Importance of coordination and a multidisciplinary approach

Although this section mainly describes social services, it is essential to realise that the *medical, educational, psychological and social needs* should be considered together. No single profession can tackle successfully all the problems and the use of an *assessment team* is important.

In young children the paediatrician, psychiatrist, child psychologist, health visitor, social worker and educationalist will all be involved as well as the family doctor. Older children need educational, social and vocational assessment. Adults may require repeated assessments from psychiatrists, clinical psychologists, general practitioners and social workers. Much of this assessment will take place in hospitals, schools, training centres, workshops or in the individual's own home.

Community social services

Many of the main social services of local authorities aim to provide a supportive community service in which the mentally handicapped persons and their families are encouraged to live a more normal life. If possible such individuals should be trained to follow a full-time occupation.

Since the introduction of the Education (Handicapped Children) Act 1971, the care of mentally handicapped children up to the age of 19 years has been transferred to the education services (see page 98).

Many varied types of assistance are provided by social services departments of local authorities including the following:

— social work support and counselling;
— practical help – home help, day nurseries, laundry services, sitters-in, etc.;
— training and day centres for adults;
— occupational therapy centres;
— workshops for adults;
— employment in ordinary industry;
— small homes (hostels);
— short-term or respite care;
— holidays and recreational activities – clubs, etc.

Social work support and counselling

Parents and families need much help to adjust to the problems of caring for a mentally handicapped child. Many professionals are involved – doctors, health visitors, teachers and social workers. Much of the domiciliary visiting in the community is undertaken by social workers especially after initial diagnosis and assessment.

Although education authorities are now responsible for the education of mentally handicapped children in special schools, much of the social work for this group, for example visiting at home, is carried out by social workers from the social services department. This has the great advantage of improving coordination between the education and social services departments and enabling continuity of care to be maintained when the child reaches the age of 19, ends formal education and then comes under the direct supervision of the social services department.

Practical help

Many families facing the problems of caring for a mentally handicapped individual may need the assistance of *home helps* (see page 336), *day nurseries* (see page 237) and *laundry services*. *Sitters-in* can be of great help to enable the parents to get a short break. *Respite care* is also invaluable (see page 309).

Training centres for adults

Adult training centres or social education centres are provided by social service departments and designed to carry on the training of mentally handicapped people who have left special school. Most are mixed but there are some single sex centres. The main task of the centre is to concentrate on training mentally handicapped people in some skill, preferably within ordinary employment. A few adult mentally handicapped people may find it difficult to adjust themselves to such training, but with the modern workshop whose tasks are more diverse, most should be able to benefit (see page 307).

Social training should continue in the adult training centres and all should concentrate on mastering the skills of helping to run a home and becoming more skilled in various hobbies and pastimes. It is very often in these training sessions that a simple concept of numbers is understood.

The importance of *inducement and constant encouragement* must be recognised. Mentally handicapped individuals must be given targets to achieve and not just left to work at their own pace. The *potential of many mentally handicapped people is far higher than usually expected*, but full potential will only be reached by training which constantly encourages each individual to improve.

Family therapy

Any training given in a centre should always be linked with home life for mentally handicapped people enjoy participating domestically. The handicapped person's family, too, may need continuing support. They should be encouraged to include their handicapped member in all their activities since stimulation and a loving and secure environment, as with all children, will help development. In addition to home visits by professionals, informal family group meetings allow ideas to be exchanged, problems to be aired and are also social occasions.

Problems occasionally arise as puberty develops in mentally handicapped people. It should always be carefully explained to parents that close supervision must be maintained on the activities of their child at home. In particular, it is most important that every parent of a mentally handicapped girl realises that her mental handicap will make her more vulnerable to the advances of unscrupulous men.

Occupational therapy centres

Some occupational therapy centres are also used to help mentally handicapped people, giving them an opportunity to become involved in many different activities. These include various handicrafts and also training in group activities. If possible evening clubs should be arranged and run in such a way that the mentally handicapped people themselves do much of the organisation (see also page 309).

Workshops

During the last few years there has been widespread development in the setting up of a *sheltered workshop* within an adult training centre by local authorities, where mentally handicapped adults are employed. The types of workshops vary greatly, but include the following.

- Carrying out simple tasks which can only be undertaken by hand; occasionally these are contracted out to the workshops by industry and undertaken by mentally handicapped people. Such tasks vary but in one group of workshops includes the following:
  — fixing a pourer into the top of a salt container;
  — stamping tight the top of another container;
  — assembling packs of picnic cups;
  — assembling ball-point pens.
- Manufacturing 'own products' such as the making of wooden and soft toys or furniture which are then sold locally.

Because of the necessity to fit the regime into that of industry, the workshop remains open for the whole of the year. Although the workshop is, in effect, a place of employment for many mentally handicapped people, the training processes still continue. This is often seen in the method of payment adopted. One successful scheme is to base weekly payment upon a 'points' system, in which points, which represent part of the maximum wage, are added for good steady work and rate and standard of production, and deducted for bad behaviour, lateness or non-attendance. In this way the mentally handicapped people employed at the workshop quickly learn the importance of hard work and good behaviour.

Inducement is an essential part of workshop training and the method of financial remuneration used should encourage better productivity, hard work and better social behaviour. It is usual to arrange that the maximum 'wage' be equal to the maximum amount each may earn without having any deduction made from income support. At present, this means each mentally handicapped person employed at the workshops may earn a small sum of money per week without any deduction being made in income support.

One of the most encouraging and remarkable changes which has always been reported following the successful introduction of workshops for mentally handicapped persons has been the great improvement in the behaviour and outlook of those attending. Almost without exception, they become better behaved, easier to control and seem to be very delighted to realise at last they are 'earning' – they obviously feel they have made a great step forward by having shown they can do a useful occupation. There is little doubt that the introduction of such workshops has done much to improve the opportunities and facilities for the adult mentally handicapped person.

Employment in open industry

Until very recently few opportunities occurred for mentally handicapped people to move on from workshops to working in ordinary industry. Successful workshops report that it is possible to find work in ordinary industry for at least 10% of the mentally handicapped who have been trained in the workshops. The success of this must depend to some extent on the employment opportunities in the district and the present high level of unemployment is making it very difficult. It is, however, important to recognise the employment potential of mentally handicapped people which, in a substantial minority, includes successful employment in ordinary industry, especially when unemployment falls to lower levels.

Small homes (hostels)

Most social services departments provide special homes where mentally handicapped persons can live when, for any reason, they have to leave home. In some cases there is a need to provide a home (hostel) where the individual can live during rehabilitation after discharge from hospital. It is most important that no-one is ever kept in hospital any longer than is absolutely necessary, otherwise they become institutionalised and further rehabilitation becomes more difficult.

The term 'home' is often used instead of 'hostel' because it is hoped that it will not give the impression of impermanence or of a certain austerity. All should provide a homely atmosphere and be friendly. The purpose of the home should be to provide a permanent substitute family home.

The size of each home varies, but it should not exceed 20 and many excellent ones are much smaller containing four to five individuals.

It is important that all mentally handicapped persons living in the home partake of ordinary duties just as if they were living with their own family. These include the cooking of breakfast and the preparation of a light evening meal.

Every effort should be made to integrate these homes completely within the community – children should attend normal special schools (i.e. not a school solely for the residents), adults should go out to work either in ordinary industry or in special workshops. The activities of the residents should be as nearly the same as those people in a normal home environment.

Short-term or 'respite' care

Very many mentally handicapped children are looked after in their own homes by devoted parents. There is, however, a great deal of strain involved and many parents find the continuous caring process produces considerable problems for the family. It is important that the devotion of such parents is not continued in such a way that matrimonial difficulties occur, and that other normal members of the family are not neglected.

One of the most useful aids in preventing this danger is for social services departments to provide 'short-term' care in which special temporary arrangements are made to look after the mentally handicapped child for a short period (two to three weeks to enable the parents and family to get a complete break). It has been found that such short-term care helps such parents considerably and enables them to return refreshed to the arduous task of looking after their mentally handicapped child.

It is also important to provide some shorter breaks for parents by arranging for experienced 'sitters in' who can look after the mentally handicapped child while the parents have an evening out. In some instances it helps to arrange residential care for one night or even for a weekend.

Holidays and recreational activities

Most social service departments provide social centres or clubs for mentally handicapped people where they can pursue pastimes and form a club. Such activities are valuable in helping them to gain confidence, to enjoy themselves and to get used to meeting people. Social workers often attend such centres and, in this way, keep in touch with their clients.

Holidays of various kinds are also arranged. Some of these are traditional type holidays but others are of a more ambitious type (i.e. adventure type of holidays, camping, etc.).

Services provided by hospitals

A certain proportion of profoundly mentally handicapped adults are unable to settle at home or in a training centre, and it may be necessary to admit them to a special hospital. A few will always have to remain there because of their inability to learn even simple social habits, or because of extreme mental instability and behavioural problems. It is always the aim of the authorities to rehabilitate people to such a degree that they can be discharged to attend adult training centres. Close coordination is always maintained between the staff of the hospital and the staff of the community mental handicap service. It is generally agreed that everything should be done to ensure that no mentally handicapped child or adult ever remains permanently in hospital.

Special legal powers covering mentally disordered people

Criminal proceedings

In criminal proceedings, courts have power to authorise the admission and detention of a mentally disordered person found guilty of offences by the Courts. A *Hospital Order* may be made if the court is satisfied that, on the written or oral evidence of two doctors (one of whom must be specially approved), the offender is suffering from mental illness, severe mental impairment, mental impairment or psychopathic disorder warranting hospital treatment. This order authorises the removal of a patient to hospital within 28 days. The Court may, if necessary, make an order for the detention of the patient in a *place of safety*, which includes residential accommodation provided by a Local Authority, a hospital or mental nursing home, a residential home for mentally disordered persons, a police station or any other suitable place where the occupier is willing to receive the patient.

Alternatively, the Court may make a *Guardianship Order* instead of a Hospital Order if it is thought that the client should be cared for within the community. It is usual in such cases for local authorities to assume the office of Guardianship.

Protection and management of property and affairs

Any person who becomes mentally incapable of managing his or her own affairs cannot legally authorise anyone else to do this. If power of attorney has been given to another person before the mental illness then such authority will probably become inoperable because of the illness. In such cases, the *Court of Protection* exists to protect and manage the affairs and property of any person who is mentally incapable of doing so. The Court of Protection usually appoints a *receiver* – often a close relative (parent, brother or sister) – to administer the patient's affairs under the direction of the Court. This will continue until the Court of Protection is satisfied, on medical evidence, that the patient is now fit again. Application to the Court of Protection (at 25 Store Street, London WC1) can be made by a close relative or by instructing a solicitor to make such an approach.

18   Care of the elderly

Proportion of elderly within the community

The proportion of elderly people in the United Kingdom has been steadily rising over the last 90 years. At the beginning of the twentieth century, about 6.25% of the population were aged 60 years and over. Today in the UK approximately 21% of the population are aged 60 years and over. Projections up to the year 2005 indicate that this will remain stationary and then begin to fall slightly at the end of the next 15 years. The largest increases are now occurring in the oldest age groups (see Table 18.1).

There are many striking differences between the proportion of elderly men and women; 58.3% of all old persons are women but this proportion is much greater in very old age (see Table 2.1, page 32). Falling birth rates during this century have accentuated the rising proportion of old persons but the main reason for the increase is associated with the *increased life expectancy of young persons today*. The life expectancy of a boy today is 71.8 years and a girl 77.8 years. In 1911 the figures were 49 years and 52 years respectively. Yet the life expectancy of a man aged 65 years is now a further 13.14 years and a woman 18.19 years (compared with 11 and 12 years respectively in 1911). There has always been much speculation about the *longevity of women compared with men*. There are probably many reasons – the majority of women are better motivated to survive for they continue to have an active job looking after their home and also seem better able to withstand the effects of chronic crippling diseases which so often occur in old age.

Figure 18.1 shows clearly who the elderly lived with in 1976. These

Table 18.1   Numbers of persons aged 75 years and over (thousands, England and Wales, 1971–87. (From Population Trends, 1989.)

	1971	1976	1981	1987
Males	749	809	951	1143
Females	1614	1770	1979	2241
Total	2363	2579	2930	3384

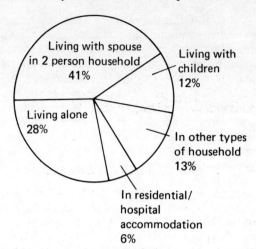

Fig. 18.1   Who the elderly live with, England, 1976.

figures come from a survey of the elderly undertaken in England in 1976. Note that *94% of all old persons live at home*, the remaining 6% live in hostels, hospitals, etc.; 28% of old persons live alone and only 12% are living with children. In fact *two-thirds of all elderly households contain no one under the age of 65 years and one-third of the elderly have never had children or their children have not survived* – they have no near immediate next generation family.

Disability among the elderly

The incidence of physical and mental disability among the elderly is high. About 70% of all physically disabled persons are aged 60 years and over while almost half are aged 70 years and over (see latest OPCS survey carried out in 1988; Table 16.1, page 271).

Prevention of social and medical problems in old age

The avoidance of many problems in the elderly lies in various preventive steps being taken, including the earliest possible recognition of symptoms and social difficulties.

Advice to the elderly

Each local authority Social Services Department employs social workers and social work assistants who help old people with advice and, if need be, visit them at home. This advisory work is carried out in close association with many other persons working in the community and especially with those in the primary health care team – doctors, health visitors and community nurses. Links are also maintained with clergymen, voluntary workers, friendly visitors and community workers so that old people in need of special help can be found quickly. Any old person living alone (on average these represent 28% of all old people) is always at special risk. Special alarms can be fixed (see page 316) but neighbours must play their part. Any person living nearby should, in some way, ensure daily that the old person is all right. In country villages and small towns, such surveillance is often natural and tragedies rarely occur; however in large cities old people living alone are at much greater risk.

Health advice

Health advice should be given on the following subjects.

- The importance of maintaining a clear cut sense of purpose in retirement.
- Physical activity and how, if this is to be effective, it must be linked to the lifestyle of the individual.
- Intellectual activity is also very important and can be crucial in maintaining a lively mind.
- Weight control. Gross overweight causes many additional problems in old people – it increases the chance of heart diseases and makes any degenerative arthritis much worse especially in hips, knees and back.
- How to deal with the increasing likelihood of various forms of degenerative arthritis. Here a balance should be maintained between conservative and radical treatment (including joint replacements) and between activity and rest.
- Nutritional problems, especially in late retirement.
- Various screening tests should continue to be carried out – cervical cytology until the age of 70 years, regular eye tests, and the importance of not ignoring any tendency to deafness, which can become very isolating to the old person, should be stressed.
- How to minimise the dangers of food poisoning – here an understanding of the dangers of incorrect food storage is essential.
- Care of the feet – many serious mobility problems have their underlying cause in much earlier neglect of the feet.
- How to cope with living on one's own. *It is essential for the individual to leave the house at least once every day.* The acquisition of a pet, such as a dog, can be a great help as the animal has to be taken for a short walk every day. Having a pet also helps as the old person starts concentrating on caring for the pet rather than becoming more and more introspective, lonely and cut off from society.

- The importance of planning so that the accommodation which is the home of the elderly person is warm and easy to run.

Planning for retirement

Many of the difficulties can be eased by some degree of *planning for old age*. Most serious mistakes are made by people about to retire. All too often they move to some unknown seaside resort for their retirement and are disappointed and find it difficult to settle down. It must always be remembered that *the older the person, the more difficult it is to readjust*. Human friendships are worth much more in old age than being in some attractive place.

Large companies are increasingly arranging pre-retirement seminars for their employees (usually lasting two days). These are normally held within 2–5 years of the pending retirement and it is always best if employees attend with their partner. Topics covered include pensions, various social security benefits available, health, the home in retirement including security in the home, leisure and possible part time or voluntary work, as well as at least two sessions on financial services – these should include advice on tax, investments and how inheritance tax can be reduced. *It is also essential to check that everyone has made a will as many further problems and difficulties can be caused to the family of anyone who dies intestate.*

Many large insurance companies now also run 'open' seminars for employees of smaller firms. It is a great help for anyone and their partner to attend such pre-retirement courses.

Housing

Housing in retirement

Not enough regard is given to the type of accommodation needed in retirement. Whatever its type – flat, house or bungalow – it should always have the following characteristics.

— Be sited on level ground. So many of the traditional seaside towns, popular with retired persons, are too hilly.
— Have an entrance which can be directly approached by car – i.e. a car should be able to drive up to the front door.
— Have a downstairs room which could be turned into a bedroom.
— Have a downstairs lavatory and washbasin (a downstairs bath is useful but often not possible, although a shower is often practicable).
— Have an effective, simple and automatic system of heating.

These five points are connected with the inevitable fact that certain physical limitations will eventually develop as the person gets older. The aim must always be *to help old persons to remain independent in their own home for as long as possible*.

It is always important that, if the old person is living in a house which is obviously too large and unwieldly, it is left for a smaller home *early in retirement or preferably before*. Old people never like the disturbance of moving and it becomes more difficult as they increase in age. If possible, elderly people should be settled in their retirement home by the age of 60 years.

It is a help to ensure that, in some way, the house is heated automatically by oil, gas or electricity. Many old people feel the cold acutely and the constant stoking of coal fires can be hazardous and may result in falls. The inability of an elderly person to arrange proper heating of the accommodation may eventually lead to the dangerous condition of hypothermia.

It is important that relatives do not take the old person permanently into their home unless this is clearly inevitable. Many kindly relatives are tempted to do this as they feel the old person is barely capable of continuing to look after him or herself. But independence is very precious, especially to older people. Relatives, such as children who precipitately take their elderly parents into their homes, may soon find it is a great mistake as the old person is not happy and begins to cause many difficulties. It is far better to arrange for the old person to stay temporarily with relatives – say for two to three weeks – and to retain their own home and independence.

It is also sensible to arrange for the old person to live reasonably near the rest of the family (say within 30 minutes to an hour's journey) so that support and surveillance can easily be maintained and yet the old person can continue to lead an independent life.

Sheltered housing

This means a flatlet or flat for elderly people with a *resident warden in attendance* to ensure that help is readily available in an emergency. A bell or alarm is fitted to each flatlet. Elderly people living in such accommodation are usually fairly frail but can look after themselves. If a midday meal is provided for them in a luncheon club close by, so much the better.

Sheltered housing is provided either by housing authorities or in accommodation built by housing trusts or voluntary bodies. The Social Services Committee usually pays a small sum per year per unit of sheltered accommodation to help pay the cost of the warden and other amenities (such as special alarms or telephones).

Supportive housing

Some local authorities are now introducing special units – supportive housing – where even more support can be given to the frail elderly person than in sheltered housing. In addition to a midday meal two or three hours of domestic help is provided daily, yet the old person retains his or her own 'front door' and identity to a greater extent than in any hostel.

Interests, hobbies, part-time work

All retired people should always be encouraged to cultivate some hobby, pastime or interest. This process should preferably have been started before retirement. It does not matter what type of extra activity is tackled provided that it gives a real sense of purpose.

It is helpful to encourage an individual to do some voluntary work, such as helping other people (elderly, handicapped or children). Occasionally it may be possible for the elderly person to undertake some form of part-time job.

For those who are in some way handicapped, perhaps because of physical limitations, it is important to encourage the continuation of their usual activities for as long as possible. Thus, a retired person should always be encouraged to look after the house even if all the work involved cannot be tackled.

Financial help

Pensions and allowances

Pensions and extra financial help are provided by the Department of Social Security. However, many old people need help in claiming their pensions and other allowances and the health and social care professionals should be ready at all times to explain and assist. It is most important that *maximum use is made of pensions and allowances and it is never safe to assume that every old person fully understands their entitlement*. Many of the elderly only imperfectly understand the range of pensions available and it is essential for professional carers to realise this and therefore discuss the matter with elderly patients in hospital. There is a special form of financial help which is often overlooked – *Housing Benefit*, which can help people on low incomes to pay their rent and/or rates (community charge).

Housing benefit

Housing benefit is a government scheme to help people on low income (whether elderly or not) pay their rent and/or community charge. The scheme is run by the local authority. It can operate in council housing, private rented accommodation, in the elderly person's own home (for rates, community charge) and in many other types of rented accommodation.

If the elderly person gets Income Support (see below) and pays rent and/or community charge, the maximum Housing Benefit will usually be paid. It is not available to anyone living in a hostel.

Retirement pension

The retirement pension is a state benefit which is paid to everyone who has:

— reached state pension age (60 years for women and 65 years for men);
— retired, or can be treated as retired from a regular job;
— paid (or been credited with) enough National Insurance contributions.

A married woman can qualify for a retirement pension either

— if she meets the above conditions; or
— on her husband's qualifications. In this instance she must be 60 years of age or over *and* her husband at least be 65 years old.

Since October 1989 anyone receiving a retirement pension can earn any amount in addition without any reduction being made in the state retirement pension.

If the elderly person goes into a National Health Service hospital the retirement pension is reduced after six weeks. If, however, the person is living in a local authority hostel (see pages 333–4), the retirement pension is reduced immediately.

Income support

Income support is a benefit anyone (elderly or not) may be able to get if their total income is insufficient. Income support is a non-contributory benefit and can, in certain circumstances, be paid to persons receiving a retirement pension.

Community services available to assist the elderly living in their own homes

Numerous special services are supplied by the social services department to assist the elderly living in their own homes. In all instances, the constant aim is to ensure that the elderly person remains as independent as possible. In most cases, it is important to provide such services early enough so that they can prevent more serious difficulties from developing. Community services include the following.

Home helps (see pages 336–7)

The main value of home helps is to assist elderly people within their own homes. It is usual for the home help, who is often a married woman, to do the housework, essential shopping and get the elderly person a meal. The home help should always help with those tasks that are beyond the elderly person's capacity, for example cleaning windows and some of the heaviest tasks within the home.

Home help service can be full-time or part-time but, apart from emergencies, most of the home helps visit two or three times per week spending 2–4 hours with the old person at each visit. Most local authorities make a charge for this service based on a sliding scale; the elderly person with a good income would pay the full charge, but for any elderly person whose sole source of income is the old age pension, the service is usually free.

The provision of home helps enables many, who would otherwise be too frail, to stay within their own home. An important part of any home help's duties is to observe the elderly person at home in a sensible but inconspicuous way so that adequate warning can be given if the individual is becoming too frail to manage on his or her own.

Applications for home helps should be made to the Director of Social Services or Area Social Services Officer (see page 234).

Good neighbour schemes

A number of local authorities have introduced 'good neighbour' schemes in which arrangements are made for someone living close by to call on an elderly person to help with many simple tasks, for example shopping, lighting the fire, simple cooking and light housework. Usually a small recompense is paid to the good neighbour if she is helping regularly (see page 337). Such services are usually given free to the elderly person, but are not provided by all local authorities.

Home care programmes

Elderly persons living on their own are particularly susceptible to rapid deterioration when they are discharged home from hospital after an illness. Home care programmes have been devised to support elderly people at such times. A typical scheme provides a home help and meals service for 20% of elderly patients discharged from hospital (selected from those at special risk) for four weeks following discharge. At the end of four weeks, if further help is needed it is provided through the normal home help service.

Meals service

Social services departments provide two types of meals services.

Meals-on-wheels provide a hot two course meal delivered to the home of the elderly person, usually three or six times per week depending on the need. A small charge is made for this service, which is heavily subsidised.

Luncheon clubs are for less frail elderly people who attend at some local hall or club from three to six times a week and there obtain a hot meal. Luncheon clubs are especially useful as the elderly person is *encouraged to meet others, gets exercise walking to the club* and not only gets the benefit of a good *hot meal*, but has the opportunity to *make friends*. A similar charge is usually made for the meal at the luncheon clubs as for meals-on-wheels.

Day care centres

These have been described as 'hostels without beds' as they are intended to look after frail elderly persons who can sleep at home but require the kind of care and attention which is usually provided in hostels. Transport collects and brings the elderly person to the centre and takes the person home in the evening. The elderly person spends the day at the centre where meals and other services (for example laundry, hairdressing) are provided.

This type of care is of particular value where a frail elderly person is living with younger relatives who go out to work during the day. It is also useful for anyone living alone and can prevent much loneliness as well as ensuring that the elderly person can remain satisfactorily at home without having to be admitted permanently to a hostel. It is usual for an elderly person to come to a day care centre two or three times per week. A small charge is usually made.

Clubs and day centres

There are many types of clubs and day centres run by social services departments and by voluntary bodies (especially Age Concern). These provide a centre which the elderly person can visit at any time for company, a light meal, tea or coffee and, in many instances, carry out some handicraft. Many social services departments subsidise such clubs. Attendance is usually free, but charges are made for meals, etc.

Holidays and outings

Most local authorities, through their social services departments, arrange special holidays and outings for elderly people and this is also widely supplemented by the work of voluntary bodies. Holidays are especially important to help the elderly living alone and also for those living with younger relatives, for holidays enable each to have a break. In this way, a holiday can be of great value to both the elderly person and the family with whom he or she is living.

Some local authorities own seaside holiday homes, but many rely on making block bookings at seaside resorts in the off-peak season (early in summer or in autumn).

Concessionary fares

Bus passes

Facilities for unrestricted free travel on buses in off-peak times of the day (09.30 to 16.30 hours) can do much to maintain the independence of elderly people. Many local authorities have introduced special schemes in which elderly people can obtain a free pass while other local authorities provide a certain number of tokens which can be exchanged for bus tickets. Schemes vary in different parts of the United Kingdom and are now mainly available to those aged 60 years (women) and 65 years (men) in receipt of a pension.

British Rail Senior Railcard

British Rail has a scheme whereby anyone who is aged 60 years or over can buy a special railcard for £16 (1991). This enables the person to obtain one-third off the price of the following fares:

— Saver returns;
— Network away breaks;
— Standard single and return fares;
— Rail Rover tickets.

In addition, the Senior Citizen Railcard holder can obtain half-price cheap day returns and certain special reductions may be available during particular times of the year.

Any holder of a British Rail Senior Citizens Railcard can also buy a Rail Europe Senior Card for £5. This offers savings of at least 30% on rail and sea travel in 18 countries including most of Western Europe.

Health services for the elderly

All community medical services provided by the general practitioners are available to the elderly person at no extra cost for there is *no charge for any prescription for women aged 60 years and over and for men aged 65 years and over*. In recognition of the extra medical work involved in providing medical services for the elderly, there is a special increased per capita fee paid to general practitioners for all patients on their lists aged 65 years and older. Social workers and health visitors usually work in very close association with general practitioners whether they are based on health centres or not. In this way, it is hoped that the supporting social services (described above) which are provided by local authority social services departments will be increasingly used.

Geriatric hospitals

Geriatric hospitals and geriatric wards in general hospitals are widely available for investigation, treatment and rehabilitation of the elderly. The main differences between geriatric and ordinary acute hospitals are the special facilities the geriatric hospital has for the following.

— Linking up with social services. The *social factors in the life of the old person often determine the seriousness of the illness and the outlook.*
— Emphasising the importance of *active rehabilitation* for all elderly people treated. There is a real danger that the bed rest necessitated in the treatment of the elderly will tend to prevent their full recovery unless very active steps are taken to assist them to become fully active during convalescence.

Day hospitals

Day hospitals have recently been developed to help with the rehabilitation of elderly patients. They act as a sort of half-way stage between hospitals and home. Patients are brought there by transport and returned home in the evening. Elderly people may attend daily or on a specified number of days per week; physiotherapy and occupational therapy services are usually provided.

The main value of day hospitals includes the following.

— They allow the elderly person to be safely discharged home earlier, thus encouraging independence.
— They assist with the active rehabilitation of the patient.
— They help to establish a better link between the geriatric unit and the community services for the elderly.

Community hospitals

In country districts community hospitals have helped develop a day hospital approach for some of their patients. It is valuable if health visitors and social workers arrange to visit the day hospital periodically and in this way improve the coordination between the two services.

These hospitals also provide *short term 'respite' care* for bedridden elderly persons being looked after at home to give the family a short break. They also are very useful for terminal cases and are staffed by the local general practitioners.

District nursing

District nurses are provided by every district health authority to give nursing care for the patient treated at home. Just under 50% of all cases dealt with by district nurses are elderly and the district nurse has a special responsibility for helping bedridden frail elderly people being looked after in their own homes. A special soiled laundry service has been developed in many areas to ensure a daily clean change of linen.

Chiropody

At present chiropody is provided by district health authorities. In many instances the service is given at luncheon clubs, day care centres, clubs or any centre where elderly people congregate.

Foot defects have a serious effect on the mobility of an elderly person (see page 328). Most people would benefit from this service, but the shortage of chiropodists makes it necessary for health authorities to provide this service only to those with obvious foot problems. There are two main ways of providing this service.

— Special chiropody sessions are arranged in clinics and old people's clubs. Health authorities also carry out home treatment where this is essential. In most instances, however, it is much better to give chiropody treatment at a nearby centre for this encourages the elderly person to get out a little. However, initial treatment may have to be undertaken at home if the elderly person's feet are so painful that mobility is seriously restricted.
— Chiropody treatment may be arranged at the private surgeries of chiropodists. In this case, the health authority meets the total cost.

To obtain the maximum value, it is important that chiropody treatment is regularly arranged *once every six to eight weeks*, otherwise the condition of the elderly person's feet may quickly deteriorate. As many elderly people are living on small pensions and find it difficult to meet extra expenses, it is best if chiropody treatment can be provided free of charge for those on low incomes.

Special problems seen in the elderly living at home

Often an illness or accident is the starting point of rapid deterioration in any elderly person living at home, hence *any illness in an elderly person must be treated seriously* even if it is trivial. Special steps must be taken to ensure that the elderly person is completely investigated, treated and rehabilitated.

Rehabilitation can be hastened by arranging for the elderly person, while recovering, to attend a rehabilitation unit run by a local authority or by a hospital. Physiotherapy and occupational therapy will assist in regaining mobility during convalescence and are very valuable to elderly people whose rheumatism or arthritis has inevitably been aggravated by them staying in bed during an illness.

Convalescence on return home can be aided by arranging a full-time home help for a fortnight, and then reducing the help, as the elderly person takes over the routine tasks. In this way, it is often possible to nurse an elderly person through a serious illness without eventual loss of function and independence.

Prevention of mental deterioration

The mental state of the vast majority of elderly people living at home is good. Surveys have shown that 82% of the elderly at home are fully normal, with about 11% showing minor problems, 4% showing clear indication of mental breakdown and the remaining 3% being classified as eccentrics.

There seems little doubt that important factors in maintaining the mental vigour of any elderly person at home are living in the surroundings they have always been used to and *having something useful to do*.

The memory of most elderly people is good except for minor difficulties of remembering names. When mental problems occur memory is one of the first factors to be affected.

Anyone living alone is always at some risk of losing some of their vocabulary because there is little or no opportunity to talk to anyone. In such cases, it is important for individuals to leave their home for a period each day if this is possible and to belong to some group activity (club etc.) which will bring them into contact with others. A friendly visitor who calls periodically is also helpful. It is useful if elderly people can keep a pet (such as a cat or dog) for they will probably spend some time talking to the pet and this can help them retain their use of language.

Domestic anxieties, loneliness and physical defects resulting in limitation of movement seem to induce mental failure. Anxieties in old age are often due to the person not properly understanding certain financial or legal problems. Careful, patient explanation by the health visitor or social worker and the sorting out of pension and legal difficulties (rent, lease or will) can often do much to help. Some elderly people may worry excessively about financial problems and may increasingly stint themselves trying to save when, in reality, their financial circumstances are quite sound. This excessive anxiety about money often tends to get worse as age increases and is best prevented by ensuring that the elderly person fully understands how many of the financial worries are groundless. It is important to point out that, today, the same type of provision is made in all elderly people's homes whether the full cost is paid or whether the elderly person is living on a pension. Much *tact* and *patience* are needed, however, and it must always be remembered that some of the very elderly people today are of a generation brought up before the concept of social security, and there is often a deep seated fear of 'living on charity'.

There seems to be a close association between the development of emotional disturbance in elderly people and either the death of a husband, or wife, or a severe fall. After either event, therefore, considerable help will be needed to assist the elderly person to overcome the effects.

When mental deterioration in the elderly living at home occurs, the symptoms often include the following.

- *Change in outlook* of the elderly person – either towards apathy or agitation.
- *Eating habits may change* – often the elderly person becomes very fussy and will eat very little.
- *Depression* is more common – as well as occasional outbreaks of verbal aggression making the elderly person much more difficult to live with.
- *Memory* – an early failure of memory is noted.
- *Talk* – any tendency to talk a lot, a characteristic of many elderly people, soon disappears.
- *Worries* which may become morbidly increased.
- There is a marked *loss in the ability* of the elderly person *to look after him or herself*.

Prompt recognition of impending early mental deterioration in the elderly at home makes early treatment possible and may prevent a serious and perhaps final mental breakdown.

The confusional states commonly seen in old age, including Alzheimer's disease, are described in Chapter 10 (see page 182).

Loneliness in the elderly

One of the most pathetic complications of old age is loneliness. *It is not always connected with living alone, rather the very lonely old person seems to have cut him or herself off from the world*.

Many social and health factors are usually connected with the problem. The most serious is the sudden loss of a beloved husband or wife. *Men seem to suffer from extreme loneliness more than women*. Extreme loneliness in widowers occurs even when they are not living alone – in other words, loneliness does not always seem to result directly from social circumstances.

Loneliness of some degree probably occurs in about 20% of elderly persons. There are many causes – bereavement, departure of children, absence of hobbies, limitation of physical activity.

It is never easy to prevent loneliness developing. Increasing social contact may occasionally help. Another approach is to encourage the elderly person to understand that he or she is of some value to others and especially to younger people. Loneliness is so often 'an attitude of mind' in which the elderly person loses interest and becomes isolated.

Although not invariable, any elderly person who has varying interests and hobbies is less likely to suffer from extreme loneliness even if their circumstances may suddenly change. Thus the encouragement of widespread hobbies and interests among middle-aged persons and those retiring within the next 2–5 years can do much to prevent extreme loneliness later in old age.

Home accidents

Elderly people living at home, either with a family or on their own, are *more liable to have accidents* – particularly falls. Recent surveys have shown that about 35% of elderly people are liable to fall. In any elderly person, *a fall is likely to be more serious than a similar accident in a younger person*, both because (*i*) it is more likely to result in serious injury, especially in the development of various fractures, and (*ii*) it may also precipitate mental deterioration.

Women are more liable to falls than men and the tendency to fall increases with age. Sheldon in his classic survey in Wolverhampton classified home falls in elderly people in four ways.

- Falls associated with *attacks of vertigo*. A sudden attack of vertigo (dizziness) occurs in the course of movement and unless there is a solid object immediately at hand, the elderly person falls head-long.
- Falls associated with *an increased liability to trip*. Women seem particularly liable to trip over small objects. Many elderly people who, when younger, never had a tendency to trip find, as they grow old, they are much more likely to do so. They trip more easily over small objects or if there is a trivial unevenness in the floor level.
- Falls due to *difficulty in recovering balance*. There seems no doubt that many elderly people find their power in recovering their balance after trivial false movement is much impaired compared with their ability to do when younger.
- Falls due to *sudden collapse*, or to *legs giving way*. This seems particularly to occur in very old people over the age of 80 years.

The elderly person suddenly collapses and often is unable to move for some time afterwards even if he or she has not been injured in the fall.

Many of these falls can be prevented and their effect diminished. The possibility – and, in people over 85 years of age, probability – of a fall should always be considered by those looking after the elderly person. The following steps should be taken to diminish the chance of falls.

- An elderly person increasingly depends on *sight* to maintain balance, as labyrinthine function is often faulty. Thus, an elderly person who is quite steady in daylight may be very liable to fall in the dark. This should be explained to the person who should always ensure that there is adequate light throughout his or her home. It is particularly important to see that the lighting of passages or staircases is really good – at least a 60 watt bulb should be used.
- Extra care should always be taken by any elderly person who changes his or her spectacles to bifocals, for these make it more difficult to focus in the area around the feet. Consequently objects seen previously may now become potential obstacles and lead to falls.
- The likelihood of a tendency to increased tripping should always be remembered and care must be taken to ensure that floor fittings, carpets, linoleum, rugs, etc. are securely fastened. In families where elderly people live, children must not leave toys around on floors over which the elderly person is likely to walk. There should never be loose electric flex across a floor.
- Wherever possible, a very elderly person should learn to walk with some support from a solid object (banister, handrail, chair, table, furniture), especially if it is known that there is a liability to fall, or should constantly use a walking aid such as a Zimmer frame.

Intelligent anticipation of the causes of a fall can do much to prevent one. This is important as a fall could easily result in the death of a very elderly person.

Rheumatism and arthritis

Most elderly people have some degree of rheumatism or degenerative arthritis.

It is interesting that many elderly persons, even with marked osteoarthritis, find that, however painful initial movement may be, the more active they are around the house the less problem the arthritis is. Hence enforced activity in an elderly woman still looking after her home often prevents her condition from deteriorating. With this in mind, *all forms of activity – physiotherapy, the carrying out of some simple tasks, occupational therapy – are useful in preventing further limitation.*

The success of *hip replacement surgery* has been very marked and any elderly person who is seriously crippled with degenerative joint disease of the hips should always consider such an operation. In most cases the operation will render the elderly person completely mobile for 10–15 years.

Some of the worst cases of degenerative arthritis occur in very stout people. The prevention of obesity in younger persons reduces the likelihood of a severe arthritis developing at a later age.

In all instances where there is a limitation in the range of movement of an elderly person, the various social services designed to help with their feeding problems (such as meals-on-wheels), with housework problems (home helps) and with shopping difficulties (friendly visitors) should be used as they are most important in avoiding the development of other medical problems.

Foot defects

Foot defects very often cause serious problems in retired people. The types of abnormalities include ingrowing toe-nails, flat foot, hallux valgus, bunions and corns, and hammer toes.

At least half of the elderly people living at home suffer from some form of foot defect. In many this leads to pain on walking and consequently often produces some limitation of movement. This can be of a serious degree and may result in the elderly person becoming more or less house bound.

Most of the foot conditions found in elderly people can be prevented, at least, from causing serious effects by arranging radical treatment for the more disabling conditions and, for the minor conditions, regular chiropody (see page 323), as well as by teaching foot hygiene.

Hypothermia

Hypothermia is a serious condition in which the body cannot maintain correct temperature control and consequently loses heat, especially in winter. It is very important that the methods used in diagnosing this condition are fully understood by all people looking after the elderly. Hypothermia is a dangerous condition if not recognised early and is particularly likely to occur in elderly people living alone in inadequately heated housing.

Hypothermia is NOT only seen in retired elderly people living in cold homes (although such conditions will always make it more likely). It may suddenly and dangerously occur in any elderly person who has been taken ill unexpectedly (as in pneumonia), even though the person may be seated in a chair in a room which is not unduly cold. It can also occur after strokes, or after a heart attack in which the elderly person may sit quietly in a chair for hours on end.

Whatever the cause, it is *most important* that the condition is *recognised early* and that all staff dealing with the elderly know the early signs of hypothermia. The person *does not usually look cold* and certainly does not shiver. The hands and face often look warm and are red or reddish purple in colour. The individual is often *drowsy, very inactive* and *speech may become slow and slurred*. The hands, feet and face feel cold and *the body temperature* (as measured on a specially low recording thermometer) *is usually well below 35°C (95°F)*.

Once the condition is recognised, emergency treatment must be started; treatment is often difficult and unsatisfactory. *Rapid warming is very dangerous to elderly people with hypothermia* and therefore must be avoided at all costs. The aim should be to limit the warming up of the elderly person to approximately 0.6°C (1°F) per hour. The room temperature should be kept warm and a few extra blankets should be applied but no direct heat.

Prevention of hypothermia

The prevention of hypothermia involves, more than anything else, realising that the condition can develop insidiously. All those looking after elderly people therefore should be on their guard. In particular three important factors should be stressed.

- Ensuring that elderly people are accommodated in warm conditions.
- Encouraging elderly people to move around and not allowing them to sit all day even if they are in a relatively warm room.
- Always realising that hypothermia is more likely to occur in an elderly person with illness. For this reason anyone nursing an elderly person, especially in their own home, should always be on the look-out.

Cardiovascular disease

About 18% of elderly people are limited in their activity on account of cardiovascular disease. Just under 5% are confined to the house, while 13% found some limitation in their activity out of doors. *Angina of effort* is the commonest single factor, with *pulmonary heart failure* and *cerebrovascular accidents* being other reasons for limitation. Angina may be helped by modern heart surgery in which a coronary artery transplant is carried out – this may be specially useful in the younger elderly person with angina of effort.

A great deal can also be done to *minimise the effect of many of these conditions by improving social and environmental conditions.* The position of the home of an elderly person often has a marked effect upon the amount of limitation caused to anyone with even an early stage of heart failure. Any hill which has to be negotiated is likely to have a most limiting effect on the heart patient. Stairs in the house are also undesirable. The best home for any aged person is on the flat, with direct access to the front door by car so that an elderly patient with heart disease can move from the house without having to go up an incline. A bungalow is much better than a house as it has no stairs.

Hearing loss

About 30% of the elderly at home have some degree of hearing loss, but there is a much *higher incidence of deafness in the oldest age group* – in those aged 80 years and over the incidence of deafness approaches 60%. In many cases it is impossible to prevent the deafness itself, but a great deal can be done to prevent its worst effects by the provision and maintenance of a hearing aid. Many elderly people who are deaf have developed deafness over many years and have got used to a number of its disadvantages.

However deafness, more than any other single cause, leads to *isolation of the old person* – isolation from the easy and natural social contact of chatting to people. For the family living with a deaf elderly person who can hear very little the difficulty of communication greatly adds to the problems created by the elderly person. Mutual resentment soon follows with a general deterioration in the relationship between the family and the elderly person.

A properly fitted and maintained hearing aid may prevent such a situation developing and, in this way, avoid much unnecessary unhappiness. Patience and encouragement are needed, otherwise the patient soon gets fed up with the minor difficulties of the aid and ceases to use it. Chapter 16 (see page 290) provides a detailed explanation as to why most people find hearing aids difficult to get used to.

Vertigo

Vertigo (dizziness) can be an important and distressing symptom seen in some elderly people. It is most likely to occur in women aged 85 years and over but, although found in men up to 79 years of age, is rarely seen in men over 80 years of age. In the extreme cases, there is little done to prevent its occurrence except to ensure that no elderly person, who is very liable to such attacks, lives alone. The extreme likelihood of falls makes great care necessary. In the less severe cases, a full investigation should always be carried out, as well as arranging for all the precautions already mentioned to prevent falls. In particular, it must always be remembered that elderly people with vertigo are likely to have *great difficulty in the dark*. It is, therefore, most important that they never get up from bed at night without turning on the light, which should be a bright one. To ensure that the elderly person can easily find the switch on awakening, it is wise to have some form of night light in the bedroom.

Visual defects

It is usual for most elderly people to have to rely on spectacles to overcome visual defects. Well over 90% of elderly men and women require spectacles for near vision and between 50% and 60% for distant vision.

Recent surveys have shown a different assessment regarding the incidence of unsatisfactory spectacles. It is, however, still clear that a considerable proportion of elderly people are not obtaining the help they should from their spectacles because they are unsuitable and need changing. Ignorance may still play a part, for some elderly people may not realise how important it is to *retest the sight of any person regularly*. To avoid this problem it is important to ensure that elderly people have their vision tested every two years. It may not be enough just to advise retesting, it may be necessary for a social worker or health visitor to arrange an appointment and to take the elderly person to the optician.

Blindness or near blindness only occurs in 1 to 2% of the elderly living at home. The individual problems of blindness have been discussed in detail in Chapter 16 (pages 283–8).

Nutrition in the elderly

Health is only possible provided there is an adequate and well-balanced diet. This is true of all ages but the maintenance of an adequate nutrition is particularly important in all elderly persons.

A recent survey showed that, in the opinion of the investigators, 17% of elderly men and 22% of elderly women had a poor level of nutrition. Foods requiring some preparation are eaten less by elderly people living alone than by elderly people living in families or as a married couple.

Cases of extremely *poor nutrition* in elderly people are usually connected with an *elderly person living alone* who has lost interest in preparing meals, or who is not having any outside meals. Occasionally extreme difficulty of mobility (from any cause) may lead to inadequate shopping. Elderly people may find it difficult to cross a very busy road and hence find shopping an ordeal. They may unnecessarily restrict their diet rather than face crossing busy roads, even to reach essential food shops (for example a greengrocer). The realisation that such a simple cause may start a chain of events, which could eventually lead to a severe state of malnutrition, should be sufficient to suggest a simple remedy – an arrangement with a friendly neighbour to help with the shopping.

All those who are, in any way, working with elderly people whether as doctors, nurses, health visitors, social workers, voluntary workers or even just neighbours and friends, should always remember that, particularly in the case of an elderly person living alone, the monotony of preparing meals for oneself can soon lead to inadequate and quite unbalanced diet. The remedy is to try and make immediate arrangements for any of the following.

- For the elderly to go, if able, to a suitable club for three or four good meals a week (see page 320).
- To come to an arrangement whereby the elderly person regularly meets with another elderly person, also living on their own, eating their main meal in each other's homes. Taking it in turns to prepare the meal will not only relieve the monotony of eating alone but will ensure a variation in the food chosen.
- To arrange for meals-on-wheels service to be delivered three or more times a week (see page 320).
- To arrange a part-time home help service for the elderly person, part of the duties being to cook a hot meal (see page 336).

Pulmonary disease in the elderly

Bronchitis and *emphysema* together with *bronchial spasm* are the chief causes of respiratory illness in the elderly. About 20% of elderly people have some degree of bronchitis with chronic cough; these figures are from industrial areas and are likely to be lower for rural ones. Men suffer more from this than women. About 4% of the elderly are severely disabled by bronchitis and emphysema.

The prevention of bronchitis in the elderly is, of course, the same as prevention of the disease in adults. The bronchitis of the aged is only a later stage of the bronchitis in the middle aged.

Apart from the particular hazards of dust in certain occupations already discussed, there is no doubt that *persistent cigarette smoking* is the main cause of much of the irritation, chronic cough and expectoration. It cannot be too strongly stressed that any adult who is a smoker with a chronic cough and with winter attacks of bronchitis, must give up smoking at once to prevent slowly deteriorating and progressive chronic bronchitis, developing, with all its crippling invalidism. Thus, the prevention of the problem of bronchitis in old age often rests with stopping smoking as an adult. If an elderly person stops smoking it usually helps, but if he or she has already developed a severe degree of chronic bronchitis, it may be impossible to halt the disease.

Prolapse and stress incontinence

About 12 to 15% of married women over the age of 60 years suffer from some degree of prolapse with stress incontinence of urine. The highest incidence is seen in women who have had many pregnancies. Immediate gynaecological investigation should always be carried out as, in many, a simple operation can help.

Enlarged prostate

About 25% of men over the age of 65 years have symptoms of an enlarged prostate. Symptoms usually include frequency of micturition by day or night and dribbling with overflow.

The prevention of both conditions consists of *early diagnosis and treatment*. Transurethral resection of the enlarged prostate is, today, the operation of choice and is probably the best form of treatment in most patients. Drug treatment with phenoxybenzamine has also given beneficial results but the side effects of dizziness and postural hypotension have precluded its use in some men.

Incontinence

Incontinence is a difficult problem with some elderly people. Its management involves the following.

* Making certain that medical or surgical treatment will not help.
* Encouraging elderly people to empty their bladder regularly. There is much evidence that a number of those who suffer from incontinence just 'forget' to go regularly to the lavatory. In hostels where attendants remind the elderly people from time to time the level of incontinence is always less.
* The use of suitable clothing. A number of elderly people have urgency and cannot undo their clothing in time. There is a wide range of special clothing designed and available from the Disabled Living Foundation or aids centres which can help in this problem. Buttons are replaced by 'velcro' and many garments have special front openings although they are designed in such a way as to look normal.

Residential services

Hostels for elderly people

Every local authority has to provide, through its Social Services Committee, hostels for elderly persons. Most of the modern hostels are specially designed and newly built. A few have been converted from large houses.

The modern elderly person's hostel is usually designed for from 35 to 55 elderly people. Hostels larger than this are now not built as it is difficult to maintain a friendly personal atmosphere in them. Each new hostel has a majority of single rooms but a few twin-bedded ones. A hostel usually has lounges of varying size, situated on each floor. A lift must be provided so that all the accommodation is of the 'ground floor type', in other words, can be reached without the elderly person having to climb any stairs.

A resident matron and staff are in charge, and minor illnesses are usually looked after by them but, in the case of more prolonged or serious illness, the elderly person should be admitted to hospital and return to the hostel when fit again.

Each hostel provides a high standard of care for those living there and it is usual for all the needs of the elderly people to be provided, including clothing.

One very special arrangement in elderly persons' hostels is that every person contributes to their cost. Each hostel has a standard charge – a usual present day figure is between approximately £120 and £140 per week which represents the economic cost of keeping an elderly person in the hostel. Each person is asked if they can afford to pay this charge. If they can, they do. If not, then each person must pay a proportion of their retirement pension. This portion is calculated so that the elderly person is always left with pocket money for personal spending. The local authority is responsible for the additional cost.

Old people's homes today should be happy places. They, of necessity, take the frailer elderly who cannot manage at home.

Hostels are also provided by many voluntary and church organisations. In many instances, local authorities will assist the voluntary body by paying a per capita grant based on the weekly cost of keeping the elderly person.

Emergency compulsory removal of an elderly person from home

Occasionally it is necessary to consider removing compulsorily an elderly person from home because it is dangerous for the individual to stay at home and they refuse to enter a hospital or old person's hostel. Fortunately few elderly persons are removed in this way as most readily agree or can be persuaded. Cases that have to be moved are those who have badly neglected themselves and include those suffering from late cancers and others who are afraid to go into hospital.

Action is taken under Section 47 of the National Assistance Act 1948, and the Amendment Act 1951, which give power for the compulsory removal of aged and certain other people to hospitals or other institutions. It is only possible to remove those who are:

— suffering from grave chronic disease or being aged, infirm or
   physically incapacitated, are living in insanitary conditions; *and*
— are unable to devote themselves, and are not receiving from other
   persons, proper care and attention.

The social services department arranges the removal but first the
District Medical Officer must arrange for a doctor to certify that it is in
the interests of the person to do this. If the magistrate (or Court) is
satisfied, the removal to hospital or hostel is then carried out.

19 Other community social services

Home helps

Every Social Services authority (County Councils, Metropolitan District Councils and London Boroughs) has a duty to provide a home help service adequate for the needs of the area. The aim of the home help service is to provide assistance in the home where because of age, acute or chronic illness (physical or mental), the individual cannot look after the home. The service is also used in some maternity cases.

Most (about 88%) of the work of the home help services is with the care of *elderly people* (see page 319) but other groups are also covered including those with *chronic illness* (accounting for nearly 6% of the work).

Home help services are also used in caring for *mentally or physically handicapped children*, allowing a parent more time to spend teaching the child. This is especially important for a child who is born deaf. Provision of a home help to assist with housework and shopping can allow the parent to spend more time teaching the child lip reading – this is particularly important while the child is aged 1½ to 5 years.

Home helps also assist families with young children especially when sudden illness arises, or when either parent is away, perhaps in hospital, and when such help would enable the parent to rejoin the family more quickly.

Approximately 665 000 persons receive home help assistance each year in England. It is usual to make a charge for the service, but there is a sliding scale according to income; those on income support or those receiving the pension as their only income are given the service free.

The duties of a home help vary with each case but include many of the normal tasks associated with housework – cleaning rooms, preparing food and meals, shopping, lighting fires and, in a family, looking after the children.

Home help services can be provided full or part-time to the client depending on the circumstances. Apart from emergency work, in the United Kingdom most of the service by home helps is provided part-time, perhaps amounting to two or three sessions per week. This is particularly important when assisting *elderly people* over long periods as it is *essential to encourage these people to continue to do as much housework as they can themselves*, thus helping them to keep active for as long as possible.

In emergency illness or maternity cases, a full-time help for a short period may enable a young family to be kept together and thus avoid the need to take children into short-term care. This type of support is particularly valuable where there are no relatives or family to help (apart from the father of the family who has to continue to go to work).

Links between home helps and a coordinated community team

The home help soon gets to know very well the client or family he or she is visiting and learns a great deal about their personal problems. It is, therefore, important that *all home helps form part of a balanced and coordinated community social work team* and, in particular, *work in close contact with social workers*. Because of this, most social services departments have arranged for home help services to be organised within their area social services teams and any useful information the home help has learnt about his or her charges can easily be passed on to the social workers so that the fullest possible social support can be arranged.

For the same reasons, the local organiser of home helps must *coordinate closely with general practitioners, community nurses* and many others who need the assistance of home helps from time to time in their practices.

Occasionally the home help has to tackle a particularly difficult, dirty or heavy task to clean up a home which has become extremely dirty due to the neglect or illness of the occupant. Many social services departments arrange special teams to do this special work and many provide special equipment. In a number of instances, male home helps are used for these tasks. It is usual for those tackling such exceptionally difficult tasks to be given extra remuneration for such work.

Good neighbour schemes

Usually the demand for home helps outstrips the provision and some authorities have experimented with alternative methods of help such as 'good neighbour schemes'. Local volunteers are sought, often from among fit elderly people, who will agree to carry out a number of light duties, for example shopping, cooking, light cleaning. Most schemes rely on recruiting such volunteers from members of the public living close by so that little or no travelling is involved.

Most schemes arrange for the volunteer to be paid a small sum, say £5–7 per week as an honorarium, provided help is given on most days of the week.

Care of homeless families

Since the introduction of the Housing (Homeless Persons) Act, 1977, the main responsibility and duty for providing temporary or permanent accommodation for those who are homeless rests with the local housing authority (metropolitan and other district councils). Social Services authorities are required to cooperate by giving homeless clients support and advice.

The 1977 Act introduced two new concepts.

- Those who are *homeless are divided into priority cases and others*. Priority cases indicate anyone who has one or more children living with them, anyone made homeless because of an emergency (fire, flood, etc.), and any household which includes one or more people who are elderly or mentally handicapped or suffer from a physical disability. Battered wives and pregnant women are also priority cases.
- The homeless are also divided into those made *homeless by chance* and those made *homeless intentionally*.

Duties of housing authorities to those who are homeless

For those with a priority need

Provided the homelessness is not intentional, the housing authority has a duty to provide permanent accommodation which enables the family to live together as soon as possible.

If the homelessness is intentional, the local authority is obliged to (*i*) provide accommodation for the household on a temporary basis; and (*ii*) to give advice and assistance.

For those who do not have a priority need (whether intentional or not)

For these cases the housing authority have a responsibility to give advice and assistance, as they consider appropriate, in any attempts the homeless person may make to obtain or retain accommodation for him or herself. The Code of Guidance published with the Act indicates that such assistance should include registering the family on the housing list, giving assistance through a housing aid centre or referring the case to housing associations or voluntary bodies. Advice should also be given regarding lists of accommodation agencies, hostels and possible accommodation in the privately owned sector.

Many homeless families need much continuous help and support. Some are difficult to help – perhaps due to the low intelligence of the mother or father. Careful after-care work often needs to be carried out after rehousing, otherwise the family may inevitably fall into debt and repeat their mistakes.

Initially some homeless families are rehoused in sub-standard housing and then progress towards normal council housing. This usually occurs once the family has shown themselves capable of managing their own affairs. Even at this stage, such families need much support from social workers, family service units, health visitors and others.

Prevention of homelessness

The prevention of homelessness is, in many ways, more important than its treatment. There are two special problems: (*i*) the avoidance of large rent arrears; and (*ii*) the support and help given to homeless families immediately after their rehousing.

Avoidance of rent arrears

The avoidance of large rent arrears involves a number of actions which should be taken by housing and social services departments without having to resort to eviction. The following are important.

— An early warning system after a few missed payments should be instituted to enable special arrangements for rent collection to be made, and for social services advice to be sought.
— If rent arrears are still accumulating, housing authorities should check whether the tenants are eligible for housing benefit.
— There should be a vigorous pursuit of rent arrears and this should include selective visiting in certain areas to prevent the arrears becoming greater.
— If the family are receiving income support, this will contain a sum equivalent to the rent and arrangements can be made for this to be paid directly to the local authority.
— If there are serious family and social problems, it may be possible to assist by payment of rent arrears, using powers of Section 1 of the Children's and Young Persons Act 1963.
— Transfer to cheaper accommodation to help reduce the rent problems. Care has to be taken in such cases to see that there is not undue concentration of families with social difficulties rehoused in the same district.

Family planning

Family planning (see page 65) in all homeless families should always be carefully considered as too many children at too short intervals in any family are likely to aggravate problems. In the most intractable problem families, it is best to arrange a domiciliary family planning service to ensure the mother receives correct family planning advice, otherwise few will attend clinics.

Bed and breakfast accommodation

In some urban areas, there is a grave shortage of temporary accommodation and families have to be housed for the time being in 'bed and breakfast' accommodation. This arrangement *must* be made by the social services department. It is always an unsatisfactory expedient and housing authorities should always attempt to rehouse such families as quickly as possible.

Care of unsupported mothers

The care of the unsupported mother (including the unmarried mother) is also the responsibility of social services departments who can make arrangements, often in conjunction with voluntary bodies, for the residential care of some mothers. As with other types of homelessness, it is important to do everything to educate the mother to prevent further problems. It follows from this that *the unsupported mother needs a considerable amount of supporting social work*; most will also require much advice and teaching which is best arranged by social workers in conjunction with the health visitors (see page 64).

Hospital social workers

In the reorganisation of 1974, the control of hospital social workers was transferred from the health services to local authority social services departments. The number of hospital social workers has steadily increased in the last 25 years and their tasks have altered. At present there are approximately 2200 hospital social workers and most of these work in district general hospitals or in geriatric and paediatric units. Those who work in psychiatric hospitals are usually specially qualified *psychiatric social workers*.

There are four main areas of work for hospital social workers.

• *Medical casework* concerned with the adjustment of the patient and family to the patient's disease. This is the largest and most important aspect of hospital social work. It mainly involves working with the patient in hospital (including in-patient and out-patient work) but may also necessitate the hospital social worker visiting the patient's home. All types of cases are covered: work with children including child abuse; much work is also undertaken with the elderly, many of whom live alone and are consequently very vulnerable (see page 324). Terminal cases are included, especially cancers. Illness in the parent of a one-parent family often produces many extra difficulties which the hospital social worker will try to solve. Another important group of cases are accident patients and especially those suffering from chronic disabling diseases such as rheumatoid arthritis. Many social problems occur in mental illness and the rôle of the hospital social worker in such cases is often a crucial one.

- *Environmental help* involves arranging how the patient's home can be improved to help him or her to cope with the illness. This may involve the complete rehousing of the patient or the adaptation of the home either structurally or by the introduction of certain aids.
- Arrangements for *immediate assistance* to the patient or his or her relatives. This includes financial help, convalescent arrangements, provision of escorts or accommodation for relatives visiting dangerously-ill relatives.
- *Liaison* with various other social work agencies (including the social services department of the area where the patient lives) to enable long-term care and rehabilitation of the patient.

20 Alcohol and drug abuse

Alcohol abuse

Alcohol abuse (formerly called alcoholism) can be defined as 'dependence upon alcohol to such a degree that the person shows noticeable mental disturbance or an interference with bodily or mental health'. It is both a medical and social problem in its origins and manifestations – it interferes with interpersonal relations and with the normal economic and social functioning of the individual and the family.

There has been a large increase in the consumption of alcohol in Great Britain over the last 25 years and approximately double the amount of alcohol is consumed today compared with the mid-1960s. Estimates indicate that at least one million people have a serious alcohol problem with more than 10 000 premature deaths being connected with alcohol abuse.

Causes of alcohol abuse

It is important to understand that alcohol abuse is *not* a specific disease – in certain circumstances *anyone can be affected. Social factors are always very important* and there is a higher incidence in persons who are single, widowed or divorced. The usual average age for men to begin to show alcohol abuse is the mid-40s while in women it is higher. In serious cases of alcohol abuse men outnumber women in the ratio of 4–5:1. Certain occupations are at special high risk – commercial travellers, business executives, lawyers, publicans and seamen while the level in doctors is higher than average. No particular personality is especially susceptible although there is a higher incidence in both excessively shy people and gregarious extroverts. All sections of society contain persons with alcohol abuse but the greatest incidence is found in Social Classes I and V.

Development of alcohol abuse

Alcohol abuse usually develops gradually over a lengthy period of time. Many cases start as social drinkers who gradually extend the amount they consume. In an attempt to measure the amount of pure alcohol taken regularly (the essential factor in the development of alcohol abuse) the '*unit of alcohol*' is now used as an indicator.

1 unit of alcohol = ½ pint of ordinary beer (or lager)
               = 1 single measure of spirits (whisky, gin, vodka, etc.)
               = 1 glass of wine
               = 1 small glass of sherry
               = 1 measure of vermouth or aperitif.

All the above contain approximately the same amount of alcohol.

A safe amount of alcohol consumption per week is up to 21 units for men and 14 units for women. If the drinking is evenly spread during the week then up to 36 units for men and up to 21 units for women is unlikely to lead to any long-term harm. However the individual is on the borderline limit and any gradual drift towards heavier drinking, which can easily occur, may mean that the person will soon become a heavy drinker with consequent dangers to his or her health. Any man drinking more than 36–49 units regularly per week, and any woman drinking more than 21–36 units per week runs a serious risk to their health.

Note that the *safe limit for women is less than that for men.* The water content in the body measures 55–65% in men but only 45–55% in women, and, as alcohol is spread throughout the body fluids, the higher water content in men means that the alcohol is more diluted than in women. Hence higher concentrations of alcohol accumulate in women than in men and therefore there is more chance of damage to essential organs such as the liver.

Serious alcohol abuse

Two main types of serious cases of alcohol abuse have been described: (*i*) problem drinkers and (*ii*) dependent drinkers.

Problem drinker

This is an *individual who experiences serious physical and/or mental symptoms.* Loss of appetite and poor food intake often follow. This stage may last a long time and is often accompanied by numerous social, family, occupational, mental and financial difficulties. If effective treatment is undertaken early, it may be possible to reverse the increasing list of problems but relapses are common and the developing family and social difficulties often mean that support diminishes, which itself often accelerates the worsening of the situation.

Dependent drinker

Such an *individual has a compulsion to drink*. In the early stages there is increased tolerance to alcohol, but this later changes to reduced tolerance. If alcohol is then stopped withdrawal symptoms occur; these symptoms are relieved by more drinking. Soon drinking seems to take precedence over other activities. Even if drinking is stopped for a period such persons tend suddenly to start drinking again.

In both types of serious alcohol abuse, the late stages see much illness including cirrhosis of the liver and/or peripheral neuropathy. Severe memory loss with dementia occurs and finally serious withdrawal symptoms (dementia tremens).

Prevention of alcohol abuse

The prevention of alcohol abuse depends on the following steps being taken.

- Early careful *control of the amount of alcohol consumed*. If the amounts mentioned on the previous page are adhered to, permanent health problems will not occur.
- *Avoidance of drinking alone*.
- *Simple disciplines* when taking alcohol regularly – the couple who like a late evening drink realising that it is best to limit this to a drink or two about half an hour to three quarters of an hour before going to bed. The earlier such drinks are taken, the more likely it is that too much alcohol will be consumed.
- The substitution of *non-alcoholic drinks* at times in a social atmosphere. Mixer drinks or sparkling mineral water are useful as it is impossible at a glance to see that they are non-alcoholic. It cannot be too strongly emphasised that most alcohol abuse starts with careless 'social drinking'.
- Strict adherence to the *'no drink and drive principle'*. Public opinion is increasing the pressure on everyone to control the drink/drive problem; and of course the consequences for anyone who loses their driving licence can be serious.
- The *example of parents* is crucial in moulding the drinking habits of their children.
- The care and *vigilance of doctors, nurses and social workers* in diagnosing and recognising the various problems of those showing the early signs of alcohol abuse at a stage when it may be possible to reverse the process.

Diagnosis of alcohol abuse

Effective early diagnosis of alcohol abuse depends on the recognition of a combination of social and medical signs. *Increasing absenteeism, decline in job efficiency, worsening marital disharmony, and self neglect* are always suggestive of alcohol abuse. A clear indication of an inability to keep to a sensible drinking limit, missed meals, blackouts and nocturnal sweating followed by early morning drinking is usually confirmation of serious alcohol dependence.

Treatment of alcohol abuse

Treatment is never easy and success depends on:

— obtaining the complete cooperation of the drinker;
— an acceptance by the individual concerned that a serious drinking problem exists;
— early diagnosis; and
— support from the family.

The first aim of treatment is to reverse any physical, mental and social damage. Next, any alcohol dependence must be tackled. In the United Kingdom 18 *special detoxification units* have been set up and their use should be combined with *home detoxification* where the general practitioner helps to coordinate the care. Here voluntary bodies such as Alcoholics Anonymous (AA) and special Community Alcohol Teams can be a great help, especially during rehabilitation and after-care. This is essential as relapses may easily occur.

Drug abuse

Drug abuse is serious as it can lead to drug dependence. The World Health Organisation defines drug dependence (the term which has replaced drug addiction) as 'a state, psychic and sometimes physical, which results from the interaction between a living organism and a drug which is characterised by behavioural and other responses that always includes a compulsion to take the drug on a continuous or periodic basis in order to experience its psychic effects and sometimes to avoid the discomfort of its absence'.

Three types of drug dependence occur.

- *Intermittent consumption* without the development of tolerance.
- *Daily use of drugs*, often by injection, to obtain their psychic effect.
- In patients receiving *drugs prescribed medically*. In this instance, the drug is taken to avoid psychological and/or physical withdrawal

symptoms. Drugs producing such reactions include barbiturates, tranquillisers and hypnotics.

Contributory factors of drug abuse leading to drug dependence

The following contributory factors are usually connected with the misuse of drugs.

- *Personality*   Immature, inadequate and unstable individuals who often come from a broken family or who have had an unhappy childhood and who may have shown truancy and/or criminal tendencies are more likely to become drug abusers.
- *'Peer pressure'*   Few want to be the 'odd one out' in any group and a number of young people start to take drugs for this reason.
- *Availability of drugs*   Anyone who has easy access to drugs may begin to abuse them. Consequently, there is a *higher incidence of drug abuse in doctors and nurses* than in the general population. Although this danger is now well known, it still occasionally occurs in spite of the various precautions and safeguards which have been introduced.
- *Experimentation*   A number of young persons start to use drugs from curiosity; to experience for themselves the effect of these drugs. In those who are wealthy enough to afford to buy them easily, or who belong to an unconventional group in society, the temptation to experiment widely may be too great and this can become the starting point of serious drug abuse.

Although much drug abuse is linked to certain sections of society, it is important to realise that *drug dependency occurs in all social classes and the range of behavioural problems which are caused is very wide*.

Types of drugs abused

A large number of different drugs are abused, including the following:

— narcotics – heroin, morphine, methadone;
— cocaine;
— amphetamines;
— lysergic acid diethylamide (LSD);
— barbiturates;
— cannabis;
— solvents (glue, butane, petrol);
— tranquillisers.

The use of the most dangerous habit forming drugs, such as the narcotics and cocaine, in health care are very carefully controlled by law. Their use must always be recorded and they must be stored under lock and key. Barbiturates are also controlled and changes in prescribing practices have very largely reduced their medical use. Tranquillisers are not so strictly controlled and their widespread use has also become a problem, although adverse symptoms are only produced when attempts are made to change or withdraw the drug.

Narcotics remain the most dramatic and potentially dangerous drugs because of the problems of dependence which often destroys the normal life pattern of the dependent individual and also has a devastating effect on his or her family. A further problem, which has got much worse in the last decade, is *the increased danger of AIDS and hepatitis* (see Chapter 8) as many of these narcotics are conveniently given by injection. Unless new sterile syringes are always used for each injection HIV or the hepatitis B virus can be very easily spread. Shared syringes amongst drug abusers has been one of the recognised causes of the spread of these diseases especially in AIDS (see Table 8.2). Note that 15.7% of all HIV positive cases recorded in the United Kingdom are in drug abusers sharing syringes. Narcotic abusers have increased significantly in many countries during the last 15–20 years. Present estimates suggest that the likely number of drug abusers in the United Kingdom exceeds 100000 – most of these are to be found in London and other large conurbations such as Edinburgh, Glasgow, Manchester and Merseyside and their satellite communities.

Aspects of drug dependence

Drug dependence can show many aspects, including the following.

- *Physical dependence*   Physiological changes in the body eventually occur, hindering any attempts to stop taking the drug as *serious withdrawal symptoms* develop, most of which can only be relieved by further consumption of the drug. These physiological changes in the body of a chronic abuser of narcotics are the basis of drug dependence or addiction.
- *Psychological dependence*   This is commonly found in all types of drug abusers. It may be present in combination with physical dependence as in the case of narcotics or may be the main reason for the dependence as with tranquillisers and barbiturates. Psychological dependence develops because the *individual mistakenly believes it would no longer be possible to exist without the drug*. The symptoms which then follow any attempt to withdraw the drug are mainly psychosomatic.
- *Tolerance*   When a drug is *consumed on a regular basis, the same dose produces less effect*. This is commonly seen with most narcotics hence the need to increase dosages with a drug like morphia to produce the desired effect. This, in turn, heightens dependency.

Diagnosis and recognition of drug abuse

The diagnosis of drug abuse depends on (*i*) recognition of suggestive signs and symptoms of drug dependency; (*ii*) recognising the social problems which commonly follow drug dependency; and (*iii*) a doctor or nurse realising that any patient already receiving treatment with a drug known to be able to produce dependency is at some risk.

- *Signs and symptoms* The medical signs and symptoms include malnutrition (with vitamin deficiencies), extreme anxiety, insomnia, fits, blackouts, recurrent infections, repetitive incidences of trauma (falls etc.), peripheral neuritis and/or symptoms of liver disease.
- *Social problems* These include all forms of *family and/or marital disharmony*. Many cases are first recognised by the family who should always be consulted and carefully listened to as, in this way, many suggestive signs may come to light which would otherwise be missed. The possibility of drug abuse should be raised when any *young person suddenly shows criminal tendencies*. Association with criminal behaviour, especially in young persons, is a common drug-related social problem as this is often the only way they can obtain enough money to buy more drugs.

  It is always wise to consider the possibility of drug abuse in the 'at risk' groups of the population, including anyone from a family already known to have a history of drug abuse as the incidence of drug abuse in the children of drug abusers is much higher than normal.
- *Drug dependency in patients* Any patient who is a *frequent attender* at the general practitioner's surgery, either for minor complaints or for certificates for absence from work, should be considered as a possible drug abuser. Any *elderly person who has been on any drug (which is known to produce drug dependence) for a long time* should be considered to be at risk – in everyone all drugs are metabolised less effectively as the individual gets older.

  Any doctor who suspects that he or she is treating a person with drug dependence must notify the Chief Medical Officer of the Home Office Drugs Branch within seven days (The Misuse of Drugs Act, 1971).

Prevention of drug abuse

A better understanding of the potential dangers of all forms of drug abuse is crucial for the prevention of the condition. This is particularly important in anyone such as a nurse or doctor who, in their occupation, has an opportunity to obtain access to drugs which can produce dependence. *Any experimentation in such individuals is very danger-*

ous and this must be emphasised early in the training of nursing and medical students.

Health education is also important and is most effective when it is reinforced by sound family life. It is important never to give the impression that it is only the 'hard drugs' (the narcotics) that are dangerous. Most chronic drug abusers who are dependent on 'hard drugs' started by using the so called 'soft drugs' such as cannabis. Having enjoyed the feeling of well being which cannabis commonly produces, they can soon be persuaded to try other drugs and, in this way, eventually become dependent on narcotics. *Health education must stress that ANY drug abuse is potentially dangerous*. It should also emphasise that *the effects of many solvents can be very dangerous especially when used in a confined space* i.e. when a plastic bag is placed over the head. Solvents have resulted in a number of accidental deaths in young persons. Television can be most helpful in getting this message over, especially when repeated in different forms such as drama episodes.

Probably one of the most effective forms of prevention is a stable and happy family. Certainly there is a much greater incidence of drug abuse in broken families or where both parents work full time and leave their children on their own for long periods. *Young persons who run away from home and often end up in the large conurbations are always at special high risk*. Many voluntary bodies help prevent such youngsters from being drawn into drug abuse by helping them when they arrive in large cities and by providing them with hostels, day centres and support and counselling.

Treatment and management of drug abuse

The treatment of drug abuse may involve special drug dependency clinics, day centres and includes specialist social services and/or the general practitioner and primary health care team.

An essential prerequisite for successful treatment of any person in whom drug dependency has developed is their determination to stop taking drugs. Without such motivation success is most unlikely. Therefore, the first stage should always be to emphasise this and to obtain *a written statement (the contract) which is signed by the individual*. The objective of the treatment is then absolutely clear. At the same time anyone involved in the management and treatment must realise the following.

- *Moralistic and judgemental attitudes must always be avoided* for this would be totally counter-productive.
- Although the person being treated may genuinely want to give up the drug habit, this will be difficult and *relapses may occur*. Therefore, as well as any positive treatment prescribed, *the social*

life pattern of the individual and his or her family must be carefully considered. Much of the danger of relapses may be closely connected with past contacts and friends of the person involved. In many instances, once the initial stages have been overcome, it is better for the *patient to move away from the area where the dependence started.* A move to a new district enables a fresh start to be made. In any such move, it is also important to avoid those heavily populated places where drug abuse is most commonly found.

The basis for treatment in the early stages is to keep the person in some specialist unit and to substitute a less dangerous drug for the original one, slowly breaking the dependence. An example of this technique is the use of methadone in individuals dependent upon heroin.

Once the person has come off all drugs, *close follow up and support are essential.* A number of useful self help agencies can help at this stage, for example Narcotics Anonymous and Families Anonymous.

Index

Criminal behaviour and drug abuse 348
in maldjusted children 101
Cross infections 115
in obstetric units 135
Crown immunities abolished 22

Day care centres for elderly 320
in child abuse 263
Day centres, and elderly 184
Day hospitals, for elderly 322
Day nurseries, and dysentery 134
and unmarried mothers 64
main functions of 237–8
Deaf and Dumb Associations 267
social services for 289
Deafness, high frequency 86
in schoolchildren 98
Death Rate (crude) 34
Dental care in pregnancy 54
care in schoolchildren 91
caries in developing countries 189
Dental Services Committee 14
Department of Employment and ERCs 97
and special problems of handicapped 227–8
Designated Area 12
Detoxification Units (alcohol) 345
Developmental stages in children 77–8
Diabetes 162–3
Diarrhoeal diseases, and WHO 196–7
Diphtheria, prevention of 120–1
virulence test in 122
Diploma on Social Work (Dip.SW) 233
Director of Social Services-main functions of
231–3
Disability and age 271
general principles for helping 273–4
incidence of 270–3
Disabled Persons (Employment Acts) 1944
and 1958 268
Disabled Persons (Services, Consultation and
Representation) Act 1986 and 270
Disablement Resettlement Officer (DRO) and
handicapped schoolchildren 96
District General Manager 1
responsibilities of 8
District Medical Officer and health education
185
relationship to District General Manager 8
District Health Authorities – and community
midwifery 50
duty to inform parents in the case of a
handicapped child 94
and health education 185
membership of 21
organization and functions of 7–9
responsibilities re school health 84, 91
District nurse and elderly 174
role in health education 174
District Nursing Officer 8
District Treasurer 7
Domino scheme 49
Down's syndrome and age of mother 304
and genetic counselling 303

and health education 177
screening for 57
Dried milks, in infant feeding 70
Drug abuse 345–350
and AIDS 142–3, 192
and WHO 192
aspects of dependence 347
diagnosis of 348
prevention of 348–9
treatment of 349–53
Drug dependency clinics 349
Duchenne Muscular dystrophy and
amniocentesis 57, 177
Dysentery, types of 134
Dyslexia 102

Ear piercing, and viral hepatitis B 149
Ectopic pregnancy 59
Education Act 1981, details of 92–7
Education (Handicapped Children) Act 1971
305
Education Supervision Order 243
Electronic alarms – to prevent cot deaths 76
Emergency Protection Orders 241–2
and child abuse 255, 259, 262
Employment Rehabilitation Centres (ERCs)
and handicapped schoolchildren 97, 283
Emotional abuse (children) 252, 254
Encephalitis (acute) and prevention of 125–6
viruses responsible for 126
Enterotoxin, in food poisoning 129
Environmental health – and WHO 192
inspectors 216
Epilepsy, colonies for 101, 292
general epidemiology of 165
in children 101–2
social services for 291–2
special hospitals for 292
Exemption from vehicle excise duty
(handicapped persons) 276
Expectation of life in UK 312
in world 205
Extrinsic factors, in mental health 109–110

Falls and vertigo in elderly 330
causes of in elderly 326
Families Anonymous 350
Family Assistance Orders 244
Family Health Service Authorities
organization of and functions of 5, 11–14
membership of 21
Family breakdown in child care 244
in group homes 245
placement 243, 245
Family history, and congenital abnormalities
76
Family Planning and WHO 190–1
Family therapy, for mentally handicapped
persons 306
Family Welfare Association 224
Fibre and colonic disease 152
and ischaemic heart disease 44, 152
Finger bruising, in child abuse 260

Remploy Workshops 277
Rent arrears and homelessness 339
Residential nursery 246
Residence Order 241
Respite care for relatives of elderly 183
 of mentally handicapped 309
Restricted Area (in general practice) 12
Retirement, planning for 315–17
Retrolental fibroplasia 69
Revenue expenditure 3
Review of child abuse cases 263–4, 266
Rhesus factor 52
 incompatability 52
Rickets 211
Royal Commission on NHS (1979) 2
Royal Association for Disability (RADAR) 267
Royal National Institute for the Blind
 and blind children 97
 and blindness generally 267
Rubella in pregnancy 52
Rural Community Councils 225

Safety in children 81
Salmonellosis (food poisoning) 130–2
Sampling – of foods 213–14
 of milk supplies 215
Scabies in schools 90
School – clinics 91
 doctor duties of 85–90
 follow up clinics 87
 health service aims of 84–5
 nurses duties of 85–7, 90
 special types of 95
Scottish Health Education unit 16
 Health Service Planning Council 15
Screening tests for cervical cancer 44
 in infants 74–5
 in schools 90
Seat belts 82
Secondary Prevention, definition of 150
 and health education 172, 179–80
 in elderly 180–1
Secretary of State for Health, functions of for
 health 1–4
 and community care 228–30
 functions of for social services 225–7
Secretary of State for Scotland, responsibilities
 for health services 15
Secretary of State for Wales, responsibilities
 for health services 17
Serious suspicion (child sexual abuse) 265
Sex linked conditions 57
Severe mental impairment-definition of 301
Sex education – in schools 83
Sexual abuse in children 254, 264–6
Sexually transmitted diseases 145–8
 and WHO 198
Shell-fish and typhoid fever 216
Sheltered employment, for blind 285–6
 for handicapped generally 277
Sheltered housing, for elderly 316–17
 for mentally handicapped 295
 for unmarried mothers 66

Sight testing, in children 86
 in elderly 331
Sitters-in, for mentally handicapped 309
Slum clearance 220
Smear test in cervical cancer 154–5
Smoking and incidence of low weight babies
 68
 in cancer of the lung 156
 in ischaemic heart disease 151
 and primary prevention 172
 in pregnancy 55
 in schools 89
Social Class and child abuse 253
 and cot deaths 76
 and ischaemic heart disease 44
 and Standardised Mortality Ratio 46
 definition of 45
Social isolation and deafness 181
 in elderly 325–6
 Social Service Authorities and Committees
 and child care responsibilities 237–47
 main functions of 230–1
 map of those in England and Wales 235
Social Service Departments, main duties in
 child protection 257
 main responsibilities 224, 228–33
Social Work Departments (in Scotland) 230
Social workers and handicapped 277
 and health education 185
 and training (specific grants) 229
Solvents (glue, petrol) abuse 346
Specialist Assessment Team (in child sexual
 abuse) 266
Special Educational Needs 93–4
 assessment of 95–6
Special schools, types of 95–6
Specialists in Community Medicine 8–9
 (Child Health) 84
 (Social Services) 235–6
Specialists in Community Nursing 8
Specific grants for mentally ill 229
 for training social workers 229
Specific Issue Orders 241
Speech defects and emotional difficulties 102
 development in children 78
Standardised Mortality Ratios, definitions of
 and examples 34
 for various diseases 46
Standing Advisory Committees 2
Staphylococcal infections, types of 120
Sterilised milk 215
Streptococcal infections, types of 120
Substitutes for reading (for blind people)
 287
Sudden infant death syndrome (cot death)
 76–7
Suffocation in children 82
Suicide and mental illness 294
Sunbathing – excessive and cancer of the skin
 153
Sunshine Homes 97
Supervision Orders 241
 and child abuse 262